CHANGE
AND
CONTINUITY

•

A READER ON

PRE-CONFEDERATION

CANADA

•

*From the reference
library of*

_____

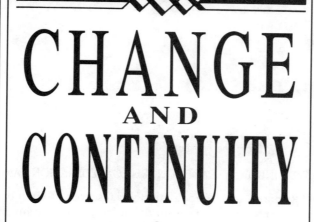

CHANGE
AND
CONTINUITY

•

A READER ON

PRE-CONFEDERATION

CANADA

•

CAROL WILTON

MCGRAW-HILL RYERSON LIMITED

Toronto   Montreal   New York   Auckland   Bogotá
Caracas   Lisbon   London   Madrid   Mexico   Milan
New Delhi   Paris   San Juan   Singapore   Sydney
Tokyo

CHANGE AND CONTINUITY: A READER ON PRE-CONFEDERATION CANADA

1 2 3 4 5 6 7 8 9 0   AP   1 0 9 8 7 6 5 4 3 2

Printed and bound in Canada

Care has been taken to trace ownership of copyright material contained in this text. The publishers will gladly accept any information that will enable them to rectify any reference or credit in subsequent editions.

SPONSORING EDITOR: CATHERINE A. O'TOOLE
SENIOR SUPERVISING EDITOR: ROSALYN STEINER
PERMISSIONS EDITOR: NORMA CHRISTENSEN
COVER & TEXT DESIGN: SHARON MATTHEWS/MATTHEWS COMMUNICATIONS DESIGN

Canadian Cataloguing in Publication Data
Main entry under title:

Change and continuity: a reader on pre-Confederation Canada

ISBN 0-07-551151-7

1. Canada–History–To 1763 (New France).
2. Canada–History–1763-1867.   I. Wilton, Carol.

FC161.C53 1991   971   C91-094543-8
F1032.C53 1991

For my daughter
Margaret

Contents

Preface

Several people have contributed to the appearance of this book. Catherine O'Toole, sponsoring editor at McGraw-Hill Ryerson, has been enthusiastic and encouraging. It has been a pleasure to work with Rosalyn Steiner, senior supervising editor. Professor Jane McLeod at Brock University and Barbara Braun provided willing assistance on short notice. Peter Oliver offered advice and cheered me on. My greatest debt, however, is to my students at York University, the University of Toronto, and Brock University.

Introduction

The pre-Confederation period is fundamental to our understanding of today's Canada. Developments that occurred before 1867 continue to exert a compelling influence on Canadian life. These are still apparent in French cultural, religious, and legal traditions, in British forms of government and courts of justice, and in the economic structure of this country. These influences continue to pervade our literature, art, and music, as well as the conventions and habits that shape the lives of thousands of Canadians. On a darker note, some of the less admirable features of our society find their roots in pre-Confederation times, including the circumstances of our native peoples and the destruction of our natural environment. The history of pre-Confederation Canada, therefore, deserves careful examination, not least because of its links to the present.

This book differs from other pre-Confederation readers in emphasizing the lives of ordinary Canadians through an examination of a number of recurring themes. While important landmarks like the Conquest, responsible government, and Confederation receive separate treatment, the heart of the volume consists of topics devoted to the subjects of nature and the environment, popular politics, and work. Each of these requires a word of explanation.

Native peoples and the environment receive more attention here than is customary in introductory texts. These themes are related, not only because of the degree of popular interest they currently enjoy, but because in pre-Confederation times the link between natives and the fur trade raised important questions about the conservation of natural resources, as Topics 1 and 10 indicate. Natives appear in another context as well, in articles exploring the subject of the effects of European contact from sixteenth-century Acadia to nineteenth-century British Columbia. Particularly significant is the question of the effects of the twin ravages of alcohol and disease on native populations, a subject that is explored in depth in Topic 6, *The Extinction of the Beothuks*.

The subject of popular politics is central to an understanding of pre-Confederation society. Before 1867, and for many years thereafter, politics was fundamentally undemocratic. Quebec, for example, lacked an assembly before 1791. Even after that date, property qualifications limited the electorate essentially to affluent white males, not all of whom exercised the franchise.[1] In Canada West, as late as the 1850s, less than 15 percent of the population, perhaps 40 percent of the males of voting age, had the franchise.[2] This did not mean, however, that those outside the centres of power were entirely excluded from participation in the political process. On the contrary, the disfranchised were able to make their views known, sometimes through institutional channels such as petitioning, sometimes by extraconstitutional and even violent methods like rioting. Governmental authorities, in turn, were required to respond. Whether they answered with constructive solutions or with repression, the fact that they reacted at all was implicit acknowledgment of the necessity of coming to terms with popular participation in politics. This book, then, considers politics in the broadest sense, taking into account instances in which "private" concerns—whether economic, social, or political—entered the public sphere, however "irregular" that participation may have been.

Life is about love and work, or so said the father of psychoanalysis, Sigmund Freud. Love has probably not received its due here, but the work of ordinary Canadians is central. The selections on natives and fur traders, farmers and fishers, lumberers and shipyard workers illustrate the human side of the staples approach to Canadian economic history. Indeed, the subject of the role of natural resources in the Canadian economy is particularly important in the pre-Confederation period, and these selections can serve not only as readings in social history but also as a point of departure for more detailed discussions from the perspective of economic history. One of the traditional themes of Canadian economic history, the role of railways, is given new treatment in Topic 14. Recent research has shifted the focus away from railways as part of the economic infrastructure servicing the staples trades, and examines instead questions such as the role of railways as manufacturers and the business methods and contacts of railway promoters.

The forerunners of white-collar workers also appear in this volume: missionaries and nuns, teachers and lawyers, merchants and bureaucrats.

---

1. See David De Brou, "Voter Turnout in Haute-Ville de Quebec, 1814–1836," paper presented at the Annual Meeting of the Canadian Historical Association, Winnipeg, June 7–9, 1986.
2. See Elwood Jones, "The Franchise in Upper Canada, 1792–1867," paper presented at the Annual Meeting of the Canadian Historical Association, Winnipeg, June 7–9, 1986.

Many of the workers who appear in this volume are middle-class women; their lives are much better documented than those of their working-class sisters. At least until recently, the history of the middle class more generally has been a sadly neglected subject. It is now being reclaimed from obscurity by historians of the professions, among others, and by writers interested in middle-class culture.

Beyond the three key themes of natives and the environment, popular politics, and work, a number of subtopics receive considerable attention here. First there is the role of religion. In the late twentieth century, secularized Canadians are in danger of overlooking religion's centrality in shaping the attitudes and behaviour of people in the past. The largest church in pre-Confederation Canada was Roman Catholic, with Protestantism splintered into a number of different churches and sects, the largest of which were Anglican, Presbyterian, and Methodist. Selections in this volume concentrate on the Roman Catholic Church, reflecting its central place in historical writing on New France and in early nineteenth-century Quebec. Some articles focus on the role of church leaders, while others examine aspects of popular religion. Space constraints limited coverage of the equally significant role of religion in English Canada, represented here primarily in George A. Rawlyk's article on the role of the preacher Henry Alline in eighteenth-century Nova Scotia; some suggestions for further readings point to an important literature on Protestant culture.

Immigration is another subtheme. Immigration from Europe formed the backdrop to encounters between natives and newcomers, whether the latter were fur traders, missionaries, nuns, or settlers. The British Conquest of the mid-eighteenth century confronted the French with an influx of administrators and merchants; this tide became a flood with the Loyalist migrations of the 1780s. Irish immigration to Upper Canada in the 1830s provides the background to the articles on Peter Aylen and Ogle Gowan in Topic 8. Ogle Gowan's cousin, Judge J. R. Gowan, dispenses informal justice to Gaelic-speaking settlers in Topic 15, and in the same section the story of "Poor Gaggin" illustrates the unfortunate career of another immigrant from Ireland. The articles in this book, then, provide some basis for comprehending the immigrant experience over two hundred years of Canadian history.

A related theme is the evolving relationship between colonies and mother country. The colonies examined here, whether under French or English authority, were part of an empire whose interests they were expected to serve. For most of the period 1600–1867, they were part of a mercantilist system, providing raw materials such as fish, furs, lumber, and wheat to the mother country, and receiving in return such manufactured goods as china, metal objects, wine, and cloth. The economic control of the mother country was parallelled by political control: colonial governors and administrators generally came from abroad and were charged with the task of supervising colonial affairs in the interests of the mother country.

The colonies experienced varying forms of government during the two and a half centuries covered by this book. These included the paternalist autocracy of New France and early Quebec; limited forms of representative government featuring assemblies with severely restricted powers; responsible government in the mid-nineteenth century; and finally, in 1867, Confederation and a federal system. The selections that follow trace these changes, keeping the colonial status of the new world settlements firmly in focus. It is important to keep in mind throughout that the influence of the mother country was not limited to economics and politics, but was clearly evident in colonial religion, architecture, and even settlement patterns, as many of the following articles indicate.

Change and Continuity aims to take an innovative approach to a few of the significant themes, primarily in social history, that have transformed the writing of Canadian history, and to present them to students in introductory courses in Canadian history. Each topic consists of three readings; most of the articles, for reasons of space, received extensive editing. Two of the readings in each topic are generally from secondary sources, books written by historians about the past. The third selection is usually a short excerpt from an original document or primary source. Ideally, the topics can be read and understood by students who do not have the benefit of tutorials or seminars; at the same time, these readings can serve as a basis for weekly discussion in courses that permit the use of one of those formats. The book was prepared for use with *Colonies: Canada to 1867*, but may, of course, stand alone as an introductory text.

The readings listed at the end of each topic enlarge on the themes covered in the topic, or deal with related subjects. The "Further Readings" are a very small sample of the work available on pre-Confederation Canada. For additional materials, students might want to consult D. A. Muise, ed., *A Reader's Guide to Canadian History 1: Beginnings to Confederation* (Toronto: University of Toronto Press, 1982), as well as bibliographies and footnotes in the books listed.

P A R T

1

THE
FRENCH
REGIME

TOPIC 1

Natives and the Environment

From the fifteenth century, the native peoples of what are now the Atlantic provinces and Quebec were in contact with Europeans who came to fish and to trade for furs. In the long run, the results were disastrous for the natives, who fell prey to European diseases and the effects of alcohol, while their cultural framework was severely undermined. Historians, however, caution against assuming that those alterations were an immediate consequence of contact with the Europeans. L. F. S. Upton's article on the Micmacs of the Maritimes stresses the continuity of Micmac life over almost two hundred years of contact with the Europeans. The theme of the continuing autonomy of native culture is examined with reference to the natives of British Columbia in the article by Robin Fisher in Topic 10.

The fur trade was one of the principal reasons for the French presence in North America. In addition to its effects on the natives, the fur trade adversely affected the environment, leading to the virtual disappearance in some areas of certain fur-bearing animals. For example, by 1630 overhunting had led to the extinction of the beaver in Huron tribal territories.[1] It was the natives themselves who hunted fur-bearing animals to extinction, a fact which may surprise contemporary observers who consider the natives to have been the first environmentalists. This problem was examined by Calvin Martin in his controversial Keepers of the Game[2]; his conclusions are summarized in the first article in this section. The related

1. Bruce G. Trigger, *Natives and Newcomers: Canada's Heroic Age Reconsidered* (Kingston and Montreal: McGill-Queen's University Press, 1985), p. 207.
2. Calvin Martin, *Keepers of the Game: Indian-Animal Relationships and the Fur Trade* (Berkeley and Los Angeles: University of California Press, 1978).

subject of the conservation of fur-bearing animals is treated in A. J. Ray's article in Topic 10.

A first-hand account of relations between natives and newcomers from the French point of view is provided in the excerpt from the Jesuit Relations *(in* Black Gown and Redskins *by Edna Kenton). The* Jesuit Relations *were annual reports from Jesuit missions in North America which were published in France between 1632 and 1673 in order to publicize the work of the Jesuit missionaries. The excerpt describes the hospital at Sillery, the first native reservation, founded by the Jesuits in 1637 in the hope that the natives would more easily be Christianized if they adopted a sedentary way of life. The hospital there was opened in December 1640 and staffed by Hospitaller nuns under the direction of Marie Guenet, dite de Saint-Ignace. Iroquois raids forced the nuns to retreat to Quebec in May 1644.*

THE WAR BETWEEN INDIANS AND ANIMALS

CALVIN MARTIN

Over the past five centuries the American Indian has been called every-thing from "noble savage" to "besotted alcoholic"—epithets that say as much about the conscience of contemporary white society as they do about the state of the Indian. So it was that in the heat and froth of the 1960s environmental movement, yet another title—"ecological Indian"—was conferred on the idealized native American, who was paraded out before an admiring throng and hailed as the high priest of the Ecology Cult. According to law professor Rennard Strickland, "*It is not an accident that the idea of ecology and the ideal of the Indian should emerge simultane-ously as national issues,*" and former Secretary of the Interior Stewart Udall concurred. Both Indian activist Vine Deloria, Jr., and Kiowa novelist N. Scott Momaday urged white Americans to "adopt Indian ways to survive."

Critics of the ecological Indian were quick to respond. In 1972 the frontier historian W. H. Hutchinson expressed a strongly negative opin-ion in his "Dissenting Voice Raised Against the Resurrection of the Myth of the Noble Savage." A past master of sarcasm and metaphor, Hutchin-son blasted the dewy-eyed romantics who would claim for the Indian such a delicate ecological conscience "as to make the Sierra Club seem an association of strip miners by comparison." Nature, as he cogently put it, "is *not* a benign bovine with a teat for every questing mouth!" Hutchinson went on to say that the Indian revered nature because he had no other choice; that he perceived nature as being controlled by supernatural forces that he was obliged to propitiate if he hoped for success in life; failure to perform the proper rituals, adhere to taboos, and conduct ceremonials was tantamount to inviting disaster. We ought to dry our eyes and recognize that the Indian was above all a self-centered pragma-tist when it came to land use.

Hutchinson ended his assault with a troubling question: "If the Amer-ind was a truly dedicated ecologist, why did he so succumb to the artifacts offered him by Europeans that he stripped his land of furs and pelts to get them?" His answer: "He did so because he was only human. The white

CALVIN MARTIN, "THE WAR BETWEEN INDIANS AND ANIMALS," *AMERICAN MUSEUM OF NATURAL HISTORY* (JUNE/JULY 1978).

man offered him material goods—iron and woolens and gewgaws and alcohol—which he could not resist. These riches, which is what they were, gave his life an expanded dimension it had never known before. No power on earth could keep him from getting these things by raid or trade, once he had been exposed to them. To ask him to have refrained from making his material life fuller and richer is to ask him for far more than we ever have asked of ourselves." Hutchinson had identified the ecological Indian's Achilles' heel.

Hutchinson's response is essentially that of most other ethnohistorians who have pondered the Indian's role in the fur trade—the most notorious and unequivocal case of resource abuse by native North Americans. There can be no denying that the native hunter was the principal agent of wildlife destruction in most theaters of the fur trade, particularly in Canada where whites operated mainly as brokers rather than as hunters and trappers. In Canada, where the evidence against the Indian is most damaging, there were, in fact, mitigating circumstances that make the Subarctic Indian's motive in wildlife extermination considerably less crass than scholars such as Hutchinson have conceded. Without denying the essential validity of Hutchinson's statement that Indians were initially impressed with the items proffered them by Europeans—and at the risk of being accused of ennobling the "savage" once more—I would give a somewhat different, localized version of what happened when all those marvelous items of Old World origin first reached the native hunters of eastern Canada.

Put succinctly, the fur trade throughout eastern Canada was a paradox. Native hunters felt a sense of spiritual kinship with major game animals, including those sought for their pelts—a relationship tempered by genuine awe and fear of these powerful animal beings and their spiritual wardens, or game bosses. Historic evidence seems to corroborate the modern ethnographer's claim that Subarctic Indians have traditionally been obsessed by the responsibilities of the hunter and the hunted toward one another. Included among these responsibilities has been the understanding between man and animal that game can be harvested only in modest quantities. Animals have always considered immoderate slaughter to be presumptuous. According to present-day tribesmen and their early historic ancestors, game animals voluntarily surrender themselves to be slain by the needy hunter. The injunction against overkill could not be circumvented by disposing of the animal remains in a manner pleasing to the slain beast, after which regeneration would normally occur. Such procedures worked only when the hunter restricted his take to a reasonable quota agreed upon between his spirit being and that of the animal he yearned for, and communicated with, in his dreaming, singing, drumming, and sweating—all of this prior to the actual hunt.

Subarctic hunters also considered animals to be persons with whom humans could talk and enjoy other forms of social intercourse, including the right to harvest these "animal persons" on a limited basis. In sum, man and animal have traditionally had a relationship of mutual courtesy: intelligent animal beings and intelligent human beings had contracted long ago not to abuse one another. Animals took offense not only when they were slaughtered in excessive numbers but also when they were subjected to other forms of disrespect: when humans failed to address them by the proper titles of endearment or when their remains were defiled by being thrown to the dogs or when their flesh was consumed by menstruating women. Humans, in their turn, were offended when animals refused to be taken in their traps or otherwise eluded the famished hunter and his family. Whenever one side transgressed the bounds of propriety the other side unleashed its arsenal of weapons to chastise the offenders and bring them back into line. For their part, animals could punish humans by fleeing their hunting areas, rendering their weapons impotent, or afflicting them with disease.

The paradox emerges in the early records, which describe how Canadian Indians hunted fur-bearers and other mammals with abandon. One would think that their hunting ethic would have precluded the orgiastic destruction of wildlife. But that ethic was apparently suspended during the heyday of the Canadian fur trade. The Indian described in these records is peculiarly hostile toward animals: he hunts the beaver and other large game with a vengeance; his mood is vindictive. Furthermore, he has clearly lost touch with much of the spirit world that sustained him prior to the coming of Europeans. Sometime in the early contact period, nature—the universe—seems to have become inarticulate and the dialogue between human persons and animal persons ceased, at least temporarily. The French surgeon-botanist Sieur de Dièreville conveyed in 1708 the essence of this sentiment in some wretched verse on the art of beaver hunting:

> They [the natives] take precautions in regard to all
> The varied needs of life. The Indian race,
> Well qualified to judge the point, because
> Of its familiarity with all their arts,
> Believe that they [beaver] have been endowed
> With an abounding genius, and hold too
> It is pure malice that they do not talk.

Or as the Recollet priest Chrestien Le Clercq explained it in 1691, the Micmac Indians, who still insisted that the beaver had "sense" and formed a "separate nation," maintained that they "would cease to make war upon these animals if these would speak, howsoever little, in order that they might learn whether the Beavers are among their friends or their enemies." Near the turn of the nineteenth century, surveyor David Thompson and fur trader Alexander Henry, the Elder, encountered Cree and Ojibwa in southern Manitoba and the upper Great Lakes region who referred to some sort of conspiracy of animals against mankind for which the beaver, at any rate, were "now all to be destroyed." Together with these cryptic remarks on the overt antagonism between man and animal, there is considerable explicit and inferential evidence proving that the man-animal relationship had gone sour.

Indian hunters now tracked game remorselessly; no thought was given to the animals' welfare as the beaver and other fur-bearers were hounded to near extinction in parts of the north woods. What made the Indian apostatize? I believe the answer lies in the devastating impact of diseases on these people.

The early records contain frequent references to eastern Canadian Indians, in common with native Americans throughout the hemisphere, being decimated by a variety of Old World contagions, most significantly, smallpox, influenza, and plague. Folkloric and circumstantial evidence place the arrival of these diseases well before the date of first recorded European contact. In all likelihood coastal Indians were exposed to deadly bacteria and viruses carried by Bristol, Norman, Basque, and other European fishermen who were working the various banks off the Canadian Maritimes some years before the Genoan-born merchant John Cabot "discovered" and officially took possession of the area for the English king, Henry VII, in 1497. Transmitted by infected natives, the diseases rolled inland. And the death rate was appalling. In the early seventeenth century the Jesuit Pierre Biard recorded that the Micmacs "are astonished and often complain that...they are dying fast, and the population is thinning out." Similar testimonials occur throughout the *Jesuit Relations* and other early records of New France. The victims had never encountered these diseases until the Europeans arrived, and the high mortality was due to the natives' lack of adequate immunological protection.

Eastern Canadian Indians have always interpreted major illness as punishment for some sort of transgression, generally meted out by offended wildlife spirits. Fitting the ethnographic and historic records together, I conjecture that prior to sustained contact with whites, who subsequently would be correctly suspected of being responsible for this calamity, the eastern Canadian aborigine followed conventional logic and blamed these mysterious, devastating epidemics on angered wildlife. Here was the "conspiracy" of animal against man alluded to by Cree and Ojibwa sources: wildlife had decided, for some obscure reason, to direct their most potent weapon against man, who now felt himself imperiled by their terrible wrath. Wildlife had broken the compact of mutual courtesy. The dialogue between man and animal became acrimonious and then simply ended for many individuals.

Such was the emotion-charged setting that European traders and missionaries penetrated in the seventeenth and eighteenth centuries. Gently urging the Indians to furnish furs for the European market and renounce their "superstitions" for the sake of the Gospel, the Europeans could not have found a more receptive audience. The Indians were predisposed to respond positively to both requests. Their spiritual complex a shambles, they now turned on their former colleagues, the game, with a vengeance and an improved hunting technology. The Indians were, as some Micmac aptly phrased it, literally making war upon the beaver.

The Canadian Indian may well have been a conservationist of animal resources as long as he considered them articulate and congenial beings— a hunting ethic that has been revived in this century by Indians in many parts of Canada. The message for those environmentalists who have looked to the Indian for spiritual inspiration, however, is not encouraging. The northern hunter conserved animals only when the two engaged in courteous dialogue. It is unlikely that Western societies will ever duplicate this particular, functionally conservationist vision of the universe. Nature, it seems to me, will be forever deaf and dumb in the presence of Judeo-Christian societies.

ACADIA: THE FIRST CONTACT

L. F. S. UPTON

With the coming of the white man, the Micmacs entered into a process of acculturation that has continued to this day. This experience, common to all Amerindians, falls into two main phases: non-directed and directed acculturation. At first, two different cultural systems meet on a nearly equal footing and each chooses from the other those traits and materials that are of the most use to them; neither side is in a position to advance its culture by force. In the second stage, directed contact, one group develops the power to force change on the other and to decide what course that change will take.[1] Under the impact of white traders, missionaries, and settlers, many native people have passed from non-directed to directed acculturation within a generation. The Micmacs were able to resist that passage for almost two hundred years. From the first contact with white fishermen early in the sixteenth century until about 1700, they were able to absorb and to utilize European innovations which modified their behaviour in a manner they were able to control to a large extent. Outwardly they appeared to have maintained their traditional life within their accustomed territories, but contact with the French had in fact undermined their society.

Lack of power, not of desire, prevented the French from directing the acculturation of the Indians to European society. The first French to write of the Micmacs had no doubt that they were an inferior people who had wantonly wasted their opportunities and "through the progress and experience of centuries ought to have come to some perfection in the arts, sciences and philosophy...ought to have produced abundant fruits in philosophy, government, customs and [the] conveniences of life."[2] No educated European could approach the Amerindians without preconceptions based on an already extensive sixteenth-century literature concern-

---

1. Robert F. Berkhoffer, *Salvation and the Savage* (Lexington: University of Kentucky Press, 1965), p. ix.
2. R.G. Thwaites, ed., *Jesuit Relations* (Cleveland, 1886–91), 3: 111.

ing the New World. At one moment the Micmacs were accorded the honour of living in the manner that "was in vogue in the golden age"; at another they were dismissed as beggars, poor hypocritical people.[3] Europeans, accustomed to a class system and a hierarchical ordering of authority, inevitably saw societies less structured than their own as primitive. Frenchmen needed a regular supply of food and shelter and clothing and the institutions that guaranteed such necessities; the Micmacs apparently needed none of these things, for they lived under four sticks in the ground, alternately feeding and starving.[4] The Indian fitted nowhere in the European scale of things: more intelligent than a peasant; measured and deliberate where the white was always in a hurry, equable where the French were quarrelsome.[5] It was quite obvious that such people should be moulded into something comprehensible.

Some Frenchmen had a perfectly clear idea of what they wanted to do with the Micmacs. Champlain hoped to pacify them and stop their intertribal wars in order that his country "might derive service from them, and convert them to the Christian faith."[6] He explained as much to a group of Indians in September, 1604, and promised to send them settlers to teach them how to cultivate the soil and free them from the miserable life they led.[7] When the Sieur de Monts settled at St. Croix, the Indians showed a proper deference by making him "judge of the debates, which is the beginning of voluntary subjection, from whence a hope may be conceived that these people will soon conform themselves to our manner of living."[8] On leaving his new establishment at Port Royal in 1607, de Monts promised the local Micmacs that he would return with "households and families. . .wholly to inhabit their land, and teach them trades for to make them live as we do." The promise "did somewhat comfort them."[9] Not for a moment did French visitors show any desire to accept the Micmac way of life as it stood, and they blithely assumed that their hosts would be happy to see it thoroughly overhauled.

For their part, the Micmacs were generally unimpressed by the self-assurance of the Europeans they met. Frenchmen bragged of their riches yet haggled incessantly until they had struck a mean bargain for the

---

3. Fr. Chrestien LeClerq, *Gaspesia* (Toronto, 1910), p. 116; *Jesuit Relations*, 2: 79.
4. Marc Lescarbot, *Acadia* (1609; reprinted London, 1928), pp. 161–63.
5. *Jesuit Relations*, 6: 231; 3: 12.
6. Samuel de Champlain, *Works* (Toronto, 1912–36), 1: 272.
7. Ibid., p. 292.
8. Lescarbot, *Acadia*, p. 24.
9. Ibid., p. 139.

simplest goods; men who were truly rich would bring splendid gifts to those they visited. Whites boasted of the wonders and comforts of home yet voyaged for weeks over dangerous seas to beg for furs that were too old to wear. Could France really be a terrestrial paradise if men were willing to abandon their families to visit the land of the Micmacs? The Indians were not so discontented with their lot that they wished to visit France.[10] Obviously, the actions of the whites belied their words, and the Micmacs could reply confidently to every criticism: "That is the Savage way of doing it. You can have your way and we will have ours."[11]

The first to bring European ways to the Micmacs were fishermen, many of whom, but by no means all, were from France. Trade with the coastal Indians was as old as the North Atlantic fishery, and its beginning cannot be placed more precisely than at some time in the first quarter of the sixteenth century. The trade must have started as part of the ritual of gift exchange that the Indians required on first meeting strangers. The fishermen found a ready market for the furs they acquired and were ready to exchange whatever goods they had at hand, including those parts of their ships' equipment that could be written off as lost on the voyage. Ships' masters and crews could make a profit at the expense of the owners, who, as soon as they realized what was happening, sent out trade goods on their own account. The resulting returns became an important auxiliary source of profit. Since the Micmac bands went to the same coastal sites each summer, they could be located easily and traded with on a regular basis. The value of this commerce was well enough established by the end of the century to become the financial justification for the first settlements and the first missionaries. But though both settlers and missionaries were occasional visitors for years to come, the fishermen returned year after year to barter with the Micmacs. Even at the end of the seventeenth century the fishing boats were still carrying off the bulk of the furs and hides collected by the Micmacs.[12]

The Indians incorporated the seasonal arrival of the fishermen into their annual life cycle. As the range and quantity of European goods increased, the bands were able to live through the summer with progressively less dependence on the gathering of local food. They awaited the

---

10. Ibid., p. 260; LeClerq, *Gaspesia*, pp. 104–5.
11. *Jesuit Relations*, 3: 123.
12. Nicholas Denys, *Description and Natural History of the Coasts of North America (Acadia)* (Toronto, 1908), pp. 445–49.

arrival of one boat after another, consuming what they acquired from each. Brandy, introduced on these occasions, had a demoralizing effect and was of considerable assistance to the fishermen in their relations with Indian women.[13] The "French trade," as these seasonal visits came to be known, affected Micmac life at several levels. It changed the pattern of sustained food-gathering to one of summer hunts for moose hides, punctuated by long periods of relaxation; to greater dependence on a foreign rather than a country diet; to reliance on goods acquired and not made. Further, the traders promoted miscegenation and spread new diseases. Long before the first land-based merchant set up his post, the fishermen had introduced the Indians to the realities and abuses of the commercial world.

The French trade harmonized with Micmac life insofar as it required nothing new of a people who already hunted and traded through the medium of gift exchange. On the surface, European goods simply reinforced the old ways by permitting the Micmacs to do what they had always done more efficiently. A single discharge from a musket could kill five or six ducks where an arrow could only take one; a cooking pot saved endless hours of hollowing out tree stumps and heating water with red hot stones; an iron knife facilitated everything from skinning animals to making snowshoes. By using European tools in the traditional context, the band could now travel further and faster, feed and clothe itself better. The new implements could also be absorbed into the spirit world of the Micmacs, for it was the "spirit" of iron, not the metal itself, that made it superior to stone, the "spirit" of the kettle that determined its efficiency. As long as these innovations could be explained within the traditional pattern of thought, they were not necessarily a challenge to it. But such adaptations were doomed to failure in the long run, for the desire to acquire new goods made it impossible to use them simply in the traditional context. To buy European goods the Micmacs had to adapt to European demands and, imperceptibly, year by year, European standards. The result was a gradual disruption of every aspect of Micmac life, from the spiritual world to the daily routine.[14]

When animals became an item of commerce, the bond that had once

---

13. Ibid.
14. A.G. Bailey, *The Conflict of European and Eastern Algonkian Cultures, 1504–1700*, 2 ed. (Toronto, 1969), pp. 13, 14, 46–52; Denys, *Acadia*, pp. 399–422; Martin, "European Impact on the Culture of a Northeastern Algonquian Tribe...," *William and Mary Quarterly*, n.s., 31 (1974): 3–26, passim; Eleanor Leacock, "Montagnais-Naskapi Band," in *Cultural Ecology*, ed. B. Cox (Toronto, 1973): 81–100, passim.

united hunter and hunted was made nonsensical. The Micmacs lost their special relationship to the fauna as they adopted a more materialistic and European concept of the environment. What had been a resource for the use of the whole people became an opportunity to be exploited for the benefit of the most aggressive hunter. Once this notion was accepted, the way was open for an end to the idea that the land itself was for all to use. As the years of contact lengthened and trade was conducted with men outside the group, these outsiders became more important to the Micmacs' survival than their fellows. In the pursuit of the means to acquire European goods, certain lands were delimited as the preserve of one family rather than another. No longer was it imperative to co-operate with other band members, and the division of the land into hunting areas for individual families became all the more acceptable for that reason. Further, the European goods made the Indians more independent and more capable of moving and hunting and surviving in small groups. Hunting moose and beaver had never demanded the co-operation of large numbers of men: the moose was a solitary animal best stalked by the fewest hunters while the beaver was almost stationary and could be killed at leisure. European goods intensified the small-group nature of the Micmac hunt.[15]

Although the demands of the trade led to a greater individualization of economic enterprise, the Europeans preferred to do business with one acknowledged leader rather than with a conglomerate of individuals. Generous to a fault when it came to making gifts, the Micmacs were less than punctilious when it came to making payments for goods received. The Europeans found it necessary to hold one man accountable. If the existing chief was not amenable, then the whites would pick another person and conduct trade through him. Micmac society was pulled in two opposing directions: towards and away from a concentration of authority. Some of the chiefs with whom Europeans dealt tried to reach an accommodation between the two extremes; one, for example, abased himself before his fellow band members, conspicuously dressing in the most ragged clothes and consciously undervaluing his share of the total yield in order to avoid arousing jealousies. At the same time, the trading chief

---

15. Eleanor Leacock, *The Montagnais "Hunting Territory" and the Fur Trade*, American Anthropological Association Memoir 78, [1954]; Rolf Knight, "A Re-examination of Hunting, Trapping, and Territoriality among the Northeastern Algonkian Indians," in *Man, Culture and Animals: The Role of Animals in Human Ecological Adjustments*, ed. A. Leeds and A.P. Vayda, American Association for the Advancement of Science Publication 78 (Washington, D.C.: the Association, 1965), pp. 27–42.

could demand some formal courtesies from the whites: a gun salute on approaching a trading post and feasts of welcome and farewell.[16] By virtue of this recognition he gained an authority within his own band that had no place in pre-contact society. If one man could become chief by choice of outsiders, so might another. The way was opened to a multiplicity of chiefs, who could now be defined as the leaders of the smallest groups with which Europeans cared to trade. Thus the determination of who was in authority passed out of the hands of the Indians and into the power of the French.

The emphasis on killing animals for commercial reasons distorted a way of life in which hunting had been only one of the seasonal activities in an annual cycle of food-gathering. Time spent hunting and trapping, even with efficient new tools, was time taken at the expense of the traditional routine. Moose were hunted in summer when they were the hardest to catch, and beaver were taken in the coldest weather when their fur was thickest and they were most difficult to approach. European goods had to make up the resulting deficiencies, but for all practical purposes the new products were inferior to the old ones. No European clothing could provide as much protection against the climate as fur, and European foods such as dried peas and prunes, even if they did not spoil on the Atlantic crossing, were less nutritious than country foods. Of course, the more animals killed for their skins, the more meat that was eaten; but overall the effect of trade was to leave the Micmacs less well-fed and clothed than before. The result was a general decline in health, more sickness, and less resistance to new ailments. Sickness diminished men's ability to hunt and, thus, to buy the new goods required to make up the new deficiencies, and this inefficiency promoted a further decline in physical well-being. And, since the physical and spiritual were never far apart in Micmac life, the traditional interrelation of man and spirit was also harmed by these new conditions.

The fur and skin trade introduced change to the Micmacs; their lives slowly altered over generations in a way frequently beyond their comprehension. The trader laid the groundwork for the missionary, who came to answer the unsolved riddles of white contact by propounding an alternative explanation for the whole of life. The missionary directly challenged the spiritual complex that had already been undermined by the economic impact of the French trader. The missionary's role was perfectly familiar to a people conscious of the spirit world and of the need to have an

---

16. LeClerq, *Gaspesia*, p. 246; Sieur de Dièreville, *Relation* (Toronto, 1933), pp. 150–52.

intermediary to maintain contact with it. Sickness, for both missionary and buoin, was a matter of spiritual concern, and the role of priest as healer was nothing new. Missionaries early appreciated the situation and were able to manipulate this coincidence of their functions and the buoin's to preach their own viewpoint. The Micmacs were able to verify the missionaries' claims about the superiority of their god without reference to Christian doctrine and only accepted what they had first screened through the filter of their own perceptions. Having selected only those ideas they found agreeable, the Micmacs were able to translate Christian beliefs into their own terms. As with the trader, so with the missionary, acculturation was a lengthy process.[17]

The first missionary, the Abbé Jessé Fléché, arrived with de Monts' settlers at Port Royal. Two Jesuits, Fathers Biard and Massé, went out with Poutrincourt's group and set up their own establishment at Mt. Desert Island. Both left in 1616, and among the more important of their scattered successors was another Jesuit, Barthélemy Vimont, who built a chapel at an inlet on Cape Breton that he named for St. Ann, mother of the Virgin Mary, who was to become the Micmacs' patron saint. But there was no continuous contact with the Indians. One of the longest established missions was founded by Father Maitre de Lyonne at Chedabucto in 1657; it was still in existence thirty years later. There were also missions on the mainland side of the Bay of Fundy, the most important being that of Father Chrétien Le Clerq, who began his work in Gaspesia in 1676 and stayed for almost a decade.[18]

The most striking attributes of the missionary were that he was white and French and therefore of the same kind as the fishermen who had frequented the coasts for many years before his arrival. Being to this extent a known quantity, the missionary had little difficulty in approaching the Micmacs. The formalities that governed the arrival of a guest allowed him the opportunity to state his business at length, and the gift of even a small amount of tobacco was enough to win an attentive audience.[19] The Micmacs regarded the first missionary, Fléché, as they did other newcomers, with a cautious curiosity and an eye to his usefulness. Since the French were apparently set on coming over in numbers, it was prudent to ally with them. When Fléché showed himself anxious to

---

17. For an overview of the missionary impact, see Robert Conkling, "Legitimacy and Conversion in Social Change: The Case of French Missionaries and the Northeastern Algonkian," *Ethnohistory* 21 (1974): 1–24.
18. Angus A. Johnston, *A History of the Catholic Church in Eastern Nova Scotia*, 2 vols. (Antigonish, N.S.: St. Francis Xavier University Press, 1960, 1972), 1: 8–25.
19. LeClerq, *Gaspesia*, pp. 288–89.

perform a ceremony that involved mysterious signs and sounds and water, 140 Micmacs were happy to oblige him; they saw baptism as a pledge of friendship and alliance with the newcomers.[20] Although later missionaries refused to baptize on this scale, the link between the French and the new religion remained basic to the Micmacs' acceptance of the missionary. He was useful, the only person who could communicate with the French, whether they were traders, settlers, or, later, soldiers. As the importance of the Europeans increased, so did the status of the one who performed the rituals recognized and respected by the whites.

The missionary had other uses beyond acting as an intermediary. One of the basic functions of the buoin was to predict where food might be found for the band. The missionary spent much time in prayer, communicating with his spirit. Could that spirit make useful predictions? Chief Membertou was impressed when, under Biard's direction, he prayed for food and found a good run of smelt on the following day. He checked on other occasions and found to his satisfaction that the Christian God had directed him at one time to moose and at another to herring.[21] Even after several generations of Christian contact, the new spirit was still expected to serve this old function. When LeClerq refused to predict where the next game animals would be found, his guide triumphantly pointed out that since his spirit had given him clear directions he was obviously in touch with a superior power.[22] Over the years, however, the missionary was able to make a claim to spirit power of the same order as the buoin's. Nothing loath to pray for plenty, the priests were correct on enough occasions to prove the usefulness of Christianity.

Catholic practices also paralleled those of the buoin in medical matters, sometimes with an uncanny exactness. Just as the buoin carried bits of bone and other apparently everyday objects imbued with mystic power, so did the missionary. The frequent use of the crucifix as a healing agent was totally comprehensible to the Micmacs. When Membertou's son fell sick, "we put upon the sufferer a bone taken from the precious relic of the glorified Saint Lawrence, archbishop of Dublin in Ireland."[23] The man recovered, and the lesson learned was that the missionary's curative powers were at least as great as the buoin's. . . .

The fact that the missionaries were able to pass such basic tests in the arts of prediction and medicine meant that the Indians were willing to

---

20. *Jesuit Relations*, 2: 89, 155.
21. Ibid., 1: 167.
22. LeClerq, *Gaspesia*, pp. 172–75.
23. *Jesuit Relations*, 2: 19.

gratify them by observing the formalities of the Christian religion. . . . As the years passed, Christian ideas gradually melded with traditional beliefs and the Micmacs began to talk of an afterlife that was miserable for the wicked and blissful for the good. A rough equivalence between Christian and native beliefs took shape: Jesus was the sun, guardian spirits were saints, tricksters were the devil.[24]

The success of the missionary took place at the expense of the buoin, who was hard pressed to maintain his traditional ascendancy. Honours were about even in the matters of prediction, and this fact itself meant a diminution of those powers that the buoin had once held as uniquely his own. The appearance of new diseases, some of which came with missionaries, totally confounded the buoin. A crucifix was no more able to cure smallpox than the entire contents of a medicine bag, but the missionary was demonstrably protected by his spirit power from an illness that could kill the buoin as easily as anyone else. Both sides continued to agree on the spiritual nature of the physical world, and the contest was fought along mutually recognized lines. When LeClerq reproved some Indians for licking the bodies of the sick and breathing over them, he was told that they were doing as he did at baptism: chasing out sin.[25]

The logical course for the buoin to adopt, if they wished to survive, was to incorporate some of the Christians' powers into their own rites by obtaining similar relics and performing similar rituals. LeClerq noted one instance where a picture traded from the French was being venerated as an image from heaven and another where Indians were hearing confession. . . . These attempts to adapt to the changing times did little to help the buoin and simply illustrated the Christianization of powers that were in an irreversible decline.

There was no need for the missionaries to dissemble or compromise their faith in paralleling Micmac experience. Both Indians and French saw culture and religion as a unit and neither expected them to operate independently of each other. Both believed in direction by a supernatural power which could be ritualistically consulted, and their common faith in the reality of mystical experience was an important bond. Missionaries could unabashedly pit the authority of their dreams against those of the buoin. Christian revelations were a viable form of persuasion. The ultimate experience in mystical contact, spirit possession, was prized by the

---

24. LeClerq, *Gaspesia*, p. 220; Bailey, *Conflict*, p. 145.
25. LeClerq, *Gaspesia*, p. 220.

Micmacs but feared by the missionaries as evil, a known evil with which they were prepared to cope.[26]...

As an element in white contact, the missionaries contributed to the decline of the traditional forms and beliefs of Micmac society, but not in the way they might have wished. Their success was as much the result of their being French as of being Christian. It was not Christian doctrine that persuaded the Micmacs, but the ability of the missionaries to perform on terms set down by those they wished to convert. A full century after the arrival of the first missionary the Micmacs described themselves as Christian, but their knowledge of the new belief remained rudimentary and suffused with their old concepts and attitudes. By then the missionary had replaced the buoin and his power had to be accepted, in a utilitarian sense, as the superior one. Persuasion operated through demonstration, not doctrine.

The activities of the missionary complemented those of the trader, and in many parts of North America both combined together to pave the way for the settler, the final agent in the destruction of the Indian. But as with trader and missionary, the impact of the settler on the Micmacs was so gradual over so many years that the changes might almost pass unnoticed....

When the British took control of Acadia for the third and last time, capturing Port Royal in 1710, there were just over 1,500 native-born Acadians with roots going back from two to four generations.[27] The Micmac population stood at about the same number, having declined from the 3,000 or so at the beginning of the seventeenth century. In one hundred years the French had been able to establish a white population only one-half the size of the Micmacs' at their first arrival.

The legal forms under which the French took possession of Acadia were those of the seigneurial system: the king owned the land and could theoretically dispose of it at will. There was never any question of treating for the cession of Indian lands, no concept that the Indians had rights that had to be bargained for, no thought that they should be treated as a separate nation. Vast grants were made to individual Frenchmen for their profit: between 1632 and 1635 the Company of New France disposed of 3.7 million arpents. By the end of the century there were fifty-five grants of

---

26. Bailey, *Conflict*, p. 137; Cornelius Jaenen, *Friend and Foe* ([Toronto]: McClelland and Stewart, 1976), pp. 50–57, 65.
27. Andrew H. Clark, *Acadia* (Madison: University of Wisconsin Press, 1968): 113–21.

a seigneurial character still in existence.[28] As the French saw it, the Indians had no land they could legally call their own. When Récollet missionaries tried to establish farming communities to assist in the conversion of the Micmacs, they arranged to purchase the necessary lands from one of the French grantees.[29] But whatever the technicalities of form, the Acadian settlers themselves obtruded scarcely at all on Micmac territory. Farming on tidal flats that were dyked to permit cultivation, they were adding new land rather than destroying old hunting grounds. As far as the Acadians were concerned, there could be no question of dominating the Micmacs and bending them to their will. Mere survival dictated that they live in harmony with the natives. The king of France might claim ownership of all the land, but the realities of life made the claim meaningless.

At first glance, the Acadians appear to have been much less of a challenge to Micmac life than the traders and missionaries. The settlers tended to acculturate to the Micmacs, adopting their habits of dress and transportation. Many of the early French took Indian wives, and the community at La Have, for example, was a métis settlement. The relationship proved to be a source of security as well as population to the settlers, for blood ties ensured their protection and good treatment at the hands of the Micmacs. This mingling of the Micmacs with a settled population, however, tended to subtract from their numbers. Whether the children of mixed descent became hunters or farmers depended on which parent had the major responsibility for their upbringing. The white male settlers had an interest in retaining control of their children, if only as labourers on their farms. By contrast, the fishermen who preceded them had had no interest in the offspring of their casual liaisons, and those children were raised by their mothers totally within the Micmac culture. Hence the Acadian settlers presented a non-violent but very real threat to native survival; the half-breed child who stayed on the farm eventually assimilated to white society.

---

28. Ibid., pp. 91, 115; Jaenen, *Friend and Foe*, p. 160.
29. The purchase was never completed (W. F. Ganong, "Richard Denys, Sieur de Fronsac, and his Settlements in Northern New Brunswick," New Brunswick Historical Society, *Collections* 7 [1907]: 7–54).

Of the Hospital

[Lately removed from Kebec to Sillery.]

FROM THE *JESUIT RELATIONS*

...But let us come to what has occurred in this house of Mercy.

Besides the adornment and consolation which it gives to the whole Colony, it serves as a strong support to the settlement of the Savages, and bears a good part of the expenses and burden thereof. The Village of Sillery is still small, but I doubt very much if, without this house which has been established there, it could have reached the state in which it is; and I know not yet if it could subsist without this help. It has indeed cost inconveniences to these good sisters; the day's time of a man has often been employed for going to Quebec in quest of a few herbs or a half dozen of eggs for the sick; but the desire that they have had to exercise their offices toward the Savages, and to contribute to their settlement, in accordance with the scope of their vocation, has caused them to abandon their building at Quebec, with all its conveniences, as that desire had caused them to abandon France,—seeing, especially, that the French, when sick, have no difficulty in going to Sillery; but the sick Savages are unable to go to Quebec, and thus it would have been a hospital for Savages, without Savages.

The fear of the Hiroquois not having hindered so many worthy persons of both sexes from going to Montreal and other places on the great River— though the Hiroquois are near by, and prowl all about,—it was not likely to have effect a league or two from Quebec, so as to impede a Religious community in its offices, and in a benevolence for which alone it came into the world, and which the Savages were ardently desiring. Moreover, their building at Quebec is being finished, little by little,—so that, if any accident occurs, they can prudently and advisedly retreat thither; and, if the French multiply further, they can establish a little separate Hospital

EDNA KENTON, ED., *BLACK GOWN AND REDSKINS: ADVENTURES AND TRAVELS OF THE EARLY JESUIT MISSIONARIES IN NORTH AMERICA (1610–1791). FROM JESUIT RELATIONS.*© 1954 BY VANGUARD PRESS. REPRINTED BY PERMISSION OF VANGUARD PRESS, A DIVISION OF RANDOM HOUSE, INC.

THE WORD "REDSKINS" WAS PART OF THE ORIGINAL TITLE OF THE BOOK AND DOES NOT REFLECT THE ATTITUDE OF THE EDITOR OF THE PRESENT VOLUME. SIMILARLY, THE USE OF THE TERM "SAVAGES" IN THE FOLLOWING SELECTION IS A REFLECTION OF SEVENTEENTH-CENTURY FRENCH ATTITUDES TO THE NATIVES, WHICH IS NOT ENDORSED BY THE EDITOR.

for their succor, which would not injure that of the Savages, and would advance the colony.

The Nuns have received and assisted in the Hospital, this year, about one hundred Savages of various nations: Montagnais, Algonquins, Atticamegues, Abnaquiois, Hurons, those of Tadoussac and the Saguéné, and of some other nations, more distant. At the time I write this report, there is a woman afflicted with a slow disease, whom Father Buteux lately brought hither, on returning from Tadoussac. She is from a region above thirteen or fourteen days distant, far within the lands of the Saguéné. Five or six French workmen have also been relieved in this house of charity; they had been stricken with the land disease, at the fort of Richelieu, and were in danger of dying from it, if they had not found kind help.

A good widow called Louyse had a daughter named Ursule, who was married to a Captain of Tadoussac. This young woman fell sick, and, after two or three years of debility, finally took to bed at Sillery and retreated to the Hospital, staying now in the common ward, again in the neighboring cabin. It was necessary to give her the viaticum; she was then in her cabin near the door of the Hospital. The good Louyse adorned this little house with bark, like an oratory; but, quite in the savage fashion, she hung all round it robes of Beaver or Moose, wholly new and finely embroidered. She put the most beautiful one on the bed of the sick woman; she covered the whole floor with leaves, and also the top of the cabin; she went to the Nuns to borrow a Crucifix and two candlesticks, with the tapers, and put them near her daughter's bed. The whole neighborhood accompanied the Blessed Sacrament with great respect and devotion. Her mother had her buried with all the solemnity possible to a Savage, and put in her grave all that she had most precious in the way of Beaver, Porcelain, and other articles of which they make account. When the Nuns pointed out to her her poverty, and that that availed nothing for the dead, she said, "But you people certainly buried your sister Religious" (it was mother de sainte Marie, deceased two years ago) "with her beautiful robe, and with all the honor that you could."

I will relate how the Socoquiois made prisoner by the Algonquins arrived at this house last year. As soon as he had landed opposite the Hospital, the Savages of Sillery went forward to receive him with Charity. They led him into all their houses and cabins, one after the other, and made him dance in all,—but with gentleness and friendship. He obeyed throughout, although he had his body all covered with wounds and sores. After that, two of the principal Savages led him to the Hospital, where he was received by the Nuns with great joy. They called the Surgeon; the whole ward was full of Savages, in order to see what state his wounds were in. . . .I was present at this sight; the first view made us chill with horror. He had endured the dressing of his wounds without ever saying a word or showing any sign of pain; he made known by signs the manner in which they had treated him, without betokening any displeasure against those who had put him in this pitiful condition. By good luck there was at the Hospital a sick Abnaquiois, baptized, and called Claude, who well understood Socoquiois. This poor wretch was extremely comforted to meet him; and, as he was astonished, at first, to see the Nuns show him so much charity, this good Christian explained to him how their whole occupation was only to assist and succor the poor and sick, and that they observed virginity all their life. That greatly impressed his mind. He was restored in a fairly short time, and sent back to his own country, in order to show the affection of the French and Savages toward him. These are so many precursors of the Gospel.

FURTHER READINGS FOR TOPIC 1

C. E. Heidenreich. *Huronia: A History and Geography of the Huron Indians, 1600–1650*. Toronto: McClelland and Stewart, 1971.

Cornelius Jaenen. *Friend and Foe: Aspects of French–Amerindian Cultural Contact in the Sixteenth and Seventeenth Centuries*. Toronto: McClelland and Stewart, 1976.

Bruce G. Trigger. *Natives and Newcomers: Canada's "Heroic Age" Reconsidered*. Kingston and Montreal: McGill-Queen's University Press, 1985.

L. F. S. Upton. "Contact and Conflict on the Atlantic and Pacific Coasts of Canada." *Acadiensis* 9 (1980): 3–13.

Topic 2

New France: Aspects of Paternalism

*P*aternalism flourishes in conditions of political, social, and economic
inequality. It is the face of generosity masking the reality of
subordination and making it more palatable. Paternalism characterized
the society of New France, where an autocratic state and a hierarchical and
somewhat authoritarian church operated without many institutionalized
channels of popular participation. This did not mean, however, that the
authorities showed themselves indifferent to the welfare of the population.
On the contrary, as W. J. Eccles's article shows, officials of the church and
state around 1700 took steps to cope with the destitute, ill, and abandoned
members of society on an ongoing basis as well as in emergency situations.

A similarly paternalist response was elicited from the state by movements
of popular protest which erupted in New France between 1700 and 1763,
and which form the subject of Terence Crowley's article. The authorities
generally treated protesters with leniency, provided their disturbances did
not fundamentally challenge the stability of the state; perhaps this tolerance
resulted from the knowledge that there was no alternative method for
calling attention to grievances such as food shortages and high commodity
prices. This article provides an interesting contrast to the selections on
popular politics in Topics 8 and 13.

The role of the Roman Catholic Church in New France was so significant
that English-speaking historians such as Francis Parkman once thought
that the colony was a virtual theocracy, ruled by priests who permitted no
freedom of thought within its boundaries. This view has now been
discredited by work such as Cornelius Jaenen's, which indicates that

although the colonists generally conformed to official doctrines, they also retained their folk beliefs and superstitions whether or not these were sanctioned by the church. The article by J.-P. Wallot in Topic 5 on the role of the church in early nineteenth-century Quebec provides a useful point of comparison.

Social Welfare Measures and Policies in New France

W. J. ECCLES

From the first establishment of Royal government in New France in 1663 until the Conquest in 1760 the basic premise, not merely of royal policy but of all the social institutions—indeed the basic premise upon which society in New France rested—was individual and collective responsibility for the needs of all. In the King's official instructions to Jean Talon, the first intendant to serve in New France, dated 27 March 1665, the concept of social responsibility was made plain:

> The King, considering all his Canadian subjects from highest to the lowest as though they were virtually his own children, and wishing to fulfil the obligation he is under to extend to them the benefits and the felicity of his rule, as much as to those who reside in France, the Sieur Talon will study above all things how to assist them in every way and to encourage them in their trade and commerce, which alone can create abundance in the country and cause the families to prosper.[1] . . .

This, then, was the official policy: avowedly paternalistic. It remained, however, for the officials in Canada, the governor-general, the intendant, their subordinates, and the Sovereign Council at Quebec to implement the policy; to cope with the myriad problems that beset the King's subjects in their day-to-day existence.

During most of the seventeenth century the colony existed under virtual siege conditions, with the powerful Iroquois confederacy striving to destroy it. Thus the underlying military basis of French society was, of necessity, emphasized in Canada. Custom and conditions, therefore, required the close regulation by the royal officials of many aspects of day-to-day colonial existence. Dependent on imports from France of essential supplies, and with communications severed during half the year, the colonial officials had to regulate prices and distribution. The number of

---

W. J. Eccles, "Social Welfare Measures and Policies in New France," in *Essays on New France* (Toronto: Oxford University Press, 1987): 38–49. Reprinted by permission of the publisher.
1. *Rapport de l'archiviste de la Province de Québec, 1930–1931,* 9; Mémoire du Roy pour servir d'instruction à Talon. Paris, 27 mars 1665.

tradesmen—butchers, bakers, millers, tailors—was closely regulated, and a close check on both the quality and price of their goods was maintained to protect the consumers. In times of short supply, hoarding was penalized and rationing frequently resorted to. When, in 1691, the Intendant Champigny advocated the abandonment of price regulation, claiming that only freedom from restraint could create abundance and with it lower prices,[2] Louis XIV and the people of New France overruled him. The King stated: 'It is a good thing to conserve the freedom that commerce requires, but when the avarice of individuals goes too far and proves detrimental to the well-being of the country it is necessary to curb it by every practicable means, even by legal sanctions, when other means fail.'[3] And two years later, when the intendant declined to regulate the price and supply of meat, the Sovereign Council insisted that a public assembly be called to discuss the matter. At the meeting the consensus of opinion went against the intendant; he thereupon bowed to the popular will.[4] Regulations were duly imposed and the practice continued until the Conquest.

The fundamental institution upon which society in New France rested was the seigneurial system of land tenure. This system, consciously modelled on the ancient Roman *praedia militaria*,[5] was well calculated to settle a great many families on the land and to bring it into production with the minimum of delay. Too intricate to be discussed in all its ramifications, it must suffice to say that the seigneurial system afforded a large measure of social and economic security for the lower ranks of society, and also of social mobility.[6] The relative ease with which persons, originally of the peasant class, who possessed intelligence, ability and initiative, could amass capital in the fur trade, acquire a seigneury, and with it the status of the colonial *petite noblesse*, was a remarkable feature of social development in seventeenth-century New France.

In his plans for the rejuvenation of the French economy, Colbert assigned an important role to New France. One of the prerequisites for the

---

2. Paris, Archives Nationales, Colonies, Series C11A, XI, f. 292, Champigny au Ministre, Que., 12 nov. 1691.

3. *Rapport de l'archiviste de la Province de Québec, 1927–1928*, 139; Mémoire du Roy au Gouverneur de Frontenac et à l'intendant Bochart Champigny.

4. Ibid., *1928–1929*, 324, Mémoire du Gouverneur de Frontenac et de l'intendant Bochart Champigny au Ministre. (26 oct. 1696).

5. *Ordonances des intendants et arrêts portant règlements du Conseil Supérieur de Québec.* Québec, 1806, II, 128 ff. Projects et règlements faits par Messrs de Tracy et Talon au sujet de l'établissement du pays du Canada...

6. On the Canadian seigneurial system see Marcel Trudel, *Le régime seigneurial*, Brochure Historique no. 6, Publication de la Societé Historique du Canada. Ottawa, 1956.

implementation of these plans was a rapid increase in the colony's population; hence, from 1663 to 1672 the Crown sent to Canada each year some 500 men and up to 150 marriageable girls. The original intention was that the men should be given a concession of land on a seigneury, two arpents of which would have been cleared and seeded ready for them, along with tools, seed, food and clothing enough for the first year.[7] It would then be up to them to clear the forest from the remainder of their concession and bring it into production. In practice, however, this proved unworkable. Conditions in the New World were too different from those in France and men thrust onto the land in such a fashion would have starved to death before the first winter was over had they been left to themselves. The Sovereign Council at Quebec therefore decreed, in 1664, that all *engagés* would be required to work for three years for the previously established settlers at wages of 60 to 90 *livres* a year. At the end of this time it was expected that the *engagés* would have garnered the experience needed to cope with Canadian conditions and would then be granted tools, seed, clothing and food enough for a year, and land of their own on an established seigneury.[8] In the distribution of these indentured servants the members of the Sovereign Council, their fellow seigneurs, and the religious orders engaged far more than their share of this labour force, but then few of the *habitants* could, at that time, have afforded a hired hand.[9] Yet three years was not a long time, and it must also be remembered that these were years of war with the eastern tribes of the fierce Iroquois confederacy. The first harsh lesson that anyone in Canada had to learn was how to elude their scalping knives.

Within this social and economic framework the settlers, once established, were expected to provide for themselves and to care for the members of their own families who, for one reason or another, needed help. When parents became too old to work, for example, their children were expected to look after them. The customary procedure here was for a meeting of all members of the family to be held before a notary to decide which of the children would care for the parents and how much the others would contribute. The agreement was then given the official seal by the notary, who retained a copy.[10] . . .

---

7. Projects et règlements faits par Messrs de Tracy et Talon. . .op. cit.
8. *Jugements et délibérations du Conseil Souverain de la Nouvelle France* (Québec, 1885), I, 201–6.
9. Louise Dechêne, *Habitants et marchands de Montréal au XVIIe siècle* (Montreal, 1974), 61–3.
10. For examples of such contracts see, *Jugements et délibérations du Conseil Souverain de la Nouvelle France*, I, 118.

It was inevitable, however, given the hasty manner in which many of the emigrants had been recruited in France, that some of them would find conditions in Canada too arduous and would abandon the attempt to wrest a living from the wilderness. Thus, within a few years after the establishment of royal government, Quebec was beset by beggars. In all probability Montreal encountered the same problem, but few of the local records have survived for this period. In August 1677 the Sovereign Council issued an *ordonnance* forbidding all begging in Quebec, ordering the mendicants to quit the town within a week and return to their neglected farms. At the same time the colonists were forbidden to grant alms at the door of their homes under any circumstances, on pain of a ten-*livres* fine.[11]

This rather draconian law appears to have had the desired result. But some six years later, in April 1683, Quebec was once again plagued by beggars who refused to work; this at a time when the established settlers were desperately short of labour. Worse still, these vagabonds raised their children in idleness and inhabited a vile collection of huts on the outskirts of the town, making it the site of all manner of scandalous disorder. To remedy the situation, while there was time for those causing it to re-establish themselves on their land before the onset of winter, the intendant ordered them to return to their concessions within a week. Anyone caught begging in future was to be placed in the stocks, and flogged if caught a second time. Once again, no one was to grant alms at the door of his home to beggars on pain of a ten-*livres* fine.[12]

This legislation was clearly designed to cope with the social and economic problem posed by the indolent, the undeserving poor. There still remained the problem of the deserving poor, those who through no fault of their own were unable to provide for themselves. During these years the only recourse they had was the charity of the more fortunate members of society. To maintain some sort of control of this situation, which past experience had shown could all too easily lead to abuse, these unfortunate individuals were required to obtain a mendicant's license, attesting to their need, from their local curé or judge.[13] As long as there were not too many beggars the system sufficed, but when economic conditions worsened then other measures had to be taken.

Such was the case in 1688. Throughout the history of New France, and more particularly in the seventeenth century, the fur trade was the

---

11. *Jugements et délibérations du Conseil Souverain...*, II, 870–2.
12. Ibid.
13. Ibid., III, 219 ff.

economic life blood of the colony. For the three years preceding 1688 no furs had reached Montreal from the west owing to the Iroquois war. This had hit the colonists hard; not just the fur trading fraternity, but virtually everyone in the colony felt the effects, a great many being reduced to penury. To make matters worse, an epidemic of the tertian ague in the summer of 1684 had resulted in a very heavy death toll, leaving many widows and orphans. In consequence, what appears to have been hordes of people were reduced to seeking alms in the streets of the three towns and throughout the countryside. Moreover, the authorities were convinced that some indolent people were taking advantage of the situation to maintain themselves in idleness by begging, even though work was available for them.

It was clear that the reiteration of the *ordonnances* of 1677 and 1683 forbidding begging and ordering the mendicants to return to work would not suffice. Fortunately the intendant at this time, Jean Bochart de Champigny, was both an efficient administrator and a very humane person. On 8 April 1688 he called a special meeting of the Sovereign Council to deal with the situation. The resulting *règlement*,[14] a lengthy and detailed document, shows the French colonial system in quite a good light. A social problem is seen to exist, it is carefully analysed, and an honest attempt is made to solve it.

In drafting the legislation the intendant and the Sovereign Council had three main aims in view: to see to it that no one starved, to find useful work for all those capable of working, and to put an end to the public annoyance created by the horde of mendicants. In attempting to achieve these aims they distinguished between two types of poor, the deserving and the undeserving; the former were to be helped to help themselves, the latter were to be coerced into ceasing to be charges on, and sources of annoyance to, the other colonists. In the rural areas each seigneury was required to care for its own without calling for outside help; but in the three towns, Quebec, Montreal, and Trois-Rivières, where the situation was the most acute, a new institution, the *Bureaux des Pauvres*, offices of the poor, was to be established forthwith. These bureaux were to be staffed by the local curé and three directors who were to hold meetings once a month, and oftener if circumstances required. One director was to serve as treasurer and keep a careful account of all alms received and dispensed, another was to act as secretary and keep a journal of the office's deliberations and transactions. They were empowered to investi-

---

14. Ibid.

gate the need of all applicants for aid, to seek employment for them, and, lest some of them should demand exorbitant wages to avoid being hired, the directors were required to come to an agreement with those offering employment on the wages to be paid, and the poor were to accept the stipulated rate without argument. . . .

With this legislation enacted, the Sovereign Council felt able to reimpose the earlier stringent measures against unlicensed begging and the practice was once again forbidden on pain of corporal punishment. Only if some exceptional misfortune had descended upon a family could its members ask the curé in a country district or the directors of a town bureau of the poor for permission to solicit alms. The directors were also empowered, when a family overburdened with children requested help, to put the children out to work for as long as was deemed advisable rather than allow them to become a charge on the public, but contracts of service were to be drawn up by a notary and the conditions were to be made as advantageous as possible for the children. In other words, the indolent were not to be allowed to take advantage of circumstances to avoid work, and the circumstances were not to be used by anyone to take advantage of the deserving poor. . . .

But the question remains: how well did this poor law function? A document dated 1698, ten years after the bureaux were first established, states that there had been objectionable consequences. Some individuals had taken advantage of the institution and had come to depend more on charity than on their own efforts; thus the bureaux had, in some measure, contributed to the perpetuation of the problem rather than to its removal. Worse still, many *habitants* suspected that the contributions they were called on to make were, in effect, a subsidy to laziness or bad management, hence some of them refused to give anything. These circumstances inevitably led to bad feeling on the part of all concerned; and this, the Quebec authorities felt, was more detrimental to the people's souls than the alms were of benefit to the bodies of the needy.[15]

This same document also indicates that by 1698 the *Bureaux des Pauvres* were no longer functioning. It is possible only to surmise why they had, at this time, a short existence. The main reason for their establishment, dire poverty in the colony, ended a little over a year after the *règlement* was enacted. In August 1689 the fur brigade returned from the West with 800,000 *livres* worth of furs. The colony was prosperous

---

15. Archives Judiciares de Montréal, Extrait des registres du Conseil Souverain, 22 fevrier 1698.

again. Then, too, shortly before these furs arrived at Montreal the colony suffered a ferocious and damaging assault at the hands of the Iroquois, marking the reopening of hostilities with this powerful confederacy and with the English colonies as well. For the ensuing eight years New France was kept fully occupied by these foes, and at the same time the governor of the colony, the comte de Frontenac, embarked on a policy of fur-trade expansion. Each year after 1689 hundreds of men were sent west to trade with the Indian tribes. Doubtless many of the able-bodied poor who had not found work in the colony to their liking were willing enough to embrace the arduous, but profitable and exciting, life of the *coureur de bois*.

By 1698, however, the war was over, the fur trade was in a very depressed state and voyages to the West were expressly forbidden by royal edict. Thus it is not really surprising to find in that year the Sovereign Council grappling once more with the problems occasioned by beggars and vagabonds. In February the council issued an *arrêt* stating that idlers and riffraff were, on the pretext of poverty, causing annoyance to the residents of Quebec by begging from door to door instead of working, as many of them were well able to do. The remedy for this situation, the *arrêt* stated, was easily to be found in the re-establishment of the *Bureaux des Pauvres*, and this was now ordered to be done. The local curés and four other directors in the towns were ordered to see to the nourishment of the deserving poor by conforming to the *règlement* of 1688 in all its particulars.[16]

The *bureaux* were duly re-established and it is known that they functioned effectively for over a year, and likely much longer.... At the meeting held on 14 July 1698 it was decided, without any reasons being given, that the bureau would meet only once a month in future.... The last meeting for which the minutes have survived is that held on 15 July 1699. There is no hint given that the bureau was suspending its activities. How much longer it continued to function, or how active the other bureaux were, is not known. Further research may well provide the answers.

These *Bureaux des Pauvres* were intended mainly to cope with emergency situations, but there still remained the chronically indigent who could not help themselves and who had no one to care for them. A decade or more of war, along with both the rise in population (approximately 15,000 by 1700) and the aging of the immigrants of the 1660s, had resulted

---

16. Ibid.

in enough such persons to constitute a distinct problem. This time it was the clergy, aided by the secular authorities, who took steps to solve it. In Montreal, the main theatre of war, the problem was the most acute, and here the colony's first almshouse, the *Hôpital Général*, was founded by Jean-François Charon and a group of lay brothers....That the almshouse was functioning by 1698 we know....

Useful though it undoubtedly was, the Montreal almshouse catered only for male indigents, at least while the Charon lay brothers had charge of it. After 1692 older women who could not support themselves other than by begging were sent to Quebec where Bishop St Vallier had, in that year, established an almshouse with an endowment out of his own pocket. The terms of the royal charter granted the *Hôpital Général* at Quebec are of some interest. In the preamble it is stated that as such institutions had proven very useful in the majority of the towns in France, there was every reason to believe that they would have the same utility in Canada. It is made plain that their main purpose was to eradicate the mendicant problem. Those placed in the care of the *Hôpital* at Quebec, both men and women, were to be given work to do in the institution's workshops or on its farm land. Here too the view is expressed that the majority of beggars were mendicants through choice, preferring to beg rather than to seek gainful employment. Consequently able-bodied beggars were to be placed in the almshouse by the authorities and made to help care for the chronically ill, and for those other deserving souls who were unable to maintain themselves by their own efforts.[17] The aim was to solve a social problem as much as, or more than, to provide Christian charity.

One group that received particular attention from the Crown were foundlings. The authorities always made every effort to discover the parentage of abandoned babies. Any woman found guilty of having concealed her condition and given birth to a child clandestinely was dealt with harshly by the courts—the death penalty being invoked in many cases. All too frequently, however, babies were found abandoned on the steps of a church, or of a private home, and it then remained for the royal officials to care for them. In 1726 the Intendant Bégon ruled that such children had to be cared for at the expense of the seigneury where they were found, rather than by the Crown.[18] But by 1736 it had become established practice for the Crown to accept this responsibility. In that

---

17. *Edits, ordonnances royaux, déclarations et arrêts du conseil d'état du Roi concernant le Canada* (Québec, 1854), I, 271.
18. *Arrêts et règlements du Conseil Supérieur de Québec...*(Québec, 1854), 310.

year the Intendant Gilles Hocquart decreed that the *procureurs du roi* would in future pay only seven *livres* a month for the care of abandoned illegitimate children between the ages of eighteen months and four years, by which time it was expected private families would be found who would agree to care for them. Twelve years later, in March 1748, Hocquart issued another *ordonnance* which, although dealing only with the situation in Montreal, throws a good deal of light on the manner in which this social problem was dealt with in Canada.[19]

The *ordonnance* begins by stating: 'The King, having been most desirous in the past that foundlings should be nourished and reared at the expense of, and be a charge on, the Royal domain, it is our responsibility to redouble from time to time our attention for their safe keeping, particularly since we have just been informed that a considerable number of the said children have perished in the past.' The intendant then declared that he would not go into the causes of this unfortunate state of affairs and proceeded instead to lay down detailed regulations for the proper care of the *enfants du Roi*. The local Crown prosecutor was instructed to make sure that the wet-nurses to whom the infants were first entrusted were capable of nursing them; a certain midwife was to be engaged to act as consultant in this connexion, be paid a retainer of 60 *livres* a year, and be exempted from the billeting of soldiers for her services. The wet-nurses were to be paid 45 *livres* for the first three months for each child, and ten *livres* a month after that until the child attained eighteen months. Since this was, the intendant declared, more than the townspeople were accustomed to pay for the nursing of their own children, the Crown prosecutor should have no difficulty in obtaining the services of nurses, who were to be paid cash in advance. When the infants were eighteen months old, and before if possible, the Crown prosecutor was required to have them cared for by honest families who would be made legally responsible for them until the age of eighteen or twenty. These foster-parents were to be given a grant of 45 *livres* upon taking a child into their care. Those children who had not been taken by private families at eighteen months were to continue to be cared for by their nurses, who would be paid seven *livres* ten *sols* a month. Every quarter the Crown prosecutor was required to send the intendant a list of all the children being cared for at the Crown's expense, with the date of their birth; another list being of the children being cared for privately, and by

---

19. *Inventaire des ordonnances des intendants de la Nouvelle France* (Québec, 1919), II, 203; *Arrêts et règlements du Conseil Supérieur...*, 395–6.

whom; and a third list giving the names of any children who had died, along with the date of their demise. . . .

There now remains only the medical services to be discussed. The colony was relatively well provided with both surgeons and doctors. One of them at least, Michel Sarrazin, as well as being highly regarded as both surgeon and doctor, enjoyed an international reputation as a scientist, being elected a corresponding member of the *Académie Royale des Sciences* along with Sir Isaac Newton.[20] The Intendant Champigny remarked of him that for every patient from whom he received a fee, he treated ten without charge.[21] Some of the more well-to-do citizens insured themselves against mishap by a means that is common today: the pre-paid medicare plan. In Montreal some forty-two citizens contracted with a master surgeon in such a scheme. For a fee of five *livres* each a year they and all members of their families were to receive medical care until completely recovered from all accidents or ailments except the plague, small pox, epilepsy, and lithotomy.[22] Although this is the only private medical contract so far to come to light, there is passing reference to another such in the records of the Sovereign Council.[23] Further research in the notarial records would very likely disclose more.

The more seriously ill were cared for at the colony's three hospitals: the *Hôtels Dieu* established at Quebec in 1639, Montreal in 1659, and Trois-Rivières in 1702. All three, and particularly the *Hôtel Dieu* at Quebec, enjoyed high reputations for the calibre of medical service they afforded to all, regardless of ability to pay. Separate endowments were maintained for the treatment of the poor, and the intendant insisted on a strict accounting of these revenues.[24] At Montreal the *Hôtel Dieu* contracted with two master surgeons to visit the wards every day, each for three months in turn, at a fee of 75 *livres* a year, to care for the charity cases.[25]

This, then, is as much as is presently known of the social-welfare measures in New France. Until a good deal more research is done, only tentative conclusions can be formed. All that presently can be said is that

---

20. Maude E. Abbot: *History of Medicine in the Province of Quebec* (Toronto, 1931), 25–6.
21. *Jugements et délibérations du Conseil Souverain. . .*, IV, 312–15.
22. A.D. Kelly: 'Health Insurance in New France,' in *Bulletin of the History of Medicine*, XXVIII, Nov.–Dec. 1954.
23. *Jugements et délibérations du Conseil Souverain. . .*, I, 436–7. (In this case, heard on 1 August 1667, a surgeon sued a citizen of Trois Rivières for non-payment of medical bills, for the treatment of the defendant, his family and servants, amounting to 465 *livres*. The defendant claimed to have a yearly medical contract and was required to produce proof.)
24. *Ordonnances des intendants et arrêts portant règlements du Conseil Supérieur de Québec*, II, 278–9, 7 juin 1727.
25. A.D. Kelly, op cit.

in the paternalistic, hierarchical society of New France, poverty was not regarded as a sin but as socially undesirable and, under certain conditions, as economically reprehensible. The people of the colony were, in many respects, much more fortunate than the mass of the people in Europe. There was an abundance of free land, fishing and hunting were open to all, and both fish and game abounded. Except during the early years of the eighteenth century, the fur trade flourished and brought considerable wealth into the colony, providing a relatively high standard of living to all ranks of society. The Church, in this age of Vincent de Paul, eventually to be canonized, played its traditional role of caring for the sick, and for the aged who had no one to care for them. It was thus left to the royal officials to enact mainly *ad hoc* measures to alleviate hardship resulting from temporary conditions, and to make provision for such special cases as foundlings, who were wards of the Crown.

It was not assumed, as it was in the England of that age, that a sizeable segment of the population would always be paupers. In New France no one starved—and of few parts of the world in that era could this be said. Steps were taken to prevent ne'er-do-wells from being a charge on society, and those unable to fend for themselves through no fault of their own were afforded some measure of security. The Crown accepted this as its proper responsibility and some at least of the colonial officials made sincere efforts to discharge the responsibility.

"THUNDER GUSTS":

Popular Disturbances in Early French Canada

TERENCE CROWLEY

Popular disturbances in the form of crowds, mobs, and armed uprisings were an intrinsic part of society and government in the Western world during the seventeenth and eighteenth centuries. Although the word "revolt" was often used by those in authority to describe these momentary but frequently violent upheavals, such a term is generally inappropriate at least before the 1760s when revolutionary ideas became more widespread. . . .

[In general, they fit the pattern identified by] George Rudé, the foremost student of popular protest in this period, [who] has attempted to differentiate those popular disturbances he calls the "pre-industrial" crowd from what became more characteristic in the nineteenth and twentieth centuries. Eighteenth-century popular disturbances, Rudé writes,

> tend to take the form of direct action and the destruction of property rather than of petitions or peaceful marches or demonstrations; and this was as true of peasant rebellion as it was of industrial machine-breaking, the imposition of the 'just' price in food riots or the 'pulling-down' of houses or the burning of their victims in effigy in city outbreaks. Yet such targets were generally carefully selected and destruction was rarely wanton or indiscriminate. Such movements tended to be spontaneous, to grow from small beginnings and to have a minimum of organization: they tended, too, to be led by leaders from the 'outside' or, if from 'inside', by men whose authority was limited to the occasion. They were generally defensive, conservative and 'backward-looking', more concerned to restore what had been lost from a 'golden' age than to blaze a trail for something new; and, accordingly, such political ideas as they expressed were more often conservative than radical and they tend (with some notable but rare exceptions) to be borrowed from conservative rather than radical groups.[1]

Rudé also notes that political issues tended to play a relatively insignifi-

TERENCE CROWLEY, " 'THUNDER GUSTS': POPULAR DISTURBANCES IN EARLY FRENCH CANADA," IN CANADIAN HISTORICAL ASSOCIATION, *HISTORICAL PAPERS* (1979): 11–31. BY PERMISSION OF CANADIAN HISTORICAL ASSOCIATION AND THE AUTHOR.

1. George Rudé, "Popular Protest in 18th Century Europe", Paul Fritz and David Williams, eds., *The Triumph of Culture: 18th Century Perspectives* (Toronto, 1972), p. 278.

cant role in early eighteenth-century protest and that England, with its measure of political democracy, witnessed disturbances that were more militant, sophisticated, and coloured by political concerns than were their counterparts in France.[2] The same observation may also be applied to the English colonies in North America where the frequency of crowds and mobs increased as the conflict with the mother country intensified in the 1760s and 1770s.[3] . . .

The nature of settlement in New France and the small number of colonists precluded popular protest on the scale or frequency of that witnessed in France, while the absolutist inspiration of French colonial government inhibited the formation of political disturbances that were seen in England and her colonies. France and England had total populations of over thirty million people by the early eighteenth century; Paris had grown to one-half million residents by 1700 and London to 575,000 by 1750.[4] In contrast, the population of the Quebec colony, generally referred to as Canada, numbered only fifty-five thousand in 1754, with some eight thousand people residing in the town of Quebec and four thousand in Montreal. The population of the French colonies on Prince Edward Island (Ile Saint-Jean) and Cape Breton (Ile Royale) amounted to 8,596 in 1752, with nearly one-half residing in the capital of Louisbourg.[5]

Conditions that often fomented popular discontent in the mother country were not present in her colonies. Settlement in New France was greatly dispersed and there were only six villages outside of the towns. The most common cause for French peasant revolt, high taxes, was absent from the colonies. Taxes on the export of beaver pelts and moose hides

---

2. George Rudé, *Paris and London in the 18th Century, Studies in Popular Protest* (London, 1970), pp. 8, 18.
3. Jesse Lemisch, "The American Revolution Seen from the Bottom Up", Barton J. Bernstein, ed., *Towards a New Past: Dissenting Essays in American History* (New York, 1969), pp. 3–45; Jesse Lemisch, "The Radicalism of the Inarticulate: Merchant Seamen in the Politics of Revolutionary America", A.F. Young, ed., *Dissent: Explorations in the History of American Radicalism* (De Kalb, Ill., 1978), originally published as "Jack Tar in the Streets: Merchant Seamen and the Politics of Revolutionary America", *William and Mary Quarterly*, 3rd ser., XXVII (1970), pp. 3–35; Pauline Maier, *From Resistance to Revolution: Colonial Radicals and the Development of American Opposition to Britain, 1765–1776* (New York, 1972), especially Chap. I; Gordon S. Wood, *The Creation of the American Republic, 1776–1787* (Chapel Hill, N.C., 1969), especially pp. 319–28. On colonial Latin America, see Chester Lyle Guthrie, "Riots in Seventeenth-Century Mexico City: A Study of Social and Economic Conditions", *Essays in Honor of Herbert Eugene Bolton* (Berkeley, 1945), pp. 243–58.
4. Rudé, *Paris and London*, pp. 35–6.
5. Canada, *Censuses of Canada 1665–1871* (Ottawa, 1876); J.S. McLennan, *Louisbourg: From Its Foundation to Its Fall* (London, 1918), p. 372.

were removed in 1717, leaving the 10 per cent customs duty on wine, spirits, and tobacco imported into Quebec as the only continuing form of taxation.[6] Seigneurial obligations in Canada were controlled by contract and subject to regulation by the intendant. Seigneurial dues appear to have been relatively light during the French regime and *corvées* were rare.[7] The tithe for the church was not heavy either, for although it had originally been set at one-thirteenth of the fruits of human labour and production of the soil, it was subsequently reduced to one twenty-sixth.[8] "Si, en France", Louise Dechêne concluded in her study of seventeenth-century Montreal, "la paysannerie d'Ancien Régime est définie par rapport à la classe qui l'exploite et la domine, au Canada, la population rurale est autre chose: des petits propriétaires parcellaires, à qui le régime demande un certain nombre de tributs—redevances, corvées, milices—mais qui, sur le plan matériel, bénéficient d'une sorte de trêve."[9] Nor in the towns were there large numbers of journeymen apprentices who were a frequent source of disturbances in England. Only at the St. Maurice forges, the Quebec shipyards, and Louisbourg were there any concentrations of skilled craftsmen. In Quebec that gave rise in 1741 to the first recorded strike in Canadian history, but among craftsmen recently arrived from France rather than among the Canadian workers.[10]

Despite these differences the distinction between the colonies and the mother country can be exaggerated. New France was far from being a pastoral paradise inhabited only by prosperous farmers and freedom-loving coureurs de bois. Demands placed on the people, especially by means of the three tributes of seigneurial dues, *corvées*, and militia service mentioned by Dechêne, did produce discontent. Runaways among apprentices and indentured servants and desertions from the ranks of the colonial regulars also testified to grievances but, apart from the Louisbourg mutiny of 1744, such discontent did not assume collective expres-

---

6. W.J. Eccles, *The Canadian Frontier 1534-1760* (Toronto, 1969), p. 81. Taxes were even lower at Louisbourg. See T.A. Crowley, "Government and Interests: French Colonial Administration at Louisbourg, 1713-1758", (Ph.D. thesis, Duke University, 1975), pp. 256-7.
7. Richard Colebrook Harris, *The Seigneurial System in Early Canada* (Quebec, 1968), pp. 63-70. Allen Greer, "Seigneurial Tenure in Quebec: The Examples of Sorel and St. Ours, 1670-1850", (paper presented to the Canadian Historical Association Annual Meeting, Saskatoon, June, 1979).
8. Cornelius Jaenen, *The Role of the Church in New France* (Toronto, 1976), pp. 84-90.
9. Louise Dechêne, *Habitants et marchands de Montréal au XVII siècle* (Paris, 1974), p. 486.
10. Peter N. Moogk, "In the Darkness of a Basement: Craftsmen's Associations in Early French Canada", *Canadian Historical Review*, LVII (1976), pp. 399-439.

sion in the form of mobs and crowds.[11] It was the conditions created by war that were most likely to lead the people to protest in New France, just as in the mother country the increased tax burden during periods of military conflict was the most conspicuous harbinger of opposition from French peasants. In the century and a half of settlement in Canada during the French regime, there was only one period of extended peace between 1713 and 1744, and even that was marked by localized conflicts such as the Anglo-Abenaki and Fox Wars. Militia service was compulsory for all men sixteen to sixty, a heavy burden on the population and one which certainly caused resentment, but surprisingly little is known about the operation of the militia organization on the local level.[12] The billeting of regular soldiers in the towns of Quebec and Montreal also caused disputes. More significantly, however, war interrupted shipping to the colonies and aggravated the unstable economic situation created by pre-industrial agriculture and rudimentary communications systems.

On at least a dozen occasions, people in New France took to the streets, paraded to the walls of towns, or otherwise assembled for direct action in defiance of the law. Food shortages were the root of at least four demonstrations and commodity prices were at the centre of an equal number. Religious issues and resistance to forced labour for the government accounted for other forms of collective action. In several instances, officials and the middle classes used such disturbances or collective violence for their own purposes, but more often the motivation and leadership came from within the crowd than from without.

Demonstrations were the only collective means by which the habitants and lower classes could influence those in authority, although they were sometimes used for political purposes. Governmental structures in New

---

11. Jean-Pierre Hardy and David-Thiery Ruddel, *Les apprentis artisans à Québec 1660–1815* (Montreal, 1977), pp. 74–80; André Lachance, "La désertion et les soldats déserteurs au Canada dans la première moitié du XVIII siècle", *Mélanges d'histoire du Canada français offerts au professeur Marcel Trudel*, Cahiers du Centre de Recherche en Civilisation Canadienne-Française (Ottawa, 1978), pp. 151–61; T.A. Crowley, "The Forgotten Soldiers of New France: The Louisbourg Example", French Colonial Historical Society, *Proceedings of the Third Annual Meeting*, Alf Andrew Heggoy, ed. (Athens, Ga., 1978), pp. 52–69. Allen Greer, "Mutiny at Louisbourg, December 1744", *Histoire Sociale/Social History*, XX (1977), pp. 305–36 suggests that the desertion rate among colonial regulars on Cape Breton was lower than in France, but uses a specious comparison in which the French figures cover a time period during two wars, when desertion was highest, while those for the colonies cover only a period of peace.

12. Dechêne, *Habitants et marchands*, pp. 356–61, has advanced our knowledge of the militia on the local level, but has found no generalized discontent in Montreal before 1715.

France were highly autocratic, just as they continued to be during the opening decades of the British regime. Power was concentrated in the hands of the governor and intendant who reported to the Ministry of Marine in France. Merchants, seigneurs, and favoured individuals were able to exercise a continuing though informal influence on the administration by virtue of their economic power, social prestige, or proximity to decision-making; but the lower classes were totally excluded except when the intendant authorized a local assembly to discuss a specific matter, such as the construction of a church or the price of beaver.[13] Otherwise, assemblies were unlawful in a time and place where there were no political rights, only privileges inherited through custom or bestowed by the king. . . .Collective petitions were also prohibited although they appeared occasionally.[14] In New France the Church alone provided the only continuing means for collective popular expression and representation when parishioners gathered annually to elect churchwardens for their parish. . . .

Collective protest in New France was. . .more common than historians have previously recognized. Popular disturbances were not simply spasmodic reactions of mindless people succumbing to momentary whims or losing themselves in the collective identity of the crowd. As in Europe, people in New France assembled to seek remedy to immediate but well-defined grievances, to "representer la misère de la Coste", as one witness to the disturbance of 1714 admitted.[15] Demonstrations emanating from the countryside appear to have originated among the local residents themselves rather than had leadership from outside the area. They were not declarations of political principle, but requests for official intervention or indignant reactions against what were perceived as unfair practices or unjust impositions by government. The discussions preceding the 1714 march, the steadfastness of the men of Longueuil protesting the royal *corvée* in 1717, the impudence of women confronting Governor Vaudreuil

---

13. Representation in various forms is discussed most fully in Gustave Lanctôt, *L'administration de la Nouvelle-France* (Montreal, 1971, reprint of 1929 edition), Chap. VII, "La participation du peuple dans le gouvernement". On the influence of factions and interest groups, see Guy Frégault, "Politique et politiciens", *Le XVIII siècle canadien: études* (Montreal, 1968), pp. 159–243; and Crowley, "Government and Interests", pp. 283–316, 367–81.

14. Colbert to Frontenac, 13 June 1673, *Rapport de l'Archiviste de la Province de Québec* (1926–27), p. 25 (hereafter RAPQ). See also Francis Hammang, *The Marquis de Vaudreuil, New France at the Beginning of the Eighteenth Century* (Bruges, 1938), chap. 1.

15. Archives Nationales du Québec à Québec, NF 13–1, Matières de Police, 30 September 1714, 98 ff.

in 1757, and even the reactions of the officials themselves suggest that such forms of collective behaviour were accompanied by some notion of legitimatization, which revealed that the protestors were supported by the consensus of the larger community or were defending a traditional right.[16] But in contrast to Europe, no disturbances associated with popular festivities or feast days have been uncovered in New France. The charivari, or mock serenade of newly married couples, was imported into the colonies from the mother country and created the raucous behavior normally associated with that public ritual. Although the charivaris did not burst into anti-government or anti-Church activity, Bishop Laval found that they led to "désordres et libertés scandaleuses" where "des actions très impies" were committed, and he officially banned them in 1683.[17]

The study of collective protest quickly turns to an examination of the society which first produced and then reacted to it. The essentially non-political character of most of these disturbances and the absence of large-scale popular protest fomented by the middle classes reflects not only political structures during the French regime, but also the mentality of the middle classes and their numerical weakness in the social structure.[18] There were no Bacon's or Leisler's rebellions, nor any Regulators, in New France as there were in the English colonies. At the same time the strong military presence in the French colonies accounted for at least part of the restraint shown by demonstrators. New France was an armed camp where authorities could threaten effective counter-violence through the use of garrisoned regulars. There were no police forces as such but, unlike officials in England and her dependencies, French colonial administrators did not have to rely on only the "hue and cry", the *posse commitatus* or the militia for law enforcement in such situations. Towns were garrisoned with colonial regulars ready for the call and French officials showed that they were prepared to use force if disturbances persisted or became unruly. Officials even argued that the garrisons should be increased

---

16. E.P. Thompson, "The Moral Economy of the English Crowd in the Eighteenth Century", *Past and Present*, L (1971), pp. 70–136.

17. See Henri Têtu and C.O. Gagnon, eds., *Mandements, lettres pastorales et circulaires des évêques de Québec* (Quebec, 1887), I, pp. 114–5; and Jaenen, *Role of the Church*, p. 140. For France, see Yves-Marie Bercé, *Fête et révolte, Des mentalités populaires du XVI siècle au XVIII siècle* (Paris, 1976).

18. The character and composition of the bourgeoisie in New France continues to be hotly contested. For an introduction to the debate, see Dale Miquelon, ed., *Society and Conquest: The Debate on the Bourgeoisie and Social Change in French Canada, 1700–1850* (Toronto, 1977).

because soldiers were necessary "pour maintenir l'ordre de la Colonie et reprimer L'insolence des habitans."[19]

Popular protest in New France was sparked more by a sense of injustice, a fear of privation, and a desire to invoke government protection than it was prompted by any single economic factor. There is no mechanical correlation between the incidence of popular disturbances and the price of the dietary staple, wheat. Demonstrations in 1704 and 1705 occurred when wheat prices were falling, while those in 1714, 1717, and 1757–58 transpired within the context of advancing prices being paid to producers.[20] More important than the price of wheat was the nature of markets during the *ancien régime* and its effects on popular psychology. Markets in the colonies demonstrated the same characteristics as those described by Pierre Goubert for France: limited in extent, poorly provisioned, inelastic, and subject to speculation. As a result, the popular mind was haunted by [fear of famine].[21] New France did not experience famine where people died as they did in Europe, but shortages due to interruptions in shipping or poor harvests and rapid escalations in prices were sufficiently numerous to alarm people when such indicators first appeared. For this reason protests erupted in the fall or spring when the prospect of a difficult winter loomed ahead, or when shortages were beginning to be perceived before the arrival of ships or the appearance of spring crops.

Fears that a difficult situation might suddenly deteriorate further, or indignation that others had denied them access to essential commodities, were nurtured by the fundamental instability of pre-industrial markets. Fears and indignation as elements of popular psychology help to explain why popular protest erupted more over food or prices than actual instances of destitution or starvation. Similarly, Charles Tilly has concluded that in modern Europe conflicts over the food supply occurred not so much where people were hungry, but where people believed that others were depriving them of food to which they had a moral and political right.[22] That such conflicts in New France never reached the level of great societal redressing rituals that they attained in Europe is indica-

---

19. Vaudreuil and Bégon to Pontchartrain, 20 September 1714, *RAPQ* (1947–48), p. 277.
20. Wheat prices are discussed and charted in Dechêne, *Habitants et marchands*, pp. 324–36, 521; and in Jean Hamelin, *Economie et société en Nouvelle-France* (Quebec, 1960), pp. 58–62.
21. Pierre Goubert, *L'Ancien Régime*, Tome I: *Le Société* (Paris, 1969), p. 42.
22. Charles Tilly, "Food Supply and Public Order in Modern Europe", Charles Tilly, ed., *The Formation of National States in Western Europe* (Princeton, N.J., 1975), p. 389.

tive of better economic conditions in the New World and a lesser degree of social antagonism. It also testifies to the success of government regulation of the economy of New France. Older historians of New France such as Francis Parkman, George Wrong and L.H. Gipson, who were imbued with the principles of nineteenth-century *laissez-faire* liberalism, saw such government activity as a fettering of trade, excessive benevolence, and a paternalism which hampered the untrammelled free spirit.[23] W.J. Eccles, in contrast, has more recently argued that government intervention in New France was inspired by the aristocratic ethos of the age and dictated by the nature of the colony's economy.[24]...

That New France did not witness popular protest on the scale or frequency observed elsewhere may therefore be partially attributed to the activities of her officials. Through intervention in the marketplace they by-passed the buyers and their agents, who filtered through the country-side to purchase farm products, and either moderated or prevented speculation and price collusion among decidedly small merchant communities in Montreal and Quebec. Official regulation of the food supply in New France was made easier and was ultimately more successful than that in many areas of France for two reasons. As settlement during the French regime was strung out along the avenues of the St. Lawrence and the Atlantic, the colonies did not experience the transportation difficulties encountered in parts of France where there were few waterways and only poor roads. Secondly, despite the weaknesses inherent in agriculture at the time, Canadian agriculture was at least as efficient as that in France as a whole, although it was dependent on clearing new lands.[25] Even with poor harvests, early Canadian agriculture was able to feed a rapidly expanding population and export surpluses of wheat and other foodstuffs to Louisbourg and the West Indies from the 1720s to 1751. Only in 1743 and 1744 was it necessary for Quebec officials to import wheat from France and the English colonies to feed the Canadian population.[26]

---

23. For a review of these interpretations, see Yves F. Zoltvany, *The Government of New France: Royal, Clerical, or Class Rule?* (Scarborough, Ont., 1971), pp. 36–55.
24. W.J. Eccles, *Canada Under Louis XIV 1663–1701* (Toronto, 1964), pp. 57–8; *Canadian Society During the French Regime* (Montreal, 1968), pp. 13, 43–4; *The Canadian Frontier 1534–1760* (New York, 1969), p. 75.
25. Dechêne, *Habitants et marchands*, pp. 326–8; W.J. Eccles, *France in America* (Toronto, 1972), pp. 121–2.
26. Alice J.E. Lunn, "Economic Development in New France, 1713-1760" (Ph.D. thesis, McGill University, 1942), p. 101.

These procedures to avoid popular disturbances and the leniency with which the protestors were handled suggest that colonial authorities, like their English counterparts, unofficially recognized the legitimacy of demonstrations as long as they acted within certain bounds.[27] Governors and intendants were overtly hostile to such manifestations in their correspondence with their superiors in France, but their actions belied their words. "Sedition", "mutiny", "revolt", and "riot" were terms they used to describe popular disturbances, but punishments were never harsh. This is explained not only by the non-destructiveness of the crowds, but also by the opinion among colonial officials that the people had no other way to express their plight. Officials in France, especially early in the eighteenth century, feared outbreaks as violent as those seen in the mother country and argued for stiffer sentences. Their subordinates in New France chose, rather, to remedy the complaint and exact only enough punishment to reinforce the appearance of authority.

In 1768 the *New York Journal* referred to the popular tumults that occasionally erupted as "Thunder Gusts" which "do more Good than Harm."[28] By providing a channel for collective expression with a minimum of violence, popular demonstrations can be said to have had a beneficial effect in New France.

---

27. David Grimstead, "Rioting in Its Collective Setting", *American Historical Review*, LXXVII (1972), p. 362.
28. Cited in Maier, *From Resistance to Revolution*, p. 23.

The Role of the Church in New France

CORNELIUS JAENEN

Were the *habitants* concerned about religious ideas or were they content with mere external conformity to inherited traditional observances, rites and forms which, they believed, would assure them the salvation they ultimately desired? During the closing decades of the French period, the church in France was shaken by deism, skepticism and indifference, yet so critical an appraiser as Pontbriand declared that there was no trace of error in his diocese. Those Canadians who communicated with France would surely have encountered some of the current religious thought of the metropolis. Just as astonishing is the fact that in the 1740s when communication with New England was frequent, there is no mention in New France of the Great Awakening. Perhaps to avoid all mention of Protestantism was a reflex action.

Wayside shrines dotted the countryside testifying the beliefs of those who erected them; few people ever passed them without at least some acknowledgment of their significance. Family prayers were recited morning and evening, and in the majority of homes grace was said before and after meals. The belief in the efficacy of relics, pilgrimages, novenas and the exposition of the Blessed Sacrament was firmly rooted in the popular mind. The shrine of Ste. Anne de Beaupré early became a centre of pilgrimage, and, by the end of the seventeenth century, there were scores of miracles attributed to her intervention. The relics of the Jesuit martyrs, though few in number, soon had miracles attributed to them—one nun claimed that a particularly stubborn Huguenot had become docile and converted readily after being given a broth in which a small fragment of Father Brébeuf's skull had been placed. Supernatural events were also connected with the tombs of Bishops Laval and Saint-Vallier. Reverence and awe were paid to Catherine Tekakwitha, Marie de l'Incarnation, Jeanne le Ber and Marguerite Bourgeoys—but a few of the outstanding women pioneers of the faith in New France. It was commonly believed that the blessed bread, which the parishioners presented in turn, and which engendered some competition among the women who prepared it, possessed special attributes. It could aid in "chasing demons" from the

Cornelius Jaenen, *The Role of the Church in New France* (Toronto: McGraw-Hill Ryerson, 1976): 144–51. Used by permision of the author.

body of the possessed, in healing sickness, and giving strength. According to the *Rituel*, "the great Saints employed it successfully to these ends." To sell it at a higher price than ordinary bread was declared an act of simony. Stories of the Host stopping a fire at Quebec, or curbing a plague of caterpillars were fervently repeated. Although, to date, the church of New France has not produced a single Canadian canonized by Rome,* Bishop Saint-Vallier was certain that Brother Didace's intercessions had obtained for him the cure he sought at Trois-Rivières.

It is always difficult to establish the extent to which a folk-belief may be a survival of the "old religion", that is, of pre-Christian paganism, or to determine whether it is a localized accretion with no particular religious connotation. Studies of European religious mentality and survival of magical pagan beliefs and practices would seem to indicate that the cultural baggage of colonists to the New World included a great variety of such beliefs and practices. The inhabitants of New France placed great stock in magical formulas, in healing waters, in natural phenomena as omens of Divine intervention, in the observation of taboos, and in the efficacy of witchcraft and sorcery. Such acceptance was not in any way separated from religious belief as evidenced by the fact that prayers and pilgrimages, along with religious processions and the public display of the Host in its sun-shaped ostensory, were employed to stop plagues of caterpillars and grasshoppers, to put out fires, to protect from violent storms and earthquakes. Although it might be noted that the earthquakes of 1663, remarkable for their severity, had no more long-range effect in bringing about a reformation in fur traders' and merchants' morals than did the fiery celestial apparitions which were widely reported at that time.

The Feast of St. John the Baptist was observed, as in France, with all the pagan observances recorded for the festivities of the night of June 23–24. Grasses long reputed to have magical qualities were tossed into the flames, the common people danced around the community bonfire, and the ashes were later carefully gathered, according to ancient Western European custom. In 1646, for example, the Jesuits accompanied the governor to the great bonfire at Quebec, which he lit, and they sang an appropriate hymn and prayer for the occasion before leaving the people to their celebrations. Each year thereafter, the clergy was present for the ceremonies, until, in 1650, the Jesuit Superior refused to attend—not wishing to light the fire himself—and set a precedent, although another member of the order attended in surplice and stole. Thereafter, the Jesuit

*IN OCTOBER 1982 MARGUERITE BOURGEOYS WAS CANONIZED.

made no mention of these festivities, and apparently they withdrew discreetly from participation in celebrations which took on more mundane characteristics.[1] This did not prevent the observances from developing into a sort of colonial national holiday.

A colony where popular religious belief sometimes bordered on the superstitious can be expected to have experienced serious outbreaks of witchcraft and to have engaged in the judicial pursuit and exorcism of sorcery. It is essential to recall that, during the Middle Ages, witchcraft was regarded as a superstition inspired by the devil. Pope Gregory VII, for example, condemned the popular belief that natural calamities were caused by diabolical intervention. The Council of Trèves (1310) decreed that the "sabbaths" did not exist but were mere hallucinations inspired by Satan; belief in their existence was therefore a sin. This attitude changed, notably among theologians and the educated elite, during the period between 1560 and 1620, when challenges from Protestantism and the old surviving pagan customs of the countryside coincided with witch-hunting. Suppression of witchcraft in France and the colonies fell entirely within the jurisdiction of the secular power from the 16th century forward, and from 1500 to 1670 not one year passed without some sorcerers being executed by orders of the Parlements. There were publicized cases of "possession" of nuns at Aix, Loudun and Chinon which greatly worried Mother Marie de l'Incarnation that the hysteria would spread to New France and to her convent in particular.[2] By the seventeenth century, the Catholic revival brought the *dévots* to question these supposedly Satanic rites and powers, and there was a return among a religious elite to the mediaeval interpretation of witchcraft. Bishop Laval and most of his clergy in the colony tended to believe that mental disorders and the power of suggestion had much to do with popular belief in witchcraft. The essayist Montaigne had condemned superstitious practices, and had postulated mental derangement as the explanation for apparent devil possession. The Belgian doctor, Jean Wier, had called into question the medical evidence given at witch trials and each passing decade saw a greater number of medical authorities share his skepticism. The Ordinance of 1682 put an end, for practical purposes, to witchcraft trials in France.

Marie de l'Incarnation, Jérôme Lalement and Paul Ragueneau all saw in

---

1. *Journal dés Jésuites* (Montreal, 1892), pp. 53–54, 89–90, 111, 127, 141–142.
2. R. Mandrou, *Magistrats et Sorciers en France au XVIIe siècle* (Paris, 1968), pp. 221–226.

the "possession" of a young girl who was probably subject to epilepsy, the "malignity of certain magicians and sorcerers come from France." The caterpillars which plagued Canada in 1646 were described in some texts as "nefarious spirits", the Amerindian religious leaders were regarded as "sorcerers" and some soldiers who were reputed to possess knowledge in bone-setting and healing were considered to be under diabolical influences. The inhabitants of Beauport and Bellechasse were reported to watch the goblins tripping away under the direction of Satan himself at sabbaths held on the island of Orleans.

At a time when witchcraft trials were shaking Connecticut and Massachussetts, authorities in New France showed a marked tendency to discredit popular belief in this form of supernatural activity, or to simply avoid prosecuting suspects. Bishop Laval and the Sulpician superior, Tronson, were influential in quieting alarms about diabolical possession and witchcraft. The clergy, as a whole, had a firmly rooted belief that the grace flowing from the sacraments could be employed against dangers of uncertain origin. Finally, there was a growing weight of informed opinion in France which discredited what sometimes passed for sorcery. The *Rituel* which Saint-Vallier gave the colony warned that charges of witchcraft were to be dealt with prudently; nevertheless, it did not deny its existence and provided that burial in consecrated ground be refused to sorcerers. The service of exorcism in the *Rituel* warned against "suspecting neighbours and other persons of having procured this evil", and cautioned the faithful "not to listen to vain promises made by certain people who hasten to assure them that they will discover the author of the spell."[3]

One of the popularly believed diabolical powers was that of *nouer l'aiguillette*, that is rendering a marriage barren and the couple impotent by a spell. In 1657 a rejected suitor and corporal of the garrison was said to have cast a spell on the marriage of Marie Pontonnier and the gunsmith Pierre Gadois. When no children were procreated, the troubled couple sought the advice of their parish priest, who—on the bishop's suggestion—had a new nuptial blessing given.[4] The results were still negative; therefore, the church annulled the marriage after three years of enquiry provided for in the sacred canons "for cause of and in consequence of perpetual impotence caused by witchcraft." René Besnard, the corporal in

---

3. Rituel du diocèse de Québec (Paris, 1703), pp. 570–572, 589.
4. *A.J.M.*, *Documents Judiciaires*, "Interrogation of René Besnard Bourjoly," November 2, 1658.

question, meanwhile, was charged in the seigneurial court of Montreal with the attempted seduction of three women, and it developed during his trial that he was believed to have been responsible for the aforementioned barren marriage. He escaped with a heavy fine and banishment from Montreal. If any needed further proof of the power of the spell he was supposed to have cast, it was provided by the fact that when Marie Pontonnier and Pierre Gadois each re-married, they both had very fruitful marriages blessed by numerous offspring. . . .

There was disinclination to proceed with formal charges of witchcraft and sorcery in the courts. In 1666 one of the Hospital Nuns at Quebec reported the theft of some consecrated hosts from their chapel and suggested that it resembled similar thefts which had preceded the appearance of black masses in the Paris region the previous year. The Sovereign Council took no action. In 1671 occurred the trial for "the child strangled by the Galbrun woman and other acts of witchcraft", but the Sovereign Council elected to prosecute only for infanticide and not for witchcraft. In 1682 a Mme. de Folleville, who ran a thriving cabaret in Montreal where such well-known traders as Duluth and Le Gardeur de Repentigny came to drink and play cards in a back room, was accused of furtively keeping a book on black magic. She was banished from Montreal but was able to have the sentence quashed. A few years later a Marie Godet claimed that a Jean Campagnard had tried to bewitch her by giving her a gift. He managed to give a pound of butter to her servant so that she eventually came into possession of this "gift"; when she later fell ill she concluded it was an evil spell. Although witnesses testified that Campagnard caused cattle to die and that he brought illness to several individuals, he was not convicted.[5]

Then in 1676 there were rumours of an outbreak of witchcraft and sorcery at the Sulpician mission and reservation of La Montagne. The *Abbé* Guillaume Bailly, posted there as director and schoolmaster, had become deeply interested in visions and dreams. Other Sulpicians became affected by Bailly's belief in witches to the extent that an inquiry had to be launched. The Superior in Paris sent a cautionary note of advice in March, 1680 in dealing with Amerindians who were allegedly "possessed":

First, do not question at all on this matter those persons who do not accuse themselves thereof.

---

5. *Archives Nationales de la Province de Québec (A.P.Q.), Procédures Judiciaires*, Vol. I, "Case of Jean Campagnard," February 20, 1685.

Secondly, do not interrogate too scrupulously on certain useless details even those who accuse themselves.

Thirdly, do not believe too readily what they say unless you are in possession of definite proofs that it is not imagination at all but is reality. Fourthly, treat them the same as other sinners in granting them or refusing them the sacraments.[6]

The source of this unusual behaviour appears to have been the priest Bailly, for in 1689 he and two Sulpician companions became involved with a visionary nun who claimed to receive spirit messages from the other world. The three priests were recalled to France for "consultation" and soon Bailly was forced to leave the community of Saint-Sulpice.

In 1742 there was a great scandal in Montreal when a soldier employed a religious book and a crucifix as accessories in an act of prognostication and divination. A shoemaker named Robidoux had asked a soldier of the Montreal garrison named Havard to employ his occult powers by using a mirror to make appear the face of a thief who had robbed him of 120 livres. A large crowd assembled to watch the several hours of dramatic incantations which included smearing a mirror and a crucifix with oils and coloured powders, and lighting and snuffing of candles. Soon gossip had it that Havard was of Jewish origins—for profanation of churches was popularly attributed to Jews, Protestants and dabblers in the occult. Some asserted that he had outraged the crucifix, that he had pierced it with a knife and that blood had spurted from the wound. Havard and Robidoux were arrested and tried; Havard was sentenced to make a public confession and to spend five years in the galley fleets, while Robidoux was to be pilloried and banished from Montreal for three years. An appeal to the Sovereign Council resulted in Havard's sentence being reduced to three years in the galleys, and in Robidoux's being levied a fine of three livres payable to charities for prisoners. Bishop Pontbriand was making his pastoral visitation of Montreal at the time of the trial; he found that the sense of outrage and public indignation was so intense that he issued a *mandement* expressing the town's horror and distress over the incident of the "outraged crucifix". By way of public penance and compensation, a general procession was organized from the parish church to the chapel of Bonsecours where the ceremonies of the adoration of the cross would be observed. Because so many parishes now wished to possess this "out-

---

6. *Bibliothèque de Saint-Sulpice, Paris (B.S.S.P.), Tronson Correspondence*, Vol. I, No. 97, "Tronson to Dollier de Casson," March 20, 1680, pp. 166–167.

raged crucifix" as a sort of relic, the Bishop decided to give it to the safekeeping of the Hospital Nuns of Quebec.[7]

At least a majority of the colonials, like the common people of the mother country, seem to have practised their religion, more out of social convention and habit than out of any over-zealous conviction or superstitious fear. Most performed their Easter duties and took part in midnight mass at Christmas, although fewer attended mass faithfully each Sunday. Even those who did attend regularly did not always show the respect and attention that one might expect of them. In every decade there were priests who complained to the bishop and to the secular authorities about the laxity of religious practice. Nevertheless, the Canadians seem to have been a generally religious people. Their chief fault was that they performed their religious obligations in much the same way as they performed their social obligations, and in this they followed rather well the example of their Kings. Anyone who refused to conform to the conventional life-style was quickly marked; be that as it may, few entered into the religious observances with either deep and fervent conviction or mystical fanaticism. Peter Kalm observed in mid-eighteenth century that the colonials—even the garrison troops—were faithful in reciting their morning and evening prayers, in saying grace before and after meals, and in saluting various shrines and memorials. He wrote:

> It was both strange and amusing to see and hear how eagerly the women and soldiers said their prayers in Latin and did not themselves understand a word of what they said. When all the prayers were ended the soldiers cried *Vive le Roi*! and that is about all they understood of the prayer proceedings. I have notice in the papal service that it is directed almost entirely toward the external; the heart representing the internal is seldom touched. It all seems to be a ceremony. In the meantime the people are very faithful in these observances, because everyone tries by these means to put God under some obligation and intends by it to make himself deserving of some reward.[8]

It would be erroneous to suppose that religion was the chief motivational force behind all aspects of everyday living. Such an interpretation could

---

7. *Archives du Séminaire de Québec (A.S.Q.), Polygraphie XIII*, Nos. 5–10; *A.J.M., Procès Fameux, 1734–1756.* "Case of Havard," June 30, 1742; H. Têtu and C.O. Gagnon (eds.), *Mandements* (Québec, 1887), Vol. II, pp. 19–21.
8. Adolph B. Benson (ed.), *Peter Kalm's Travels in North America* Vol. II (New York, 1966) p. 422.

only come from an unwarranted association of early seventeenth-century eschatological thought and *dévot* revivalism, and the projection back into early times of nineteenth-century ultramontanism, with the general tone of colonial Catholicism. While it is true that, during the early missionary period when the religious foundations of the colony were laid, a mystical and even fanatical Catholicism made itself felt, it did not dominate thought and action after 1663. Utopian visions and eschatological dreams faded into the romantic background; and by that standard, religiosity declined as settlement progressed, as more aspects of French life were transferred to the colony, and as the metropolitan sources of ecstatic religiosity dried up. The episcopacy of Saint-Vallier seems to have marked a low point in religious conviction, although Pontbriand was certain that the church in his own day was disorganized and undisciplined beyond comparison. These were far cries from the fervently practised Catholic uniformity that some historians have erroneously seen in New France.

FURTHER READINGS FOR TOPIC 2

W. J. Eccles. "The History of New France according to Francis Parkman." *William and Mary Quarterly*. Third Series, vol. XVIII, no. 2 (April 1961): 163–75.

W. J. Eccles. *The Canadian Frontier 1534–1760*. Albuquerque: University of New Mexico Press, 1969.

Allan Greer. *Peasant, Lord and Merchant: Rural Society in Three Quebec Parishes, 1740–1840*. Toronto: University of Toronto Press, 1985.

Dale Miquelon. *New France 1701–1744: "A Supplement to Europe."* Toronto: McClelland and Stewart, 1987.

Marcel Trudel. *The Beginnings of New France 1524–1663*. Toronto: McClelland and Stewart, 1973.

TOPIC 3

New France: European or North American?

The extent to which colonial peoples of European origin continue to be dominated by metropolitan influences emanating from the mother country, as opposed to environmental influences and frontier life, is endlessly fascinating. One school of historians, inspired by the work of American historians such as Frederick Jackson Turner, stresses the importance of the "frontier" environment of the "new world" to the evolution of new institutions and a new culture. The reluctance of Canadian historians to overemphasize the significance of the frontier is reflected in the selection from Dale Miquelon's book on New France. Miquelon examines elements of French society which were reproduced, with some modifications, in New France, including a hierarchical social order, the Roman Catholic Church, and the institution of the family. While recognizing the impact of native North Americans and the modifying effects of colonial life, Miquelon concludes that the society of New France was essentially derivative of French society.

A different answer is supplied by the work of Serge Courville, a historical geographer whose article focuses on the interplay between structures imposed by France, particularly the seigneurial system, and the behaviour of the colonial population. The framework for this discussion is provided by the concepts of urbanité and territorialité, which are defined in the footnotes. Courville argues that New France produced a "distinctive way of life" which provided the basis from which French Canadian society later evolved.

Luc Hoppen's article provides a concrete illustration of the interplay of metropolitan and frontier influences in the context of domestic architecture. Between 1608 and 1760, the homes of New France evolved from metropolitan models, with modifications occasioned by the use of local materials, colonial weather conditions, the limitations of local pocketbooks, and, of course, the fear of fire. Both European and North American influences, then, are evident in the realm of material culture, no less than on questions relating to social structure and social values.

NEW FRANCE 1701–1744:

"A Supplement to Europe"

DALE MIQUELON

Orders and families; relationships governed by the *coutume*, by *rente* and seigneury, by tithe and parish; authority and obedience (and perhaps a dialectically related individualism); old-fashioned notions of the virtues of clergy, military, and judiciary: these are the linkages of the Old Regime. The extent to which they were indeed transferred "bodily from one country to another" defines the extent to which Canada was indeed an Old Regime society.

Those at the apex of Canadian society were status conscious to a degree. Quarrels over precedence, such as the confrontation of Crisafy and Champigny, remained standard behaviour for officials, French and Canadian. In particular, that constant procession that was Old Regime society was sorted out and fought over in the church, the one place where the entire community assembled. There were always arguments over the right to have *prie-Dieu* and to place them in prominent locations. In 1710 the churchwardens of Notre Dame de Montréal demanded that a *prie-Dieu* used by the local commander and by the king's attorney be removed from their church, and they took their case to the Superior Council. In another instance, in 1719, the Marine Council, no less, ruled that Governor Vaudreuil was not to permit his son to use his *prie-Dieu* in the Montreal church in his absence, "something that besmirches the character of the local Governor of Montreal," and he was himself no longer to worship, as he was accustomed to, with an entire retinue of soldiers. In the same year, the Marine Council also doused the pretensions of Louvigny to receive the palms and ashes within the chancel of the church in the same manner as the Governor General.[1]

DALE MIQUELON, *NEW FRANCE 1701–1744: "A SUPPLEMENT TO EUROPE"* (TORONTO: MCCLELLAND AND STEWART, 1987): 231–39, 245. USED BY PERMISSION.
1. Canada, Assembly of the Province of, *Edits et ordonnances*...(Quebec, 1854), pp. 433–34, 25 juin 1710, 276–77, 30 juin 1710; Archives des Colonies (AC), B 41: 535v, Conseil de Marine à Vaudreuil, Paris, 24 mai 1719, fol. 544, Conseil de Marine à Louvigny, Versailles, 24 mai 1719.

Many questions of precedence had been settled by an omnibus regulation of the King in Council in 1716.[2] The most arcane matters were considered, including who should have torches to light bonfires on festive occasions and who should receive incense at mass, but in particular it dealt with rights to *prie-Dieu* and precedence in processions. It is a testimony to the power of rank that human ingenuity kept on devising ever more ingenious manifestations of dignity requiring the subtle adjudications of a royal council. . . .

To what extent were people of all walks of life—out of range of the example of imported officials—imbued with a sense of rank and hierarchy? In a famous dispatch of 1707, Jacques Raudot wrote of the Canadian people that, "never having any education because of the laxity that results from a foolish tenderness that their fathers and mothers have for them in their childhood, imitating in that the Indians," they grew up without discipline and developed a "hard and ferocious character."[3] They lacked respect for their parents and their superiors, including their *curés*. For this reason, there was "no decency in their conduct towards one another." Raudot claimed that he tried hard to draw them from this barbarism by fining their acts of violence and ferocity but felt himself engaged in a losing battle. The bonds of society unravelling and the pernicious Indian example: Raudot provides a contemporary and negative anticipation of Turner's frontier thesis as it has been reworked in the hands of a modern Canadian historian[4] For all his decrying of colonial mores, however, Raudot did not despair of Canadians. He pinned his hopes on the efficacy of education. He supported François Charon's school at Montreal. In every parish he hoped someday to see schoolmasters who in addition to the instruction they would give Canadian children "will teach them early to be submissive." At the same time, Raudot did not give up on their parents. By exalting the position of the local captains of militia—giving them subaltern rank in the regular troops and honoraria—the habitants, he argued, would be brought into a greater dependence. Over thirty years later, his argument still held sway. The King approved Beauharnois's act of sending an officer among the parishes to ensure that the militiamen were learning their drills, "as nothing is more appropriate to maintain discipline and subordination among them."[5] . . .

---

2. *Edits et ordonnances*, pp. 352–54 règlement, 27 av. 1716.
3. AC, C11A 26: 167–68, Raudot père au Ministre, Québec, 10 nov. 1707.
4. W.J. Eccles, *The Canadian Frontier, 1534–1760*, Histories of the American Frontier (New York, 1969), Chap. 5.
5. AC, B 72: 382, Mémoire du Roi, Marly, 12 mai 1741.

Our pursuit of the question of rank...takes us...right into the nave of the parish church....To the extent that Canadians had access to the teaching, preaching, and sacraments of the Church, they affirmed both rank and community while they affirmed faith. Access to the church becomes a fundamental question for the interpretation of Laurentian social history.

Townsmen were well integrated into the liturgical cycle of the church year and enjoyed ample access to confession and the sacraments. In the earlier eighteenth century, 80 per cent of the clergy lived in the towns, although only a quarter of the population was urban. Because of the presence of many religious orders, there were chapels in addition to the parish churches. The obvious counterpart of this was that the three quarters of Canadians who lived in the countryside were served by only 20 per cent of the clergy. Not only were the clergy in short supply but many of them were also loath to live in the countryside where they were often poorly housed and received little from the tithe....

Thus while the influence of the Church upon the urban communities seems to have been considerable from the colony's earliest days, its influence in the country parishes remains problematical. The historian must balance rural society's long period of social incubation during which the Church was a fugitive influence against the growth of an ecclesiastical presence as the countryside became more settled and more affluent. He must also consider the equally uncertain influence of the town and urban leadership upon society as a whole.

The religious orders were an element of urban leadership and urban society that merits attention. The ideas of social linkage shown to have animated the communities of nuns, for example, were decidedly hierarchical and can only have been a reflection of secular society. It would be difficult to argue that they reflected a metropolitan influence that flew in the face of a colonial egalitarianism. A mother superior governed her community armed with the power of a kind of temporary excommunication, excluding impenitent sisters from the communion rail. The main body of nuns were the choir nuns, who sang the holy office and who were equal within the community yet observed an order of seniority determined by years since profession. But beneath them were the *soeurs converses*, the Cinderellas of the convents, country girls who were to be *robuste* and *docile*. It was they who shouldered the heavy work of the stables, gardens, kitchens, and laundries. They were the perpetual tail end of the conventual procession. They might not sing in church, might read only with the approval of the mother superior, and if they were unable to read were not to be taught. And if they were poor, they were not to seek equality of riches in a convent, the principle being that "those who had nothing in the world may not seek in the convent what they never had outside it."[6] The different religious orders were themselves ranked in the esteem of the community. Jesuits were admired more than liked. Récollets were liked more than admired. To oversimplify somewhat a complex analysis of the populations of the Quebec convents, the Hôpital-Général attracted a disproportionate number of aristocratic women; the Ursulines, of the daughters of the bourgeoisie; and the Hôtel-Dieu, of the daughters of artisans.[7]

The Church saw as one of its major functions keeping fast the bonds of society, both horizontal and vertical. In Saint-Vallier's catechism, for example, the idea of subordination varies from implicit assumption to explicit lesson as one follows the chain of questions and answers designed for those who were ignorant of the faith, according to his preamble, the usual condition of children, artisans, and servants.

It is, of course, at the fourth commandment, "Honour thy Father and thy Mother," that the doctrine of obedience is most fully addressed. Everything follows from an initial explanation: "Not only does God wish that we honour them, but He also orders us to be submissive towards and to have respect for those who represent Him and who are clothed with His authority; for those who resist the order He established in the world, become worthy of eternal damnation."[8] From this it was clear that servants were to serve masters with respect and fear, that all persons were to be submissive to kings, princes, and governors, to bishops and pastors. "Be submissive, says Saint Peter." "Saint Paul says obey your pastors." What lesson can be drawn from this commandment? the catechist asks. "That we are obliged to become well informed of what we owe to our superiors."[9]

The fifth commandment provides another opportunity to reinforce the lesson. After explaining that a person attacked can defend himself with means proportionate to the need, the equivalent of the common law's doctrine of reasonable defence, the catechist is to continue with a second, and at first sight redundant, question:

---

6. Micheline D'Allaire, *L'Hôpital-Général de Québec, 1692–1764* (Montreal, 1971), pp. 149–55 (quotation, p. 152).
7. Ibid., Chap. 1.
8. Jean-Baptiste de La Croix de Chevrières de Saint-Vallier, *Cátechisme du diocèse de Québec*, fac. of 1701 ed. (Montreal, 1958), p. 177.
9. Ibid., pp. 179–80.

If we are mistreated with blows, can we not return them and avenge ourselves?

No, vengeance is forbidden us, and God has reserved it to Himself.[10]

One can only assume this is a qualification inserted for the benefit of wives, children, and servants.

The Church's support of authority, of state authority, and of the cult of kingship was a repeating pattern in the fabric of daily life. And at times of crisis, there was always an episcopal *mandement* to support the government. For example, when in 1742 the Superior Council ordained that habitants surrender their hidden grain for urban consumption, Bishop Pontbriand reminded the flock that "those who contravene the Council's regulations will render themselves grievously guilty before God and before men...it is not permitted to pass the limits prescribed by a legitimate authority," and, to clinch the argument, "he who resists the authorities resists God's order, and those who resist it render themselves worthy of eternal damnation." The only recourse of good Christians was to remain "amenable [*docile*] to the instructions of your pastors."[11]...

Quantifiable data provide another avenue to the solution of the problem of rank and social solidarities in New France. A researcher in the notarial archives tells us the answer is to be found in marriage contracts. The key is the value of the *douaire préfix*, an amount of money that was to be taken from the estate of a deceased husband by his widow to permit her to live, to quote an eighteenth-century jurist, "according to the condition of her husband."[12] It was a value arrived at by both families in concert and subject to the censorship of the large number of relatives and sometimes friends who always signed marriage contracts—one did not want to look ridiculous. It was a direct reflection of rank and a sense of rank, a good measure in a society in which rank was manifested more by expenditure than by income.

The result of tabulating *douaires* is a table of rank remarkably in accord with metropolitan ideas but simplified, compressed, and highlighting the

---

10. Ibid., p. 185.
11. Henri Têtu and Charles O. Gagnon, eds., *Mandements, lettres pastorales circulaires des éveques de Québec*, 2 vols. (Quebec, 1887, 1888), II: 22-23, 15 oct. 1742.
12. Peter N. Moogk, "Rank in New France: Reconstructing a Society from Notarial Documents," *HS/SH* 8 (1975): 34–53. The quotation, p. 41, is from Claude de Ferrière (1770). Contrary to Moogk's contention, the *douaire* of 1,000 livres, p. 44, indicates considerable respect for the rustic seigneur, since it places him among the honourable employments, which neither his paltry display of wealth nor his real power would indicate.

stratification of trades not much noticed by the jurists Loyseau and Domat. Individuals are classified in groups: an elite of military, judicial, and administrative officers, followed by honourable employments, good trades, modest occupations, and base occupations. The plain habitant farmers placed themselves at the very bottom of the list, which may not have been at all in accord with their wealth.

The lamentations of Raudot over the presumed Indianization of Canadian upbringing and character are hard to interpret. Those in the upper ranks of society, who embraced the fur trade, the wilderness, and the guerrilla, also embraced the notion of hierarchy. Hierarchy was enjoined upon the people, built into their institutional life, and, as the evidence of the *douaire préfix* demonstrates, found acceptance among them. Quarrels of precedence occurred at the parish level as well as among high officials and captured the interest of rustic seigneurs and captains of militia. Lording it over others, if not subordination, had a distinct appeal. This was certainly Hocquart's conclusion. "They love distinctions and attentions," he wrote, "pique themselves on their bravery, are extremely sensitive to slights and the least punishments." These special qualities of Canadian individualism were reflected in the comments of a host of contemporary French officers and officials. The common denominator of their disapproving social analysis was that, to continue quoting Hocquart, Canadians were "naturally ungovernable [*indocile*]."[13] The testimonial avalanche is irresistible. Canada was, in Pontchartrain's phrase, "a land of another spirit, other manners, other sentiments."[14] It is as though one half of the social testament of the Old Regime were cherished and the other utterly forgotten.

Both Indian society, with its essential equality of persons, and White society, with its history of hierarchical structure, made room for slavery. Isolated instances of slavery can be found in Canadian society from early in the seventeenth century. Toward the end of the seventeenth century, the argument was made that Black slavery would solve Canada's perennial labour shortage. Although the King agreed to this in 1689 and 1701, nothing came of it. Bégon was repeating the arguments in favour of Black servitude in 1716 and 1719, and in 1721 the Regent actually invited the

---

13. AC, C11A 67: 97 [Hocquart?] "Détail de toute la colonie," 1736. The refrain is constant, for example Saint-Vallier's similar comment, "M. Bégon connait aussi bien que moi la disposition de leurs esprits, peu portés à se soumettre et à reconnaitre leurs supérieurs temporels, de même que les spirituels [10 Sept. 1726]," in Auguste Gosselin, *L'Eglise du Canada depuis Laval* (Quebec, 1911), I: 392.

14. See above, Chap. 2 at n. 15.

Indies Company to send a cargo of Blacks to Quebec. There was, in fact, no great influx of Black slaves. But Indians taken in war by Canadian allies and sold to Canadians made their appearance in the central colony. Large numbers of these were of the Pawnee tribe situated in what is now the state of Nebraska, and their name in French, *Panis*, became a synonym for Indian slave. That they served mainly as domestics, were often indistinguishable from free servants, and were often Christianized and well integrated into Canadian households can lead us, erroneously, to discount the foundation of their condition: unfree and subject to sale and purchase.

The legal foundation of slavery in Canada was Raudot's 1709 ordinance proclaiming the legality of the slavery of "Panis et Negres." That not everyone was at ease with the concept of slavery is evident from Raudot's specific denial that France's constitutional freedom from slavery could apply to a colony and also from a curious challenge to slavery that occurred in 1733. A fur trader whose slave had been confiscated to satisfy a debt and subsequently sold to a third party challenged the whole proceeding on the grounds that a Christian could not be sold. The council referred the matter to Hocquart, who ruled that both confiscation and sale were legitimate. Following the advice of the King's memorandum of 1735, he further ordained that slaves could only be freed by a written act before a notary.[15]

Slaves were never a large group in New France. Only from 1710 do the annual additions to the Indian slave population in the White colony reach double digits, the average annual additions for the period 1710 to 1744 being slightly more than twenty-six. From 1700 to 1742, annual additions to the Black slave population averaged slightly in excess of two. In 1742, the increase was fifteen, and from that date double digits prevail for Blacks as well.[16] The condition of slavery as understood by Canadians must have been an amalgam made up of the Indian notion of slavery resulting from capture in war, traditional class notions of the servant, and the idea of the human chattel, the classic conception of slavery associated with the development of Black slavery in the Americas. . . .

Colonial social structure bore very much the same relation to metropolitan social structure as did Canadian architecture to French architecture. It was smaller in size and much less grand. It lacked the variation and fine detailing of the original. Nevertheless the relationship was unmistakable. Canadian society was a ranked society of the Old Regime type, but it was

---

15. M. Trudel, *L'Esclavage au Canada Français: histoire et conditions de l'esclavage* (Quebec, 1960).
16. Ibid., tables, pp. 84–85, 89, 96.

compressed, simplified, and oddly skewed to emphasize prickly dignity and autonomy at the expense of due subordination. The lower orders of society, in particular, lost much of the institutional embodiment that existed in France. But family, the principal institution of Old Regime linkage, lost none of its vigour and gained in importance from the absence of other linking institutions. In the bosom of the family, the individual flourished.

SPACE, TERRITORY, AND CULTURE IN NEW FRANCE:

*A Geographical Perspective**

SERGE COURVILLE

The countryside of Quebec in the seventeenth and eighteenth centuries is often considered only in terms of the structures put in place by France as it established its Laurentian colony. This short essay aims to reveal another type of territorial organization and, in so doing, to point towards a fuller understanding of Quebec's landscape and culture. Based on recent research in history and geography, it addresses old questions about the relationships between people and place, colonizers and the colonized, official worlds and lived realities. It intends to show that the development of Quebec during the French regime and later can be read at many levels.

In effect, the human geography of the lower St. Lawrence Valley before 1760 comprised at least two territorial frameworks. Their co-existence reflected the distance that separated New France from Old. Along an axis from the heights of Quebec City to the Island of Montreal, with higher population densities in the oldest settled areas, there existed a thin strip of settlements embedded in a geometric landscape. This was structured space, the result of careful planning uncommon in North America at that time. But this space was also locally organized. Beyond the administrative divisions of the land into seigneuries, parishes, and *censives* (long lots) was another reality, a multitude of domestic spaces created out of the close relationship between habitants and their physical and human environments.

Divided between the political will of the colonizer to subordinate the development of the colony to metropolitan needs and the immigrants' desire to take advantage of new-world opportunities, the St. Lawrence

SERGE COURVILLE, "SPACE, TERRITORY, AND CULTURE IN NEW FRANCE: A GEOGRAPHICAL PERSPECTIVE," IN *PEOPLE PLACES PATTERNS PROCESSES: GEOGRAPHICAL PERSPECTIVES ON THE CANADIAN PAST*, ED. GRAEME WYNN (TORONTO: COPP CLARK PITMAN, 1990): 165–76. USED BY PERMISSION OF THE AUTHOR.

* TRANSLATED BY PATRICIA KEALY WITH THE ASSISTANCE OF COLE HARRIS, FROM "ESPACE, TERRITOIRE ET CULTURE EN NOUVELLE-FRANCE: UNE VISION GÉOGRAPHIQUE," *REVUE D'HISTOIRE DE L'AMÉRIQUE FRANÇAISE* 37, 3 (1983): 417–29. A PRELIMINARY VERSION OF THIS TEXT WAS SUBMITTED TO JEAN-CLAUDE ROBERT (DEPARTMENT OF HISTORY, UNIVERSITÉ DU QUÉBEC À MONTRÉAL) AND NORMAND SEGUIN (DEPARTMENT OF HISTORY, UNIVERSITÉ DU QUÉBEC À TROIS-RIVIÈRES). THE AUTHOR WISHES TO THANK THEM FOR THEIR COMMENTS. HE ALSO WISHES TO THANK ALL THOSE WHO CONTRIBUTED OBSERVATIONS AND SUGGESTIONS, PARTICULARLY MARCEL BÉLANGER (DEPARTMENT OF GEOGRAPHY, LAVAL UNIVERSITY), JACQUES MATHIEU (DEPARTMENT OF HISTORY, LAVAL UNIVERSITY), AND HEATHER PARKER, WHO HELPED WITH AN EARLY TRANSLATION OF THIS PAPER.

Valley expressed two logics: *urbanité*,[1] of French origin and the source of macro-forms and macro-structures; and *territorialité*,[2] originating in the intimate local places shaped by habitants out of the structured space that the French state imposed. From these logics emerged a cultural space, or cultural region, that would survive the British conquest of 1760 and leave its mark on all subsequent development of this area.

A Structured Space

For France in the seventeenth and eighteenth centuries, the first step towards the conquest of the new world was control of the St. Lawrence Valley, the principal access to the wealth of the vast hinterland of North

---

1. The concept of *urbanité* refers to characteristics of civilization as expressed in the areas of law, the arts, science, and religion. See M. Bélanger, "L'urbanité de Québec," *Cahiers de géographie du Québec* 25, 4 (1981): 11–16. In the specific process of colonization, *urbanité* denotes the transplantation both of institutions intended to govern colonial development and, more generally, of everything deriving from the nature of the state itself. By extension, it means a way of being, acting, and feeling that is different from that associated with *territorialité*.

2. The concept of *territorialité* refers to the actual content of civilizations, to their own specific nature, and to their internal equilibrium. Claude Raffestin and others have defined it as the sum of relationships that arise within a given three-dimensional system (society-space-time) in order for civilizations to achieve the greatest possible autonomy within the limits of that system's resources. It reflects the multidimensional nature of a group's territorial reality, the way in which human societies satisfy their material and spiritual needs at a given time, in a given place, with a given population and a given set of tools. In this context, relationship is seen as a process of exchange and communication. Space itself is not important; what is important here is the use that people make and the knowledge they have of the reality that we call space.

   Territorialities, not territoriality, thus arise from the sum of the variety of relationships that people have with their social and physical environment, whether they are seigneurs, habitants, merchants, solicitors, or craftspeople. This sum is not mathematical; it is bio-social. It refers to the totality of interconnecting relationships or, more precisely, to the dynamic totality of those relationships, since the components can vary in time. The territory in which these relationships are expressed is in fact the product of the interconnection among actors, starting from a primary reality—space—which is perceived as a support, a resource, a reward, and a mediator in human exchange.

   The concept of territoriality thus points the way to a true geography of difference, but invites us to consider it not solely with respect to concrete forms of landscape and culture, but in that richer light of "constituent fields" of language, power, economy, and territorial organization. These fields are interwoven, have their own durations, and together define areas in which a group's originality is expressed. For a more complete analysis, see C. Raffestin, *Pour une géographie du pouvoir* (Paris: Librairies techniques, 1980); and R.D. Sack, *Human Territoriality, Its Theory and History* (Cambridge: Cambridge University Press, 1986).

America.[3] The idea of colonization for exploitation took hold early, and as soon as the limits of a coastal establishment became evident, the French state began to move inland.[4] Although its early settlement efforts were hesitant and produced only mediocre results, its power remained extraordinarily effective. In less than half a century, the colonial world was structured by institutions that would govern economic and social relationships, and by a system of land division (developed in the 1630s) that formed the framework for rural settlement.[5] The territory was divided into seigneuries and *censives* perpendicular to the St. Lawrence River, and an early network of towns was created, each, even then, with administrative, military, and commercial facilities.

This intense colonizing effort followed from a single, integrating rationality. The seigneury, the *côte* (a discrete line of farmhouses along the river), and the *Coutume de Paris* (the code of French civil law that prevailed in Canada) represented more than a simple juxtaposition of familiar institutions that might be expected to contribute to colonial development. They were part of a common enterprise, which helps to explain why they were transplanted to the new world in the first place and why they spread throughout the colony.[6] In the St. Lawrence Valley, France sought complete territorial control through the establishment of a stable rural society capable of reproducing itself. To achieve this, officials chose a combination of structures that would lead not only to the effective settlement of colonists around the seigneur, defined as the state's partner in the colonization effort, but also to their collective adherence to values appropriate to the ideal of a land-owning society under the old regime.[7]

Although mitigated for a time by the initial difficulties of colonization, this ambition strengthened under royal government after 1663, as administrative reforms established the state's power in all areas of economic and social life. Land ownership, the distribution of settlers, demographic

---

3. See S. Courville, "Contribution à l'étude de l'origine du rang au Québec: la politique spatiale des Cent-Associés," *Cahiers de géographie du Québec* 25, 65 (1981): 197–236.

4. J. Hamelin, ed., *Histoire du Québec* (Sainte-Hyacinthe: Edisem, Privat, 1976).

5. This theme has already been treated by several authors, including R.C. Harris, *The Seigneurial System in Early Canada* (Quebec City, Madison, Milwaukee, and London: Les Presses de l'Université Laval, University of Wisconsin Press, 1968); and M. Trudel, *Les débuts du régime seigneurial au Canada* (Montreal: Fides, 1974).

6. S. Courville, "Contribution à l'étude de l'origine du rang au Québec," 198–99.

7. See F. Ouellet, "La formation d'une société dans la vallée du Saint-Laurent: d'une société sans classes à une société de classes," *Canadian Historical Review* 62, 4 (1981): 407–50.

behaviour, religion, civil law, and trade were only some of the areas that, henceforth, would be controlled by the administration. Through the years, the regulatory apparatus was fortified as new regulations were added relating to fishing, hunting, farming, settlement, statute labour, payment of seigneurial dues, and the fur trade. At the same time that officials were attempting to concentrate the population in villages and to restrict the size of seigneuries (which grew considerably in number between 1663 and 1760), a settlement policy was established. Bonuses were paid for early marriages and large families, bachelors and their parents were fined, aid was provided to soldiers who had been sent to pacify the country and who decided to settle there, and young women known as *filles du roi* were sent to be quickly married off to pioneers.[8]

Despite the creation of a parish system at the beginning of the eighteenth century, officials paid scant attention to the local setting. An entire colony, after all, had to be settled and developed. The development of individual seigneuries was left to the initiative of the seigneurs, subject to the regulatory control of the state. A metropolitan logic gave the colony its initial shape and framed its subsequent development. This logic was rooted in medieval tradition, but steeped in the rationalist thought of the Renaissance and touched by the new economic theories that were taking hold throughout Europe. It gave rise to structures and standards intended to ensure the success, and to define the form and function of, colonization. According to the precepts of French mercantilism, the Laurentian colony would never be more than a planned offshoot, a satellite region, of France.[9] Shaped in a mould intended to ensure a solid foundation for continental development, the colony appeared "prefabricated," closed to change.[10] Yet change would come, not as a result of government decisions but of the actual conditions of life in New France.

As soon as it was established, colonial society escaped the regulatory control of the state and deviated from imposed models. Deviance began with the seigneurs, who did not wholly share the state's goals, preferring the city and the fur trade to the development of their seigneuries.[11] The

---

8. See G. Paquet and J.-P. Wallot, "Sur quelques discontinuités dans l'expérience socio-économique du Québec: une hypothèse," *Revue d' histoire de l'Amérique française* 35, 4 (March 1982): 483–521.

9. See L. Dechêne, *Habitants et marchands de Montréal au XVIIe siècle* (Montreal: Plon, 1974).

10. See S. Diamond, "Le Canada français au XVIIIe: une société préfabriquée," *Annales* 16, 2 (1961): 317–53.

11. This topic has been treated most thoroughly by C. Nish in *Les bourgeois-gentilshommes de la Nouvelle-France 1729–1748* (Montreal: Fides, 1968); and by R.C. Harris, *The Seigneurial System.*

habitants, for their part, managed to come to terms with the demands of seigneurs and priests, seeking not so much to remove themselves from established spatial structures and the role reserved for them, as to take advantage of those structures and to live according to their own priorities. This transformation was rapid and resulted in the emergence, alongside the world of the towns, of a parallel system that evolved at its own pace.[12] One world was dominated by the colonial elite and structured by trans-Atlantic trade and culture; the other was dominated by the habitants themselves, who lived in a much closer relationship with the land. There was no clear dividing line between the two, but there were enough points of contrast to allow one to speak of different actors, of different social groups, methods of production, and trade.[13] Thus, quite early, a new type of spatial organization, the product of people establishing themselves in space, became interwoven with the institutional structure imposed from above.

A Mosaic of Domestic Spaces

Retarded at first by Iroquois raids and the small number of settlers, rural settlement was soon accelerated by overproduction of furs at the end of the seventeenth century, the resulting reduced demand for labour in the fur trade, and a rapid increase in population from under 10 000 in 1681 to nearly 52 000 in 1739. By the latter date, less than a quarter of the population lived in towns and within a few decades, the empty spaces between Quebec City and Montreal were largely occupied. New territories such as Charlevoix and the lower valleys of the Chaudière and Richelieu rivers were settled, as populations spilled beyond the borders of earlier settlements and people migrated well away from their native regions.

The influence of seigneurs may have accounted for the choice of some new settlement locations, but in most cases the decision was taken by individuals and families and had nothing to do with seigneurial boundaries. When settlers colonized an area near the one from which they had come, they usually settled on land their parents had acquired and reserved for the purpose. Settlement in such areas was more rapid, and it was facilitated by the presence of neighbours from the same region, many of whom were kin. In the case of migrations to more distant places, people

---

12. L. Dechêne, *Habitants et marchands*, 482.
13. G. Paquet and J.-P. Wallot, "Sur quelques discontinuités," 497.

settled on newly acquired land that was divided among different groups coming from different regions. Settlement in these areas was more difficult, depending as it did on neighbourhood relationships established among the newcomers. It appears, in fact, that for individuals who shared no common background with other settlers, the first two years were crucial. Either they managed to make a fortunate marriage, thus becoming integrated into the community, or they remained outsiders, in which case they would probably have to leave, the fate most often of bachelors and isolated couples. On the other hand, members of established families would settle permanently on adjacent lots.[14]

Although initially open to arrivals from outside, these settled areas had a tendency, once organized, to close in upon themselves and to rely on a locally defined system of relationships. Without ever being completely broken, connections with the original settlements became weaker and were soon limited to family ties. And while new communities (*solidarités*) were taking shape, formed through combinations of marriages among the founding families,[15] fewer newcomers arrived. They were discouraged both by the scarcity of land and by already established settlers' more or less overt distrust of anyone who might represent a threat to their land holdings. Land represented wealth to the settlers, of course, but it was equally important as the principal mediator of social relationships: ties with neighbours were forged both through the land and for it.

Although they were somewhat hampered by the obligation to live on their own concessions (*tenir feu et lieu*) and by the speculative practices of certain seigneurs, the settlers' greatest efforts during the settlement phase were directed towards acquiring land by buying or trading wooded or abandoned lots, by combining inheritances, and by requesting further concessions intended to provide for their children's future. The majority of pioneer families engaged in such land acquisition, prizing land not for

14. See J. Mathieu, François Béland, Michèle Jean, Jeannette Larouche, and Rénald Lessard, "Peuplement colonisateur au XVIIIe siècle dans le gouvernement du Québec," in *L'homme et la nature. Actes de la société canadienne d' étude du dix-huitième siècle*, ed. R.L. Emerson, W. Kinsley, and W. Moser (Montreal: Société canadienne d'étude du dix-huitième siècle, 1984), 2: 127–38.

15. See L. Lavallée, "La famille et les stratégies matrimoniales dans le gouvernement de Montréal au XVIIIe siècle," in *Société rurale dans la France de l'Ouest et au Québec (XVIIe-XXe siècles)*, Actes des colloques de 1979 et 1980 (Montreal: Université de Montréal, École des Hautes Études en sciences sociales, 1980), 141–47; see also J. Mathieu, C. Cyr, G. Dinel, J. Pozzo, and J. St-Pierre, "Les alliances matrimoniales exogames dans le gouvernement du Québec 1700–1760," *Revue d' histoire de l' Amérique française* 35, 1 (1981): 3–32.

its exchange but for its use value,[16] and the practice soon spread through-out the territory and even beyond, thus creating permanent settlements from what had been nothing more than formal spatial structures imposed by the state. Within these settlements, people developed a strong sense of belonging to place. Felt most strongly in relation to land holdings and, secondarily, where social cohesion was strongest,[17] this attachment was long expressed locally by place names that were heavily charged with spatial and social meaning (the "Rang du Bord de l'Eau" and the "Rang des Caron," for example). Parishes—which like the seigneuries were the result of the state's political goals, but appeared only after settlement was established and land holdings assured—introduced a new level of spatial order and identity. Yet they never completely superseded the earlier, locally expressed sense of belonging felt by habitant families. . . .

A Dense Cultural Area

By the time of the English conquest, the territory of Canada was struc-tured by a rational division of land into seigneuries and censives, but organized by the geography of its domestic spaces. The territory was settled by people who were relatively homogeneous in place of origin, language, and religion, and composed of a multitude of family holdings established within the structures introduced by the colonizer. It thus became the place where a culture was forged,[18] and patterns of collective behaviour defined—patterns that would be spread by rural expansion in the late eighteenth and nineteenth centuries.[19]

Originally encouraged by state initiatives, settlement in the seigneurial lowlands quickly became autonomous, stimulated by local social and environmental circumstances and increasingly cut off from the type of

---

16. Land was valued as a means of providing farms and a future for sons and daughters, rather than as a commodity for the realization of profit. We lack meticulous studies of this particular subject, but on the general point see L. Dechêne, *Habitants et marchands*, 296.

17. J. Mathieu et al., "Les alliances matrimoniales," 26.

18. See M. Bélanger, "Le Québec rural," in *Études sur la géographie du Canada*, 22ᵉ Congrés international de géographie (Montreal: University of Toronto Press, 1972), 31–46.

19. See G. Bouchard, "Les systèmes de transmission des patrimoines et le cycle de la société rurale au Québec, du 17e au 20e siècle" (Paper given at the University of Ottawa, June 1982).

contacts generated by the fur trade. The result has sometimes been seen as a rather introverted world, insensitive to trade and closed to innovation. Population was sparse, and a coherent urban network that might have encouraged trade had not developed. Only a few small centres appeared; aside from the two major commercial towns of Quebec City and Montreal, the urban framework of the Laurentian colony consisted of nothing more than a skeletal network of small port villages.[20]

Closer analysis reveals, however, that this world was surprisingly dynamic. It was hostile to outside intrusion, which was seen as a potential source of constraint, but much more open to external contacts than is generally recognized—provided such contacts coincided with domestic goals. While not denying their origins, Canadian habitants took advantage of the opportunities offered by the new world to assert the differences between themselves and French peasants,[21] rejecting the norms of the metropolis in favour of a North American way of life. (This process of social change was also exemplified in the English colonies to the south.) Because land was abundant, habitants were able to develop an economy based on extensive agriculture that was productive enough to provide a fairly comfortable living. Nevertheless, its maintenance depended upon the movement of children away from the family farm when they married.[22] Resulting from the need to maintain the balance between family and farm and the availability of new lands, migration engendered a form of agricultural development that, while sensitive to profit, was essentially the product of the migrants' experience, resourcefulness, and ability to fend for themselves. The argument advanced by some as evidence of the backwardness of New France, that when iron tools became scarce they were replaced by wooden ones, only illustrates this. Though it reveals the limited means of the population and the colony's difficulty in ironwork-

---

20. Research in progress on the development of villages in Quebec in the eighteenth and nineteenth centuries indicates that by 1760 only about twenty such establishments existed, most of them located on the edge of a seigneury.
21. The difference between the French peasant and the Canadian habitant is one of territoriality. The French peasant's territoriality is entirely saturated by information coming from his or her own territory, where he or she has always lived, whereas the habitant's territoriality has also absorbed new information originating from territory that she or he has settled. The attitude and behaviour of the two groups may appear to be similar and part of a continuity, but may in fact be seen to be different in that they have different underlying contexts and systems of relationships.
22. J. Mathieu et al., "Les alliances matrimoniales," 34–35.

ing, it also says much for the ability of farmers to meet their own technological needs.[23]

Seen from this point of view, the history of the St. Lawrence colony appears to have been, above all, that of group adhesion to territory. Relationships among people, relationships with nature, and the intensity of these relationships within the local setting were all significant or determining factors in the colony's development.[24] Of course, there were obstacles. One can cite, for example, France's policy of requiring settlers to clear and work the land they owned, or the fact that many settlers abandoned their land. The attachment of people to place does imply, however, that territoriality was based on domestic priorities, which reinforced family strategies to the detriment of official needs and subordinated external stimuli to local requirements. It also goes a long way to explain the hold that some family groups had on the territory, shown clearly by certain place names, and the impact that the expansion of trade between New France and the Antilles in the 1730s had on the development of local agriculture.[25]

The Laurentian colony was created as the land was cleared, and set within the framework of a seigneurial system that eventually monetarized property relationships. Within this realm, domestic and commercial spheres tended to coincide. The farm, the farm house, the neighbourhood, and the *rang* were aspects of a single environment, or habitat. The assemblage of people and houses had a social significance that outweighed its economic functions. When economic activity extended beyond this local space it was always to satisfy domestic needs, even in the face of official disapproval. In the seventeenth and eighteenth centuries, this outreach turned to the fur trade and in the early nineteenth century to the timber trade to support the family farm. The process eventually generated seasonal migrations to the forests of Maine and Ontario and permanent migrations to the towns and cities of Quebec and the United States.

---

23. This hypothesis was principally developed by R.L. Séguin in *La civilisation traditionnelle de l'habitant aux 17e et 18e siècles* (Montreal and Paris: Fides, 1967).
24. M. Bélanger, "Le Québec rural," 32ff.
25. See J. Mathieu, *Le commerce entre la Nouvelle-France et les Antilles au XVIIIe siècle* (Montreal: Fides, 1981).

Such mobility did not reflect a simple desire to move[26]—other things being equal, new places were usually more threatening than old. It had its origin in a method of colonization based on exclusion and the constant forced migration of a certain part of the population to new territory. For some, forced migration became permanent; for others it was a temporary adventure that would eventually enable them to establish themselves on their own land. It is necessary, in this context, to distinguish between the real voyageurs, for whom the fur trade was a career, and the more numerous participants in the fur trade who sought to accumulate a small nest egg in order to establish a farm. After 1700, however, few farmers' sons found employment in this essentially urban-based activity.[27] Because the St. Lawrence Valley was far from the territory of the fur trade, rural settlement tended to become increasingly removed from it, and was materially and morally supported by strong family ties that favoured the re-creation of farms similar to those the settlers had just left. Because relations between habitants and seigneurs seem generally to have been distant and characterized by distrust, if not contempt, these pioneer settlements not only became economically autonomous but were also cut off socially from everyone who was not directly involved with the concerns of the group.

By 1760, the colonial period had lasted long enough to establish attitudes and forms of behaviour that would be passed on to future generations.[28] The seigneurial space in the St. Lawrence Valley, a generally artificial entity superimposed on a dense network of local spaces, was no longer an abstract formulation, but a place where a human tradition and a physical environment converged, an intensely lived-in space that expressed the colonizer's logic much less than it did the habitants' life. It was a setting for a human society based on new relationships among people and things, and these new relationships defined a type of civilization that is better understood in terms of individual and familial spaces and times than of official institutions.

Conclusion

New France was structured by France but organized by the people who

---

26. See C. Morissonneau's theory on this subject in "Mobilité et identité québécoise," *Cahiers de géographie du Québec* 28 (1979): 29–38.
27. L. Dechêne, *Habitants et marchands*, 386–487.
28. M. Bélanger, "Le Québec rural," 33.

lived there. It was shaped by two logics, which were expressed not only by the evolution of forms in space but also by the distance that, very early, separated habitants from everyone connected with European culture and trans-Atlantic trade. Already firmly entrenched by the end of the French regime, the distinctive way of life that emerged from these circumstances did not really come into its own until the century following the conquest. By then a new francophone middle class (*moyenne bourgeoisie*) had appeared, supported by seigneurial property, government positions, and parliamentary office. Thus cut off from a new elite that was soon to prove as distant as the previous one, country people closed themselves off and found their own way to adapt to change and to life on the periphery of an urban world they rejected. (They had nevertheless to come to terms with it, occasionally at the risk of endorsing its values.) Contacts with the outside world increased, and there were new migrations that took habitants and their way of life to new places, but local domestic space in the St. Lawrence Valley remained apart, still incorporated within the traditional framework of familial experience. From all this grew a truly local culture that reflected the originality of settlement in the St. Lawrence Valley much better than did the culture of the elite. This local culture would also favour the development of a fairly rigid set of beliefs, values, and standards that political leaders would later exploit in promoting their own ideas of collective development.

FEAR OF FIRE

LUC HOPPEN

One week later than usual, the inhabitants of Montreal lined up for the annual Corpus Christi procession on June 19, 1721, when suddenly disaster struck. "One of the musketeers, instead of firing into the air, accidently [sic] aimed at the church, setting the roof on fire." The flames spread wildly, reducing 125 houses to ashes.

No lengthy investigation was needed to determine why the fire spread so fast. "These buildings were roofed with cedar shingles," an observer recorded. "Moreover, the heat being excessive and the wind considerable, the whole roof went up in flames like straw."

It was the desire to prevent such damage that led to the *canadianization* of the house in New France. It was fire—and the fear of fire—that determined how houses were built. When fire struck a city, a few sparks could turn into a torch. Jumping from wooden roof to wooden roof, racing from one end of a street to the other, both sides taking flame at the same time, fire was the scourge of the colony, causing many deaths and much destruction.

On the recommendation of an engineer dispatched to Montreal immediately after the 1721 fire, Intendant Michel Bégon issued a new building code: Houses were to be built of stone and roofed with tiles or slate. But the necessary materials being unavailable, Bégon was forced to relax the regulations and allow roofs made of "a double covering of boards".

Then fire struck again, this time in Quebec City in 1726, causing Claude-Thomas Dupuy, Bégon's successor, to issue new regulations. He renewed the ban on wooden buildings in cities, and decreed that cedar shingle roofs had to be replaced by overlapping boards or slates. He also required that houses be built with cellars, and prohibited mansard roofs.

Heavy frames were to be replaced by lighter structures that could be easily dismantled in case of fire. As an example, Dupuy pointed to his palace which had just been rebuilt according to the plans of Gaspard-Joseph Chaussegros de Léry, the engineer Bégon had sent to Montreal after the fire of 1721. As well, chimneys were to be set in firewalls projecting above the roofs.

LUC HOPPEN, "FEAR OF FIRE," *HORIZON CANADA* 1, NO. 10 (1984): 237–40. BY PERMISSION OF LUC HOPPEN, ARCHITECTURAL HISTORIAN, LAVAL UNIVERSITY, QUEBEC.

It Took 200 Years

The results substantially modified the exterior of the house. Thus, nearly two centuries after the arrival of Jacques Cartier, the Canadian house acquired a distinctive style that would dominate the urban landscape of New France before spreading into the rural areas.

Three main phases can be distinguished in the evolution of domestic architecture in New France. First came the era of the pioneers, lasting from 1608 to 1660. It was natural for the first colonists to transplant in New France the style of home that was familiar to them. Champlain, for instance, described his house downriver from Quebec at Cap Tourmente as being like a Normandy farm-house. The problem in recreating this style of building was that suitable materials and manpower were lacking. Wood, of course, was plentiful, and the first European builders introduced sawed boards and the half-timbered style of construction in which the spaces between upright posts were filled with stone, brick or daubing.

Early dwellings in New France were cold, drafty places. Marie de l'Incarnation (1599–1672), first superior of the Ursuline convent in Quebec, described a house in Quebec City's lower town in which she lived shortly after her arrival in the New World in 1639: "It is so poor that we can see the stars through the roof at night, and it is hard to keep a candle lit because of the wind."

Later, she described the convent itself: "Our building has three floors, in the middle of which we have our cells made like those in France. Our fireplace is at the end to heat the dormitory and the cells whose walls are only of pine; for otherwise we would not be able to keep them warm.

"Don't think that we can go for very long in winter without being close to the fire; one hour would be too long, even with hands hidden and being well covered up.

"Except for the services, the usual place for reading, writing and studying is, of necessity, by the fire.... Our beds are of wood and are closed like cupboards, and although they have double covers of serge, you can barely keep warm."

Constant efforts to keep warm and to keep candles burning in drafty homes contributed greatly to the risks of fire in these tinderboxes.

Descriptions of early buildings in Quebec and Montreal testify to a great variety of materials and designs but none have survived.

The second phase, from 1660 to 1720, saw a major transformation in domestic architecture, dictated by the realities of weather and population growth. Added to this was the political determination to visibly assert the French presence in North America. When King Louis XIV took the colony in hand in 1663, making it a province of France, Canada was exposed to the direct influence of royal tastes. This meant an architecture which respected the principles of French classicism while adapting itself to suit various social classes.

Architecture in this period was well advanced, allowing artisans to build both palaces and private homes. But architecture in Canada, and that meant basically the house, had to yield to the socio-economic reality: Manpower and materials were expensive, plans were ambitious, but means were slight; and above all, fire was a constant threat.

Humble Abodes

While it was difficult in a colonial town to build according to principles laid down at Versailles, it was even harder to do so in the sparsely populated countryside. *Seigneurs* and *habitants* were usually forced to build in wood. A few dared to try a modest stone foundation, waiting for favourable circumstances to enlarge it.

The home of the *habitant* was generally quite small, measuring about six metres by 4.5. Some were two storeys, all had a chimney with an open hearth. The roof was made of boards or thatch, and door and window openings were few and narrow. Only a few wealthy or important individuals could afford to hire master carpenters and masons to build them larger homes of stone with a slate roof.

The third phase of domestic architecture, running from 1720 to 1760, was characterized by the desire to reduce, if not to eliminate completely, the risk of catastrophic fires. The type of house that evolved during this period, with its chimneys and fire walls, had to be built by experienced master masons. They could not simply use the homes built between 1660 and 1720 as models because the fire risks presented by these houses were exactly what the new constructions were supposed to do away with. But most of these skilled workmen were Canadian-born and it was only natural for them to look to local models rather than to academic architecture. Thus, the first buildings modified to conform to Dupuy's building regulations of 1727 became the "model homes" of the first domestic architecture truly adapted to the particular conditions in New France.

Changes to the Cityscape

From 1720 to 1760, Quebec City, Montreal and Trois-Rivières underwent a major facelift. More, yet safer houses were crowded into the same limited space. The building regulations, as well as the limited training workers got, left little room for initiative; so that by the time of the British conquest of the colony, New France exhibited a largely standardized style of domestic architecture.

There were, of course, some differences, stemming from the varied origins of the colonists, the local scarcity or abundance of particular materials, and the environment. The homes in Quebec City were somewhat different from those in Montreal, for instance. The crumbly limestone of the Quebec City region required whitewashing or some other protective surface, while the more resistant sandstone of Montreal stood up better to the elements. Elsewhere, the absence of stone and of skilled workers to assemble it promoted the development of wooden architecture.

Moved to the Country

Finally, while the urban environment reached maturity during the first half of the 18th century, it was not until the second half that the canadianization of the rural house occurred. The population was growing rapidly. The old style of house was considered too small and fell out of favour. Larger houses, and more of them, were needed. This is when the master builder, who had acquired his experience in the city, was able to transplant to the country the urban-type housing that had resulted from the successive fires of 1721 and 1726.

For many Canadians today, surviving houses of this period are striking reminders of the French era in our history. But these old relics are not all French—they bear traces of English influence, especially in their windows and roofs. And even more, they are properly Canadian because even before the Conquest, the style of housing construction brought over from France had undergone drastic modifications.

FURTHER READINGS ON TOPIC 3

W. J. Eccles. "The Social, Economic and Political Significance of the Military Establishment in New France." *Canadian Historical Review* 52 (March 1971): 1–22.

Richard Colebrook Harris. *The Seigneurial System in Early Canada*. Quebec and Madison: Les Presses de l'Université Laval and University of Wisconsin Press, 1966.

Allan Greer. *Peasant, Lord and Merchant: Rural Society in Three Quebec Parishes, 1740–1840*. Toronto: University of Toronto Press, 1985.

Naomi Griffiths. *The Acadians: Creation of a People*. Toronto: McGraw-Hill Ryerson, 1973.

Topic 4

Work in New France

*A*lthough historians have been preoccupied with the role of the fur trade *in New France, in fact the fisheries were of greater economic importance. As Brian Young and John Dickinson note,[1] "Until the end of the French regime in 1760, France imported far more cod than fur and the fishery employed many more seamen and ships than all other French colonial trade combined." Hence the inclusion in this volume of Christopher Moore's moving account of the life of the Norman fisherman Charles Renaut. Renaut's biography provides the focus for Moore's observations on the working life of fishermen, the question of seasonal migration from Europe in pre-industrial times, and the role of Cape Breton as an outpost of Empire. Readings on other workers in the staples industries can be found in Topic 11.*

The role of women in New France, like that of the fishermen, is too often overlooked. Jan Noel's pioneering article, which explores the contributions of women to military life and commerce in New France, indicates that some women's horizons extended surprisingly far beyond the immediate demands of hearth and home in the seventeenth and eighteenth centuries.

The realities of day-to-day living are highlighted in an excerpt from the letters of Marie de l'Incarnation, a French Ursuline nun who immigrated to Quebec in 1639 and took a leading role for the next 33 years in establishing the French presence in North America. In this selection, Marie de l'Incarnation discusses her work and that of her associates on behalf of the native peoples. The epidemics to which she refers continued to be a

---

1. Brian Young and John Dickson, *A Short History of Quebec: A Socio-Economic Perspective*, (Toronto: Copp Clark Pitman, 1988), p. 23.

major killer of native peoples until well into the twentieth century. The work roles available to women in later periods are discussed in Topic 15.

CHARLES RENAUT'S LETTER

CHRISTOPHER MOORE

I

Charles Renaut's letter crossed the Atlantic in the spring of 1731, a single sheet of heavy parchment paper folded twice and sealed with a blob of wax. Across one side an address was inked in large and laboured characters: "to be given to Charle Renaut at the abitation of ian filepot[1] at Scaterie on Cape Breton". It was another letter from his wife.

Writing late in April in their Norman fishing-village home, Marie-Joanne Renaut had sent off the letter as the annual migration of the fishermen was reaching its springtime peak, leaving towns like hers populated by women, children, and the old as the New World cod catch drew their men westward in thousands. From Basque seaports in southwestern France, from Brittany and the Channel ports of Normandy, flotillas of tiny fishing boats and larger merchantmen were sailing west, crammed with supplies for a season's work, crammed also with fishermen and shore labourers. Some would catch the cod of the open waters of the Grand Banks. Others would go to deserted shore-stations in Newfoundland or Labrador or on the Gaspé coast. Others sailed for Ile Royale, seeking shore space in one of the outport harbours or steering for Louisbourg, where the captain could trade his cargo while his passengers sought employment. . . .

Raised in a fisherman's town, Charles Renaut had found his career more by inheritance than by choice. The cod fishery that occupied his village was France's great economic interest in North America, more valuable than the fur trade, source of an important foodstuff, great employer of ships and men. It gave the nation an esteemed product to export and consume at home, and every naval strategist stressed its contribution to the training of seamen. In fishing ports like the one that raised Charles Renaut, the cod trade was the vital livelihood that sustained a way of life. For two hundred years—since time immemorial, Renaut would have

---

CHRISTOPHER MOORE, ABRIDGED FROM "CHARLES RENAUT'S LETTER," *LOUISBOURG PORTRAITS: LIFE IN AN EIGHTEENTH-CENTURY GARRISON TOWN* (TORONTO: MACMILLAN, 1982), PP. 118–27, 144. REPRINTED BY PERMISSION OF MACMILLAN OF CANADA, A DIVISION OF CANADA PUBLISHING CORPORATION.

1. "Abitation of ian filepot" was a crude spelling for "The fishing property of Jean Phelipeaux."

said—his Norman forefathers had been sailing to the harbours and headlands of North American shores they lumped together as Terre-Neuve, the New World. The elders of the community could boast of forty or fifty voyages to Terre-Neuve, six to eight months of each year devoted to the catching and shipping of precious cod. . . .

A fisherman by his ancestry and heir to the tradition of his people, Charles Renaut took up his community's seagoing vocation in his teens. Though he probably began in menial shore jobs, Renaut soon left these to inlanders. He graduated to small-boat fishing, the heart of the industry, where, by the mid 1720s, prowess proven in several seasons of work gave him a place among the veterans.

Thus established, Charles Renaut married and began a family—one he would leave behind to go with the fishing fleet each spring. Some years he sailed as early as February, for to be first on the fishing grounds was both a professional triumph and a commercial advantage. The fishing grounds kept him until September, and then the transatlantic migration began to reverse itself, to carry the summer's catch to market and take the migrant fishermen back to their families. Spring to fall at work in the New World, fall to spring at home in the old—like generations before him, Renaut was settling into the rhythms of the migratory fisherman, enduring half a year of privation to earn half a year in the security of his ancestral home.

In the fall of 1730 Renaut broke the pattern. Instead of sailing home after a summer in Ile Royale, he stayed on to take winter work. In the coldest months of the year, the fishermen who were settled in the colony extended their catches and revenues by sending boats out from November through January, pausing only when the ice drifting down from the north drove them ashore. One of those committed to this harsh winter fishery was Jean Phelipeaux, settler and fishery proprietor at the island outpost called Scatary, a few leagues east of Louisbourg. Catches had been good in the summer of 1730, and Phelipeaux wanted workers to expand his winter campaign. That fall he persuaded Charles Renaut and his brother Mathurin to winter in Ile Royale and work the second season with him. When the letter from France reached Jean Phelipeaux's fishing station at Scatary in the spring of 1731, the Renaut brothers' families had not seen them for a full year.

II

Close by the easternmost tip of Ile Royale the triangular island of Scatary lies cruelly exposed to the wild Atlantic, but the ecology that seemed so unwelcoming to human habitation drew schools of cod to the surrounding waters. Drawn in their turn by this rich resource, Renaut's forebears had noted the island's wood, fresh water, and snug harbours, and it was one of the first places settled when the colony took root. Seen from a shallop pitching in the Atlantic rollers, Scatary harbour in 1731 was little more than a series of wharves projecting from the rocky shore of a sheltering cove, with clusters of sheds and houses behind each wharf and the spruce woods closing the rear. Scatary existed only for the fishing, and only a mission priest and a surgeon lived there by other trades. The wives and daughters of a dozen proprietors were the community's only women. Migrant workers like the Renauts made up most of the population of about two hundred and fifty, and sea-links to Louisbourg provided most of their scant needs in exchange for fish. At Scatary Renaut and his fellows lived the plain life of hired fishermen through weeks and months dominated by the demands of their work.

For all the brevity of the fishing seasons, fishing businesses needed large catches to ensure their profits. The fishermen worked every day they could, and the church even spared them the obligation of observing holy days in the summer season. Every morning that weather permitted, in fog or rain or just in morning chill, Charles Renaut sailed from Phelipeaux's wharf with two companions. Their craft was an open boat called a shallop, a broad-beamed vessel perhaps thirty feet long and equipped with sails and oars. Before the dawn departure, someone had gone out to tend bait nets near the harbour. Now the shallop's bait barrels were packed with fresh herring or mackerel. Stashed near by were long, multi-hooked lines, a heap of weights, and a grapnel. A chart and compass, spare clothing, bread, a keg of spruce beer or watered wine—all the sundry supplies of a day's work—were stowed beneath the bows.

Each morning Renaut's shallop might run several miles under sail to a favoured fishing ground, and every trip tested the seamanship, skill, and endurance of the three-man crew. A misjudgment of weather or a trivial piloting error could be a death sentence to the men who faced the ocean in these heavy-laden open boats, so the shallopmaster needed sailing ability as well as the knack of finding where the cod would swarm. A crew reputed for finding cod would rarely be left alone on the sea, for Scatary outfitted dozens of shallops ready to follow the lead of a successful fisherman.

Come safely to their chosen spot, their shallop anchored or drifting over their prey in twenty fathoms or less, Renaut and his fellows baited and dropped as many multi-hooked lines as they could tend. If their choice of site was good, they would be busy all day, hauling in the heavy lines, dropping the fish into compartments in the floor of the shallop, then baiting and casting out their lines once more. The long day of labour and risk was an unremitting test of the boatmen's endurance. They might pause to eat or drink, to hail their fellows or a passing ship, or even to hunt seals and seabirds, but pay as well as pride held them to their work, for hired fishermen were paid by what they caught.

The fisherman's work was gruelling even when warm sunshine lit an almost gentle ocean. More often weather exacted a further test of their hardiness, as squall lines and fast-moving fogs swept down upon the shallops. Even in high summer the intersection of warm land and cool ocean brought winds and damp fogs to chill them. The array of capes, caps, and gloves that every boat carried could never completely shelter the fishermen. In winter storm, frigid salt spray and ice-rimed gear were chronic hardships. It was a harsh career and a risky one. Each year storms and ice claimed a few shallops; each year collisions and accidents exacted their toll of lives and vessels.

If all went well, mid afternoon of the fishing day saw Renaut and his crew hauling in their lines to hoist sail and find their way back to Scatary, their shallop now laden down with several hundredweight of fish. At Jean Phelipeaux's wharf, a rustic structure of poles, planks, and heavy wharfing spikes, Renaut helped pitch his catch to the shore crews, who began to prepare the fresh fish for preservation. Catching the cod was only half the job; now a careful curing would ready it for transport and marketing. . . .

The labour of men like Charles Renaut in the catching, curing, and selling of cod was the engine that drove the economy of Ile Royale. In Renaut's years there, his boat was only one among four hundred shallops gathering in the cod that teemed over the inshore banks, and the ports of Ile Royale also fitted out sixty or seventy ocean-going schooners to pursue the fish to banks as distant as Saint-Pierre and Sable Island. Several thousand fishermen and shoreworkers worked at the catch. Toward the end of summer there might be 150,000 hundredweights of dry cod ready for shipment along with 1,600 barrels of valuable cod-liver oil—enough to pay the wages of thousands of men, enough to meet all the debts incurred for mountains of supplies, enough to fill the holds of all the trading vessels crowding Louisbourg's broad harbour.

It was not just fishermen who cared about the catches of the little fishing ports up and down the coast of Ile Royale. Almost all the trades of Louisbourg and its colony fasted or grew fat according to the progress of the fishing industry. Cod paid for the goods that occupied merchants and shopkeepers and their clerks and employees. It hired the transport that employed boatmen and builders. It drew the trading vessels of distant seaports, and the ships made work for the sailors and warehousemen and brokers whose wages supported the inns, taverns, and shops of Louisbourg. Ultimately it was cod that generated the colonial revenues that justified the King's growing investment in the rising fortifications of Louisbourg. . . .

Indeed, Charles Renaut's humble product could claim global influence. He would return to Normandy with his pay, but his catch might be sold in the Caribbean, around the Mediterranean, or almost anywhere in northern Europe. Though Ile Royale's production was only part of France's cod catches, which competed in international markets against abundant British and American supplies of the same commodity, the little colony's cod still formed a significant portion of the world's cod supply, in turn an important contribution to the food resources of a burgeoning European population. A global economy that the nations often found worth warring over, the cod trade and the wealth it produced had fired the imagination of New World explorers, colony-builders, and naval theorists. It still depended on the daily labour of obscure fishermen like Charles Renaut.

Like nearly everyone in Ile Royale, Charles Renaut shouldered a working day that filled most of his waking hours. After spending the day in his shallop and part of the evening helping to clean the catch, he might still have boat-caulking or net-making duties to attend to. Even when such chores were not pressing, a man there only for the work lived austerely, his horizons circumscribed by Jean Phelipeaux's fishing station. Renaut lived close by the worksite, rarely escaping the sound and smell of the fishermen's labour. He slung a straw-filled *paillasse* and stowed a padlocked sea-chest in a bunkhouse provided by his employer, a simple structure adjacent to the worksheds and flakes and perhaps roofed only with sailcloth. . . .

Still, the fishermen did not work without cease. Merchant Bertrand Imbert of Louisbourg tells of walking out of the town to inspect a stock of cod in the middle of an August afternoon. The summer work should have been at its peak, yet after closing his deal, Imbert joined several unhurried fishermen for a drink at their quarters. Employers could tolerate occasional interruptions of this sort, for they were merchants to their men. Most employers sold liquor and other merchandise to their fishermen, deducting the price of all they sold from the employee's wages. In seasons when catches were small and profits smaller, some proprietors earned more from rum sales than from their fish. . . . For Renaut. . . eating and drinking were probably the major diversions with which he passed his scarce hours of leisure. . . .

Music and dance, contests and gambling could add to the group's entertainment, but simple talk was probably the major diversion of hard-labouring men completing long days of work. In the isolation of the worksite, common origins and outlooks sustained the bonds between the workers. There was nothing unusual in the partnership of brothers like Charles and Mathurin Renaut, and since Jean Phelipeaux's roots were Norman like theirs, many of his employees had probably travelled out together from the brothers' homeland. Renaut likely had friends and cousins near by, and such comradeship helped knit the fishing stations together. . . .

When Marie-Joanne wrote in April 1731, Charles Renaut was already four months dead. [He had drowned three days after Christmas, 1730.] He would never eat the cheese and butter she was sending, never see his daughter walk. When some messenger faithfully delivered the letter to Scatary that summer, Jean Phelipeaux could only add it to the papers of the dead brothers and go on with the hard routines of his trade. Because he died without seeing it, Charles Renaut's useless letter still lies in the registers with a note on his belongings and how he died, as if the cold Ile Royale waters that closed over his head in December 1730 had conferred on this obscure transient visitor some small and unsought immortality.

New France: Les Femmes Favorisées

JAN NOEL

Economic Opportunities

Even more than demographic forces, the colonial economy served to enhance the position of women. In relation to the varied activities found in many regions of France, New France possessed a primitive economy. Other than subsistence farming, the habitants engaged in two major pursuits. The first was military activity, which included not only actual fighting but building and maintaining the imperial forts and provisioning the troops. The second activity was the fur trade. Fighting and fur trading channelled men's ambitions and at times removed them physically from the colony. This helped open up the full range of opportunities to women, who had the possibility of assuming a wide variety of economic roles in *ancien régime* society. Many adapted themselves to life in a military society. A few actually fought. Others made a good living by providing goods and services to the ever-present armies. Still others left military activity aside and concentrated on civilian economic pursuits—pursuits that were often neglected by men. For many this simply meant managing the family farm as best as one could during the trading season, when husbands were away. Other women assumed direction of commercial enterprises, a neglected area in this society that preferred military honours to commercial prizes. Others acted as sort of home-office partners for fur-trading husbands working far afield. Still others, having lost husbands to raids, rapids, or other hazards of forest life, assumed a widow's position at the helm of the family business.

New France has been convincingly presented as a military society. The argument is based on the fact that a very large proportion of its population was under arms, its government had a semi-military character, its economy relied heavily on military expenditure and manpower, and a military ethos prevailed among the élite.[1] In some cases, women joined their menfolk in these martial pursuits. The seventeenth century sometimes

---

Jan Noel, from "New France: Les femmes favorisées" *Atlantis* 6, no. 2 (Spring 1981), pp. 80–98. Used by Permission.
1. W.J. Eccles, "The Social, Economic and Political Significance of the Military Establishment in New France," *Canadian Historical Review*, L11 (March, 1971) pp. 8–10.

saw them in direct combat. A number of Montrealers perished during an Iroquois raid in 1661 in which, Charlevoix tells us, "even the women fought to the death, and not one of them surrendered."[2] In Acadia, Madame de la Tour took command of the fort's forty-five soldiers, and warded off her husband's arch-enemy, Menou D'Aulnay, for three days before finally capitulating.[3]

The most famous of these seventeenth-century *guerrières* was, of course, Madeleine de Verchères. At the age of fourteen she escaped from a band of Iroquois attackers, rushed back to the fort on her parents' seigneurie, and fired a cannon shot in time to warn all the surrounding settlers of the danger.[4] Legend and history have portrayed Madeleine as a lamb who was able, under siege, to summon up a lion's heart. Powdered and demure in a pink dress, she smiles very sweetly out at the world in a charming vignette in Arthur Doughty's *A Daughter of New France, being a story of the life and times of Magdelaine de Verchères*, published in 1916. Perhaps the late twentieth century is ready for her as she was: a swash-buckling, musket-toting braggart who extended the magnitude of her deeds with each successive telling, who boasted that she never in her life shed a tear, a contentious thorn in the side of the local curé (whom she slandered) and of her *censitaires* (whom she constantly battled in the courts).[5] She strutted through life for all the world like the boorish male officers of the *campagnard* nobility to which her family belonged.[6] One wonders how many more there were like her. Perhaps all trace of them has vanished into the wastebaskets of subsequent generations of historians who, with immovable ideas of female propriety, did not know what on earth to do with them—particularly after what must have been the exhausting effort of pinching Verchères' muscled frame into a corset and getting her to wear the pink dress.

By the eighteenth century, women had withdrawn from hand-to-hand combat, but many remained an integral part of the military élite as it closed in to become a caste. In this system, both sexes shared the

2. F.-X. Charlevoix, *History and General Description of New France*, vol. 3 (New York, 1900), p. 35.
3. Ethel Bennett, "Madame de La Tour, 1602–1645," in M. Innis, ed., *The Clear Spirit* (Toronto, 1966), p. 21.
4. G. Brown et al., eds., *Dictionary of Canadian Biography* (hereafter *DCB*), vol. 3 (Toronto, 1966–), pp. 308–13.
5. Ibid., R. Boyer, *Les Crimes et Châtiments au Canada Française du XVIIIe au XXe siècle* (Montréal, 1966), p. 338–39.
6. For a splendid description of the attitude and lifestyle of this class in France, see P. de Vaissière, *Gentilhommes compagnards de l'ancienne France* (Paris, 1903).

responsibility of marrying properly and of maintaining those cohesive family ties which, Corvisier tells us, lay at the heart of military society. Both also appealed to the ministry for their sons' promotions.[7]

What is more surprising is that a number of women accompanied their husbands to military posts in the wilderness. Wives of officers, particularly of corporals, traditionally helped manage the canteens in the French armies.[8] Almost all Canadian officers were involved in some sort of trading activity, and a wife at the post could mind the store when the husband had to mind the war. Some were overzealous. When Franquet rode into Fort Saint Frédéric in 1752 he discovered a terrific row among its inhabitants. The post was in a virtual state of mutiny because a Madame Lusignan was monopolizing all the trade, both wholesale and retail, at the fort; and her husband, the Commandant, was enforcing the monopoly.[9] In fact, Franquet's inspection tour of the Canadian posts is remarkable for the number of women who greeted him at the military posts, which one might have expected to be a male preserve. Arriving at Fort Sault Saint Louis he was received very politely by M. de Merceau and his two daughters. He noted that Fort Saint Frédéric housed not only the redoubtable Madame Lusignan but also another officer's widow. At Fort Chambly he "spent the whole day with the ladies, and visited Madame de Beaulac, an officer's widow who has been given lodging in this fort."[10]

The nuns, too, marched in step with this military society. They were, quite literally, one of its lifelines, since they cared for its wounded. A majority of the invalids at the Montreal Hôtel-Dieu were soldiers, and the Ursuline institution at Trois-Rivières was referred to simply as a *hôpital militaire*.[11] Hospital service was so vital to the army that Frontenac personally intervened to speed construction of the Montreal Hôtel-Dieu in 1695, when he was planning a campaign against the Iroquois.[12] In the colony's first days, the Ursulines also made great efforts to help the

---

7. G. Frégault, *Le Grand Marquis* (Montreal, 1922), pp. 74–75; A. Corvisier, *L'Armée française de la fin du XVIIe siècle ou ministère de Choiseul* (Paris, 1964), p. 777.

8. Ibid., pp. 762–63, 826.

9. L. Franquet, *Voyages et memoires sur le Canada* (Montréal, 1974), pp. 56, 67–68, 200.

10. Ibid., pp. 35, 76, 88.

11. Louise Dechêne, *Habitants et marchands de Montréal au XVIIe siècle* (Paris, 1974), p. 398; Franquet, *Voyages*, p. 16.

12. *DCB*, 2, p. 491

Governor seal Indian alliances by attempting to secure Iroquois students who would serve as hostages, and by giving receptions for Iroquois chiefs.[13]

Humbler folk also played a part in military society. In the towns female publicans conducted a booming business with the thirsty troops. Other women served as laundresses, adjuncts so vital that they accompanied armies even on the campaigns where wives and other camp followers were ordered to stay home.[14] Seemingly indispensable, too, wherever armies march, are prostitutes. At Quebec City they plied their trade as early as 1667. Indian women at the missions also served in this capacity.[15] All told, women had more connections with the military economy than is generally noted.

While warfare provided a number of women with a living, it was in commerce that the *Canadiennes* really flourished. Here a number of women moved beyond supporting roles to occupy centre stage. This happened for several reasons. The first was that the military ethos diverted men from commercial activity. Second, many men who entered the woods to fight or trade were gone for years. Others, drowned or killed in battle, never returned.[16] This left many widows who had to earn a livelihood. This happened so often, in fact, that when women, around the turn of the eighteenth century, overcame their early numerical disadvantage, the tables turned quickly. They soon outnumbered the men and remained a majority through to the Conquest.[17] Generally speaking, life was more hazardous for men than for women[18]—so much so that the next revolution of the historiographic wheel may turn up the men of New France (at least in relation to its women) as an oppressed group.

At any rate, women often stepped in to take the place of their absent

---

13. J. Marshall, ed., *Word from New France* (Toronto, 1967), pp. 27, 213, 222–23, 233.
14. Dechêne, *Habitants et marchands*; p. 393; Franquet, *Voyages*, p. 199; I. Foulché-Delbosc, "Women of Three Rivers, 1651–1663," in A. Prentice and S. Trofimenkoff, eds., *The Neglected Majority* (Toronto, 1977), p. 25; Corvisier, *L'Armée française*, p. 760.
15. Boyer, *Crimes et châtiments*, pp. 349–51; Dechêne, *Habitants et marchands*, p. 41. Dechêne concludes that, considering Montreal was a garrison town with a shortage of marriageable women, the degree of prostitution was normal or, to use her term, *conformiste* (pp. 437–38).
16. Eccles, "The Social, Economic and Political Significance of the Military," pp. 11–17; Dechêne, *Habitants et marchands*, p. 121.
17. J. Henripin, *Trends and Factors of Fertility in Canada* (Ottawa, 1972), p. 2; R.-L. Séguin "La Canadienne aux XVIIe et XVIIIe siècles," *Revue d'histoire de l'Amérique française* (hereafter *RHAF*), 13 (mars, 1960), pp. 495, 503.
18. Marcel Trudel, *Montréal, la formation d'une Société* (Montréal, 1976), p. 163; H. Charbonneau, *Vie et mort de nos ancêtres* (Montréal, 1975), p. 135.

husbands or brothers. A surprising number of women traders emerge in the secondary literature on New France. In the colony's earliest days, the mere handful of women included two merchants at Trois-Rivières: Jeanne Enard (mother-in-law of Pierre Boucher), who "by her husband's own admission" was the head of the family as far as fur-trading was concerned; and Mathurine Poisson, who sold imported goods to the colonists.[19] At Montreal there was the wife of Artus de Sully, whose unspecified (but presumably commercial) activities won her the distinction of being Montreal's biggest debtor.[20] In Quebec City, Eleonore de Grandmaison was a member of a company formed to trade in the Ottawa country. She added to her wealth by renting her lands on the Île d'Orleans to Huron refugees after Huronia had been destroyed. Farther east, Madame de la Tour involved herself in shipping pelts to France. Another Acadian, Madame Joybert, traded furs on the Saint John River.[21]

With the onset of the less pious eighteenth century, we find several women at the centre of the illegal fur trade. Indian women, including "a cross-eyed squaw named Marie-Magdelaine," regularly carried contraband goods from the Caughnawaga reserve to Albany.[22] A Madame Couagne received Albany contraband at the other end, in Montreal.[23] But at the heart of this illegal trade were the Desaulniers sisters, who used their trading post on the Caughnawaga reserve as an *entrepôt* for the forbidden English strouds, fine textiles, pipes, boots, lace, gloves, silver tableware, chocolate, sugar, and oysters that the Indians brought regularly from Albany.[24] Franquet remarked on the power of these *marchandes*, who were able to persuade the Indians to refuse the government's request to build fortifications around their village.[25] The Desaulniers did not want the comings and goings of their employees too closely scrutinized.

These *commerçants*, honest and otherwise, continued to play their part until the Conquest. Marie-Anne Barbel (*Veuve* Fornel) farmed the Tadoussac fur trade and was involved in diverse enterprises including retail sales,

---

19. Foulché-Delbosc, "Women of Three Rivers," p. 25.
20. Trudel, *Montréal*, p.163.
21. Bennett, "Madame de la Tour," p 16. Madame Joybert was the mother of the future Madame de Vaudreuil. *DCB* 1, p. 399. For E. de Grandmaison, see *DCB*, 1, p. 345.
22. Jean Lunn, "The Illegal Fur Trade Out of New France, 1713–60," Canadian Historical Association Report (1939), p. 62.
23. W. J. Eccles, *Canadian Society*, p. 61.
24. Lunn, "Illegal Fur Trade," pp. 61–75.
25. Franquet, *Voyages*, pp. 120–21.

brickmaking, and real estate.[26] On Franquet's tour in the 1750s he encountered other *marchandes* besides the controversial "Madame la Commandante" who had usurped the Fort Saint Frédéric trade. He enjoyed a restful night at the home of Madame de Lemothe, a *marchande* who had prospered so well that she was able to put up her guests in splendid beds that Franquet proclaimed "fit for a duchess."[27]

A number of writers have remarked on the shortage of entrepreneurial talent in New France.[28] This perhaps helps to account for the activities of Agathe de St. Père, who established the textile industry in Canada. She did so after the colonial administrators had repeatedly called for development of spinning and weaving, with no result.[29] Coming from the illustrious Le Moyne family, Agathe St. Père married the ensign Pierre Legardeur de Repentigny, a man who, we are told, had "an easy-going nature." St. Père, of another temperament, pursued the family business interests, investing in fur trade partnerships, real estate, and lending operations. Then in 1705, when the vessel bringing the yearly supply of French cloth to the colony was shipwrecked, she saw an opportunity to develop the textile industry in Montreal. She ransomed nine English weavers who had been captured by the Indians and arranged for apprentices to study the trade. Subsequently these apprentices taught the trade to other Montrealers on home looms that Madame de Repentigny built and distributed. Besides developing the manufacture of linen, drugget, and serge, she discovered new chemicals that made use of the native plants to dye and process them.[30]

Upon this foundation Madame Benoist built. Around the time of the Conquest, she was directing an operation in Montreal in which women turned out, among other things, shirts and petticoats for the fur trade.[31] This is a case of woman doing business while man did battle, for Madame Benoist's husband was commanding officer at Lac des Deux Montagnes.

The absence of male entrepreneurs may also explain the operation of a

---

26. Lilianne Plamondon, "Une femme d'affaires en Nouvelle-France: Marie-Anne Barbel, Veuve Fornel," *RHAF*, 31 (septembre, 1977).

27. Franquet, *Voyages*, pp. 156–58.

28. For example, Hamelin in "What Middle Class?" The absence of an indigenous bourgeoisie is also central to the interpretation of Dechêne in *Habitants et marchands*.

29. Séguin, "La Canadienne," p. 494.

30. For accounts of Agathe de Saint Père, see *DCB*, 3, pp. 580–81; Fauteux, *Industrie au Canada*, pp. 464–69; Massicote, *Bulletin des Recherches historiques* (hereafter *BRH*) (1944), pp. 202–7.

31. H. Neatby, *Quebec: The Revolutionary Age* (Toronto, 1966), pp. 72–73. Neatby refers to this activity in the early post-Conquest era; Franquet encountered Madame Benoist in 1753 (*Voyages*, p. 150).

large Richelieu lumbering operation by Louise de Ramezay, the daughter of the Governor of Montreal. Louise, who remained single, lost her father in 1724. Her mother continued to operate the sawmill on the family's Chambly seigneury but suffered a disastrous reverse due to a combination of flooding, theft, and shipwreck in 1725. The daughter, however, went into partnership with the Seigneuress de Rouville in 1745 and successfully developed the sawmill. She then opened a flour mill, a Montreal tannery, and another sawmill. By the 1750s the trade was flourishing: Louise de Ramezay was shipping 20,000-*livre* loads, and one merchant alone owed her 60,000 *livres*. In 1753 she began to expand her leather business, associating with a group of Montreal tanners to open new workshops.[32]

Louise de Ramezay's case is very clearly related to the fact that she lived in a military society. As Louise was growing up, one by one her brothers perished. Claude, an ensign in the French navy, died during an attack on Rio de Janeiro in 1711. Louis died during the 1715 campaign against the Fox Indians. La Gesse died ten years later in a shipwreck off Île Royale. That left only one son, Jean-Baptiste-Roch; and, almost inevitably, he chose a military career over management of the family business affairs.[33] It may be that similar situations accounted for the female entrepreneurs in ironforging, tilemaking, sturgeon-fishing, sealing, and contract building, all of whom operated in New France.[34]

The society's military preoccupations presented business opportunities to some women; for others, the stress on family ties was probably more important. Madame Benoist belonged to the Baby family, whose male members were out cultivating the western fur trade. Her production of shirts made to the Indians' specifications was the perfect complement. The secret of the Desaulniers' successful trade network may well be that they were related to so many of Montreal's leading merchants.[35] The fur trade generally required two or more bases of operation. We saw earlier in our discussion that this society not only placed great value on family connections but also accepted female commercial activity. It was therefore quite natural that female relatives would be recruited into business to

---

32. For discussion of the De Ramezays' business affairs, see Massicote, *BRH* (1931), p. 530; J.-N. Fauteux, *Essai sur l'industrie au Canada sous le Régime Français* (Québec, 1927), pp. 158–59, 204–15, 442.
33. *DCB*, 2, p. 548.
34. Fauteux, *Industrie au Canada*, pp. 158, 297, 420–21, 522; P. Moogk, *Building a House in New France* (Toronto, 1977), pp. 60–64.
35. Lunn, "Illegal Fur Trade," p. 61.

cover one of the bases. Men who were heading for the west would delegate their powers of attorney and various business responsibilities to their wives, who were remaining in the colony.[36]

We find these husband-wife fur trade partnerships not only among "*Les Grandes Familles*" but permeating all classes of society. At Trois-Rivières women and girls manufactured the canoes that carried the fur trade provisions westward each summer. This was a large-scale operation that profited from fat government contracts.[37] In Montreal, wives kept the account-books while their husbands traded. Other women spent the winters sewing shirts and petticoats that would be bartered the following summer.[38]

The final reason for women's extensive business activity was the direct result of the hazards men faced in fighting and fur-trading. A high proportion of women were widowed; and as widows, they enjoyed special commercial privileges. In traditional French society, these privileges were so extensive that craftsmen's widows sometimes inherited full guild-master's rights. More generally, widows acquired the right to manage the family assets until the children reached the age of twenty-five (and sometimes beyond that time). In some instances they also received the right to choose which child would receive the succession.[39] In New France these rights frequently came into operation, and they had a major impact on the distribution of wealth and power in the society. In 1663, for example, women held the majority of the colony's seigneurial land. The *Veuve* Le Moyne numbered among the twelve Montreal merchants who, between 1642 and 1725, controlled assets of 50,000 *livres*. The *Veuve* Fornel acquired a similar importance later on in the regime. Some of the leading merchants at Louisbourg were also widows. The humbler commerce of tavernkeeping was also frequently a widow's lot.[40]

Thus, in New France, both military and commercial activities that

---

36. See Moogk (*Building a House*, p. 8) for one case of a husband's transfer of these powers.
37. Franquet, *Voyages*, p. 17.
38. Dechêne, *Habitants et marchands*, pp. 151–53, 187, 391; Séguin, "La Canadienne," p. 494.
39. Charbonneau, *Vie et mort*, p. 184; G. Fagniez, *La Femme de la société française dans la première moitié du XVIIe siècle* (Paris, 1929), pp. 111, 182–84. A recent study by Butel ("Comportements familiaux") has documented the phenomenon of widows taking over the family business in eighteenth-century Bordeaux.
40. Marcel Trudel, *The Beginnings of New France* (Toronto, 1973), p. 250. This was largely due to the enormous holdings of Jean Lauzon's widow. Dechêne, *Habitants et marchands*, pp. 209, 204–5, 393; Plamondon, "Femmes d'affaires." W.S. Macnutt, *The Atlantic Provinces* (Toronto, 1965), p. 25.

required a great deal of travelling over vast distances were usually carried out by men. In their absence, their wives played a large role in the day-to-day economic direction of the colony. Even when the men remained in the colony, military ambitions often absorbed their energies, particularly among the upper class. In these situations, it was not uncommon for a wife to assume direction of the family interests.[41] Others waited to do so until their widowhood, which—given the fact that the average wife was considerably younger than her husband and that his activities were often more dangerous—frequently came early.[42]

Conclusion

New France had been founded at a time in Europe's history in which the roles of women were neither clearly nor rigidly defined. In this fluid situation, the colony received an exceptionally well-endowed group of female immigrants during its formative stage. There, where they long remained in short supply, they secured a number of special privileges at home, at school, in the courts, and in social and political life. They consolidated this favourable position by attaining a major role in the colonial economy, at both the popular and the directive levels. These circumstances enabled the women of New France to play many parts. *Dévotes* and traders, warriors and landowners, smugglers and politicians, industrialists and financiers: they thronged the stage in such numbers that they distinguish themselves as *femmes favorisées*.

---

41. This happened on seigneuries as well as in town, as in the case of M. de Lanouguère, "a soldier by preference," whose wife, Marguerite-Renée Denys, directed their seigneury (*DCB*, 1, p. 418).

42. The original version of this paper was written as the result of a stimulating graduate seminar conducted by Professor William J. Eccles at the University of Toronto. My thanks to him and to others who have offered helpful comments and criticisms, particularly Professors Sylvia Van Kirk and Allan Greer at the University of Toronto. The revised version printed here has benefited from the detailed response of Professor Micheline Dumont to the original version published in the Spring 1981 volume of *Atlantis*. For Professor Dumont's critique of the article, and my reply, see *Atlantis*, 8, 1 (Spring, 1982), pp. 118–30.

LETTER TO A LADY OF RANK

Quebec, 3 September 1640

MARIE DE L'INCARNATION

Madame:

...We have had eighteen girls, not to speak of the Savage women and girls, who have permission to enter the place set aside for the instruction of the French and the Savages and come there very frequently.

After instruction and prayers we feast them according to their fashion. Their own hunger is the clock by which they judge when it is time for a meal, so when we prepare food for our seminarians, we must also provide for any others that might unexpectedly arrive. This is the case particularly in winter when the old people cannot accompany the other Savages to the hunt, for if they were not cared for at that time they would die of hunger in the cabins. God granted us the grace to be able to succour them till springtime so that they kept us good company, and it will be a singular consolation to us to be able to continue to do this with the help of charitable persons in France, failing which it will be absolutely impossible, our little seminary not being able to suffice by itself for the great expenditures required for the maintenance of seminarians and assistance to the other Savages as well.

I assure you, Madame, that the expenditure for all this is not believable. We brought clothes sufficient for two years; it has all been used this year so that, having nothing more in which to dress our girls, we have even been obliged to give them some of our own things. All the linen Madame our foundress gave us for our own use and part of what our Mothers in France sent us has likewise been used to clean and cover them.

It is a singular consolation to us to deprive ourselves of all that is most necessary in order to win souls to Jesus Christ, and we would prefer to lack everything rather than leave our girls in the unbearable filth they bring from their cabins. When they are given to us, they are naked as worms and must be washed from head to foot because of the grease their parents rub all over their bodies; and whatever diligence we use and however often their linen and clothing is changed, we cannot rid them for a long time of the vermin caused by this abundance of grease. A Sister

WORD FROM NEW FRANCE: THE SELECTED LETTERS OF MARIE DE L'INCARNATION, TRANS. BY JOYCE MARSHALL (TORONTO: OXFORD UNIVERSITY PRESS, 1967): 74–77. REPRINTED BY PERMISSION OF THE PUBLISHER.

employs part of each day at this. It is an office that everyone eagerly covets. Whoever obtains it considers herself rich in such a happy lot and those that are deprived of it consider themselves undeserving of it and dwell in humility. Madame our foundress performed this service almost all year; today it is Mother Marie de Saint-Joseph that enjoys this good fortune.

Besides the Savage women and girls, whom we receive in the house, the men visit us in the parlour, where we try to give them the same charity we do their women, and it is a very sensible consolation to us to take bread from our mouths to give it to these poor people, in order to inspire them with love for Our Lord and for his holy Faith.

But after all it is a very special providence of this great God that we are able to have girls after the great number of them that died last year. This malady, which is smallpox,[1] being universal among the Savages, it spread to our seminary, which in a very few days resembled a hospital. All our girls suffered this malady three times and four of them died from it. We all expected to fall sick, because the malady was a veritable contagion, and also because we were day and night succouring them and the small space we had forced us to be continually together. But Our Lord aided us so powerfully that none of us was indisposed.

FURTHER READINGS FOR TOPIC 4

Marie-Emmanuel Chabot, O.S.U. "Marie Guyart, *dite* Marie de l'Incarnation." *Dictionary of Canadian Biography*, Vol. 1. Toronto: University of Toronto Press, 1966.

W. J. Eccles. "A Belated Review of Harold Adams Innis's *The Fur Trade in Canada*." *Canadian Historical Review* 60, no. 4 (December 1979): 419–41.

R. Ommer. "The Cod Trade of the New World," in *A People of the Sea: The Maritime History of the Channel Islands*, ed. A. G. Jamieson. London: Methuen, 1986: 245–68.

Lilianne Plamondon. "A Businesswoman in New France: Marie-Anne Barbel, the Widow Fornel." In *Rethinking Canada: The Promise of Women's History*, ed. Veronica Strong-Boag and Anita Clair Fellman. Toronto: Copp Clark Pitman, 1986.

---

1. Smallpox, which spread as far as Huronia, broke out at Quebec in August 1639, shortly after the arrival of the French ships. It reached epidemic proportions in November and continued until February 1640.

P A R T

2

Change
and
Continuity
After
the
Conquest

TOPIC 5

The Conquest: Cataclysm or Continuity?

A s a result of the British Conquest and the Treaty of Paris in 1763, New France became a British rather than a French colony. What were the consequences for the inhabitants of the new province of Quebec? This question is one of the most controversial in Canadian historical writing because of its implications for the politics of twentieth-century Quebec. Clearly, the French controlled the economy before the Conquest. When and how did they lose that control to businessmen of British descent?

Adherents of the extremely nationalist "Montreal school" such as Michel Brunet, some of whose work is excerpted here, argue that a colonial bourgeoisie existed in New France. This bourgeoisie was reduced in number by post-Conquest migration back to France; those who remained were quickly relegated to a position of economic inferiority by British merchants with close ties to the London metropolis whose domination was to be long-lasting and far-reaching. Fernand Ouellet, on the other hand, stresses the degree of social and economic continuity after the Conquest, arguing that the French remained important in business into the 1780s. As Ouellet sees it, British domination of the fur trade and later the lumbering industry was not so much a direct result of the Conquest as a testament to British business aggressiveness and expertise.

Of course, much more than the economic life of Quebec was affected by the inauguration of British rule. The Church was required to adapt to a regime overtly hostile to Roman Catholicism and to the loss of the direct tie with the French church. Nevertheless, as J.-P. Wallot's article argues, there was a good deal of continuity in the religious life of the habitants in the decades before and after the Conquest, as a comparison with the article by Cornelius Jaenen in Topic 2 confirms.

The Legacy of New France Restored to Favour

FERNAND OUELLET

By the Royal Proclamation of 1763, England had brought about a sort of social revolution in Quebec. The promoters of this radical transformation had believed that, through the superior business techniques of the British and a massive wave of immigration from New England, it would be possible in a few years to institute a "Mercantile State" in Quebec, populated by an Anglo-Saxon majority. The measures they had adopted in 1763 would then be justified. However, this was merely a utopian dream: the situation prevailing some years later led to the opposite result. The British authorities were forced to confirm the social and institutional heritage left by New France. The history of the Royal Proclamation of 1763 is simply the history of its disintegration. In 1774, England sanctioned this reversal by adopting the Quebec Act.

Between 1765 and 1774 there was no revolutionary change in the economy. Any reconstruction was faced with a tangle of problems that affected all levels of society. Although very real progress was made in all sectors of the economy—the fur trade, agriculture, fisheries and the Saint Maurice foundries—and new enterprises were begun, the economic situation remained essentially that of the French era. In this respect, the consequences of the change of political control were scarcely important. The slight quantitative gains that were achieved were based firmly on the traditional economic structure. The revival of the fur trade immediately raised again the traditional rivalry between Montreal and Albany; both wished to control the western trade. The British who had settled in the country allied themselves spontaneously with the French Canadians in the bitter competition. The struggle became so intense that the government instituted a policy which was, in fact, favourable to Albany and detrimental to the interests of the French-Canadian and British fur traders. The restraints placed on the ambitions of the inhabitants of the Saint Lawrence Valley were essentially those used by the administration of New France.

FERNAND OUELLET, "THE LEGACY OF NEW FRANCE RESTORED TO FAVOUR," CHAPTER 14 IN *UNITY IN DIVERSITY*, ED. P. G. CORNELL (HOLT, RINEHART AND WINSTON): 154–58, 160, 163–64. BY PERMISSION OF FERNAND OUELLET, DEPARTMENT OF HISTORY, YORK UNIVERSITY.

The reinstatement of these controls had several causes. The government administrators were convinced that the irresistible attraction that the fur trade held for the inhabitants had in the past hindered harmonious economic development. Also, the administration had been placed under considerable pressure, both in Canada and in London, by the fur trade merchants of New England and by the shareholders of the Hudson's Bay Company, who were trying to secure supremacy in the lucrative fur trade. The boundaries laid out in 1763 were the result of these factors. Finally, the governors, in their desire to maintain the stability of the trade in the West, had adopted a series of restrictive measures all of which were unfavourable to the local fur trade. Trading permits were brought back into force, and security equal to twice the value of the merchandise to be carried on a given expedition had to be posted to obtain such a permit. In addition, the traders were forbidden to go into an Indian village and extend credit to Indians. These decisions, which effectively confined the traders to the environs of the posts, clearly favoured Albany, since the businessmen of New England were in a better position, having the advantages both of lower transportation costs and a greater supply of trading goods.

Albany's favourable position in the fur trade not only enabled most of the furs to be channelled toward the port of New York, but also gave this port a considerable advantage in the provisioning of the western posts with trade goods. In effect, Quebec ran the risk of becoming a dependency of New England, but Canadian businessmen of both origins wanted to establish themselves independently in the English and West Indian markets. To become well rooted in the West Indian market, the Canadian merchants needed the support of established fisheries, a thriving timber trade and a stable agricultural production. With these assets, they could have controlled their import trade themselves.

In spite of these handicaps, the fur trade continued to expand after 1763, and the records of the French Regime were rapidly exceeded. Nevertheless, after 1770, the resources of beaver began to be exhausted in the areas exploited since the Conquest. The Quebec Act, which returned the far West and the Ohio Valley to Canada as fur reserves, made possible an extension of the area that could be exploited and a further increase in the fur trade. Montreal's dominance was henceforth assured.

Although agriculture was also beset with problems, it made considerable progress as well. After 1763, production rose. The cycle reached its ceiling by 1770—in 1774 the surplus of wheat was estimated at more than one-half million *minots*. All levels of society benefited from this increase, which, however, was not consistent. In 1765–1766, and again three years later, bad crops and epidemics brought hard times.

Aside from the attempts to diversify production through the introduction of new crops, such as potatoes, hemp and flax, the most interesting feature of this agricultural evolution was the development of an external market. The colony made considerable efforts to dispose of its surpluses by provisioning the fisheries, and by entering the West Indian market and even, on occasion, the markets of the mother country. These sales did not, however, entirely alleviate the persistent over-production, and as a result agriculture was not as prosperous as it might have been.

Low prices and the lack of currency indicated a stagnation in the economy, but it was in other areas that difficulties were more prolonged. The merchants had to fight long and hard to secure the abolition of the restrictions imposed upon the sedentary fishery by the Proclamation of 1763, for this industry lay on the fringes of the great Atlantic cod fishery which was minutely regulated to conform with the British mercantile system. By attaching these fishing posts either to Newfoundland or to Nova Scotia, England theoretically excluded the inhabitants of the Saint Lawrence Valley from this area of business, and limited the prospect of a well organized and diversified trade with the Antilles and Great Britain.

Although the Saint Maurice iron industry was in a fairly advantageous position, such was not the case with lumbering. Strong competition from the countries of Northern Europe and from New England considerably reduced the possibilities of expansion in an industry that was later to become one of the most important resources of Canada. In the meantime, it had to be content with modest development.

In short, the Canadian economy expanded slowly in spite of the efforts of the businessmen. The gains made could not mask the durability of the older centres of competition; the great economic changes still lay in the future.

The Enduring Social Structure

After the Conquest, the French Canadians remained the chief source of population expansion. After the Seven Years' War, the population increase returned to normal because of a heavy wave of marriages and a rapid lowering of the death rate. Between 1767 and 1775 the birth rate fluctuated around fifty-four per thousand, the marriage rate about 8.3, and the death rate about 26.7. The population doubled in less than twenty-eight years. This exceptional growth contrasted strongly with the light immigration.

Clearly, local economic conditions and the situation in the mother country scarcely favoured the initiation of mass immigration. Immigration was in progress, but at a desperately slow pace in the opinion of those who wanted to make the colony British. On the other hand, the colonists who settled in the Saint Lawrence Valley were ambitious and full of initiative, and wished to play a role in the colony far out of proportion to their numbers.

The repercussions of the Conquest, the policy of the Proclamation of 1763, the economic situation and the attempts to implant a large English population had all been unable to upset the social structure of the French Regime. Socially, the replacement of the French bureaucracy by a group of administrators who were predominantly English hardly constituted a shaking of the basic structure. The elite remained the same, and the masses conserved their traditional characteristics.

The clergy and the seigneurs were still the dominant groups. The clergy continued to occupy a prominent social position in the colony. It controlled 26 per cent of the seigneurial lands; was firmly established in the parishes; and held exclusive jurisdiction over education, hospitalization, and aid to the poor. Its moral influence and privileged status within the State contributed powerfully to its assurance of a continued position as a dominant class. The lay seigneurs were in essentially the same category.

The aura of attraction around aristocratic values and the monarchic nature of the political regime were the reasons for the lasting prominence of the landed aristocracy. It saw its social utility in relation to the defence of the country, and felt that such social functions should form the basis of its political importance and justify its privileged status in the economy and the administration. However, the new regime's proclamation of freedom of trade deprived the seigneurs of State protection in the fur trade and thus generally restricted them to the development of their fiefs. Economically speaking, the seigneurs soon realized that their future, because of their customs and because of lack of business acumen, was not bright.

This society had been created to incorporate the social usefulness of the various groups and was based on the seigneurial system. The demarcation between "seigneur" and "censitaires" was indicative of the relative importance of each group. The first group charged the rent and the second paid it. Clearly, the acquisition of a seigneurie by a merchant or a rich habitant contributed to his rise in the social scale. The prestige already enjoyed by the nobility and the social significance of real property drove the bourgeoisie to acquire seigneuries. Although these periodic recruitments renewed the seigneur class, they did not help the cause of the bourgeoisie. Once he had achieved his ends and had become a seigneur, a businessman often lost the dynamism that he showed in his business enterprises, and adopted the attitudes and style of life appropriate at the time to the nobility. This lack of dynamic motivation had, during the French Regime, prevented the local bourgeoisie from becoming truly great and developing lasting traditions. This characteristic remained under the English regime, and continued to influence the majority of French Canadians and even claimed victims among a minority of British.

However, under the English regime the development of the bourgeoisie did take a different turn. The British immigrants brought different business traditions and different ideals. They believed in free enterprise and distrusted State intervention. In addition, they were convinced that only parliamentary institutions would enable the bourgeoisie to fulfill its socio-economic role, and a great many French-Canadian businessmen were willing to accept their viewpoint, in whole or in part.

The bourgeoisie was small in numbers to begin with but was continually gathering strength all through the period. It was no more English than French-Canadian. The fur trade attracted investments quite readily and was, until 1775, dominated by the French Canadians by virtue of their experience, numbers and invested capital. Nevertheless, the British showed a more marked inclination to coördinate their interests, seeking means to develop partnerships and to invest the money gained in the fur trade into other channels like the timber trade, fisheries, grain trade, the Saint Maurice foundries and import trade in general. The French Canadians seemed to remain too absorbed in fur.

Although both French Canadians and British were well entrenched, and fought together against the State and foreign competition in the fur trade and the fisheries, such was not the case in most other areas. The British seem to have been the prime movers of new enterprises. This efforts to commercialize agriculture and to stimulate and diversify production are well known, and they did the same thing for lumbering. In the long run this superiority of initiative had decisive results.

As a group, the bourgeoisie grew in force and influence. If it did not obtain the reforms it demanded or promote objectives in its own interest, it was because it did not have a sufficient weight of numbers. The bourgeoisie remained, in spite of its demands, a group that was active enough, but in the last analysis marginal and not representative of the interests of the majority. Its sense of frustration is understandable.

Between 1760 and 1775 the evolution in economic and social affairs contributed as much as the military situation to the continuing predominance of the elite groups from the *Ancien Régime*; both ensured the decline of the policy of 1763.

The Decline in the Policy of 1763 and the Quebec Act

The economic conditions and the slow immigration made the governors, already predisposed to absolutism, realize that the British regime would have to rely on the French Canadians. There could be no doubt that their overwhelming numerical superiority, though not permanent, would continue. The unleashing of radical agitation in New England raised urgent questions about the current policies. In these circumstances, it was not only the numerical superiority of the French Canadians that was valued, but all the social and political structures inherited from the French Regime. The seigneurial system, the *Coutume de Paris*, the status of the Church, and even the French criminal law were seen as the bases of an hierarchical society wherein the people moved at the will of the upper strata and were filled with the strongest military traditions. Thus, the administrators were inclined to see the functions of the clergy and the lay seigneurs as of more than ordinary importance, and endeavoured to impose their views in England.

That England recognized the tithe in law, abolished the Test Oath, and accepted in practice the union of the Catholic Church to the State is all understandable in the light of the thinking of the era. By officially restoring the *Coutume de Paris*, maintaining the seigneurial system and refusing to establish parliamentary institutions, she showed her willingness to ensure the survival of the traditional organization of the colony. The solution reached in the question of boundaries in the West and in the fishing zones reflected similar preoccupations. These decisions had been dictated by the circumstances and by consideration of the unusual situation in the Saint Lawrence Valley, but made reforms necessitated by later developments very difficult indeed. . . .

The Society

It might be said that the Quebec Act and the American Revolution confirmed the entrenchment of the *Ancien Régime's* social structure. The clergy benefited most from this affirmation. As landowners and as members of a dominant and privileged social class, the clergy could face the future with confidence.

The lay seigneurs understood that the military situation, because it emphasized their military role, gave them unparalleled relief from pressure. From this time on, their pretensions knew no bounds. They were firmly convinced that the Quebec Act was the first step in a restoration and reinforcement of their privileges. They made no effort to disguise their contempt for the bourgeoisie; nor did they have the slightest fear of inducing discontent among the peasants by raising seigneurial rents. This exaggerated attachment to their social status was not a healthy sign. They were vulnerable on the economic level, and were equally so in other respects: the American invasion had tested the precise measure of their influence on the people. The habitants' resistance to the seigneur's propaganda threw serious doubt on the latter's popularity.

The most important social changes occurred among the merchant class. The bourgeoisie grew in numbers, power and wealth. New merchants came, of course, from the local inhabitants, but they were also drawn from among the immigrants. Some, such as Dobie, Forsyth and Gregory came from England and Scotland and others came from New England. E. Ellice, Simon McTavish and Peter Pond were the most representative of this second group.

The importers and the grain dealers, as well as those engaged in the transport business, were the first to benefit from the expanded economy produced by the American Revolution. Quite prominent were a group of individuals having interests in all areas, including the fur trade and the fisheries. In the fur trade, moreover, blocks of capital took shape. The once vague concentration of efforts and means became quite clearly outlined.

The expansion of the area of exploitation, the rise in transportation costs and salaries, the general inflation, and the disastrous consequences of the competition among traders made a regrouping of interests into more extensive organizations imperative. It was in the Northwest, where the factor of distance was even more crucial, that this tendency was most strongly asserted. In 1775, talk arose about forming an organization to be known as the Northwest Company. In the southwest, although less pressing, the same evolution was occurring. Four years later, eight societies with interests in the Northwest trade did join forces. Then in 1783, a reorganization took place that gave the McTavish-Frobisher group the dominant position. This group had fully grasped the possibilities in the Northwest, and accelerated the tendency toward concentration.

As these movements towards a vast monopoly progressed, the French-Canadian enterprise was gradually outdistanced by the British in the exploitation of the West. The prolonged hesitance of the French Canadians to accept the necessity to organize seemed to be responsible for this change. For the most part, they continued to develop alone or in small groups, and thus made themselves increasingly vulnerable to the competition of the more complex enterprises. In addition, their comparative weakness in the import field at a time when trading commodities were rather scarce served them particularly badly. Whatever the reasons, the American Revolution marked the end of their primacy in the fur trade. From this time on, French-Canadian enterprise was widely outdistanced by the English-Canadian.

The British Conquest and the Decline of the French-Canadian Bourgeoisie

M. BRUNET

...Becoming members of a rich and powerful empire [after the Conquest], the *Canadien* businessmen who stayed in the country believed they were bound to make alluring profits. With Bigot and his cronies gone, they imagined that the country's trade would thenceforth belong to them, and that the new colonial government, with their counsel, would keep a paternal eye on the furthering of their interests. They refused to realize that the Conquest had put them in an even more painfully inferior position than they had suffered in the last years of French rule. Great disappointments were in store for them.

The colony was not long in prospering, but the biggest profits did not go to the *Canadiens*. As early as the capitulation of Montreal, Amherst had invited the merchants of England and the American colonies to settle in the conquest. About a hundred responded to the appeal from 1760 to 1770. The newcomers did not intend to be last in line. After a struggle of more than seventy years New France had finally been taken. The rich commercial empire of the St. Lawrence Valley, the Great Lakes and the Mississippi would henceforth belong to the conquerors. They had not made their conquest to let the *Canadiens* exploit it....

A series of misfortunes befell them [the *Canadien* traders]. The French government's bankruptcy partly ruined the businessmen of Canada. The bills of exchange on the public treasury and paper notes represented virtually all their liquid assets. They would recover only a small percentage. It is not known exactly how much they lost in that unhappy adventure....

Ill fortune continued to dog the merchants of Canada. A number of them had placed large orders in France during the war. These goods had not arrived. At the time trade resumed its normal course after the capitulation of Montreal, their warehouses were empty. They made desperate attempts to get the British authorities' permission to take delivery of the goods they had ordered before the end of hostilities in

M. BRUNET, "THE BRITISH CONQUEST AND THE DECLINE OF THE FRENCH-CANADIAN BOURGEOISIE," IN *SOCIETY AND CONQUEST: THE DEBATE ON THE BOURGEOISIE AND SOCIAL CHANGE IN FRENCH CANADA, 1700–1850*, ED. DALE MIQUELON (TORONTO: COPP CLARK, 1977): 146–54. BY PERMISSION OF THE AUTHOR.

America. These commitments had frozen the little credit they had. With nothing to sell, they could not resume the business that war had interrupted. A truly alarming situation. . . .

The colonial traders were generally unable to pay cash for the goods they did import. Their European suppliers had to extend generous terms. Moreover no trading activity of any significance can be imagined without the use of credit. By the Conquest, the former markets where they obtained credit as well as the merchandise they needed were closed to the *Canadien* businessmen. It took them some small time to realize what was happening, since for a while they kept trying to reopen trade relations with France. They were in a totally confused state. Weeks after the signing of the Treaty of Paris, François Baby was again attempting to place an order in France. His former supplier wrote him at some length to make him understand how hard it was to continue their business contact:

> I have received your favour of the 7th of this month [Baby was then in Europe]. I foresee numerous difficulties as to your proposed dispatch of a ship of 100 to 120 tons for Quebec. It is not feasible to find French ships to charter for that country since French ships would be impounded with their cargoes. I think you are not unaware that entry to Canada is prohibited for all the goods of French factories, as well as wines, brandy and other beverages. And if these are brought in at present it is by smuggling, unless they leave directly from England with their duties paid.

One by one, the French exporters took leave of their *Canadien* correspondents, who asked them to recommend them to London traders and transfer to London the meagre credits remaining to them in France. The Montreal merchant Etienne Augé parted regretfully with one of his suppliers, and told him he would like "to be in a position to continue the French business." A letter from François Baby to Simon Jauge sums up the difficulties that had to be faced by every *Canadien* trader:

> I repeat the request I made to you last year, to have the goodness to send me news of you. You must realize that it is an absolute necessity for me to know the state of my accounts with you. I have reason to expect you to extend to me the benefit of the privileges of a British subject. For heaven's sake, Monsieur, send me through Messrs Guinaud and Hankey of London a general and detailed accounting of the funds I left with you as well as those I authorized you to withdraw from M. Havy [a La Rochelle merchant]. My family, involved with all this business, has been pressing me for two years to give them an accounting, and I am not in a

position to do so, and in consequence am obliged to face many difficult moments.

Advised and recommended by their French correspondents, the *Canadien* merchants approached London businessmen: Joseph and Henry Guinaud, Daniel and Antoine Vialars, Ponthieu and Co., Isidore and Thomas Lynch, Robert Hankey. A number of them were Frenchmen who had settled in England. They appeared well disposed to their new customers. It did not take them long to discover, however, that these were nothing but very small fry in business, without contacts or credit, and with no influence in their own country. And the London merchants with whom the *Canadiens* corresponded were not among the most important in the City. These modest businessmen—those of London and those of the colony—were not substantial enough to compete with their English rivals. For example, Henry Guinaud, the London merchant to whom three *Canadien* dealers unfolded their ambitious future plans in 1765, declared bankruptcy four years later....

The *Canadien* merchants saw their profits fall. Several became unable to meet their obligations. A Montreal merchant given the job of recovering the money owing to François Baby did not have an easy time of it. Certain traders became embittered towards their more favoured English rivals. The Montreal dealer Adhémar reported to François Baby: "They tell me that Duperron and St. Martin do nothing but curse the Londoners [English merchants] and are always at loggerheads with the notorious trader at their post." Hervieux, Pierre Guy, François Baby and Saint-Georges Dupré were deep in lamentation. In their view, economic conditions had never been so bad. Saint-Georges Dupré was in a black mood: "If God abandoned me I would soon put an end to this most unhappy life."

Was the colony going through a depression? Quite the reverse. From 1765 to 1771, the trade of Canada experienced years of plenty. The end of Pontiac's war lent new impetus to the fur trade. The American colonies' agitation against the Stamp Act and the Townshend duties benefited the traders of Canada, especially those of Montreal. The American patriots' boycott of English goods had the result of increasing British exports to Canada. Montreal replaced Albany as the storage and distribution centre for English products sold in the north of the continent. From Montreal, this merchandise took the trail of the trading posts and even headed for the American colonies. The boycott called by the "Sons of Liberty" was not always effective. Most Americans had not given up the products of England. Farm prices held at an excellent level. As early as 1771, Quebec exports of food began to rise. Even the price of furs was going up; Saint-

Georges Dupré, who would contemplate suicide in October of 1771, had informed his cousin of this that same summer.

The *Canadien* businessmen had shown themselves incapable of holding their own against their English competitors. The Conquest had forced them to complete with unequal weapons. This fact dominates the whole of the economic history of French Canada after the Conquest. While La Naudière, François Baby, Pierre Guy, Etienne Augé, Saint-Georges Dupré and their colleagues fought desperately to obtain credit and merchandise, the newcomers had no difficulty tapping the English market. The importers and exporters from England and the American colonies were quite naturally more inclined to do business with their fellow countrymen than with impecunious foreigners, yesterday's enemies and the vanquished of today. In business, only the rich can borrow. The *Canadiens* had to locate new suppliers. These were not always reliable in filling orders placed with them. Often they simply could not do so. The *Canadien* merchants were forced to change their business patterns, to learn new methods, familiarize themselves with English products. The time of groping and uncertainty lasted a number of years.

The financial losses they had suffered had in addition made them extremely timid. When a businessman's capital is limited, the slightest risk makes him afraid. Little by little, the *Canadien* merchants chose to buy from their English competitors in Montreal and Quebec. A number of their own customers had been going to the English stores for a long time. The traders decided it was wiser to sell their furs on the local market. The profits might have been more modest, but they seemed less risky. A great number looked for safe, gilt-edged investments. They dared not expose their meagre economies to losses in profitable but chancy speculation. Moreover they knew that the most lucrative speculation was not for them. Saint-Georges Dupré would be happy to invest his money at five or even at four per cent. He advised Baby to do the same. The *Canadien* businessmen had had to give up the great export-import trade, the only significant road to wealth in that period. They left the large profits to others, and sought refuge in an honest mediocrity.

Obliged to abandon external commerce to the English merchants, the *Canadiens* also lost control of the fur trade. The two formed a whole. The fur trade was still the great wealth of the colony. It would be so until the end of the eighteenth century and into the first years of the nineteenth, when great Anglo-Canadian fortunes would be built in the timber business. On their arrival, the conquerors showed their interest in the fur trade. For a long time they had been bent on seizing the monopoly from New France. At last they could fulfil their ambitions, satisfy their desires!

They were not found wanting. As early as 1762, Malcolm Fraser obtained the monopoly for the Murray Bay posts. In the same year, the officer commanding at Michilimackinac gave Alexander Henry the exclusive fur-trading privilege west of Lake Superior. Also in 1762, Dunn was granted the King's posts of the Saguenay, and Grant acquired the tract that had been Vaudreuil's.

The sequel is really not hard to understand. The fur trade called for large money commitments. The canoes sent to the interior had to be fitted out, the men paddling them paid. Almost totally cut off from credit, the *Canadien* dealers were gradually ousted from the trade. They had to accept the limited role of small traders, providing they were allowed even this by a not over-brutal competition. As for the *Canadien* boatmen and voyageurs whose frugality, obedience and working spirit were so admired by the English explorers and businessmen, their brawn belonged to those with the cash to pay. In 1767, the first year in which the trade was totally open, 121 canoes left Michilimackinac between July 7 and September 12. They carried goods to the value of £ 39,000 Sterling. Of 80 traders, 70 were *Canadien*; yet the list of businessmen who gave their guarantees of the good conduct of traders and hired men contained only 23 French names in a total of 40. . . .

The careers of La Naudière, Saint-Georges Dupré and François Baby deserve a close look. These *Canadien* dealers and traders managed to maintain a higher standard of living than the farming folk by becoming civil servants of the conqueror. In his letter of July 24, 1773, La Naudière told his cousin that his father had given him the seigneurie of Ste. Anne de la Pérade as part of his inheritance. He was proposing to develop it. There was beginning to be talk of a return to the land. Agriculture offered itself as a refuge for *Canadiens* cut out of their country's trade. Numerous former dealers and merchants became farmers out of necessity; not by vocation. Those searching their family trees have often noted this phenomenon: in the eighteenth century several members of their family were in trade; in the nineteenth, the vast majority were on the farm. Do not suppose that they had freely chosen that existence. It had been imposed on them by the Conquest.

During the Revolution in the neighbouring colonies, the young La Naudière competed in loyalism. His business affairs continued in jeopardy. He attempted to obtain compensation from the British government by invoking losses supposedly suffered during the American invasion. He asked to be appointed a councillor. Not to be discouraged, he laid siege to his official protectors. Carleton's return brought him luck: he became a surveyor and a member of the Council. These two sinecures yielded £ 600. Saint-Georges Dupré, whose qualities as a businessman La Naudière had already praised, passed a succession of lean years after the Conquest—until the day when he was made commissioner of militia and put in charge of organizing the forced labour for military transport. His obedience and loyalty to the conquerors had reaped dividends. He had made a good investment. François Baby, a member of the two Councils, surveyor and adjutant-general, was also to bask in Carleton's and Haldimand's bounty.

These *Canadien* bourgeois had managed to find their niche. They were part of the very small minority, the favourites of the regime. But all the rest? To imagine their painful condition, we have only to scan the hundreds of petitions and appeals in the archives! Conquered in the economy because their native land had been defeated on the field of battle and then occupied by the victors, cut off from the vital influence of their motherland, most *Canadien* businessmen had sunk into wretchedness or mediocrity. A scant few stayed afloat, veritable islets exposed to the all-powerful influence of their English competitors, who were the unchallengeable masters of the colony's economic life.

The forming of the North-West Company indicates how modest the *Canadien* share of the country's business was. In 1780, two of the 16 company shares belonged to French-speaking entrepreneurs in partnership, Wadin et Cie. Jean-Etienne Wadin was even a Swiss merchant who had settled in Canada after the Conquest. His associate was called Venant St. Germain. In 1783, Nicolas Montour was the only *Canadien* shareholder, with two shares only. Wadin had died in the previous year, and Venant St. Germain was vegetating as an ordinary company agent. The Gregory, McLeod Company that gave hard competition to the North-West Company from 1783 to 1787 had not a single French-speaking shareholder. French names are found only among the minor employees.

The businessmen of English origin did not restrict themselves to the furs and external trade. They invaded every area. Stephen Moore and Hugh Finlay, who was destined to play an important part in the colony's economic and political life, asked the government for grants of land in the Lower Town of Quebec. John Collins, Benjamin Price and Thomas Dunn made a request for land at the water's edge in Quebec, with the purpose of building wharves. Some competitors had the same plan. John Gray and William Grant too needed land in the Lower Town. A company was formed to obtain the leases on the King's Posts. No point in adding that it included no *Canadiens*. A certain John Marteilhe was interested in the St. Maurice Forges, and disclosed his ambitions to the Board of Trade. Murray seems to have preferred Simon Mackenzie. In 1767 Carleton would rent the Forges to a company of nine shareholders for a period of 16 years. Among these shareholders were three with French names.

The grain and flour trades brought rich profits for the colony's exporters from 1771 to 1775. In 1770, Canada had exported 51,822 bushels of wheat. Exports rose to 460,818 bushels in 1774. In 1776, they returned to normal. Scarcity of wheat had forced the British Parliament to lower duties on imports in 1773. The price of the product doubled on the Quebec market. The farm people profited from this unexpected manna. It helped create a feeling of satisfaction in the mass of the population that served the English propagandists admirably well. Events seemed to vindicate those who claimed that the conqueror had brought prosperity. His business sense and concern for the general good were supposed to be its causes! Freed from a mother country and colonial administrators who had exploited it, the colony could finally develop!...

The farmers had sold their wheat well. They were all pleased about that. A few woollen socks contained a few extra coins. However, who had skimmed off the biggest profits? The wheat producers? We must doubt that. Would it not rather be the merchants and exporters? These were not *Canadien*. A certain Jacob Jordan, a Montreal businessman who was closely involved in a number of profitable transactions during the American Revolution, made a fortune as a wheat and flour broker. He had had the necessary capital and contacts to take advantage of the windfall. The *Canadien* merchants had been satisfied to follow his successful operations admiringly. Jordan was not the only English merchant to specialize in the export of agricultural products. It must be recalled that external trade had passed into the newcomers' hands. They also controlled the timber and fishing industries. . . .

RELIGION AND FRENCH-CANADIAN MORES IN THE EARLY NINETEENTH CENTURY

JEAN-PIERRE WALLOT

The French Canadians' Religion and Mores

If the church's lack of legal status enhanced the habitants' traditional independence towards it, the lack of priests among a greatly expanded population impeded the propagation of religion and morality. The ensuing problems inevitably affected religious conduct in the province, particularly in distant and neglected parishes which saw a priest only irregularly....

The Canadian faithful did not live up to the hallowed myth which was later painted in pious colours by folkloric pride and religious historians. On the whole, one can detect a great continuity with the French regime.[1] In any event, at the beginning of the nineteenth century, the *Canadiens* were religious to the extent that they partook of a general Christian conception of man's destiny, and that they usually went to church on Sundays, when there was a priest: the latter was not only a religious, but a social event, an occasion to meet neighbours, discuss crops and politics. A systematic perusal of travellers' accounts, of the clerical correspondence, and of numerous other sources reveals that French Canadians were as much superstitious as pious. Was not the bishop forced to condemn publicly so-called healers?[2] The Canadian men, recorded John Lambert, were less religious than women and did not kneel any more at the foot of crosses along the roads.[3] Like peasants elsewhere, the habitants were hard-hearted, disobedient, and independent, very close with their cash as

---

J.-P. WALLOT, "RELIGION AND FRENCH-CANADIAN MORES IN THE EARLY NINETEENTH CENTURY," CANADIAN HISTORICAL REVIEW LII (MARCH 1971): 76–89. REPRINTED BY PERMISSION OF UNIVERSITY OF TORONTO PRESS.

1. See, in particular, W.J. Eccles, *The Canadian Frontier, 1534–1760* (New York 1969), chap. 5.
2. Eg, Mgr Plessis's mandement to the parish St-Pierre, Ile d'Orléans, 17 March 1808, Archives de la province de Québec [APQ], gr.coll., livres de mandements, par. St-Pierre. On superstition, see also J. Lambert, *Travels* (London, 1810), I, 179, *passim*; Mgr Têtu and C.-O. Gagnon, eds., *Mandements, lettres pastorales et circulaires des évêques de Québec [Mandements],* 6 vols. (Quebec, 1887-90), II, 457–8, *passim*.
3. Lambert, *Travels,* I, 11 ff, 179; II, 12. 'They are religious from education and habit, more than from principle. They observe its...formalities, not because they are necessary to their salvation, but because it gratifies their vanity and superstition' (*ibid.,* I, 154).

far as religion was concerned, always trying to evade, in an incredible number of ways, the payment of the tithes and necessary repairs to the churches or presbyteries.[4] Most of the time, the priests had to bestow many gifts to their parishes, while the ungrateful habitants, if and when they paid their tithes, brought their worst wheat.[5] To that one must add secular and religious ignorance, although the church invested a lot of energy in the editing of thousands of books of prayers and catechisms.[6]

In many parishes, the faithful seemed to devote themselves to contriving numerous troubles for their priest:[7] they not only demurred at imparting the required and necessary material aid; they did not hesitate to smear a priest, if they wanted to get rid of him.[8] In some cases, they might even resort to more violent means. . . . The Canadiens' well-known vanity[9] induced some of them to decline becoming churchwardens, under the

---

4. See note 7. '. . .they [French Canadians] love money. . .' (*ibid.*, 155).

5. '. . .le blé de dime. . .est généralement le plus mauvais. . .' (Letter from Rev. Clément, in *Letters from the Curates of the Respective Parishes of Lower-Canada*. . .(Quebec 1823), 85–6). More often than not, the faithful relied on the priests' generosity to get the necessary sacred vases, ornaments, candeliers, for their churches. Sometimes, they even tried to dump on their curé the burden of the cost of repairs to the church or the presbytery (eg, APQ, pet.coll., Rev. Chouinard's Papers, notes dated 23 Dec. 1798 and 1 Nov. 1799). In the course of many years, the Rev. Panet endowed the vestry of Lislet with more than 3000 french livres in gifts of all kinds. But he was accused of being rich and hiding his money! (APQ, gr.coll., Rev. J. Panet's Papers). See also note 7.

6. From 1765 to 1791, the church had 19,000 catechisms printed (M. Tremaine, *A Bibliography of Canadian Imprints* (Toronto 1952), nos 59, 76, 255, 373 A and B, 700, 701). By 1810, 40,000 catechisms had been published since 1760 (Hare and Wallot, *Imprimés*, nos 54, 134, 135, 136, 192, and 244). Unless the printers and the church deliberately set out to lose money, one must conclude that the French Canadians' ignorance, at that time, has been exaggerated by the historiography (J. Hare, 'Les Imprimés, le vocabulaire et la diffusion des idées,' paper presented to the first colloquium of GRISCAF, Montreal, September 1969, to be published in *Annales historiques de la Révolution française*). The bishop admitted that children sometimes learned the words without understanding their meaning: '. . .néanmoins je ne crois pas qu'on puisse faire un catéchisme assez simple, pour que les enfants l'entendent sans explication' (Mgr Panet to Mgr Plessis, Rivière Ouelle, 17 May 1813, Archives de l'Archevêqué de Québec [AAQ], cartable: évêques de Québec, 4: 40).

7. Eg, AAQ, registre G, 139r, 140r, 141r, 143r, 147v, 166r, 167v, 169r, 181r, 182r, 195r; *Mandements*, 11, 523, ff. 'Les services que vous avez rendus à la paroisse de St-Antoine pendant plus de 50 ans, ne devraient pas vous attirer tant de tracasseries pour le tiers des dîmes. Je vous exhorte à les regarder comme une part de la croix de Jésus-Christ. . .' (Mgr Hubert to Rev. Noël, 3 Aug. 1792, AAQ, copies de lettres, 5: 143).

8. Rev. Beaumont narrowly missed being the victim of 'la haine et la vengeance de quelques *malheureux*, de quelques *scélérats* à qui il n'est devenu odieux que par son zèle à s'élever contre les désordres dont ils sont les auteurs' (Mgr Denaut to Mgr Hubert, Longueuil, 12 Oct. 1796, AAQ, copies de lettres, 5: 479–80).

9. Lambert, *Travels*, 1, 153–4; Observations on Canada, C.1800, MG II, Q. 57–2: 410

pretext that younger men had preceded them in this position.[10] Other
faithful lived near the United States, so they went there to marry *in
fraudem legis* to save money and inconvenience, particularly in the case of
relatives who really required a special dispensation. As the bishop admitted, in those cases he had to consent to a dispensation, otherwise the
couples would make a quick trip to the States, then live in *concubinage*
right in their parishes, to the great scandal of the other faithful. The priests
were asked to fight this disorder with ecclesiastical sanctions, 'quelque
chose de fort...qui put les effrayer salutairement.' This policy had little
success because of the parishioners' small faith.[11] In a parish near Montreal, habitants had simply taken over a rarely-used chapel, but still
consecrated, and converted it into a stable, putting cattle in the vestry and
horses in the sanctuary![12]....In a situation somewhat similar to the French
regime, the House of Assembly was obliged to vote a law to preserve order
during religious services, on Sundays, and holidays. In fact, some parishes
even selected muscular strongmen to impose order in their churches and
throw out the interruptors.[13]

The picture comes more clearly into focus by adding the French
Canadians' undeniable propensity for merriment, drinking, dancing, and
the rest,[14] the result partly of their French heredity, partly of their relative

---

10. 'Si Pierre refuse impunément d'être marguillier, Paul en voudra faire autant et on ne
saura plu où s'arrêter' (Mgr Plessis to Rev. Cherrier, Quebec, 8 April 1807, AAQ, registre
des lettres, 6: 2).
11. Mgr Plessis to Rev. Roux, Quebec, 16 Jan. and 12 Nov. 1809, *ibid.*, 322–3; 7: 71. There
were also *mariages à la gaumine*, 'a form of "do it yourself" marriage ceremony' (Eccles,
The Canadian Frontier, p. 98).
12. Mgr Plessis to the habitants of Pointe-Claire, Quebec, 10 Dec. 1809, AAQ., registre G, 182r.
13. See APQ, Justice [QBC-28], 42: 26 Aug. 1811 (nomination of constables for those purposes
in the parish of St-Laurent); 'Acte qui pourvoit au maintien de bon ordre les jours de fêtes
et dimanches dans les paroisses...(1808),' *Le Courier de Québec*, 25 May 1808 and *Journal
of the House of Assembly of Lower Canada* [JHALC] (1808), 283–5, 299–301, 443, 537–41,
625–33; Eccles, *The Canadian Frontier*, p. 98. *The Quebec Mercury* protested that the law
was unnecessary, for the church had simply to suppress religious holidays. These evils
'would not take place were the offenders not taught to suspend their daily labours on
such days...Such a loss of time cannot only not be afforded by the labouring classes, but
is totally incompatible with a spirit of commercial enterprize, particularly in a country
where the season of business is so very circumscribed' (21 March and 11 April 1808; see
the answer of *Le Courier de Québec*, 9 April 1808). 'Les marguilliers décident de charger
deux personnes de bien surveiller dans l'Eglise pour qu'il n'y ait pas de désordre,
d'arrêter les délinquants et de faire payer leur trouble par ces délinquants' (Account
books of the parish of St-Pierre-du-Portage-de-l'Assomption, 1799).
14. 'They are fond of dancing and entertainments, at particular seasons and festivals, on
which occasions, they eat, drink, and dance in constant succession. When their long fast
in Lent is concluded, they have their "jours gras," or days of feasting. Then it is that
every production of their farm is presented for the gratification of their appetites;
immense turkey-pies; huge joints of pork, beef, and mutton; spacious tureens of soup, or

affluence and of the long inactive winter months,[15] partly of the economic and social changes.[16] It may also be sharpened by a greater awareness among priests, capitalists, and political leaders of the ills of the times. The French Canadians who had sojourned in the western territories seemed the wildest: they brought debauchery to the parishes where they chose to settle down.[17] Naturally, there were good, pious, and exemplary families. But the point is they did not seem to be very numerous. On the contrary, the bishop was constantly admonishing, threatening, or punishing parishes (by recalling the priests) for not providing enough for the subsistence and lodging of their curés; for staging 'horrible' charivaris and orgies, particularly on the occasion of parish celebrations in honour of their patron saint—another occasion of feasting.[18] Some habitants seemed to be professional patron saint or marriage celebrators, going merrily from one parish to another in a seemingly endless spree, crashing—'en survenants'—local ceremonies and parties, and debauching the local population. Finally, the bishop had to suppress most religious holidays, to the great satisfaction of the Protestant British merchants who were horrified

---

thick-milk; besides fish, fowl, and a plentiful supply of fruit-pies decorate the board. Perhaps fifty or a hundred sit down to dinner; rum is drank by the half-pint; often without water; the tables groan with their load, and the room resounds with jollity and merriment. No sooner, however, does the clash of the knives and forks cease, than the violin strikes up, and the dances commence...to the discordant scrapings of a couple of vile fidlers...' (Lambert, *Travels*, I, 174–5; also Hugh Gray, *Letters* (London, 1809), p. 260 ff).

15. 'They possess every necessary of life in abundance, and, when inclined, may enjoy many of its luxuries. They have no taxes to pay...' (Lambert, *Travels*, I, 180, 154–5, 282; Gray, *Letters*, pp. 249 ff, 321–2).

16. On economic and social change, see D.G. Creighton, *The Empire of the St. Lawrence* (2nd ed., Toronto 1956), chaps. V, VI, and VII; F. Ouellet, *Histoire économique et sociale du Québec, 1760–1850* (Montreal 1966), chaps. VI, VII, and VIII; G. Paquet and J.-P. Wallot, 'La Restructuration de l'économie et de la société canadienne au tournant du XIXe siècle : une hypothèse,' paper for the Vth International Congress of Economic History (Leningrad, August 1970), mimeo., 100 pages, to be published; also Ossenberg, 'The Conquest Revisited,' p. 206 ff.

17. R.J. Ossenberg, 'The Conquest Revisited,' *Canadian Review of Sociology and Anthropology* IV (1967), p. 207; Gray, *Letters*, p. 219; Observations on Canada, C.1800, 413

18. See notes 7 and 8; AAQ, registre des lettres, 6: 2, 41, 65, 69; *Mandements*, III, 39, 55, 73, 90; Lambert, *Travels*, I, 322. Plessis has learned with 'douleur' that the habitants of Laprairie had staged an unprecedented 'affreux et horrible charivari...soit pour la durée, soit pour les injures, obscénités, impiétés de toute espèce...les travestissements, mascarades, profanations des cérémonies, ornements et chants funèbres de l'Eglise...' The Bishop compared them with the Israelites 'devenus tout à coup idolâtres et se livrant à des danses et à des jeux insensés autour d'un veau d'or.' Had not God punished them by exterminating 23,000 of those sinners 'le même jour'! The parishioners would have to make public penance (Plessis' mandement to the habitants of La Prairie-de-la-Magdeleine, Quebec, 3 Dec. 1807, AAQ, registre G, 125r; also *ibid.*, 127r).

(and perhaps a little bit jealous) at such a loss of time in merriment instead of hard work.[19] The Bishop's journal of pastoral visits mournfully lists the main sins among the population: irreligion, leaving the church during sermons, drunkenness, public disorders and scandals, dances, adultery, incest, fornication.[20] All the priests in the diocese complained that these disorders were gaining ground. . . .

The annual charges of the grand juries, reports by the governor, judges and justices of the peace, articles in the newspapers, all concur in etching the same picture. This was particularly true of the towns where prosperity, in the late 1800s, was including moral havoc and a higher rate of crime, while it rendered more arduous the task of finding justices of the peace dedicated to their duties.[21] There were, of course, many legitimate sports and amusements, such as carrioling, skating, fishing, hunting, picnicking. By encouraging horse races in Quebec, however, Governor Craig displeased the British press: races could not better Canadian horses; a six-day-week was already too short in this country; races rooted even more French Canadians in their natural laziness, and '[their] propensities to pleasure and predilection for pleasure horses it would be better to check than encourage.'[22] Dances were condemned by the bishop.[23]. . . Even the more accepted forms of recreation sometimes stirred other ills.

---

19. In the countryside, particularly in summer, religious holidays had become 'pour la plupart, des jours de débauche et de licence.' They were suppressed little by little 'pour l'honneur de la religion' and were finally unified in a single day by Mgr Plessis (Mgr Plessis to Rev. Boiret, Maskinongé, 4 July 1807, AAQ, registre des lettres, 4: 248; suppression of the feast of St. Joachim, 11 July 1804, account books of Pointe-Claire; Plessis's mandement of the 10 Dec. 1810 suppressing patron saints' holidays, APQ, gr.coll., Fréchet-Desaultels Papers; Mandements, III, 42; AAQ, registre G, 167v.; Lambert, Travels, 1, 322–3; also note 13).

20. AAQ, cahiers des visites pastorales, eg, years 1806, 1809, 1811.

21. Craig to Liverpool, Quebec, 17 May 1810, MG 11, Q. 112: 173–6. There were also complaints about irregular sittings of the courts and unpunished crimes (Minutes of the Executive Council, ibid., 183). See also the charge of the grand jury of Quebec, 30 Sept. 1808, RG 4, AI, S, 75: 119; The Quebec Mercury, 26 Dec. 1808, 2 and 9 Jan. 1809; Le Courier de Québec, 9 and 23 March 1808; Le Canadien, 30 March 1808; note 139. Governors' proclamations thundered against public and private 'immorality' (eg, 28 Feb. 1793, Public Archives of Canada [PAC], MG 24, B 1, Neilson Papers).

22. The Quebec Mercury, 19 June 1809. On carrioling and other sports and amusements, see Lambert, Travels, I, 72, 79 ff, 174, 308 ff, 320 ff, and II, 5, 45, 74 ff; Gray, Letters, pp. 164 ff, 249 ff; note 124; R-L. Séguin, La Civilisation traditionelle de l'habitant aux XVIIᵉ et XVIIIᵉ siècles [La Civilisation] (Montreal 1967), pp. 56–68.

23. Mgr. Plessis to Rev. Painchaud, Quebec, 21 March 1810, AAQ, registre des lettres, 7: 130. Dance was 'an amusement of which the French are passionately fond' (Lambert, Travels, I, 300).

Drunkenness seemed prevalent, and not only among the soldiers who, of course, with the sailors, did account for more than their share of public disorders and dissoluteness.[24] Habitants arriving at market-places at daybreak would soon leave their wives or children in charge of their carts and collect in taverns where they got drunk on rum. Or in winter they let their horses nearly freeze to death in front of taverns.[25] The habitants' drunkenness was, in fact, as proverbial as that of the British North Westers, although the latter probably learned a few tricks from the Canadiens and Indians, and would mostly confine their libations to their homes or the Beaver Club. The justices of the peace and grand juries, both in Quebec and in Montreal, complained each year of the lack of policemen, of the unnecessary proliferation of taverns,[26] 'occasioning continual scenes of riot and debauchery, particularly on Sundays, to the great scandal of society, and the ruin of lower classes of every age and sex', of the growing number of lazy and depraved mendicants and of bold prostitutes.[27]

The moral conduct of the higher classes was less open to public scrutiny, but it was probably worse. Many married men were known to chase after other women, sometimes their best friends' wives, and cases of bigamy were not unheard of: 'I have just left court where I have convicted Mrs Smith for bigamy—I am told that the Seigneur of Berthier, Mr Henri, their wives, and other members of this community are alarmed and suppose that I am preparing to attack them next...'[28] The Canadian gentlemen's daughters in the towns passed their time reading lascivious books, flirting, beautifying themselves, and parading in their windows in

---

24. Soldiers and sailors were held responsible for many public scenes of debauchery and for attacks on civilians, men and women. These brought outcries from the newspapers, one even publishing a sardonical 'Tableau d'une Ville Militaire' (*Le Courier de Québec*, 3 Feb., 12 March, and 2 April 1808).
25. Lambert, *Travels*, I, 74 ff, 160-1
26. In 1795 the Executive Council discovered that 461 licenses for selling alcoholic liquors had been signed by the governor (minutes of the 2 Jan. 1796, MG II, Q. 75–1: 126).
27. Charge of the grand jury of Quebec, 30 Sept. 1808, RG 4, AI, S, 75: 119. Taverns were 'la source de l'ivrognerie et des vices' (charge of the same jury, 19 Jan. 1811, *The Quebec Gazette*, 24 Jan. 1811). 'Le vice et l'offense d'ivrognerie dominent à un point alarmant et paraît faire des progrès' (Charge of the grand juries of Montreal and Quebec, 20 April 1810, *The Quebec Gazette*, 24 May 1810). See other charges of the same, eg, 9 May 1809 (MG II, Q. 112: 177–80), 30 Sept. 1809 (RG 4, AI, S, 79: 163), 7 Oct. 1809 (MG II, Q. 112: 183); *Le Courier de Québec*, 21 Sept 1808; also note 21.
28. Advocate General J. Sewell to his wife, Montreal, 2 March 1798, APQ, Sewell Papers, copies. The love affairs of Judge de Bonne are well known. 'Mon beaufrère court les champs, sa femme est dans un état horrible...pauvres pères!' (Chartier de Lotbinière to—, Vaudreuil, 8 July 1798, APQ, Roy Papers, no 166).

case a good husband might come shopping for them.[29] Not surprisingly, many a British merchant bagged one, not so much because of the so-called good understanding between the two races, but because they had the choice between Canadian girls and squaws. Moreover, in those classes, French-Canadian parents tended to force their children into rich marriages, where love counted for little.[30] Lambert found the children in the high classes spoiled. And, in general, they killed time in an endless round of dissipation, parties, dances, balls, gossip, and other frivolities:

> There is nothing to boast of in the morals of the higher classes of the people in Canada. The little blackening accounts of scandal are sought for, promulgated, and listened to with avidity; while good actions are often mangled, distorted, and heard with secret envy...The female parties compose a school for scandal...For a small society like that of Canada, the number of unfaithful wives, kept mistresses, and girls of easy virtue, exceed in proportion those of the old country; and it is supposed, that in the towns, more children are born *illegitimately* than in wedlock...Trials for *crim. con.* are however, unknown; neither are duels ever resorted to by the Canadian gentry, to avenge their injured honor. The husbands generally wink at the frailties of their wives, and either content themselves with increasing the number of their *horned* brethern, or fly for comfort into the arms of a *fille de chambre*.[31]

---

29. Lambert, *Travels,*, I, 289 ff, 335-6. A girl of eighteen was frowned upon if she had not a string of at least twenty 'lovers' (*ibid.*). The towns followed European fashions much more closely, although with an inevitable delay, than the countryside, which but nearly ignored them (*ibid.*, 1, 163 ff, 292 ff, 311, 318 ff; Séguin, *La Civilisation*, pp. 459–503).

30. Some openly censured that practice (*Le Courier de Québec*, 27 Feb. and 1 Oct. 1808). A younger son of a good family confessed to his friend that he hoped Americans would bring their daughters with them: '...leur qualité reconnue d'aimer les étrangers nous réjouit ici...du moins aurons-nous l'espérance de ne point vieillir si longtemps dans le triste état de célibataire, dans lequel plusieurs languissent depuis que les parents canadiens ne veulent marier leurs filles non suivant *leurs inclinaisons*, mais *suivant une rigoureuse convenance et une rigide égalité de fortunes*...' (F. Cugnet to De Lavaltrie, c.1790, Baby Papers, MG 22/6, 2: 169). For other examples, see Paquet and Wallot, 'La Liste civile,' RHAF, XXIV, 1970–1, 266–7; also Ossenberg, 'The Conquest Revisited,' p. 205.

31. Lambert also lampoons the extravagance, dissipation, gossip, and scandal common in the towns (see *Travels* I, 280 ff, 293 ff; *The Quebec Mercury*, Dec. 1806). 'The mistaken indulgence of their [upper class Canadian youths'] parents tends very much to increase the general levity and frivolity which prevail among the Canadian ladies' (Lambert, *Travels*, I, 192). 'Nous avons une partie de campagne chez Md. Ross. La tête en tourne dans les villes...' (G. de Lanaudière to his wife, Feb. 1806, APQ Tarieu de Lanaudière Papers, 2; also Mrs Lacorne de St Luc to Mrs Perrault, Montreal, 12 Feb. 1792, Roy Papers, no 166).

Although there is no reliable study of illegitimacy for the period through the parish records, which might or might not be accurate on this account, the number of foundlings seems quite high.[32] The House of Assembly voted monies each year to take care of them and to re-educate persons of easy virtue.[33] The civil laws were amended, for example in 1801, so as to cope with new or at least more acute problems, such as inheritance rights in the cases of concubines, illegitimate children in general, or those born out of incest.[34] Even smaller towns displayed the same ominous signs:

> Small as the town of Three Rivers is, the number of foundlings who are placed under the care of a poor person to bring up, are equal, in proportion to its population, to the number of children at the Foundling Hospital in London. It would be creditable to the inhabitants of Three Rivers, could I say that they are as well taken care of as in London; but the contrary is the case: for in consequence of the scanty allowance for their support, little attention is paid to them, and I am told that few live to maturity.[35]

Except for those who had been servants in the towns, the women, in the countryside, were much less prone to frivolity and immodesty than the ones in the cities.[36] They were generally religious and virtuous, members of pious lay sisterhoods where they were prompted to entice their husbands to more religion and piety 'par prières, bons exemples et autres moyens convenables,' whatever that meant.[37] Some were very pretty when young. But their physical appearance degenerated rapidly through hard work and being constantly around hot stoves.[38] They were prolific as

---

32. Parish records do not seem too reliable on this point. Moreover, contemporaries mention children born from adultery in the same numbers as those from premarital or non-marital sexual relations. A first survey of four or five parishes in the district of Quebec and of a dozen parishes in the district of Montreal suggest the following tentative figures: 4 to 5 per cent in the town of Quebec, 2 per cent in the countryside; 5 to 6 per cent in the town of Montreal, 3 per cent in the surrounding countryside. For a good study on this subject, see E. Shorter, 'Sexual Change and Illegitimacy: The European Experience,' to be published in *Perspectives in Modernization: Essays in Memory of Ian Weinberg* (University of Toronto Press).

33. Eg in 1807, when the House of Assembly voted a sum of £ 1200 st. per year to take care of foundlings and mentally disturbed persons. In 1806, 31 orphans and foundlings had benefited from the same law in the town of Quebec, 33 (of which 22 died) in Montreal (Journals of the House of Assembly of Lower Canada [JHALC], 1807, pp. 315–27).

34. JHALC, 1801, pp. 43, 51–3, 89, 189, 233, 293

35. Lambert, *Travels*, II, 49

36. 'They marry young and are seldom without a numerous family' (*ibid.*, p. 169)

37. Hare and Wallot, *Imprimés*, no 195

38. Weld, *Travels Through the States...*(London, 1799), p. 249; G Heriot, *Analyses of New Voyages* (London 1807), p. 113; Lambert, *Travels*, I, 166–8, 279, 283 ff; Observations on Canada, c.1800, 411. 'The women in Canada...do not spare themselves, especially

mothers, better educated than men, and protected by the *Coutume de Paris* in material matters. They could even vote if they met the property requirements.[39] Being not only economic partners to their husbands but also the heart of the family, French Canadians' primary value,[40] they had acquired 'an influence over their husbands, which those, who are gay and coquetish, know how to turn to their advantage.'[41] '...in Canada,' concurred Hugh Gray, another English traveller, 'it is well known, that a great deal of consequence and even an air of superiority to the husband, is assumed by them. In general. . .*the gray mare is the better horse.'*[42]

Newspapers and justices of the peace were constantly complaining about the extraordinary increasing number of prostitutes in the streets of Quebec, with estimates ranging from 400 to 600 (in a town of 12–13,000 inhabitants in 1810). They corrupted young men and perverted the whole

---

among the common people, where they are always in the fields, meadows and stables' (P. Kalm, *Travels into North America* (3 vols., London 1771 ed.), III, 56).

39. Women in Canada had always played some civil role. They often made protest rallies, eg during the American Revolution and in the early 1790s. Since the Constitutional Act of 1791 based the voting franchise on property requirements, they, as owners, could and did vote, until this right was expressly denied to them in 1834 when it was seen as a danger to their family role (Séguin, *La Civilisation*, p. 107 ff; W.R. Riddell, 'Women's Franchise in Quebec a Century Ago,' *Transactions of the Royal Society of Canada*, XXII, 1931, II, 85 ff). On their better education, see Larochefoucault-Liancourt, *Travels in Canada, 1795* (Toronto 1907), p. 104; Weld, *Travels Through the States...*, p. 194 ff; Lambert, *Travels*, I, 169 ff; R.-L. Séguin, 'La Canadienne aux 17ᵉ et 18ᵉ siècles,' RHAF, XIII, 1959–60, 502 ff. On the laws, beside Lambert and Gray, see A. Morel, *Les Limites de la liberté testamentaire dans le droit civil de la province de Québec* (Paris 1960).

40. French Canadians' first loyalty went to the family, then to the neighbours in the *rang*, and only after that, to the parish and society in general (Ossenberg, 'The Conquest Revisited...,' pp. 207–8; P. Garigue, 'The French Canadian Family,' in M. Wade, ed., *Canadian Dualism* (Toronto 1960), pp. 181–200; P. Defontaines, 'The *Rang*-Pattern of Rural Settlement in French Canada,' in M. Rioux *et al.*, *French Canadian Society*, I, 3–32; L. Gérin, 'The French-Canadian Family—Its Strength and Weaknesses,' in *ibid.*, 32–57; Lambert, *Travels*, I, 168 ff, 176 ff). The simple examination of family papers, in different archival depositories, clearly demonstrates this importance of family ties, even when members of a same family were separated during considerable time and/or by long distances. As a friend wrote another, 'un joli garçon viendra former le couple. Je le souhaite à madame et à vous. C'est une satisfaction que d'avoir des enfants; il me semble que la vie est plus douce et que c'est un plus grand lien qui unissent les époux' (B. D'Artigny to C. de Lotbinière, Quebec, 22 April 1805, APQ, gr.coll., Joly de Lotbinière Papers, no 309 ff).

41. Lambert, *Travels*, I, 169, 283, 289. Kalm distinguished the countryside, where wives appeared subservient to their husbands, from the towns, where they assumed a superior air (*Travels into North America*, pp. 81–2).

42. Gray, *Letters*, pp. 142–3. He added that the sharing of economic power through the '*communauté de biens*' between husbands and wives handicapped business.

society.[43] In May 1811 alone, eleven women were convicted of prostitution: but what was the use of condemning them to forced labour when there was no place to make them work and learn some honest trade?[44] A controversy even developed in the newspapers as to the desirability of crushing such a social evil. 'L'Ami de la Patrie' asserted that as much as three times the provincial revenue was sucked into prostitution. However, the majority opinion favoured its toleration: '...in all garrisons and seaports,' pointed out 'Cosmopolitus,' 'it must be considered not only as an unavoidable, but even a necessary evil; as, did it not exist in some degree, it requires no great stretch of thought, or knowledge of human nature to apprehend that worse might ensue.'[45]...

These jeremiads, although no doubt exaggerated, reflected the inevitable impact of demographic, economic, and urban growth,[46] but also the French Canadians' mores of the time. Naturally, the habitants in the countryside usually led a more quiet and virtuous life. Their debaucheries were more occasional and followed the fashion of what sociologists call traditional feasts or festivals or holidays, when the usually strict moral habits disintegrate for a short time and when the suppression of sexual, social, and alimentary taboos become permissible to the society if not to its religious leaders (as in marriage celebrations, some lasting many days, in carnivals, religious holidays, charivaris).[47] Perhaps, they simply loved the pleasures of life. And though they believed in their religion and in family life, they seemed to grasp very well a logic which would become quite common in our century: sin and have fun now, repent and confess later!

---

43. *The Quebec Mercury*, Jan. 1809. The grand jury of Quebec denounced 'l'accroissement alarmant de prostituées dans la ville et les faubourgs de Québec...une source de poison pour les mœurs...et pour la plus jeune classe de la société' (charge, 19 Jan. 1811, *The Quebec Gazette*, 24 Jan. 1811).
44. *The Quebec Gazette*, 9 May 1811. Such houses were necessary to force 'the idle and dissolute in the society to adopt habits of industry and application' (charge of the grand jury of Montreal, 10 Sept. 1807, RG 4, AI, S, 70: 115).
45. *The Quebec Mercury*, 26 Dec. 1808, 2 and 9 Jan. 1809.
46. See note 16.
47. D. Lemieux, 'Le Temps et la fête dans la vie sociale,' RS, VII, 1966, 282–304. For a study of the European origin and role of charivaries, see N.Z. Davis, 'The Reasons of Misrule: Youth Groups and Charivaris in Sixteenth-Century France,' to be published in *Past and Present*.

Further Readings for Topic 5

Robert Armstrong. *Structure and Change: An Economic History of Quebec*. Toronto: Gage, 1984.

W. J. Eccles. "The French Forces in North America during the Seven Years' War." *Dictionary of Canadian Biography*, Vol. 3. Toronto and Quebec: University of Toronto Press and Les Presses de l'Université Laval, 1974.

Fernand Ouellet. *Economic and Social History of Quebec*. Toronto: Macmillan, 1981.

C. P. Stacey. "The British Forces in North America during the Seven Years' War." *Dictionary of Canadian Biography*, Vol. 4. Toronto and Quebec: University of Toronto Press and Les Presses de l'Université Laval, 1974.

Pierre Tousignant. "The Integration of the Province of Quebec into the British Empire, 1763-91." *Dictionary of Canadian Biography*, Vol. 4. Toronto and Quebec: University of Toronto Press and Les Presses de l'Université Laval, 1979.

TOPIC 6

The
Extinction
of
the
Beothuks

Different groups of natives in British North America experienced contact with the Europeans quite differently. The impact of contact on some tribes, such as the Montagnais of seventeenth-century Quebec, appears to have been immediate and disastrous for the natives, while other groups, as we have seen, were protected from the loss of their autonomy by a variety of factors. Moreover, the same group of natives might experience different types of treatment from the same institutions over a period of time. In pre-Confederation Ontario, for example, natives found themselves well treated as military allies of the government before about 1830, while after that date their essential irrelevance for purposes of defence prompted the state to subject them to a program of settlement and more intensive Christianization.

Among the natives, the most tragic case appears to have been that of the Beothuks, subarctic hunter-gatherers who lived only in Newfoundland, and who were among the first natives encountered by the Europeans. Their use of red ochre on their bodies was the inspiration for the term "red Indian." The extinction of members of this tribe before 1830 has been the subject of much discussion and some distortion. How did the Beothuks disappear? Did they migrate from Newfoundland? Were they deliberately exterminated, either by Europeans or by Micmacs? Did they succumb instead to starvation and tuberculosis? The excerpt from Frederick W. Rowe's book on the Beothuks considers all these possibilities, while Ingeborg Marshall's article focuses more narrowly on disease as a factor in their extinction. John Gill's recollections, based on his mother's memories of the Beothuk "Nance

April,'' illustrate both Micmac cruelty toward the Beothuks and the artistic skills of the Newfoundland natives.

These selections invite comparison with others in this volume, including Upton's in Topic 1 and Fisher's in Topic 10.

EXTINCTION:

The Beothuks of Newfoundland

FREDERICK W. ROWE

As far as anyone has been able to determine, Shanawdithit was the last of the Beothuks. Certainly, apart from her, there were no authenticated records of contacts with Beothuks after she and her mother and sister yielded themselves up to, or were taken by, William Cull in 1823. According to Shanawdithit's figures, the 27 of her tribe who were alive the previous year had by then been reduced by sickness, starvation, murder and accidental drowning to 14 besides herself. Of these, five were men, six were women, one a "lad" and two were children. What happened to the 14 is a matter of conjecture, but it is quite probable that those who did not die of tuberculosis died from starvation which, in their weakened condition, they were unable to avert. It is most likely, therefore, that by 1826 Shanawdithit was the only Beothuk left alive.

Jukes and Bonnycastle refer to the "supposition" that the Beothuk remnant had "passed over to the Labrador coast," but the suggestion that the remnants made the long trek into the interior and then up the Great Northern Peninsula and across the Strait of Belle Isle to join Indians in Labrador remains what it has always been—a most improbable speculation. Perhaps, for once, we might accept a tradition prevalent among the Micmacs and related by one of them to Speck early in the present century to the effect that the last of the Beothuk group starved to death in a wigwam found intact near Hodge's Hill, to the north of Badger. This would tie in with what we know of Beothuk movements after 1820, and with the last evidence of Beothuk activity found by Cormack and his men in 1827 and which they attributed to the previous year.

What is certain is that as a race the Beothuks ceased to exist in Newfoundland in the 1820's—a fact which must be considered a tragedy from every aspect. And as with all tragedies of this nature, it has been followed by questions, accusations and recriminations. Paramount among the questions has been this crucial one: who or what can be held responsible for the extinction of the Beothuks? Horwood and others who have written on this in recent years have had no hesitation in pin-pointing

FREDERICK W. ROWE, *EXTINCTION: THE BEOTHUKS OF NEWFOUNDLAND* (TORONTO: McGRAW-HILL RYERSON, 1977): 142–43, 145–51, 153–57.

blame. The Beothuks were exterminated, they say, by the calculated barbarity of the European settlers in Newfoundland generally, and in the final decades of Beothuk existence, by the fishermen-trappers of Notre Dame Bay specifically. The evidence, they claim, was always with us, either directly or by implication, and if there were any doubts about the settlers' guilt they were dispelled by the Pulling and Liverpool manuscripts which contain accounts of atrocities committed against a practically helpless, dwindling group of Beothuks that included women and children. . . .

From the evidence that is available, it seems that most of the atrocities were confined to the fishermen-trappers who utilized the Bay of Exploits and the adjoining Bays, especially New and Badger Bays, for their trapping activities. Miller and John Peyton Senior must head the indictment for, apart from their personal involvement in the brutalities described, as entrepreneurs they apparently encouraged their trappers, of whom (according to Pulling) Taylor and the two Richmonds were the most notorious, to use violence against the Beothuks in order to get their skins and furs. Others directly involved in several atrocities included Matthew Ward and William Hooper. This handful of men, probably never exceeding a dozen at any one time, and representing less than one per cent of the population of Notre Dame Bay in 1790, were able, over a relatively short period of time, to do so much harm to the Beothuks largely because they were a law unto themselves, since the repeated requests made by the more civilized residents of that Bay for law-enforcement agencies continued to be ignored until no Beothuks remained.

This coterie of English and Irish settlers who were undoubtedly responsible for the killing and wounding of a substantial number of Beothuks over a period of two or three decades were in no way unique in the history of European occupation of North America. In the period we are chiefly concerned with, that is from 1750 to 1810 or thereabouts, pioneer settlers in the British colonies and what later became the United States routinely slaughtered Indians with as little compunction as they killed buffalo. In the minds of many Americans, Lewis Wetzel, whose father was murdered by the Indians of the Ohio border and who himself was seriously wounded by them when only fourteen, ranked among the heroes of the American frontier. The reason? The fact that between 1777 and 1808 Wetzel killed or tried to kill every Indian he met, a laudable preoccupation which enjoyed the moral and physical support of many of his frontier neighbours as they schemed and fought to get control of territory which had been Indian habitat for centuries. In fairness to the majority of his contemporaries, it should be noted that eventually the American conscience became outraged to the point where Wetzel was tried and imprisoned for his atrocities—something which would probably have happened to the furriers of Notre Dame Bay had there been even a semblance of police and judicial organization in that area.

Thus, no one who has studied the impressive, sometimes revolting, evidence can deny that atrocities of a most barbaric kind were committed, and that in the short period from about 1750 to 1810 an unknown number of Beothuks met their deaths from the guns of the settlers and visiting fishermen. Some were also probably killed by hostile Micmacs. It matters little, at this time, what the motivation for this violence was, whether it was a pathological fear of "Indians," a simple manifestation of human brutality, retaliation for thievery and other aggressive action by the Beothuks, or, sometimes overlooked, ordinary greed for Beothuk furs: whatever the cause, the result was the same—a reduction of Beothuk numbers. The size of this reduction must always be a matter of uncertainty and a basis for arguments. Even if it was not so extensive as some believe, and even if in any case the decline of the Beothuks was an inexorable process, the mayhem and slaughter for which some settlers were responsible most assuredly accelerated that process.

Nevertheless, recognition of the barbaric treatment accorded the Beothuks by a few settlers of the north-east coast does not imply acceptance of the charge that this treatment represented a deliberate, systematic attempt by the Europeans to exterminate the Beothuks. Descendants of the Rowsells, Taylors, Peytons, Culls, Fosters and the other early settlers abound in Notre Dame Bay today, and among their many traditions handed down from generation to generation there is nothing to substantiate such an accusation. Surely if such a policy existed for a hundred years or so, as alleged by several writers, there would have been some record, oral or written. There is none.

Similarly, the charge that killing Indians for sport was a widespread practice among the settlers is equally without competent evidence. As indicated elsewhere in this book, the settlers on the north-east coast were annually cut off from November to June from all contacts with the rest of the world. Their main concern was to feed their families—in other words, to survive. Often survival depended on their supplies of gunpowder and shot. These were the items that above all others had to be husbanded.[1]

---

1. In his Beothuk manuscript, Stanley Gillingham describes the measures taken by his 18th-century ancestors in Gander Bay to conserve their "limited" supplies of powder and shot when hunting game.

Few settlers had the time or such a surplus of precious gunpowder that they could afford, even if they had the inclination, to undertake expeditions into the heart of a hostile country to kill Indians "for sport."

Having conceded the importance of the role that European hostility played in hastening the Beothuks' extinction, many modern scholars refuse to attribute to it full or even major responsibility. In the light of what we know about the history of similar aboriginal groups elsewhere, and with increasing recognition of the importance of other environmental factors, particularly food supply and disease, they argue that it is a simplistic approach to assume that one factor was completely or even largely responsible. Here, perhaps, is the appropriate time to point out a fact frequently overlooked by those who react emotionally to the more unsavoury actions of the settlers, who feel that all the ills and woes of the Beothuks can be laid at the door of those European invaders who thrust themselves into the territory of a simple, primitive people who heretofore had enjoyed sole rights to a bountiful natural Eden, which was violently wrested from them after centuries of exclusive use:

Newfoundland was not always a paradise to which the Beothuks had sole and undisputed claim. There is some doubt as to when the Beothuks first came to Newfoundland, but it is quite possible, indeed probable, that when they arrived one or more other native groups were already there, particularly the Dorset Eskimos. It is most unlikely that the two groups would live peaceably side by side or on overlapping territory. Of a certainty, Labrador Eskimos at one period ranged as far south as the Great Northern Peninsula, perhaps farther, and here too there was traditional enmity with the Beothuks. The incursions of the Vikings most likely led to hostilities, and there is evidence that other Indian groups from Labrador and Cape Breton had a periodic interest in Newfoundland, whether for seals and other mammals and fish in the north, or caribou and fur-bearing animals in the south. In particular, as indicated elsewhere, the Micmacs from Nova Scotia were most probably in the habit of making periodic foraging expeditions across the Cabot Strait long before some of them took up permanent residence in Newfoundland. John Downing, writing to the English authorities in 1676 about conditions in Newfoundland in a "Narrative" which is now part of the Colonial Records in London, stated, "To that part of the land where the french forts are as Placentia, St. Peters [St. Pierre] and the rest, no Indians [Beothuks] come but some Canida [Canadian] Indians [Micmacs] from forts of Canida in french shallowayes with french fowling pieces all spared them by French of Canida."

Other ecological factors may have worked adversely for the Beothuks at times. Their main source of winter food was the caribou. But the caribou had other enemies, notably wolves and lynxes, and these predators may have been responsible for substantial fluctuations in caribou population from time to time. In the 1950's there was a serious decline in Newfoundland caribou population caused by a usually fatal disease transmitted to the young or partly grown caribou by the bite of the lynx. This could have happened periodically through the centuries. Climatic changes, too, may have had a serious effect on food resources, particularly caribou.

The effect on native welfare that a decline in caribou population can have was dramatically illustrated in northern Labrador in 1916. For some reason or reasons not clear, there was not only a falling off in the actual number of caribou but, possibly as a consequence of the decline, the caribou did not follow their usual migratory patterns. The result for the most northerly group of Nascopie was disastrous. The records show that but for the existence of Hudson's Bay Company stores, the starvation and mortality would have been much higher than it actually was. Had such a natural disaster occurred in 1716 instead of 1916 the group might well have become extinct. As it was, the population of the Nascopie in the northern part of Labrador declined by 50 per cent in the period between 1901 and 1926, as a direct result of the caribou shortage followed in 1919 by the influenza epidemic.

One interesting and significant modern discovery is that during the several centuries when the Beothuk population was in decline there was a deterioration of weather in the Northern Hemisphere. The November, 1976 issue of *National Geographic* carried a leading article, "What's Happening to our Climate?" by Samuel W. Matthews. The article describes the various climatic changes affecting the earth over the ages and, in particular, describes the effect of the warming and cooling of the weather on peoples and cultures in historic times. Matthews points out that during the warm period that occurred between 800 A.D. and 1000 A.D., the Vikings left Scandinavia to colonize Iceland, Greenland, and Vinland in North America. In England wine grapes could be cultivated "farther north than at any time until the present century." But by 1200 the cold was returning and "pack ice was besetting the Iceland and Greenland colonies." By the year 1500 "the Greenlanders, stunted and starved, would die to the last man." From then until the mid-1800's occurred what is known as the Little Ice Age. All over the Northern Hemisphere it was colder than at any time since the Ice Age. It is significant that the year 1816, known in New England as "the year without a summer," was part of a period when Newfoundland experienced some of the coldest weather ever recorded. Equally significant is the fact that, according to Shanawdithit, this was the time when her people suffered an acute shortage of food, with consequent malnutrition and actual starvation.

Next we should consider the role of disease in the decline of the Beothuks. Here we are on fairly firm ground. We know that Mary March and Shanawdithit's mother and sister had tuberculosis when taken by Peyton and Cull, and that all three died only months after capture. Shanawdithit herself died of this disease some five years after her mother and sister, so that it is quite possible that she too had tuberculosis when she was captured but that her otherwise robust constitution, together with the relatively good care and treatment she enjoyed in the Peyton household, enabled her to withstand the ravages of the disease for several years. It is noteworthy that Shanawdithit's account of her last years with her people indicate that illness, aggravated by lack of food, caused the deaths of several. Since at least two, and probably all three women taken by Cull in 1823 had tuberculosis, it is against the laws of probability to assume that those left behind were free of the disease, just as it would be to assume that only Mary March had the disease at the time of her capture four years earlier.

No one knows how or when the Beothuks acquired this disease. It could have been from some association either with Micmacs or Labrador Indians who had earlier acquired it from Europeans. It could even have been a legacy from a brief physical contact that Miller's men or others had with the Beothuks in the 1780's and 90's. Or if August or June had periodic contact with the tribe, as reported, one of them could have transmitted it. August, who died at a comparatively early age, may well have had the disease himself. Two things are fairly certain; first, that the Beothuks acquired the disease, directly or indirectly from Europeans, sometime during the 1700's or even as late as 1800, and second, that given their lack of immunity and their living habits, once the disease became established among them, they were doomed to total or near extinction. . . .

Tuberculosis may not have been the only disease affecting Beothuk numbers over the years. It seems most unlikely that they could have had association with Labrador Indians or Micmacs, who were in almost continuous contact with Europeans from the early 1500's on, without getting some of the other germs and viruses which plagued the Europeans periodically and which could make frightful inroads into native races. . . .

There has been little written about the marital and sexual practices of the Beothuks, and the resultant birth rate of that race. The evidence is that the Beothuks were monogamous, and that adultery was regarded as warranting death. But we don't know what the age of marriage was, what sexual practices affecting population were tolerated among the unmarried, whether there was some primitive form of birth control, and most important of all, whether intermarriage or some other biological, genetic or environmental factors had operated so as to reduce the birth rate to a danger point. Nor do we know what the infant and child mortality rate was, especially after the tribe acquired tuberculosis.

Several facts are significant. Mary March was married five or six years before having a child; both Shanawdithit and her sister were of marriageable age, yet apparently neither was married nor had had children. And nowhere is there an indication that those two women had siblings. The death rate among males no doubt was higher than among females. Did this explain the unmarried state of Shanawdithit and her sister? And did strict adherence to the practice of monogamy have a serious effect on the Beothuk population growth?

In the whole of the animal world, the chances of racial survival are inextricably bound up with numbers. It is vitally important for the long-term survival of any racial group that the population be kept above the point where ecological disasters of one kind or another, especially a combination such as a serious decrease in food supply coupled with a disease epidemic, could initiate an irrevocable process of extinction. We do not know what the apex of the Beothuk population in Newfoundland was, but it was certainly never so high as several writers have projected. Some have argued that *very* large numbers were needed to erect and maintain the extensive deer-fences on the Exploits River, but this is proven fallacious by the fact that the fences were in good repair at the time of Cartwright's journey to Red Indian Lake in 1768 at a time when it was generally agreed that the Beothuks did not exceed five or six hundred—an estimate which some students think is far too high.

If, as many scholars now believe, the Beothuks were an offshoot of the Algonquin Indians of mainland North America, it is quite possible that in the prehistoric period of Beothuk residence in Newfoundland the population was maintained by periodic or continuous migration of Algonquins from the mainland tribe. If this was so, that movement had ceased by about 1500, and had probably stopped long before as a result of other migratory developments. The question which logically follows such a speculation is whether the Beothuk group was large enough around the year 1500 to maintain itself indefinitely, given the restrictions imposed by an insular habitat and the ecological variations including occasional epidemics.

It can be argued that even without the physical brutality of Europeans and the alleged depredations of the Micmacs, the Beothuks could not be self-perpetuating once their ties with the larger Algonquin family on the mainland were severed. Of this, of course, we cannot be certain. What does seem clear, however, is that once the Micmacs and Europeans started to encroach on the Beothuks' preserves, that is the area served by the rivers of north-east Newfoundland and the coastal islands of Bonavista and Notre Dame Bays, the chances of population growth were diminished to zero. From that time, surrounded by human enemies, and with the deadly tuberculosis and probably some of the more serious childhood diseases also taking their toll, extinction was inevitable for the Beothuks.

Disease as a Factor in the Demise of the Beothuk Indians

INGEBORG MARSHALL

Introduction

At the end of the 15th century, when explorers and fishermen came to Newfoundland's shores, the island was inhabited by the Beothuk Indians. If their population density was similar to that of other subarctic hunters with a comparable subsistence pattern, then the Beothuk may have amounted to about 1,050 people at contact (Kroeber, 1965: 142; Eggan, 1968: 180).[1] Archaeological evidence of Beothuk occupation is scarce and it may well be that this native group was substantially smaller. During the historic period, that is after the discovery of Newfoundland in 1497, the aboriginal Indian population decreased and became extinct by 1829.

This fate has befallen a number of North American Indian groups and has often been attributed to disease introduced by Europeans. Sherbourne Cook (1973) has made a good case that smallpox and other epidemics reduced the New England native populations by as much as 75% and that tuberculosis, measles and other infections caused further attrition to the population at a rate of 1.5% per year which amounted to a reduction of 80% within 100 years.[2]

Cook's figures have been used to suggest a similar attrition to the

INGEBORG MARSHALL, "DISEASE AS A FACTOR IN THE DEMISE OF THE BEOTHUK INDIANS," *CULTURE* 1, NO. 1 (1981): 71–77. BY PERMISSION OF THE AUTHOR AND *CULTURE*. THE AUTHOR IS GRATEFUL TO DR. K.B. ROBERTS, PROFESSOR EMERITUS, MEMORIAL UNIVERSITY OF NEWFOUNDLAND, FOR HIS CRITICAL REVIEW AND HELPFUL SUGGESTIONS.

1. A.L. Kroeber (1965: 142); the average population density for eastern subarctic hunters and gatherers as calculated by Kroeber are 0.44 per 100 km² for Montagnais/Naskapi and Tête de Boule and 1.43 per 100 km² for Eastern Cree. If an average of these densities was applied to the Beothuk, whose subsistence pattern and environmental conditions resembled those of the former, one would arrive at a figure of 1050 for the Beothuk, population in Newfoundland, the island having an area of about 112 300 km².

   F. Eggan (1968: 180) has estimated a population density of one person per 100 km² in the north-eastern subarctic interior; this would allow for Newfoundland a population of 1123 people.

2. Cook's calculation is based on census figures for the native population on two New England islands, Nantucket and Martha's Vineyard, after 1642 and he has projected these findings to the native population of the whole of New England (1973).

Beothuk Indian population (Upton 1977) but in the absence of documentation, the impact of disease on their demography during the early contact period has been entirely assumed and there has not been a serious investigation of the relevant factors.

The purpose of this paper is to discuss the transmission of different diseases to the Beothuk and to estimate their possible effects on Beothuk demography. Attention was given to bubonic plague and smallpox, two of the most devastating epidemic diseases in England; in addition measles and tuberculosis were considered, the latter having been recorded among the Beothuk in the early 19th century.

The method has been to assemble records of disease among the European Newfoundland population, the Beothuk and other native groups, to consider the aetiology and mode of transmission of the diseases in question and to apply the collected information to the situation of the Beothuk Indians.

Beothuk Ecology and Contacts

The time span of Beothuk/European co-existence on the island of Newfoundland can be divided into two periods: the first 230 years from A.D. 1500 to 1730 were marked by avoidance of contacts with Europeans and by a drastic reduction of the Indians' territory; the second period from A.D. 1730 to 1830 was characterized as a period of further territorial confinement, increasing persecution and involuntary contacts.

The Beothuk Indians were subarctic hunters and gatherers who alternated between the coast and interior regions. In the fall they congregated at lake and river crossings of caribou to intercept the herds on their migration routes. Their winter *mamateeks* (term for Beothuk house), which could accommodate from 10 to 20 people each, were erected close by. In spring they dispersed into smaller groups to the coast. Here their major foods were seal and salmon, supplemented with porpoise, whale, seabirds, eggs, fish and other seafoods. Summer *mamateeks* were cone-shaped structures, often only large enough to house 4 to 5 people (Cell, 1982: 70–74, 194; Howley, 1915: 29–33, 85, 100, 190–92, 211).

The Beothuk had probably been in possession of most of the island at the time of discovery. During the 16th century when vessels from Europe came to fish in Newfoundland waters, the crews rarely went ashore other than to refurbish water and firewood, because most of the cod was processed and salted aboard ship. Encounters with the native population took place on the coast—usually with small groups—since neither explorers nor fishermen penetrated into the interior. It appears that the native people were initially friendly but within 30 years of first contacts acted in a hostile manner or fled at the sight of a European ship (Howley, 1915: 10, 13; Hoffman, 1961: 168, 170). For the 1500s no records of trade have been found. Nevertheless, in the early 1600s some Beothuk were in possession of metal tools. But they neither acquired firearms nor engaged in a regular exchange of goods and therefore avoided contact and remained independent of the intrusive white population.

Archaeological and written records (Tuck, 1976: 63; Howley 1915: 1–6, 10–15, 293, 288–94, 331–41) indicate that aboriginally the Beothuk had been dispersed over much of the island; consequently contacts between the different bands or groups were probably infrequent. By c. 1730 this situation changed. English fishing stations and settlements had been extended along the eastern coast as far as Notre Dame Bay and were also present on the western and southern shores. The erection of salmon posts in the Gander and Exploits Rivers and the encroachment of hunters on Indian territory led to harassments and killings of Beothuk (Marshall 1988: 63). The Micmacs from Nova Scotia came regularly to St. Georges Bay to hunt for fur, dominated the south and west coast and claimed the region of Grand Lake and White Bay (Marshall 1988: 61–67). The Micmacs were not on friendly terms with the Beothuk and their possession of firearms gave them superiority. The Northern Peninsula had become the hunting ground of Montagnais from Labrador and the area of Quirpon Island off the Northern Peninsula was visited by Eskimos during the summer season (Martijn 1990: 227; Thwaites, 1970: 334; Morandière, 1962: 18). There is no record that Beothuk groups united in an effort to resist intruders. They responded by gradually retreating into the area of Red Indian Lake and Gander Lake in the interior, travelling for food collection during the summer to the coast between Cape Freels and Cape St. Johns (Howley 1915: 33).

The Beothuks' dispersal, their pattern of migration and infrequent contact with others between 1500 and 1730 were not favourable to the spread amongst them of those diseases which have a short duration of infectivity. The situation was probably similar to that in New England as described by Cook (1973) where contacts during the first 100 years were rare and sporadic and where "there is no evidence from written records or oral tradition that serious harm to the natives resulted."

The major cause of an assumed population decline among the Beothuk during this early period was most likely the loss of territory, resulting in diminished food resources and extensive population movements. Adjustments of this nature and extent were bound to disrupt group compositions and possibly led to intergroup friction and changes in social structure and leadership, all of which would have had a negative effect on their demography.

The second period of Beothuk history, which covers the last 100 years of their existence—from 1730 to 1830—was one of territorial confinement and more frequent contacts. The hostile attitude of the expanding settler population made it increasingly difficult for the Indians to collect marine foods on the coast and eventually they were forced to remain in the interior for most of the year. This deprived the Beothuk of their traditional subsistence during spring and summer and caused food shortages and starvation. The Indians were also more actively harassed—in summer they were chased in their canoes or taken by surprise in their *mamateeks*; during the winter season parties of settlers and later of government agents ventured into the interior to seek out their camps, and this resulted in encounters and the capture of several individuals.

Estimates of the size of the Beothuk population at various intervals indicate that a drastic decline occurred in the second half of the 18th century and the rate of decline accelerated after 1811 (Howley 1915: 226–29; Marshall 1977). During the last 100 years of territorial confinement, diminishing food resources, close contact between bands and more frequent and extensive contacts with the white population, contagions could have been transmitted more easily. It is therefore suggested that disease had its greatest impact on the Beothuk population after 1730.

Diseases: Bubonic Plague

The bubonic plague caused major epidemics in western Europe until well into the 18th century, after which time it generally disappeared, though minor outbreaks have occurred after this date. Cook (1973) estimated that the average death rate among the central New England Indians in the epidemic of 1617/19 was 75%, which represents the highest average from any one disease in this region. Although these figures are documented, the presented evidence leaves considerable doubt as to whether this epidemic could have been the bubonic plague.

The bubonic plague is a rodent disease which is transmitted by a vector flea to man, after the rodent host has died. It is important that epidemics of plague can only be sustained through the presence of an infected rodent population, a rat flea and close proximity of both to humans (Shrewsbury, 1970: 5).[3]

There is no evidence of plague among the Newfoundland population at any time.[4] The rodent implicated in the European plague epidemics was *Rattus rattus*, a house and ship's rat that would not swim and could not leave a vessel that was anchored off the coast. In addition Newfoundland's climatic conditions were not suitable for the survival of the vector flea (Pollitzer, 1954).[5] Bubonic plague can therefore be discounted as an influence on Beothuk demography.

Smallpox

The situation concerning smallpox among the Beothuk is difficult to assess because there are many unknown factors. The disease is caused by the *variola* virus and is highly contagious. The infective agent is usually transmitted from an active case of smallpox by droplets in the air to the respiratory passages of another person. It is also possible to transmit smallpox in clothing that contains scabs from the smallpox sores and, below 25 °C, these scabs can stay virulent for several weeks.

Smallpox has been documented in the Newfoundland population from 1610 onwards, but no sizable epidemic has been recorded.[6] Though occasional exchange of goods with Beothuk took place, this was usually done by "dumb barter," that is in the absence of the trade partner. Items given to the natives were mostly tools rather than clothing or blankets which would have been the most likely articles to hold the contagion, and there is little likelihood of transmission of smallpox by colonists.[7]

---

3. Bubonic plague is now present in some rodent populations, particularly in the southwestern U.S., and is occasionally transmitted to a person (WHO, 1978).

4. In a letter from the English colony in Cupids, dated 17 August 1612, Bartholomew Pearson states that the "seeds the company sente over are spoyled with ratts in the shippe" yet there is no mention of disease in the settlement (Middl. Papers Mix 1/11); indeed John Slaney reported in July of that year that the health of the country surpasses that of England (Middl. Papers Mix 1/8); the only sickness which initially presented a problem was scurvy (Croute to Willoughby, Middl. Papers Mix 1/59).

5. No infected rodent population has ever been reported in Newfoundland (Marshall Laird, Professor of Biology, Memorial University of Newfoundland, personal communication).

6. In October 1610 John Guy reported one case of smallpox on his way out to Newfoundland but the man recovered and no other person became infected (Cell 1982: 60).

7. On an exploration to Trinity Bay, in 1612, Guy's party exchanged a number of items for furs, such as a hatchet, knives, points, needles and scissors, as well as hand towels, table napkins, gloves, and one shirt. Since the party was "not furnished with fit things for to trucke" they presumably chose items which they could spare (Cell 1982: 68–76).

In Labrador a presumed smallpox epidemic among a group of resident Eskimos which is reported to have occurred in 1772 on the island of Ivuktoke appears not to have spread beyond this island area (Cartwright, 1792: 1: 424; Taylor, 1974: 9). Other routes of transmission could have been seasonal fishing crews or Montagnais Indians from Southern Labrador. The latter were extensively infected with smallpox after the disease was brought to New France by the Jesuits in the 17th century (Thwaites, 1959: 24: 271; 29: 123). It has been noted that the Indians most closely associated with the missions suffered the most severe losses, implying that the effect of smallpox diminished in relation to the distance from the centres of the disease, that is the mission stations (Thwaites, 1959: 19: 91); people in isolated areas were less exposed to the virus and some camps escaped the disease altogether. Whether the Montagnais had a visiting relationship with the Beothuk of Newfoundland at the time when smallpox was prevalent among them cannot be ascertained. Traditionally these two groups had been on friendly terms and in 1719 some Montagnais endeavoured to meet with Beothuk on the Northern Peninsula to establish trade (Howley 1915: 26: 270; Morandière, 1962: 22).[8] By this route one or another group of Beothuk may well have been victim to smallpox but their geographic isolation and dispersal over a large region—at least in the 1600s and early 1700s when smallpox was most prevalent—and the infrequency of contact would have prevent the large scale and repeated epidemics experienced elsewhere. Death rate figures due to smallpox among different North American Indian groups quoted by Cook (1973) and Stearn and Stearn (1945) range from 17% to 100% with an average of 50–67% and indicate the wide variety of responses to the disease.

The likelihood that smallpox was brought to the Beothuk by European settlers or fishermen is small. However, the Beothuk's friendly relations with Labrador Montagnais may have facilitated the transmission of this disease, though such course of events remains a matter of speculation. If smallpox had reached the Beothuk in the 17th or early 18th century, the disease—for the reasons given above—would not have spread to every one of the widely dispersed Beothuk groups, and their death rate would therefore have been at the lower end of the scale recorded from other groups.

---

8. The Beothuk word for Labrador Indians is Shudamunk and was said to mean "good Indians," while Shannok stood for Micmacs or "Bad Indians" (Howley 1915: 270).

Measles

Measles, along with smallpox, is one of the most contagious of viral infections and it has caused a population decrease of up to 18% in other Indian groups.[9] Measles is transmitted in respiratory droplets from an active case through close physical proximity. Transmission to the Beothuk could therefore only have occurred in encounters with an infected individual. According to Dr. Carson, general practitioner in St. John's in the 1830s, measles and other epidemics were regularly brought to this port by new arrivals but soon assumed a milder character and seldom existed for more than a season (Carson, 1830).[10] In contrast, when measles occurred in Twillingate/Notre Dame Bay in 1827, at least half the inhabitants there were infected, which suggests that the disease had been absent from this island community for a considerable number of years (Inglis, 1827).

In this context information on epidemics from the three Moravian Mission stations in Labrador, which were founded in the 1770s and 1780s, should be considered. First mention of an unspecified epidemic in Okak was made in 1824 and the earliest measles epidemic was reported in the other two missions (in Nain and Hopedale) in 1827 (the same year measles were brought to Twillingate), that is within 50 years of regular contact with the native people who came to the mission stations. The death rate at Nain was 5.7% and at Hopedale 9.5% (Kleivan, 1966: 146), indicating that measles did not occur as frequently in Labrador as one might have expected.

I have concluded that the possibility of measles having been transmitted to the Beothuk is small. If at all, such a transmission most likely occurred during the last 50 years of the Beothuk's existence when contacts with settlers had increased.

---

9. Measles case mortality figures: 1846 Hudson Bay Indians 28% (Rollestone, 1937: 86); 1908 Indians at Oka/Quebec 55%; 1909 Indians at Caughnawaga 50% (Graham-Cumming, 1967). Population death rates: 1952 Ungava Bay Indians and Eskimos 6.9% in a population of 900 (Peart and Nagler, 1954); Alta California Mission Indians 1806: 18%; 1827/8: 12% (Keuper Valle and Valle, 1976).

10. In 1830 Carson wrote that annually eleven hundred to thirteen hundred passengers arrived from Ireland who generally carried with them the epidemic of those places from where they embarked. "Few years therefore pass without an importation of typhus fever, smallpox, measles, hooping cough, or scarlet fever and annually an abundant supply of itch" all of which soon assumed a milder character (CO 194/81: 58 Alb.Tr.).

Tuberculosis

Tuberculosis has been the major cause of death among the native American populations during the last century. Its full impact was not noted until Indians had moved into reservations and lived under closer medical observation. The largest percentage of tuberculosis infections in a population is found in the lungs but the disease may affect other sites, especially in childhood. Tuberculosis is caused through an invasion of the tubercle bacilli and a person may die within a few weeks or months of infection. More common is the development of chronic pulmonary tuberculosis, where the patient's condition may deteriorate only slowly. During this period there may be continual coughing up of tubercle bacilli. The dried sputum, mingled with dust, can easily distribute the tubercle bacilli, which remain virulent for several weeks if not exposed to sunlight. Inhaling the bacilli alone does not necessarily result in clinical disease— the susceptibility of an individual and of a population are important factors and so are overcrowding, starvation, and poor conditions of hygiene.

In Britain the incidence of pulmonary tuberculosis rose to a peak during the second half of the 18th century and it is assumed that this disease was similarly widespread in the European population of Newfoundland (Webb 1936: 14).[11] At about that time contacts between Beothuk and settlers became more frequent—Indians ventured into boats and sheds to steal sails and tools and settlers raided Indian camps in the interior. Two Indian boys were captured in the 1750s and 1760s and worked in fishing communities but were said to have visited their Beothuk families for several weeks every year (Howley, 1915: 59, 288).

If tuberculosis had not been transmitted to the Beothuk previously, it may well have reached them in the second half of the 18th century. It only needed a single individual to become infected and the bacillus could have dispersed insidiously. The status of the Beothuk as a "virgin" population, that is previously unexposed, and their way of life, provided optimal conditions for the spread of this disease.

In addition the Beothuk were confined in a small territory, causing close contacts between the groups and probably also the reuse of old campsites.

---

11. Dr. Carson affirmed in 1830 that in the Newfoundland population "tubercular consumption is most prevalent although among the poor scrofulous affections are frequently to be met with" (scrofula is tuberculosis of the lymphatic glands) (CO 194/81: 59 Alb. Tr.).

To a degree this situation could be compared to reserves which were instituted at a much later date for other native groups and in which a dramatic increase of tuberculosis was experienced. Among Indians in Saskatchewan, for instance, the death rate abruptly changed from 1% to 9% per year after they were moved into reserves (Moore, 1961: 84).[12]

Tuberculosis among the Beothuk is documented inasmuch as three Beothuk women who fell into the hands of furriers in 1823 were said to be suffering from "pulmonary consumption" at the time of their capture and all three died of this complaint (Howley 1915: 170, 175, 231). Since this is the only record of disease among the Beothuk, the presence of tuberculosis at an earlier period can only be postulated. The Beothuk population, estimated at c. 350 individuals in 1768 (Marshall, 1977), had declined to 72 in 1811, to 27 in 1820, and to 13 in 1823 (Howley, 1915: 224–29). These figures project a population reduction by 79% in 44 years at an average rate of 3.6% per year between 1768 and 1811, a decline which was probably lower in the 1760s and accelerated at the turn of the century.[13] By 1820 the population had been reduced by 92% and in 1823 by 96%; the reduction rate between 1811 and 1820 was 10% per year, and from 1820 to 1823 it was 22%. These figures cannot be explained by the few reported killings alone, but rather suggest a lack of health among the Beothuk people.

In combination with other infections, such as measles (Carey, 1965), tuberculosis could have already had a notable impact on the Beothuk population during the second half of the 18th century. Based on comparisons with figures of tuberculosis mortality rates in other Indian groups, it is suggested that between 1768 and 1811 an average of 40% of all deaths among the Beothuk were due to tuberculosis and that this percentage rose to 80% during the early 19th century.[14] This would amount to a population death rate from tuberculosis of 2% in the earlier years and of c. 11% after 1811.[15]

---

12. Between 1871 and 1899 the Canadian native population experienced a population decline by c. 3% on account of the high death rates due to tuberculosis (Wherrett, 1977: 99).

13. The exponential formula used is $P_1 = P_0 (1 - r/100)^t$ in which P_1 = the resulting population, P_0 = the original population, r = percentage of reduction per year, t = number of years.

14. Proportional mortality rate from pulmonary tuberculosis: 1835–1846 Dakota Indians Lac qui Parle—50% of deaths among those aged 10 and over; 1876–1880 Dakota Indians Fort Bertold 32%; 1878–1885 Dakota Indians Cheyenne River 52% (Williamson 1940). The mortality rate from pulmonary tuberculosis among reservation Indians in 13 different States and Territories was between 4.5% and 62.5% (Matthews, 1886; the figures are taken from U.S. census).

15. The net reduction rate from 1768 to 1811 was 3.6%; with a birthrate of c. 1.5% added the death rate would have been 5.1%. If 40% of all deaths were due to tuberculosis then the

Diminished numbers and the inability of those afflicted with disease to take part effectively in the food quest would have impaired the Indians' efficiency for making optimal use of their environment. Since malnutrition reduces resistance to infection and raises infant mortality, the Beothuk may have entered a vicious cycle, with sickness and starvation combining to ensure their extinction.

Conclusion

The Beothuk take a special position among the North American Indian groups because they lived in an isolated island habitat and persisted in their avoidance of contact with white populations. It seems unlikely that during the first 230 years after the discovery of the island by Europeans (1500–1730) imported disease would have had a significant impact on their demography. This situation is likely to have changed after 1730 when the Beothuk were confined in a small territory and were exposed to more frequent contacts.

Of the diseases that have been considered, bubonic plague has been rejected as a cause of death among the Beothuk.

It is possible that the Beothuk were exposed to smallpox, perhaps by the Montagnais from Southern Labrador, but their geographical isolation and distribution would have curbed a spread among them, resulting in a lower than average population death rate from this disease.

Whether measles had an impact on Beothuk demography cannot be ascertained, though it is possible that this infectious disease spread to them during the last decades of their existence.

Tuberculosis is documented among the Beothuk in 1823 and may already have affected their demography in the 18th century. It is suggested that the annual reduction of the population estimated at 3.6% between 1768 and 1800 and at 10% accelerating to 22% after the turn of the century was partly due to the presence of tuberculosis and that this disease played a significant role in the eventual demise of the Beothuk group.

---

population death rate due to tuberculosis would have been 2.0%. Between 1811 and 1823 the average net reduction rate was 13.3%; with a reduced birthrate of 0.5% added, the population death rate is calculated at 13.8%. 80% of this percentage is 10.64%, which represents the approximate population death rate due to tuberculosis after 1811.

References

Carey, Stuart L. 1965. A Unique Epidemic of Tuberculosis: Eskimo Point, 1963. *The American Review of Respiratory Diseases* 91 (4).

Carson, William. 1830. Answers to question proposed by the Royal College of Physicians, London, ms. report, Colonial Office Records, Series 194 Vol. 81: 56–61 (Alb. Tr.). Public Archives of Newfoundland and Labrador.

Cartwright, George. 1792. *A Journal of Transactions and Events during a Residence of Nearly Sixteen Years on the Coast of Labrador*, vol. I. Newark: Allin & Ridge.

Cell, Gillian T., ed. 1982. *Newfoundland Discovered*. London: Haklyut Society.

Cook, Sherbourne F. 1973. The Significance of Disease in the Extinction of the New England Indians. *Human Biology* 45 (3).

Croute, Henry. n.d. Letter to Percival Willoughby, ms. Middleton Papers Mix 1/59, Nottingham University.

Eggan, Fred. 1968. "Indians, North America," *International Encyclopedia of the Social Sciences*, vol. VII, David L. Sills, ed. New York: The Macmillan Company and The Free Press.

Graham-Cumming, George. 1967. "Health of the Original Canadians, 1867–1967." *Medical Service Journal Canada* 23 (2).

Hoffman, B.G. 1961. *Cabot to Cartier*. Toronto: University of Toronto Press.

Howley, James P. 1915. *The Beothuks or Red Indians*. Cambridge: Cambridge University Press.

Inglis, John. 1827. Diary, ms., microfilm A713, National Archives of Canada.

Keuper, Valle, R. and Valle, A.R. 1976. "Medicine and Health among the Alta California Mission Indians (1769–1834)." *Actes: 25ᵉ Congrès International d'Histoire de la Médecine,* Québec, Vol. 3.

Kleivan, Helge. 1966. *The Eskimos of Northeast Labrador*. Oslo: Norsk Polarinstitute, Skrifter 139.

Kroeber, A.L. 1965. "Cultural and Natural Areas of Native North America." *American Archaeology and Ethnology*, Vol. XXXVIII. New York: Kraus Reprint Corp.

Marshall, Ingeborg. 1977. An Unpublished Map Made by John Cartwright between 1768 and 1773 Showing Beothuk Indian Settlements and Artifacts and Allowing a New Population Estimate. *Ethnohistory* 24 (3).

Marshall, Ingeborg. 1988. "Beothuk and Micmac: Re-examining Relationships." *Acadiensis*, Vol. XVII, no. 2.

Martijn, Charles A. 1990. "Innu (Montagnais) in Newfoundland." Papers of the Twenty-First Algonquian Conference, ed. W. Cowan. Ottawa: Carleton University.

Matthews, W. 1886. "Consumption Among the Indians." *Transactions American Climatological Association*.

Moore, P.E. 1961. "No Longer Captain: A History of TB and its Control among Canadian Indians." *Canadian Medical Journal* 84.

Morandière, Charles de la. 1962. *Histoire de la pêche française de la morue dans l'Amérique septentrionale*, Vol. 1. Paris: G.C. Maisonneuve et Larose.

Pearson, Bartholomew. 1612. Letter to Percival Willoughby, ms. Middleton Papers Mix 1/11, Nottingham University.

Peart, A.F.W., and F.P. Nagler. 1954. "Measles in the Canadian Arctic, 1952." *Canadian Journal of Public Health* 45.

Pollitzer, R. 1954. *Plague*. Geneva, World Health Organization.

Poynter, F.N.L., ed. 1963. *The Journal of James Yonge, 1647–1721, Plymouth Surgeon*. London: Longmans.

Rollestone, J.D. 1937. *The History of the Acute Exanthemata*. London: Heinemann.

Shrewsbury, J.R.D. 1970. *The History of Bubonic Plague in the British Isles*. Cambridge: Cambridge University Press.

Slaney, John. 1612. Letter to Percival Willoughby, ms. Middleton Papers Mix 1/8, Nottingham University.

Stearn, E.W., and Stearn, S.F. 1945. *The Effect of Smallpox on the Destiny of the Amerindian*. Boston: Bruce Humphries Inc.

Taylor, J.G. 1974. *Labrador Eskimo Settlements of the Early Contact Period*, Publications in Ethnology, No. 9. Ottawa: National Museums of Canada.

Thwaites, Reuben Gold. 1959. *The Jesuit Relations and Allied Documents: Travels and Explorations of the Jesuit Missionaries in New France, 1610–1791*. New York: Pageant Book Company reprint.

Thwaites, Reuben Gold. 1970. *Lahontan's Voyages to North America*. New York: Burt Franklin reprint.

Tuck, James A. 1976. *Newfoundland and Labrador Prehistory*. Ottawa: National Museum of Man.

Upton, Leslie F.S. 1977. "The Extermination of the Beothuks of Newfoundland." *The Canadian Historical Review* LVIII: 2.

Webb, Gerald B. 1936. "Tuberculosis" (*Clio Medica*, Vol. 16). New York: P.B. Hoeber.

Wherrett, G.J. 1977. *The Miracle of the Empty Beds: A History of TB in Canada*. Toronto: University of Toronto Press.

Williamson, Thomas S. 1940. "Diseases of the Dakota Indians." *Minnesota Medicine*, Vol. 23.

World Health Organization. 1978. Weekly Epidemiological Record.

JOHN GILL'S RECOLLECTIONS

JAMES P. HOWLEY

Another old man of Exploits Bay, named Gill, gave me some further particulars about Nance and her companions. Gill's mother was also a servant in Peyton's employ at the time Nance lived with him, and he stated that he often listened with deep interest to his mother talking of her and relating other stories of the Indians.

> Nance was a married woman, according to her own account and left two children in the interior, which she used to express great anxiety about. She said her tribe were very strict about the moral law, and visited severe penalties on any one who transgressed. Burning alive at the stake being the fate of the adulterer, which was witnessed by the whole tribe who danced in a circle around the victim. Nance was fired at by a Micmac Indian once as she was engaged washing venison in the Exploits River. He waited till she turned to walk up the bank when the old ruffian deliberately fired at her across the river wounding her severely in the back and legs. The poor creature dropped the venison and limped off into the woods. In describing the incident she would act the part, limping away after being shot at. She was perfectly aware who the perpetrator of this dialolical act was,—one Noel Boss, by name, and ever afterwards entertained the greatest fear at sight of this villain or even his dog. It is said of this Noel Boss, that he boasted of having killed 99 Red Indians in his time, and wished to add one more to the number so as to complete the hundred. He afterwards fell through the ice on Gander Lake while laden with six heavy steel traps, and was drowned, by far too good a fate for such a monster.

> Nance was very pert at times and openly defied Mrs Peyton when the old lady happened to be cross with the servants. Nance would laugh in her face, and say, 'well done Misses, I like to hear you jaw, that right'; or 'jawing again Misses.' They had named her Nance April from the month in which she was captured, they did not then know her Indian name. Her elder sister was named Easter Eve, that being the day of their capture, whilst the old mother was named Betty Decker, because the party who captured them were engaged at the time decking a vessel. In personal appearance Nance was very similar to the Micmacs, being

"JOHN GILL'S RECOLLECTIONS," IN *THE BEOTHUKS OR RED INDIANS: THE ABORIGINAL INHABITANTS OF NEWFOUNDLAND*, BY JAMES P. HOWLEY (CAMBRIDGE, 1915; REPRINT TORONTO: COLES, 1974): 181–82.

about the same colour and broad featured. Her hair was jet black, and her figure tall and stout. She was a good worker, and performed the usual household avocations, such as washing, scrubbing &c. with satisfaction. At times she fell into a melancholy mood, and would go off into the woods, as she would say to have a talk with her mother and sister. She generally came back singing and laughing, or talking aloud to herself. She would also frequently indulge in the same practice at night, and when asked what was the matter would reply, Nance talking to her mother and sister. When told not to be foolish, that they were dead and she could not talk to them, she would say, 'a yes they here, me see them and talk to them.' She was very gentle and not at all of a vicious disposition, was an adept at drawing or copying anything. Capt. Buchan took her on board his man-of-war, gave her drawing paper and materials &c., he then showed her a portrait of his mother which she copied very accurately. She made very neat combs out of deers horns and carved them all over elaborately. She would take a piece of birch bark fold it up, and with her teeth bite out various designs representing leaves, flowers &c.[1] Her teeth were very white and even. She was strictly modest and would allow no freedom on the part of the opposite sex. Once when an individual attempted some familiarity he was so rudely repulsed that he never afterwards dared to repeat the offence. She would not tolerate him near her. He was a Mudty man (bad man). She seemed well aware of the difference between right and wrong, and knew if a person cursed or swore he was doing wrong, 'mudty man' she would say. She is described as a fine worker, was a good clean cook and washer. When first taken the woman had quite a job to wash off the red ochre and grease with which her person was smeared.

When she fell into one of her melancholy moods and ran off into the woods she would turn round saying, 'All gone widdun (asleep) Nance go widdun too, no more come Nance, run away, no more come.' She was fond of colours and fine clothes. Capt. Buchan sent her a pair of silk stockings and shoes from St John's in which she took great pride.''

The widow Jure, whom I met at Exploits, Burnt Island, in 1886, and who was also a servant at Peyton's, during Nancy's time gave me much information about the Indian woman. She confirmed all the above particulars. This Mrs Jure had learned some of the Beothuck language from Nance who used to compliment her on her pronunciation. Unfortunately she had now forgotten nearly all of it. But on my producing a vocabulary of the language and reading it over for her she remembered several words

---

1. I have seen a Micmac Indian perform this same feat.

and pronounced them for me. She also corrected some which were misspelt, etc.

FURTHER READINGS FOR TOPIC 6

J. R. Miller. *Skyscrapers Hide the Heavens: A History of Indian-White Relations in Canada*. Toronto: University of Toronto Press, 1989.

Donald B. Smith. *Sacred Feathers: The Reverend Peter Jones (Kahkewaquonaby) & the Mississauga Indians*. Toronto and London: University of Toronto Press, 1987.

Robert J. Surtees. "The Development of an Indian Reserve Policy in Canada." *Ontario History* 61, no. 2 (1969): 87–98.

John L. Tobias. "Protection, Civilization, Assimilation: An Outline History of Canada's Indian Policy." *Western Canadian Journal of Anthropology* 6, no. 2: 13–30.

L. F. S. Upton. *Micmacs and Colonists: Indian-White Relations in the Maritimes, 1713–1867*. Vancouver: University of British Columbia Press, 1979.

TOPIC 7

Haven in a Heartless World? The Loyalists in British North America

The Loyalists who fled to British North America during and after the American Revolution brought profound changes in their wake. To meet the demands of the more than 40,000 who came here, the British government created the province of New Brunswick in 1784, and separated Upper Canada (Ontario) from Lower Canada (Quebec) in 1791 so that the Loyalists could enjoy British laws and institutions.

In addition to examining the role of the Loyalists in shaping colonial institutions and society, Maritime historians have wondered why Nova Scotia, which had been heavily settled by "Yankees" after the expulsion of the Acadians in 1755, failed to join the American Revolution. Clearly, a number of factors are responsible, including geographic isolation and the importance of the British garrison in Halifax. George A. Rawlyk's study of Henry Alline, a preacher from New England, indicates the importance of a new religious ideology, significant in its own right, in preventing Nova Scotia from joining the rebellion against British authority.

Bruce Wilson's book on the Niagara merchant Robert Hamilton also stresses the misfortunes of the Loyalists, but regards many of their *hardships as being of their own making. Focusing on the career of John Butler, a Loyalist military leader during the American Revolution, Wilson highlights the corruption, nepotism, and constant quest for patronage which characterized the behaviour of some Loyalist officers in early Upper Canada.*

Wilson's view stands in dramatic contrast to the attitudes of many late nineteenth-century Ontarians of Loyalist descent. Unsettled by rapid social and economic change, the rise of new elites, and an influx of immigration, they reconfirmed their own identity and sense of self-importance by exalting the exploits of their Loyalist ancestors. Egerton Ryerson, the distinguished Ontario educator, was typical of this school of historians in his emphasis on the heroism with which the Loyalists faced both persecution in the former British colonies to the south and hardship in their new homes.

New Lights, Baptists and Religious Awakenings in Nova Scotia 1776–1843:

A Preliminary Probe

GEORGE A. RAWLYK

Henry Alline was a man almost larger than life and he has cast a long shadow over the religious development of the New England-Nova Scotia region until the present day. His contemporaries regarded him as Nova Scotia's George Whitefield—as a powerful instrument of the Almighty, charismatic and uniquely spiritual. Historians in the 19th and 20th centuries have been, almost to a person, overwhelmed by Alline's mystical theology, his creative powers, and his unusual ability to communicate to others his profound sense of Christian ecstasy. After experiencing a particularly disorienting spiritual crisis in the late winter of 1775, the 27 year old farmer-tanner was overwhelmed by the deep satisfaction provided by spiritual regeneration. In his *Journal* he described his conversion in the following evocative manner:

> ...O help me, help me, cried I, thou Redeemer of souls, and save me or I am gone for ever; and the last word I ever mentioned in my distress (for the change was instantaneous) was, O Lord Jesus Christ, thou canst this night, if thou pleasest, with one drop of thy blood atone for my sins, and appease the wrath of an angry God...At that instant of time when I gave up all to him, to do with me, as he pleased, and was willing that God should reign in me and rule over me at his pleasure: redeeming love broke into my soul with repeated scriptures with such power, that my whole soul seemed to be melted down with love; the burden of guilt and condemnation was gone, darkness was expelled, my heart humbled and filled with gratitude, and my will turned of choice after the infinite God...Attracted by the love and beauty I saw in the divine perfections, my whole soul was inexpressibly ravished with the blessed Redeemer...my whole soul seemed filled with the divine being.[1]

As far as Alline was concerned, the black gloomy despair of his morbid

---

George A. Rawlyk, "New Lights, Baptists and Religious Awakenings in Nova Scotia 1776–1843: A Preliminary Probe," *Journal of the Canadian Church Historical Society*, Vol. 25–26 (1983), pp. 50–55. By permission of the author.
1. H. Alline, *Life and Journals* (Boston, 1806), p. 34.

introspection had been miraculously removed. "My whole soul" he observed

> that was a few minutes ago groaning under mountains of death, wading through storms of sorrow, racked with distressing fears, and crying to an unknown God for help, was now filled with immortal love, soaring on the wings of faith, freed from the chains of death and darkness, and crying out my Lord and my God; thou art my rock and my fortress, my shield and my high tower, my life, my joy, my present and my everlasting portion.[2]

The sudden transforming power of spiritual regeneration compelled Alline to declare—and these emotionally charged words would provide the cutting edge of his Christian message until his death early in 1784—

> O the infinite condescension of God to a worm of the dust! for though my whole soul was filled with love, and ravished with a devine ecstacy beyond any doubts or fears, or thoughts of being then deceived, for I enjoyed a heaven on earth, and it seemed as if I were wrapped up in God.[3]

It is not surprising that one of Alline's major 19th century critics argued that the Falmouth resident "was converted in a rapture; and ever after he sought to live in a rapture; and judged of his religious condition by his enjoyments and raptures."[4] Rev J. Davis could have added that Alline also expected his followers to experience the intense ecstasy of spiritual rapture and to share with him his own traumatic religious experience. For Alline regarded his conversion experience as the model to be followed by those who wished to become true followers of Christ. And he carefully delineated the morphology of conversion in his pamphlet *Two Mites* and in the over 500 hymns and spiritual songs which he composed in a period of six years.[5]

Henry Alline, it is clear, was able also to perceive a special purpose for his fellow Nova Scotians in the midst of the disorienting American Revolutionary situation. He became, I have argued elsewhere, the charismatic leader of a widespread and intense religious revival which swept the colony during the war years. "The Great Awakening of Nova Scotia" was,

---

2. Ibid., 34–5.
3. Ibid., 35.
4. J. Davis, *Life and Times of the Late Rev. Harris Harding, Yarmouth, N.S.* (Charlottetown, 1860), p. 178.
5. G. Rawlyk, "Henry Alline: Reconsidered." (A paper presented at the Harvard Divinity School, February 17, 1982.)

without question, one of the most significant social movements in the long history of Nova Scotia. It was, among other things, the means by which a large number of Nova Scotians—especially the so-called "Yankees"—extricated themselves from the domination of neighbouring New England which they had left a decade and more earlier. By creating a compelling ideology that was specifically geared to conditions in the isolated northern colony, Alline enabled many Nova Scotians to regard themselves as what Gordon Stewart and I called *A People Highly Favoured of God*.[6] These people were provided by Alline with a unique history, a distinct identity, and a special destiny. A new sense of Nova Scotia identity, we have argued, had clicked into fragile place—to replace the disintegrating loyalty to New England and the largely undermined loyalty to Old England. But this was not all that Henry Alline accomplished. At one time I thought that it was, and then I re-read his *Journal* and his *Hymns and Spiritual Songs* and *Two Mites* and *The Anti-Traditionalist*. It is clear to me now that Alline also preached the simple, emotional Whitefieldian Evangelical gospel of the "New Birth" and thus provided a powerful new personal and spiritual relationship between Christ and the redeemed believer in a world where all traditional relationships were falling apart. Alline was, it is clear, obsessed with the mystical relationship of Christ with regenerate man, and because of this preoccupation he was able to use his charismatic powers to drill the reality of this insight into the minds and hearts of his thousands of Nova Scotia listeners. He was obviously a man who was obsessed with disintegrating relationships and one who therefore could relate to his fellow Nova Scotians who, too, were preoccupied with disintegrating relationships. Conversion was thus perceived as the short-circuiting of a complex process—a short-circuiting which produced instant and immediate satisfaction, solace and intense relief.

Eventually Alline visited almost every settlement in Nova Scotia, then inhabited by approximately 20,000 people, 60% of whom were recently arrived Yankees. And Halifax and Lunenburg were the only major centres of the colony unaffected by the revival Alline helped to articulate into existence. The Lunenburg area was peopled by Foreign Protestants who understood neither Alline's brand of Christianity nor the Patriot ideology of independence. Their loyalty was a mixture of self interest, indifference and splendid isolation. In Halifax, economic and military ties with Great Britain together with the heterogeneous nature of the population and the

---

6. From the vantage point of the early 1980s, it is clear to me that we overemphasized the "Sense of Mission" thesis at the expense of Alline's pietism.

influence of the elite created a consensus violently opposed both to Revolution and to Henry Alline and his Evangelical gospel.

Almost single-handedly Alline was able, by his frequent visits to the settlements, to draw the isolated communities together and to impose upon them a feeling of fragile oneness. They were sharing a common experience and Alline was providing them with answers to disconcerting and puzzling contemporary questions. For Alline, the Nova Scotia revival was, among other things, an event of world and cosmic significance. The social, economic and political backwater that was Nova Scotia had been transformed by the revival into the new centre of the Christian world. Nova Scotia had replaced New England as the "City on a Hill."[7]

In his sermons preached as he criss-crossed the colony, Alline developed the theme that the Nova Scotia "Yankees", in particular, had, because of the tragic backsliding of New England, a special predestined role to play in God's plan for the world. It must have required a special effort for Alline to persuade many Nova Scotians that they were performing a special world role. But Alline, striking deep into the Puritan New England tradition that viewed self-sacrifice and frugality as virtues, contended that the relative backwardness and isolation of the colony had removed the inhabitants from the prevailing corrupting influences of New England and Britain. As a result, Nova Scotia was in an ideal position to lead the world back to God. As far as Alline was concerned the revival was convincing proof that the Nova Scotians were "a people on whom God had set His everlasting Love" and that their colony was "as the Apple of His Eye."[8]

It would be quite wrong to stop at this precise moment—as I once did—in analyzing Alline's ideology and gospel. Henry Alline's preaching was certainly permeated with what has been called a peculiar Nova Scotia Sense of Mission. He was certainly concerned with the special place his fellow colonists had in the cosmic and secular drama then unfolding in the New World. But of greater importance, as far as Alline was concerned, was individual salvation—bringing Nova Scotians into a deep and personal spiritual relationship with Jesus Christ. If one cuts to the heart of Alline's thought and preaching, it is clear that his conceptual framework and his rhetoric were surprisingly similar to that put forward by George Whitefield and hundreds of his disciples. Of course, in many respects, Alline would go much beyond the Whitefieldian paradigm. He stressed,

---

7. G. Stewart and G. Rawlyk, *A People Highly Favoured of God* (Toronto, 1972).
8. H. Alline, *Two Mites, on some of the most important and much disputed Points of Divinity etc.* (Halifax, 1781), p. 274.

for example, that "all mankind were *actually* present with Adam;" and he refused to believe "in the vicarious sufferings of the Lord Jesus" or in the resurrection of the body.[9] Moreover, he was convinced that God had spoken directly to him and that he had actually, in a flash of insight, seen the Almighty. Yet the "New Birth" was the central reality of Alline's preaching and his theology. For Alline, genuine spiritual harmony was produced only by what he described over and over again as the "ravishing of the soul." If Alline was obsessed with one verbal image—it was that of the ravishing of the soul by the Almighty. It was a verbal image pregnant with dynamic meaning and one which blended the sexual with the spiritual to produce a powerful explosive mixture.

Alline drove a variety of Evangelical truths into the hearts and minds of his listeners largely because of his charismatic power. And furthermore, Alline was not afraid of triggering off deep emotional reactions in his hearers. He knew, from his own experience, that this was the only way to produce a profound conversion experience.

Alline was successful throughout the Revolutionary period in cultivating and sustaining the image of the supernaturally endowed charismatic leader. This was no mean accomplishment for a man, who until the age of twenty-seven, was widely regarded as a "chief contriver and ring-leader of the frolicks."[10] Almost over night Alline was transformed into a spellbinding preacher, a controversial essayist, and an unusually gifted hymnwriter. Until 1820 in New England, Alline's hymns were almost as popular as those of Isaac Watts and were frequently reprinted in hymnals which were widely used in the Second Great Awakening in New England.

It should also be kept in mind that Henry Alline adhered to no one particular church; he had no formal education; his family owned a marginal farm and possessed little social status. He therefore cannot be identified as a leader who derived his authority from traditional institutions or from traditional ideas. He and his followers insisted that his authority was derived from his close personal relationship with the Almighty. His ascendancy in the out-settlements of Nova Scotia and later in Northern New England was unprecedented and was not soon emulated. After 1783 a whole host of Evangelical preachers, many of them Baptists like the Chipmans, the Hardings, Joseph Dimock and the Mannings traversed the colony but none would attain the unique exclusiveness in

---

9. *Christian Instructor and Missionary Register of the Presbyterian Church of Nova Scotia* (March 1859) pp. 73–6.
10. Alline, *Journal*, 17.

leadership established by Henry Alline. But they tried—some tried very hard indeed.

Alline died of tuberculosis in New Hampshire in the early morning of February 2, 1784. He had made his way to New England to bring back to the land of his birth the pristine purity of the Christian gospel. Alline left behind him in Nova Scotia no Church organizational structure, no Church polity and only two ordained ministers. With his death, the movement he had played a key role in shaping threatened to fall apart. Enthusiasm without organizational discipline—and without Alline's special brand of charismatic leadership—merely led to exhaustion, confusion and doubt. Only slowly would his Nova Scotia disciples be able to breathe new life into the old Whitfieldian gospel as they began to try to transform what had become Antinomian New Lights into disciplined Baptists. But this process would be a difficult and frustrating one—and success would only come after much soul searching and much failure.

THE ENTERPRISES OF ROBERT HAMILTON:

A Study of Wealth and Influence in Early Upper Canada, 1776–1812

BRUCE WILSON

The most obvious candidate for social and political leadership at Niagara was Lieutenant-Colonel John Butler. Butler was a politically astute and ambitious man. During the war he had attempted to use the powers of his rank to select subordinate officers whose social status might be of future use to him; he had relentlessly advanced himself and his relations in the corps he commanded and, well before the end of the war, he had assumed the direction of settlement and the distribution of land at Niagara. Although he suffered setbacks in his quest for imperial patronage after the war, Butler might well expect to use his past accomplishments as leverage in his new community.

Throughout the war Butler had purposely lavished attention on his Rangers. He strove to build his corps quickly to its maximum size and to obtain for his men a high rate of pay.[1] The Rangers were important to Butler because they were his chief bulwark protecting the influence of himself and his family. The commander of the Rangers had strong opinions about their officership. His own position was to be as elevated as possible: "From my long services, the influence I have with the Indians, the rank I have held in Civil, Military, and Militia lines, and the interest I possess in the County of Albany and the Mohawk River," he wrote to Haldimand, "I am induced to hope Your Excellency will not think me unworthy of the rank of Lieutenant Colonel."[2]

Next to his own advancement, Butler placed that of his oldest sons, Walter and Thomas, and his nephews. He pushed their promotion relentlessly throughout the war. Indeed, his son Walter's callowness and his lack of experience in command were largely responsible for the Cherry Valley Massacre, the worst scandal of frontier warfare in the Revolution. Butler fought hard to prevent the introduction of experienced

---

BRUCE WILSON, *THE ENTERPRISES OF ROBERT HAMILTON: A STUDY OF WEALTH AND INFLUENCE IN EARLY UPPER CANADA, 1776–1812* (OTTAWA: CARLETON UNIVERSITY PRESS, 1983): 36–47.

1. W.H. Siebert, "The Loyalists and the Six Nations Indians in the Niagara Peninsula," *Transactions of the Royal Society of Canada*, IX, Sec. II (1915), pp. 83–92; Haldimand Transcripts, Vol. 39, p. 572, Carleton to Butler, July 9, 1777.
2. CO 42 Transcripts, Vol. 13, pp. 318–19, Butler to Carleton, June 15, 1777.

officers from the regular army into his corps and to keep all appointments
the result of his personal recommendation. Outside his own family, he
preferred, when he could find them, to appoint youths with influential
connections in colonial society. Butler's military patronage seems to have
been large. Even by 1778 his opponents at Niagara were complaining that
his dependants were too numerous to combat. A loyal clientage might
strengthen Butler in his wartime struggle and he could hope that in quieter
times his patronage of such men might redound to his and his family's
credit.[3]

Much of Butler's attention during the war was also focused upon the
possibilities of more immediate gain. The British military at Niagara
regulated all aspects of life in the war period, including agriculture. By
1780 Haldimand had decided to relieve the pressure on provisions at
Niagara by establishing a temporary agricultural settlement of reduced
Rangers and refugee Loyalists on the west bank of the Niagara River.
Superintendence of the settlement was to rest with Butler. "Lt. Col.
Butler," Haldimand wrote to the commandant at Niagara, "with whom I
have conversed fully upon this subject, has promised to give you every
assistance in his power and from his knowledge of farming, his being upon
the spot with his Rangers and his acquaintance and influence with those
who may be found to settle, I am persuaded you will find him very
useful."[4] It was a perfect opportunity for Butler to impress upon headquarters his competence and his established leadership of the Loyalists at
Niagara. Between 1780 and 1783 he wrote Haldimand a constant stream of
letters reporting on the needs and progress of the settlement.[5] Predictably,
he discovered as well a patronage value in his superintendence of agriculture. Sometime before March 1783, when it became evident peace was
near, without permission he began to lay out permanent lots in the best
locations for his favourites and admitted that by spring of 1783, "Eight of
[my] officers have already made considerable improvements."[6]

The value of Butler's influence on agriculture paled in comparison to

---

3. Haldimand Transcripts, Vol. 96, pt. 1, p. 128, Butler to LeMaitre, April 10, 1778; ibid., Vol.
216, pp. 26–27, Memorial of John Dease, July 3, 1781; ibid., Vol. 104, pp. 195–96,
Haldimand to Powell, April 11, 1781; ibid., Vol. 39, p. 572, Haldimand to Butler, July 9,
1777; on the Cherry Valley Massacre, see B. Graymount, *Iroquois in the American Revolution* (New York, 1972), pp. 183–84; Claus Papers, Vol. 26, pp. 37–39, Taylor and Duffin to
Claus, November 11, 1778; WO 28, Vol. 10, pp. 431–32, Claus to Lernoult, May 14, 1781.
4. State Records: Upper Canada, Land Board Minutes and Records, RG.1 L4, Vol. 5, pp. 9–
10, Haldimand to Bolton, July 12, 1780.
5. Siebert, "Loyalists and Six Nations Indians," p. 89.
6. Haldimand Transcripts, Vol. 105, p. 354, Butler to Mathews, March 3, 1783; ibid., Vol. 104,
pp. 430–31, Haldimand to McLean, Quebec, September 11, 1783.

the value of his influence on trade. As already discussed, Butler had entered into a profitable partnership with Richard Pollard to exploit particularly the lucrative market provided by the Indian Department. They had prospered until supplanted by Taylor and Forsyth, the firm preferred by Butler's rivals in the Indian Department, the Johnsons.

The loss of trade for Butler was a minor setback compared to those brought on by the end of the Revolution and the rebel victory. With the victory of the Revolutionary armies, Butler lost whatever chance he had of marching home to financial rewards and high position in a reconquered America. Indeed, as of June 1784 his Rangers were disbanded and he lost his direct influence and status as their commander.[7]

Haldimand's choice of Sir John Johnson to head the Indian Department had destroyed Butler's chances of further advancement as a colonial official. Although he remained deputy agent of the Indian Department at Niagara, the department contingent there was drastically cut. The reductions, besides lessening the local status of the department, left little leeway for illicit profits on the scale that Butler had previously enjoyed. To complicate matters even further, Butler's personal finances were in a distressing state; if Daniel Claus was right, Butler lost whatever profits he had made at wartime Niagara in an abortive speculation in Indian trade goods involving his old client, Edward Pollard. Butler's only immediate source of income was £ 200 Stlg per annum which he received from the Indian Department and his officer's half-pay. Even that income by at least 1786 was being absorbed by his debts to merchants.[8]

Butler's claims for war losses, moreover, were not well received: the Loyalist Claims Commissioners would not recognize his title to unsettled lands in New York valued by him at £ 5,720 which he had obtained from the Indians and for which he could produce no satisfactory deeds. On the rest of his Loyalist claim, he probably received less than the average 37 per cent allowed, since the Claims Commissioners tended to discount large claims more stringently.[9]

Much to his dismay, Butler found the promise of wealth and power that the Revolution had held out to him slipping away. Faced with the task of

---

7. Ibid., Vol. 63, p. 334 ff, Haldimand to Lt. Col. De Peyster, May 24, 1784.
8. Claus Papers, Vol. 3, pp. 22–23, Claus to [?], June 14, 1783; W. Canniff, *History of the Province of Ontario* (Toronto, 1872), p. 212; Cartwright Letter Books [transcripts], p. 229, Cartwright to Hamilton, July 18, 1786.
9. "Memorial of Lt. Col. John Butler, October 12, 1787, Quebec Land Book," quoted in E. Cruikshank, "Records of Niagara: 1784–9," *Publications of the Niagara Historical Society*, XXXIX (1928), pp. 24–27; M.B. Norton, *The British Americans: The Loyalist Exiles in England: 1774–1789* (Toronto, 1972), pp. 216, 219, 231.

re-establishing his family's influence in a new and changing society, he failed to make the necessary adjustments. He attempted to maintain his old status by relying upon his prewar and wartime contacts and influence within the military authority structure. He first attempted to draw upon the imperial government, demanding of it the prerequisites he felt were his due as an important colonial official and officer, but found the government, now the war was over, progressively less interested in the affairs of displaced officials from the lost colonies. When his petitions for patronage failed, Butler turned to the old familiar practices: corrupt supply of the Indian Department and speculation in Indian lands. The provincial government, however, was increasingly vigilant against such practices and prevented Butler from profiting by them.

Butler's natural impulse was to turn first to the imperial government, demanding of it patronage based on his past services. Even before the end of the war, Butler sought a military commission for his youngest son, a request that was refused.[10] In May 1784 he wrote to Haldimand that "my situation and circumstances not admitting of my providing for my children in a manner more suitable to my own and their wishes," he would be obliged to settle two of his sons at Niagara. This, he contended, would be an inducement to members of his corps to settle there and in order to obtain this advantage, he asked the government to give his sons the contract for portaging goods at Niagara.[11] This also was refused. Butler travelled to Quebec in the fall of 1784 to further his claims and, meeting with no success there, took ship in 1785 for England. Armed with a eulogistic summary of his services to the British government endorsed by Haldimand, he made the rounds of official society, using every advantage open to him, even to attaching himself to Joseph Brant as an interpreter to gain an audience with the Secretary of State. Butler discovered to his chagrin, however, that now it was over and lost, the imperial authorities wished to forget the war; they were deaf to the claims of importunate colonial officers. Butler returned to Quebec in the fall of 1786 empty-handed.[12]

The former Loyalist leader's only remaining strong card in his search

---

10. Haldimand Transcripts, Vol. 105, p. 376, Butler to Mathews, November 3, 1783.
11. Ibid., Vol. 105, p. 415, Butler to Haldimand, May 12, 1784.
12. Ibid., p. 418, Butler to Mathews, July 21, 1784; ibid., Vol. 215, pp. 196 ff, Narrative of Lt. Col. Butler's Services in America, May 1785; ibid., Vol. 222, pp. 70–71, Certificate by General Haldimand, May 7, 1785; CO 42 Transcripts, Vol. 26, p. 66, Butler to E. Nepean, March 17, 1786; Claus Papers, Vol. 3, pp. 108–10, P. Langan to D. Claus, June 27, 1786; Haldimand Transcripts, Vol. 76, pp. 183–85, Mathews to Haldimand, August 9, 1786; CO 42 Transcripts, Vol. 24, p. 79 ff, Petition of Sir John Johnson and others, April 11, 1785.

for patronage was his position in the Indian Department, and upon his return to Quebec, he was determined to play that card to the full. "Messrs Butler and McKee, the agent at Detroit," Haldimand's secretary reported to him, were "very lofty in their Declarations and Expectations."[13] They demanded that new restrictions on the mode of issuing provisions, which required close supervision by the commandants of the garrisons and which would curtail the possibilities for private profit, be removed and that their salaries be increased to £ 600 Stlg per annum before they would return to their posts. Butler once again demanded the portage for his sons. These demands were flatly refused and the disgruntled agents returned to their posts.[14]

Butler did gain one concession in Quebec: the appointment of his nephew Walter Butler Sheehan as Indian Department storekeeper at Niagara, the official directly in charge of Indian goods.[15] As we have seen, Butler's son Andrew along with Samuel Street was able to exploit that appointment only to a limited extent.

Butler's failure to prosper through his influence in the Indian Department forced him to turn increasingly to the possibilities of profit through the local society. In 1784 he had complained plaintively to Haldimand that "I cannot point out anything better than the Plough for my two Sons at the present."[16] Although he attempted a number of alternatives, in the end his statement proved accurate. No longer part of a profitable patronage system dependent on the military and without aid from the imperial authorities to bolster his local status or his sagging fortunes, Butler was now embarked on a long downward slide.

Despite all his setbacks, however, Butler could still take comfort at the end of the Revolution in the fact that a substantial portion of his former officers had settled at Niagara. He could still expect, with the aid and blessing of the provincial government, to consolidate these former subordinates of his into a unified leadership group; together, they might expect to reap local office as a reward for their past military service. Because they had been selected to be officers, one might assume that Butler's subordinates had been men of some substance and standing in colonial society. Such a group with both prior status and the prestige of wartime leadership would face a limited range of competition for power and place in the

---

13. Haldimand Transcripts, Vol. 76, p. 183 ff, Mathews to Haldimand, August 9, 1786.
14. Claus Papers, Vol. 4, p. 162, Sir John Johnson to Claus, October 19, 1787.
15. CO 42 Transcripts, Vol. 46, p. 395 ff, Dorchester to Johnson, January 21, 1790.
16. Haldimand Transcripts, Vol. 105A, pp. 412–14, Butler to Mathews, May 8, 1784.

Niagara peninsula. That pioneer society would produce few potential candidates for a governing elite. Early agriculture provided little base for wealth and status nor did local shopkeeping. The number of professionals within the society was minuscule. The Loyalist officers' only potential competitors for power were the major merchants with links to Laurentian supply networks. The local pre-eminence of the Loyalist officers, moreover, would seem a logical extension of the wartime authority structure. Butler had derived his powers and influence from the British military; he had attempted to entrench and extend his influence by use of his prerogatives as commander of the Loyalist forces at Niagara. Now the war was over, he could hope to continue to exercise an influence through those the military structure had formerly made his subordinates.

In fact, the status and influence of the Loyalist officers at Niagara were more apparent than real. Any effective leadership group requires an established status within its society and an internal coherence among its members. The Loyalist officers at Niagara had little of either. In the guerilla warfare that had been waged on the frontier, there had been little military hierarchy and less discipline. Most of the officers, moreover, had not enjoyed an affluence or prominence in the old colonies which would give them a precedence in the new. They were also divided by the rivalries and hostilities the war had bred among them. Once the Loyalist units were disbanded, any coherence or hierarchy the military structure had imposed on their members quickly disintegrated. Commerce was the only organized force in the new civilian settlements at Niagara and merchants would exploit that organization to exercise a potent influence on all affairs of the society.

The deciding authority in the first assignment of office in the Niagara peninsula was external to the local society. All initial offices in the new society—justices of the peace, judgeships on the Court of Common Pleas and positions on the Land Board—were appointed; and they were assigned by the government in Quebec City. These appointments proved to be extremely important because administrative power in early Niagara society was cumulative. Those who received positions in the first years of settlement were often chosen for subsequent appointments or, equally important, were consulted on such appointments.

The problems the government of Quebec faced in making the first local appointments in the upper country were essentially ones of communication. The central government in Quebec had little direct knowledge of the new citizenry at distant Niagara. It therefore turned for advice to the three organizations which had been closely connected with the upper country and which had knowledge of the new settlements: the army, the Indian

Department and, to some extent, the fur trading community. The involvement of all three of these groups with provisioning and supply meant that their most direct contacts in settlements like Niagara had been with the local merchants who had participated in Laurentian trade. Not unnaturally, they showed a predilection for merchants in their recommendations for office at Niagara.

The British army was consulted through its military commandant at Fort Niagara. The officers of the army had dealt constantly with local merchants throughout the war and possibly knew them more intimately than they knew the Loyalist officers, who were often out on distant raids. The Indian Department was also consulted on candidates through its chief local official, John Butler. Butler's recommendations, however, were more than counterbalanced by those of the new superintendent general of the department, Sir John Johnson. The government relied heavily on Johnson, who was also superintendent of the Loyalists, for advice on the new settlements. Johnson, because of their wartime rivalry, had strong reasons for favouring alternatives to Butler and his associates. The fur trade merchants were also sources of information on possible candidates because of their trade contacts along the Great Lakes and their consequent knowledge of local personnel. The major Montreal fur trade merchants favoured their local clients both from personal loyalty and because they saw obvious advantages in having their up-country contacts in control of local administration. The recommendations of their army, Indian Department, and fur trade patrons quickly gave a few merchants at Niagara control of the nascent administrative structure....

It is perhaps not surprising that the Loyalist military officers fared poorly in the postwar period. Starting with little capital, lacking entrepreneurial experience and often in middle age, they were not able to gain wealth and prestige through the local economy. Although Butler's officers received substantial land grants from the government, land, except that under cultivation, was of little value within the first generation of settlement and the amounts which could be cleared and cultivated would not make a man wealthy. Many of the original Loyalist grants passed into the hands of the merchants as payment for retail goods or collateral for mortgages. Some Loyalist families would eventually rise to prominence, in part through exploitation of their land, but the process would require at least a generation. In the occupations that might yield more immediate profit, the Loyalist military were sparsely represented: six of the twenty-four mill owners in the community as of 1792 were military, but only two of them were former officers. The Loyalist contingent in general merchandising was minuscule: the number of shopkeeper licenses per year before 1812 varied from seventeen to thirty-six with a large turnover. On the lists of shop licences for the district from 1801 to 1812, only one Loyalist officer and four rank and file appear.[17]

Butler's officers had no more success in gaining office: they represented an almost static minority within the largest group of appointed office holders, the justices of the peace. In 1789 they constituted four of eleven, in 1808 seven of twenty-eight, and in 1812 six of twenty-seven. None of the rank and file served as magistrates. No individuals bearing the family names of the officers became justices of the peace, suggesting that whatever prerogative the officers did enjoy did not extend to their offspring. Three of the five members of the Court of Common Pleas in 1789 were former Rangers and Indian Department officers and four of the eleven members of the land board in 1794. Again, none of rank and file were represented.[18]

Butler himself fared better in gaining public position than did his officers. To central government officials it was probably unthinkable that the commander of the Loyalist forces at Niagara should be entirely excluded from the management of the new settlement. By 1788 Butler had been appointed a justice of the peace, a judge of the Court of Common Pleas, and a member of the land board. Although he never attained provincial office, Butler was by 1792 lieutenant of the county, the most significant local office. Such offices, however, availed Butler but little, since he appears to have been unable to establish a loyal faction through which he could exercise their power. He perhaps took some role in forwarding the career of his nephew Walter Butler Sheehan who was appointed second sheriff of the district and, in the election of 1792, returning officer in three of the four ridings in the peninsula. Sheehan's prominence, however, was aided as much by the fact that he was a half-pay officer of the regular British army as by his uncle's influence. He eventually resigned his offices and moved to Grand River where his public prominence ended. A clearer indication of Butler's limited influence was that in his lifetime none of his three sons held a post more elevated than that of captain in the local militia.[19]

---

17. "District of Nassau Letter Book No. 2, p. 79, Statement of the Mills in the District of Nassau, by D.W. Smith, November 7, 1792," printed in *Archives of Ontario* [A.O.] *Report*, 1905 p. 325; State Records: Upper Canada, Customs: Shop, Tavern, and Still Licenses, Vol. 53–57, Shop Licences, 1802–1811.

18. *Quebec Almanac*, various years.

19. AO, Upper Canada: Journal of the Proceedings of the House of Assembly [transcripts], June 17, 1793; PAC, Indian Department: Upper Canada, RG 10 A2, Vol. 105, item 141, Memorial of W.B., Henry and George Sheehan, n.d.

There is little indication that Butler was able to use his offices for personal gain. His most significant request to local authorities, made to the land board, was for a grant of lands between Toronto and Head-of-the-Lake (Ancaster), six miles along Lake Ontario, extending back twelve miles. This he asked as compensation for his war losses and services. He was refused by the members of the board which included in its number some who had been his officers.[20]

Butler's most important office was his position in the Indian Department. Although his attempts to exploit that position for substantial personal gain after the Revolution through use of department supplies and land speculation were foiled, it is undeniable that Butler owed what postwar prominence he did enjoy to his position in the Indian Department. He played a large part in the purchase of much of southwestern Ontario from the Mississauga Indians and was significant in the diplomatic manoeuvring with the Americans and the Indians in the years before the evacuation of the border posts in 1796. The Johnson faction, however, was vigilant to prevent Butler from turning his prestige to his own advancement. As early as 1782 Sir John Johnson made an attempt to remove Butler from his post and to replace him with his own nephew; when that failed, Johnson blocked payment of Butler's personal accounts and also stepped up his family's barrage of innuendo in official circles against him.[21]

Butler had few opportunities to use his influence in the local Indian Department to respond to the Johnson offensive. In 1786 the department at Niagara was slashed from a wartime peak of nineteen officers and sixty-one staff to two officers with a staff of four. In 1790 Sir John Johnson effectively blocked Butler's further rise in the department by nominating Alexander McKee, the Indian agent at Detroit and a longtime lieutenant of the Johnsons, for the post of deputy superintendent of Upper Canada. McKee received the office in 1794.[22]

---

20. "Minutes of Nassau Land Board, July 22, 1791," printed in *A.O. Report* (1905), p. 172.

21. See, for example, Siebert, "The Loyalists and the Six Nations;" Claus Papers, Vol. 3, Haldimand to Sir John Johnson, November 25, 1782; Haldimand Transcripts, Vol. 115, p. 39, Haldimand to Sir John Johnson, December 5, 1782; ibid., pp. 121–22, Sir John Johnson to Haldimand, June 2, 1783; ibid., Vol. 102, p. 237, McLean to Haldimand, December 24, 1782.

22. *Quebec Almanac*, 1786 and 1796; CO 42 Transcripts, Vol. 46, pt. 2, pp. 395–403, Dorchester to Sir John Johnson, January 21, 1790; "Dorchester to Grenville, March 15, 1790," printed in E.A. Cruikshank, *Simcoe Correspondence*, Vol. 1 (Toronto, 1923–31), p. 10; CO 42 Transcripts, Vol. 69, p. 179, Dorchester to Dundas, September 5, 1794.

Butler's relations with the department remained strained for the rest of his life. Johnson and his officials attempted to curb Butler's actions and protested his independence; Butler in his turn complained bitterly that the department kept information from him and that his influence within it was being undermined. In Butler's last years, the Indian Department made no attempt to protect him against the scandals he had brought upon himself by speculations in Indian lands and corrupt department supply. When he died in 1796, Butler's successor was William Claus, the son of Butler's most vociferous opponent, Daniel Claus. Thus, the Butler influence within the Indian Department was decisively terminated. It is a further indication of the direction that patronage distribution was taking that, at his death in 1796, Butler's most important office in the local government, that of lieutenant of the county, did not pass to any connection of his, but to the major merchant of the Niagara peninsula, Robert Hamilton.[23]

---

23. Ibid., Vol. 50, pt. 1, p. 218, Johnson to Dorchester, March 2, 1791; PAC, Indian Department Records, RG 10 A2, Vol. 8, n.p., Joseph Chew to Alexander McKee, received September 13, 1793; "Butler to Joseph Chew, March 1, 1795," printed in Cruikshank, *Simcoe Correspondence*, II, pp. 49–50; "Green to McKee, July 7, 1796," printed in ibid., IV, pp. 326–27; "Littlehales to Hamilton, July 12, 1796," printed in ibid., p. 329.

The Loyalists of America and Their Times

EGERTON RYERSON

The Loyalists Driven from the United States to the British Provinces.

The Loyalists, after having been stripped of their rights and property during the war, and driven from their homes, and hunted and killed at pleasure, were exiled from all right of residence and citizenship at the close of the war; and though the Treaty of Peace engaged that Congress should recommend the several States to compensate them for the losses of their property, the Legislatures of the several States (with one exception) refused any compliance with this stipulation of the national treaty, and the Legislature of New York actually ordered the punishment of those Loyalists who applied for compensation. At the close of the war, therefore, instead of witnessing, as in the case of all other civilized nations at the termination of a civil war, however rancorous and cruel, a general amnesty and the restoration of all parties to the rights and property which they enjoyed at the commencement of the strife, the Loyalists found themselves exiled and impoverished, and their enemies in possession of their homes and domains. It is true about 3,000 of the Loyalists were able to employ agents, or appear personally, to apply to the English Government and Parliament for compensation for their losses; and the preceding chapter records the noble appreciation of their character and services by British statesmen, and the liberality of Parliament in making them compensation for their losses and, sufferings in maintaining their fidelity to the mother country. But these 3,000 constituted not one-tenth of the Loyalists who had suffered losses and hardships during the civil war; upwards of 30,000 of them were driven from the homes of their birth and of their forefathers, to wilderness of everlasting snow. . . .

To understand the sacrifices which the Loyalists made, and the courage and energy they evinced, in leaving their old homes and associations in the sunny parts of America, and in seeking a refuge and a home in the wilds of the remaining British Provinces, it will be necessary to notice

EGERTON RYERSON, *THE LOYALISTS OF AMERICA AND THEIR TIMES*, VOL. 2 (TORONTO, WILLIAM BRIGGS, 1880): 183–90.

what was then known, and the impression then existing, as to the climate, productions, and conditions of these provinces. . . .

Some of the officers, embarking at New York for Nova Scotia, are said to have remarked that they were "bound for a country where there were nine months of winter and three months of cold weather every year." Lower Canada was known as a region of deep snow, intense cold, and little fertility; a colony of the French; its capital, Quebec, the scene of decisive battles between the English and French under Wolfe and Montcalm, and afterwards between Murray and Montgomery, the latter the leader of the American revolters and invaders. Montreal was regarded as the place of transit of the fur trade from the Hudson's Bay Company to England.

Upper Canada was then unknown, or known only as a region of dense wilderness and swamps, of venomous reptiles and beasts of prey, the hunting grounds and encampments of numerous Indian tribes, intense cold of winter, and with no other redeeming feature except abundance of game and fish. . . .

The most common land route from New York to Upper Canada, chosen by the Loyalists at the close of the war, was to Albany 180 miles up the Hudson river, which divides into two branches about ten miles north of Albany. The western branch is called the Mohawk, leading to Rome, formerly Fort Stanwix. A branch of the Mohawk, called Wood Creek, leads towards the Oneida lake, which was reached by a portage. From Oneida Lake, Lake Ontario was reached by the Oswego river. Flat-bottom boats, specially built or purchased for the purpose by the Loyalists, were used in this journey. The portages over which the boats had to be hauled, and all their contents carried, are stated to be thirty miles. On reaching Oswego, some of the Loyalists coasted along the eastern shore of Lake Ontario to Kingston, and thence up the Bay of Quinté; others went westward, along the south shore of the lake to Niagara and Queenston; some pursued their course to the head of the lake at Burlington; others made their way up the Niagara river to Queenston, conveyed their boats over the portage of ten or twelve miles to Chippewa, thence up the river and into Lake Erie, settling chiefly in what was called the "Long Point Country," now the county of Norfolk. This journey of hardship, privation, and exposure occupied from two to three months. The parents and family of the writer of this history were from the middle of May to the middle of July, 1799, in making this journey in an open boat. Generally two or more families would unite in one company, and thus assist each other in carrying their boats and goods over the portages. . . .

The hardships, exposures, privations and sufferings which the first

Loyalists endured in making their way from their confiscated homes to Canada, were longer and more severe than anything narrated of the Pilgrim and Puritan Fathers of New England in their voyages from England to Massachusetts Bay; and the persecutions to which the emigration of the Puritans from England is attributed were trifling indeed in comparison of the persecutions, imprisonments, confiscations, and often death, inflicted on the loyal adherents to the Crown of England in the United States, and which drove the survivors among them to the wilderness of Canada. The privations and hardships experienced by many of these Loyalist patriots for years after the first settlement in Canada... were much more severe than anything experienced by the Pilgrim Fathers during the first years of their settlement in Massachusetts....The stern adherence of the Puritans to their principles was quite equalled by the stern adherence of the Loyalists to their principles, and far excelled by their sacrifices and sufferings.

Canada has a noble parentage, the remembrance of which its inhabitants may well cherish with respect, affection, and pride.

FURTHER READINGS FOR TOPIC 7

D. V. J. Bell. "The Loyalist Tradition in Canada." *Journal of Canadian Studies*, vol. 5 (May 1970), pp. 22–23.

J. B. Brebner. *The Neutral Yankees of Nova Scotia: A Marginal Colony during the Revolutionary Years*. Originally published 1937; reprint Toronto: McClelland and Stewart, 1969.

Gordon Stewart and George Rawlyk. *A People Highly Favoured of God: The Nova Scotia Yankees and the American Revolution*. Toronto: Macmillan, 1972.

Earle Thomas. *Sir John Johnson: Loyalist Baronet*. Toronto and Reading: Dundurn Press, 1986.

Bruce Wilson. *As She Began: An Illustrated Introduction to Loyalist Ontario*. Toronto and Charlottetown: Dundurn Press, 1981.

PART

3

"With Ceaseless Turmoil Seething": The Early Nineteenth Century in British North America

TOPIC 8

Popular Politics Before Responsible Government

The end of the Napoleonic Wars in 1815 resulted in the emigration from Britain to North America of many thousands of people. Among those who came to British North America in the years 1815–40 were large numbers of Irish, both Protestant and Catholic and from all walks of life. The first two selections in this volume explore the effects of this influx on popular politics.

The political career of Peter Aylen rested on the support of Irish labourers for whom he provided work in the timber industry. Aylen's politics were those of a rough and ready frontier society, and essentially bypassed or existed outside the boundaries of established political institutions. Thus he sought to control Bytown (later renamed Ottawa) by the threat of violence at the hands of his crowd of bullies. Once the violence moved beyond property damage, however, and seemed likely to result in the loss of life, civic leaders put a stop to it, and to Aylen's domination of Bytown. An illuminating contrast is provided by the career of Ogle Gowan as detailed by Donald Akenson. Gowan, a leading Orangeman of Upper Canada, operated through more conventional political channels than Aylen, though he too used violence, notably to discourage his opponents' supporters from voting at election time. These two articles, and the excerpt from James Lesslie's diary, should put to rest the hoary old myth about the entirely peaceable nature of Upper Canadian society.

The Lesslie diary contains an important primary source on the York Riots of March 23, 1832. (York became Toronto in 1834.) By that date, W. L. Mackenzie, a Reform politician and journalist of Scottish origin, had *so offended the Upper Canadian Conservatives or Tories that they had expelled him from the Assembly three times. Here we see Tory crowds resorting to rioting and to parading an effigy of the offender through the streets, a common form of popular protest. (The effigy of Mackenzie was actually burnt in front of his office.) Note that in the early stages of the disturbances, the authorities showed no great inclination to go to Mackenzie's aid, though they later became more protective of him. The alliance of government officials and members of Tory crowds was a significant feature of Toronto politics into the 1850s, as Gregory Kealey's work has shown.*

PETER AYLEN

MICHAEL CROSS

AYLEN (Vallely), PETER, timberer; b. 1799 in Liverpool, England; d. probably October 1868 in Aylmer, Que.

Peter Aylen, the "King of the Shiners," had a brief and bloody period of fame in the mid 1830s when he dominated the Ottawa valley by violence. He came to Canada about 1815, according to legend a runaway sailor. The story is given credence by his change of name: when selling land in 1837 he used what was apparently his legal surname, Vallely. Little is known of his life before the 1830s although it is clear he worked his way up to a significant position in the Ottawa valley timber trade. In 1832, by then a resident of Nepean Township, Carleton County, Upper Canada, Aylen was prominent enough to be a partner in the "Gatineau Privilege." He joined with the leading timberers on the Upper Ottawa—Ruggles, Tiberius, and Christopher Wright, Thomas McGoey, George Hamilton, and C. A. Low—to obtain a monopoly on exploitation of timber on the Gatineau River. This profitable partnership, in which each participant took out 2,000 sticks of red pine per annum, continued until 1843. Aylen's connections in the timber trade were strengthened by his marriage to Eleanor, sister of William and John Thomson, two major Nepean timberers. Her sister married another leading Ottawa timberer, Peter White.

Aylen was a man of insatiable ambition and was prepared to take any measures necessary to advance his interests. The increasingly competitive situation in the Ottawa valley timber trade of the 1830s led Aylen to adopt violence as a business tactic. He was the most vigorous of a number of timberers who raided the limits of competitors, destroyed rivals' booms and rafts, and attacked and dispersed competitors' timber crews. Aylen also capitalized on the large pool of Irish labourers left unemployed by the completion of the Rideau Canal in 1832. Setting himself up as a champion of the Irish in their struggle to obtain jobs in the French Canadian-dominated timber camps, he employed only Irishmen, thereby winning their fighting support for his violent business tactics.

In virtual control of the river by 1835, Aylen moved the struggle into the community of Bytown (Ottawa), in an apparent attempt to seize political

MICHAEL CROSS, "PETER AYLEN," *DICTIONARY OF CANADIAN BIOGRAPHY*, VOL. 9 (1861–70) (TORONTO: UNIVERSITY OF TORONTO PRESS, 1976): 13–14. REPRINTED BY PERMISSION OF UNIVERSITY OF TORONTO PRESS.

and economic control of the town. From 1835 to 1837 Aylen and a band of perhaps 200 Irishmen remained in Bytown after winter operations and terrorized the village. The "Shiners," as his followers were known, virtually controlled the working class Lower Town, and engaged freely in physical assaults and petty larceny. The lack of a professional police force allowed the Shiners to act with impunity. The pattern was set in July 1835 when Aylen was arrested for assault; the enraged Shiners went on a rampage which ended when they destroyed a canal steamer in Bytown harbour. The local magistrates soon learned that Aylen was untouchable.

Aylen's hegemony over Bytown lasted for two years, and was strengthened by his disruption of local institutions, including the Nepean Township Council, whose annual election meeting was broken up in January 1837 so that municipal officers could not be elected. Peace was reestablished on the river, however. In March 1836 the Ottawa Lumber Association was created to stop violence in the trade. Aylen was one of its first officers, apparently feeling he had gained all he could from the use of force on the river. Indeed the association provided him with early advantages. Its first cooperative venture was improvement of the Madawaska River to ease the passage of timber. Aylen's timber operations were on the Madawaska and he was placed in charge of the improvements.

In Bytown, Aylen's hold was broken in the spring of 1837. Shiner rioting reached a peak in March of that year. As a prominent Bytown merchant, James Johnston, wrote to the lieutenant governor, Sir Francis Bond Head: "Mr. Peter Aylen...has already proved to all Bytown, that he neither respects himself, nor fears God, or Man. The laws are like cobwebs to him. There are now several warrants out for his apprehension, but there is not a constable in Bytown, who will undertake to arrest him." It was Aylen's attempt to have Johnston murdered on 25 March 1837 which shocked the community into action. The magistrates, supported by a citizen organization, formed armed night patrols and swore in special constables to arrest lawbreakers. With determined community action, the Shiners were brought under control in April and May 1837.

Aylen realized that his career in Bytown was over. In 1836 he had leased out most of his property in the area when he came to reside in the town. The transactions tell something of his wealth. He rented out a property of 150 acres on the Richmond Road, three miles from Bytown, containing a two-storey house, barns, and stables, a blacksmith shop, and a store; he also let a 300-acre lot and house in Horton Township and 12 ten-acre woodlots near Bytown. After his defeat in the spring of 1837, he leased his Bytown home and store and sold his wife's dower land, 250 acres in

Nepean Township. Aylen moved to a farm on the north side of the Ottawa River, near Symmes' Landing, from which he continued his timber business.

In his new life, Aylen became a virtual pillar of respectability. The year following his move, he was one of four trustees elected to build a church in the settlement. He was a member of the Hull Township Council in 1846, an assessor of the new town when Symmes' Landing was incorporated as Aylmer in 1847, and superintendent of roads in the Ottawa County Council in 1855-56. In 1848 he had been appointed a justice of the peace. His new-found respectability was handed on to his sons, one of whom became a lawyer, one a doctor, and still another both a doctor and a lawyer.

Aylen's business grew apace; he added a saw mill at the Chats Falls on the Ottawa to his interests in the mid 1850s. His family, along with those of most major timber firms on the Ottawa, was represented on the 1849 Annexation Manifesto by the signature of his son, Peter. Aylen had not given over his old ways altogether, however. In 1851 his timber limits on the Madawaska River were confiscated by the Crown Lands Office because of his "illegal proceedings" and failure to pay the required dues. The leopard, leader of Aylmer society that he might be, had not entirely changed his Shiner spots.

The Irish in Ontario:

A Study in Rural History

DONALD HARMAN AKENSON

Beginning in 1830 and continuing for the next six years, the immigrant Irish ran amok, or at least so it seemed to the representatives of the old economic and social order. This eruption is exactly what one would expect if, just prior to 1830, the Irish had become aware that the foreign-born and their offspring were a majority locally, that they, the Irish, were the largest component of the immigrant culture, but that the local establishment was blocking their rightful economic, political, and social progress.[1]

The key figure in the local Irish eruption was Ogle R. Gowan, surely one of the most insistent figures ever to stride across the Upper Canadian stage.[2] His father was a prominent Wexford landowner, but, as a younger

---

Donald Harman Akenson, *The Irish in Ontario: A Study in Rural History* (Kingston and Montreal: McGill-Queen's University Press, 1984): 168–83. Reprinted with permission of the author and publisher.

1. The account which follows in the text of the local Irish upsurge is both detailed in narrative and nasty in its details. Two volumes might be of use in keeping it in perspective. One is Evelyn Purvis Earle, *Leeds the Lovely* (Toronto: Ryerson Press, 1951). This is the work of a local enthusiast and it emphasizes the more romantic aspects of Irish settlement. It has some delightfully evocative passages. The second volume is the sometimes underrated Durham Report, in its observations on the rise of the "emigrant" party (Lucas edition, 2: 153ff.) Durham's arguments about the emigrant party may or may not be applicable to the whole province, but they fit the Leeds and Lansdowne situation nicely. (1) He asserted that an emigrant party arose, with its origins in the heavy migration that began in 1825–6 (he used "party" in the contemporary British sense of an interest group or coalition, not in the modern sense of political party, although such interest groups often did act in politics). (2) He noted that the newcomers did not coalesce into a distinct party for quite a time after their arrival, but (3) that they were precipitated into a substantial unit by (a) a desire to assimilate the Upper Canadian political system closer to United Kingdom standards and (b) a desire to have removed the disqualifications and discriminations they experienced. (4) In the election of 1836 the newcomers from the British Isles effectively won their points. Incidentally, Durham adopted contemporary imperial usage and employed "British" to describe all migrants from the British Isles. This included the Irish, who, in fact, comprised the bulk of the migrants to Upper Canada.
2. Hereward Senior's discussion of Gowan in the *Dictionary of Canadian Biography* (DCB) is the best available. There is also valuable information in Senior's "Ogle Gowan, Orangeism, and the Immigrant Question, 1830–1833," *Ontario History* 66 (1974): 193–206. See also Walter McCleary, ed., *History of the Orange Association in the Dominion of Canada, No. 1: One Man's Loyalty* (Toronto: Committee on Orange History 1953).

(and probably illegitimate) son, Ogle became a "squireen," one of the caste most despised in Ireland, the "half-mounted gentry." Many of the Anglo-Irish ascendancy were content to remain in the countryside, acting as part-time agents for various landlords and as attenuated dependents of their own families, lording it over the Catholic peasantry but never being fully accepted by the real gentry. Gowan, though only half-mounted, tried to make his own living, or at least his own fame, in Dublin, and he did so through exploiting his family background. County Wexford was among the areas which had suffered worst from Catholic depredations in the 1798 Rising and, indeed, the Gowan family home had been burned. His father was one of the earliest local Orangemen and young Ogle had been named for his godfather, George Ogle, who was one of the grand masters of the Orange Order in Ireland. Young Ogle himself joined the Order in 1818. In Dublin, he made money and fame from the rancid underside of the Anglo-Irish character: he wrote pamphlets against the Roman Catholics and published a small anti-Catholic paper, *The Antidote*. During these years Gowan cultivated the Orange system and when, by act of the Westminster parliament, the Orange Order was dissolved in 1825, he became an "assistant grand secretary" for a benevolent society which was a surrogate for the Order, designed to keep the network together while remaining just barely within the law. Why Gowan decided to emigrate to Upper Canada is unclear, but he arrived in 1829 with a wife, seven children, and two servants, a handsome, clear-featured, aggressive twenty-six-year-old, possessed of monumental self-assurance and a deep instinctive knowledge of the drives, fears, and hatreds of his fellow Irishmen.

Within a year of his arrival, Gowan, now ostensibly a gentleman farmer from Brockville but actually a fulltime organizer and agitator, was in the centre of several troubles. Gowan operated as the hub of three concentric circles of agitation, national, provincial, and local. His national prominence came through his founding role in the Orange Order in British North America.[3] Orange lodges had sprung up in British North America well before Gowan arrived, but they were local occurrences, formed by various regiments of imperial soldiers stationed in the Canadas or by pockets of local Irish emigrés. They served as local social clubs, not as part

---

3. The standard study of the origin of the movement is Hereward Senior, *Orangeism in Ireland and Britain 1795–1836* (London: Routledge and Kegan Paul 1966). Senior continued the story in *Orangeism: The Canadian Phase* (Toronto: McGraw-Hill Ryerson 1972). A more analytic study is *The Sash Canada Wore: A Historical Geography of the Orange Order in Canada* (Toronto: University of Toronto Press 1980). For an Orangeman's view of the Order's origins, see Leslie H. Saunders, *The Story of Orangeism* (Toronto: The Grand Orange Lodge of Ontario West 1941).

of a formal network.[4] Gowan changed that. Soon after settling in Brockville, he began sounding the opinions of Orange sympathizers and on 1 January 1830 the Grand Orange Lodge of British North America was founded at a meeting held in the Brockville courthouse. . . .Gowan became the Grand Master. With remarkable energy and organizational ability, he tied together the extant local Orange lodges and expanded the network throughout Ontario and Quebec. By 1833 he had issued warrants creating ninety-one lodges in Upper Canada and eight in Lower.[5] Membership in the British North American colonies was claimed to be over ten thousand, most of them in Upper Canada.[6] This number rose continually and by 1860 the Order claimed over one hundred thousand members,[7] a number which, although doubtless inflated, indicates that the Order was a major national phenomenon.

Since the Brockville area was Gowan's home, the Orange movement had considerable adherence in Leeds county. Houston and Smyth's plotting of the residences of the grand lodge executive and grand committee members in 1833 shows that most of them came from within a twenty-mile radius of Brockville.[8] In the vicinity of Brockville, several lodges were granted warrants, the most important for our purposes being in Leeds and Lansdowne township: the lodges in Gananoque and Lansdowne were both formed by 1833.[9] In the light of the eventual clash of the Leeds county Irish with the existing political establishment, it is worth noting that there was a backlog of tension between Orangemen and the local worthies dating back to 1823. In that year, when the Orange lodges were merely individual units, not part of a national network, an attempt to ban them had been introduced into the Upper Canadian legislature. Charles Jones, one of the two members for Leeds, spoke in favour of the ban. When the vote on the second reading was evenly split, the second

---

4. See Hereward Senior, "The Genesis of Canadian Orangeism," *Ontario History* 60 (1968): 13–29.
5. Cecil J. Houston and William J. Smyth, "The Spread of the Loyal Orange Lodge through Ontario, 1830–1900" (paper presented at CHA annual meeting 1978), 4.
6. Hereward Senior, "The Character of Canadian Orangeism," in *Thought from the Learned Societies of Canada, 1961* (Toronto: W.J. Gage 1961), 177–89.
7. Cecil Houston and William Smyth, "The Ulster Legacy," *Multiculturalism* 1 (1978): 10.
8. Houston and Smyth, *The Sash*, figure 2, 31.
9. See the map mentioned in note 8 above. And in McCleary, *One Man's Loyalty* (9), it is mentioned that in 1832 the Orangemen from Gananoque had to cancel their accustomed walk, so presumably it was established by 1831, if not before. Thaddeus W.H. Leavitt, *History of Leeds and Grenville* (Brockville: Brockville Recorder 1879), 139, says Lodge No. 26 in Lansdowne is one of the oldest in central Canada, and its number indicates that it was founded by 1833 at the latest. The Orange lodge in Lansdowne officially came to an end on 13 July 1982 (*Gananoque Reporter*, 23 June 1982).

member for Leeds county, Livius P. Sherwood, as speaker had the casting vote, which he threw against the ban. This does not mean that Sherwood was favourably disposed to the Order—indeed, in the debates no one defended it—but merely that it seemed inexpedient to try to control the Orangemen with legislative monitions.[10]

If forging the Orange network was an achievement on a national scale, Gowan's activities in the legislative assembly for Upper Canada and later for the parliament for the United Canadas had province-wide reference. He was in the house off and on from 1834 until his retirement in 1861, at which time contemporaries had given him the soubriquet "the father of the house." His parliamentary activities often had a sharp local reference. Gowan, like any good politician, understood that any wider fame was contingent upon keeping his local constituents happy. In particular, the immigrant community, his natural constituency in Leeds county, needed help in obtaining clear titles to land, and he took upon himself responsibility for dealing with the often recalcitrant officials in Toronto....

All Gowan's activities had some local reference, but for the purposes of this study the most important were his election campaigns for the legislative assembly. Although these campaigns were initiated by an official call to elect members for the Upper Canada assembly, in practice the series of elections held in Leeds county in the 1830s was really about control of the local political power structure. Provincially called elections were the arena but the fight was local. In the local electoral structure there were three seats in the legislative assembly to fight over, one for Brockville, which does not require our attention here, and two for the county of Leeds proper. There were more factions than spoils, so that conflict was endemic. The two most established families were the old loyalist and very Tory ones stemming from two separate Jones clans, the descendants of Solomon Jones and his two brothers, and those of Ephraim Jones.[11] In the

---

10. On the bill and debates see Senior, "The Genesis of Canadian Orangeism," 16–18. See also Senior, "Orangeism Takes Root in Canada," *Canadian Genealogist* 3, no. 1 (1981): 14–15.

11. For want of a better term, the two Jones clans and the Sherwoods and their associates are described as Tories. This does not mean that they were Tory in the narrow sense of political party as understood in our own time. As S.F. Wise has paid, "It is impossible to disagree with [G.M.] Craig's contention that 'party' in anything but the most embryonic sense, was not a factor in Upper Canadian elections. The evidence for any substantial degree of province-wide party organization, even in 1836, simply does not exist." (S.F. Wise, "Tory Factionalism: Kingston Elections and Upper Canadian Politics, 1820–1836," *Ontario History* 57 [1965]: 205.)
    The following comments by Wise indicate that the term "Tory" nevertheless has a socio-political meaning that makes it a valid concept to use concerning the 1830s: "If

narrative which follows, Charles and Jonas Jones, sons of Ephraim, are the most important. A third loyalist family, the Sherwoods, was consequential, though of diminishing influence. In addition, another old loyalist family, the Buells, was important in local political contests, for it fought for the "reform" viewpoint with considerable vigor. The most important of this clan at the time was William Buell, editor of the *Brockville Recorder*. The dominant families in Leeds and Lansdowne township, the Landons in Lansdowne and the Stone-McDonald interests in Gananoque, did not run for provincial office and, perforce, the representation of Leeds and Lansdowne township was fought as part of the battle for control of Leeds county.[12]

When an election was called for 1830, Ogle R. Gowan, not one year off the boat from Ireland, came forward as a candidate. This was not so ill-considered as it must have appeared at the time, for we now recognize the demographic shift which immigration from the British Isles, and especially from Ireland, had caused in the late 1820s and we now know how effective Gowan had been in forming the Orange network.[13] Further, the election provided a tactical opportunity that might be exploited: only one of the sitting members, William Buell, was running and, although his seat could be taken as safe, there was an opening for the other Leeds seat. In the light of Gowan's later hyper-loyalism, it is important to recognize that he wanted to be elected more than he wanted to be elected on any

---

Upper Canad[ian] conservatism lacked uniformity and homogeneity, this is only another way of saying that it was an alliance of groups, with different interests and outlooks. It is possible to express the nature of the alliance in several ways. A Tory of the time would certainly have said that conservative leadership came from the 'respectable classes' in the community. In this sense, Toryism was the political expression of the province's small upper class, the people who considered themselves the natural leaders of society." "The core of Tory support was in the eastern counties, the area of major Loyalist settlement, and in the towns, especially Kingston, Brockville, York-Toronto, Niagara and London." "The Tory 'party,' then, was a quasi-official coalition of the central and local elites united for the purpose of distributing honours and rewards to the politically deserving." The quotations are from S.F. Wise, "Upper Canada and the Conservative Tradition," in *Profiles of a Province: Studies in the History of Ontario* (Toronto: Ontario Historical Society 1967), 24, 21, and 27 respectively.

12. On local power alignments, Elva M. Richards, "The Joneses of Brockville and the Family Compact," *Ontario History* 60 (1968): 169–84, is especially valuable. Professor Ian MacPherson has kindly permitted me to see his manuscript, "The Buell View: Building a New Order in Brockville, 1830–1850," which is very illuminating on the local power structure. A revised version is at present in press (Belleville: Mika Publishing Co.) under the title *Matters of Loyalty*.

13. There were over forty lodges affiliated with the Orange network as early as 1830 and eleven of these were in Leeds, Grenville, or Frontenac counties. (MS record book, "Records of the L.O.L. of British North America," in National Orange Archives, Toronto.)

particular principle. At first he hoped to be accepted by the reformer Buell as a *de facto* running-mate and thus to be returned virtually unopposed, but the Buells had a candidate of their own, Mathew Howard.[14] Gowan went ahead anyway. In the era before strict party politics evolved, the practice was for a series of meetings to be held in various spots in the county and each meeting (usually claiming to be non-partisan) nominated candidates. The nominations were not binding but were crudely indicative of popular feeling. Gowan, realizing that he would have to fight the Buells, announced himself as something of a backwoods Tory, thus permitting at least a tolerant relationship with Henry Sherwood, who was the candidate favoured by the old loyalist Tories. More significantly, Gowan clearly identified the social constituency for which he spoke: at a meeting at Lamb's Pond (Elizabethtown township, Leeds county, now called New Dublin) which endorsed his candidacy, a resolution was passed stating that "as there are three representative seats for the county [two for the county proper and one for Brockville]...we are decidedly of the opinion that one of these three should be an Irishman," adding, ominously, "a measure the concession of which we deem necessary to ally the rapidly increasing spirit of national animosity..."[15] At a meeting about a week later for the backwoods townships of Burgess and Elmsley, it was resolved that, as the majority of the population of the township "are Europeans by birth and education, we conceive that if a European Canadian of equal talents and integrity can be found, he should possess a peculiar claim upon our sympathy and support."[16] The meeting then endorsed the old loyalist Sherwood and the new Tory Gowan. In the actual election, the reformers Buell and Howard were elected for Leeds county but Gowan ran ahead of Sherwood, had only seventy votes fewer than the poll leader, Buell, and was just fourteen votes behind Howard.[17] The handwriting was on the wall, but the established families were slow to react.

Gowan's next step was logical (in matters of ambition he was as logical as he was relentless) for he used a by-election in neighbouring Grenville county in 1831 to turn his shotgun entente with Ephraim Jones's descen-

---

14. Senior, "Ogle Gowan, Orangeism and the Immigrant Question, 1830–1833," 195–6. See also reports in *Brockville Recorder*, 21 September 1830.
15. *Brockville Recorder*, 28 September 1830.
16. *Brockville Recorder*, 12 October 1830.
17. DCB, William Buell; Hereward Senior, "Ogle Gowan, Orangeism and the Immigrant Question, 1830–1833," 198.

dants into a formal alliance. Late in 1830 he cooperated with the Joneses in trying to form a set of "independent clubs" with the idea of uniting old loyalists and Irish Protestants and Catholics against the distant but frightening alarm of William Lyon Mackenzie.[18] This effort was not notably successful, nor was the Leeds Patriotic Club founded in early 1831 under the presidency of the loyalist George Breakenridge, with Gowan as a vice president,[19] but in these connections Gowan was establishing his own loyalty and, *mutatis mutandis*, that of his Irish followers. . . .

Gowan, like the immigrants whom he represented, was always in danger of being labelled subversive, which he and they certainly were in wishing to shoulder aside some of the established holders of power. They were not, however, disloyal to the constitution. Thus, the tour of William Lyon Mackenzie through eastern Upper Canada in the autumn of 1831 was a perfect stage-set for Gowan, allowing him to make a great show of holding his own meetings or, when possible, debating Mackenzie in person. It was particularly important that Gowan (and by implication his Irish followers in eastern Ontario) put as much distance as possible between himself and the Orangemen of Mackenzie's York constituency, and, in reaction to the Orange signatures on Mackenzie's "York requisition," Gowan intoned, "Oh how the heart sickens and the blood recoils at the idea that even one Irishman could be found who, false to his country, his religion and his God, has veered about and united with the Yankee junto of hypocrits, traitors and knaves who hold their seditious meetings at York, and fulminate from thence their poison through the province."[20] One can almost hear the old loyalist families, the various Joneses and the Sherwoods, sighing in relief and murmuring that, though our local Irish may be savages, at least in the heel of the hunt they are loyal.

The appearance of Mackenzie was doubly useful for Gowan, as not only could he trumpet his own and his followers' loyalty, but the Buell family and their electoral associate Mathew Howard were affiliated with Mackenzie, although not associated in detail with all his policies. Gowan had no scruples about tarring the Buells with the radical brush. He charged them with trying to keep Mackenzie away from areas of immigrant (read Irish) settlement and with trying to keep the Irish, even the Catholic Irish

---

18. Senior, "Ogle Gowan, Orangeism and the Immigrant Question, 1830–1833," 199.
19. *Brockville Gazette*, 26 January 1831.
20. The text is from a meeting held at the Methodist Episcopal church, Brockville, reported in the *Brockville Gazette*, 10 November 1831.

whom they were said to champion, "in the dark." A bitter controversy raged for months in the Brockville papers.[21]

...During the summer and autumn of 1832 Gowan was relatively quiet; he was in ill health, and, in any case, the populace was universally concerned with the cholera which struck in early summer.[22] The next year, however, he took up his old ways. In March of 1833 the two representatives for Leeds county, William Buell and Mathew Howard, convened a meeting at Farmersville (now called Athens) in Yonge township, on the subject of the demerits of the Anglican Church establishment in Upper Canada and the inadequacy of public education. Andrew Norton Buell, brother of William, began the meeting, but before a chairman could be chosen Gowan and a body of his supporters arrived. Accounts vary, but it seems that a great furor arose over the chairmanship and that the Irish, who were armed with "shileleaghs," beat up the reform party's chairman and generally turned the meeting into a shambles.[23]

At this meeting and at a grand procession held in Brockville later in the same month, Gowan not only had at his side the representatives of old loyalist Tories (David Jones, Charles Jones, and Henry Sherwood joined in the Brockville procession) but he also tried, with some success, to attract Irish Catholics to his van.[24] His hatred of the reformers, it seems, was ecumenical.

The Irish-Gowan alliance with the old Tories was only one of expedience, and the two sides eyed each other like two crabbit bears in a cave. The alliance had to come apart and when it did the Irish attempted to shove aside not only the Buell-reformer forces but the two Jones families

---

21. MacPherson, 140.
22. On his health, see McCleary, 9.

   The cholera epidemic, in both its provincial and local dimensions, is covered in C.M. Godfrey, *The Cholera Epidemic in Upper Canada, 1832–1866* (Toronto: Secombe House 1968) and Geoffrey Bilson, *A Darkened House: Cholera in Nineteenth-Century Canada* (Toronto: University of Toronto Press 1980). On the British background of the epidemic see Robert J. Morris, *Cholera 1832: The Social Response to an Epidemic* (London: Croom Helm 1976) and Michael Durey, *The Return of the Plague: British Society and the Cholera, 1831–32* (Dublin: Gill and Macmillan 1979).

   The local papers, especially the *Brockville Recorder*, charted the epidemic locally with considerable care. Of course the epidemic was tragic, but for anyone who savours ironies, a letter in the *Recorder* of August 1832 is worth noting: eight prisoners in the debtors' ward of the Brockville gaol pleaded to be let out as they were certain that cholera had come to be lodged in the gaol walls. Among the eight were the names of two scions of two of the oldest loyalist families, James Breakenridge and W.H. Sherwood.
23. *Brockville Recorder*, 14 March 1833, and MacPherson, 142–3.
24. MacPherson, 143–4.

and the Sherwood Tories as well. Although virtually inevitable in its dissolution, the entente with the two Jones families and the Sherwoods ended [when Gowan sprang to the defence of a friend,] "Captain" James Gray, who was particularly obnoxious to the old established families. . . .

These events, which at our distance in time seem to be merely parish comedy, were deadly serious to contemporary participants, and they precipitated in Gowan and his Irish followers the determination to go ahead on their own in the approaching general election called for the autumn of 1834. In the event, Gowan's tactics proved to be audacious, brilliant, brutal, and successful, and at least temporarily he and his immigrant followers shoved aside both the Buell reformers and all the old Tory families.

His first step was to try to reduce the effective number of seats for Leeds county from two to one, by convincing the attorney general of Upper Canada, Robert S. Jameson, a gentleman recently over from England, to stand for Leeds. A government candidate such as Jameson was in theory above mere petty politics; he ran as a government candidate, not as a party man. Jameson accepted the invitation although he loftily indicated that he would be unable to visit the constituency.[25] It was a measure of Gowan's growing power that a senior government official would stand, if not with him, at least at his invitation. In inviting Jameson, Gowan was engaging in a double or nothing gamble. Assuming that Jameson won a seat (and, although not automatic, this was a strong probability), then, if Gowan took the second seat, both sets of Leeds county families, the reformers and the Tories, would be out and the Irish would dominate the political scene. The danger was that Gowan was doubly vulnerable: if he lost to either set of old families, he would be completely eliminated.

His second tactic was to have the government change the designated spot of voting in Leeds county from Farmersville in the southeastern quadrant of the county to Beverly (now Delta) located in Bastard township, well to the rear of the long-settled riverfront townships.[26] To understand what Gowan was doing one must realize that the electoral arrangements of the time were both vulnerable and visible. Electors cast their votes publicly at pollings which lasted several days and in which electors had the privilege of voting twice, albeit not for the same candidate. The Irishmen who supported Gowan were particularly efficient at

---

25. *Brockville Recorder*, 4 July 1834.
26. Senior, *Orangeism: The Canadian Phase*, 25.

gang fighting and, both in the Old World and the New, organized their factions with a skill which bordered on the military.[27] In fact, it was reported that in the spring of the preceding year, 1833, Gowan had held a meeting in New Dublin at which his Irish followers went through the early stages of forming their own paramilitary corps.[28] The report may have been a little hysterical, but the potential of Irish organized violence was real in a county in which the Orange lodges were strong. Moreover, Beverly was a perfect piece of ground on which Gowan could fight, for it was an active Orange centre and the local justice of the peace, Joseph K. Hartwell, was an Orangeman.[29]

In dealing with the Irish threat, both the reformers and the Tories were at times naive. The reformers, in late 1833, had flirted with the idea of an alliance with Gowan. Andrew Norton Buell informed his brother William that "Gowan seems coming around to the liberal side and perhaps with a little management might be brought full over...What would you think of a union between the Canadians [meaning the reform party] and the Irish and allowing G. to go in at the next election under strong pledges? Might it not allay the bitter feeling now existing between them and tend to draw them to support the course of reform?"[30] Andrew pondered the subject further, however, and decided "to go the whole length if practicable in the good old cause of reform," by which he meant that they should run two pure-reform candidates in the 1834 election.[31] This was just as well, as any attempt to bind Gowan with "strong pledges" would have been as effective as an attempt to harness the wind. A.N. Buell, though, discarded a Gowan alliance chiefly because he underestimated the Irishman: reform meetings throughout Leeds county held early in 1834 (including one in the front of Leeds and Lansdowne) condemned the conduct of the Upper Canadian assembly and extolled Mackenzie, and Buell believed that, as far as Gowan was concerned, the Gray affair had "put a damper on his expectations..."[32]

The old loyalist Tories were equally naive. They too saw the 1834

---

27. There is a considerable historical literature on Irish factions and secret societies, but both the substance and the flavour of Irish rural violence can best be obtained by reading the contemporary stories of William Carleton, "The Party Fight and Funeral," and "The Battle of the Factions," found in his *Traits and Stories of the Irish Peasantry*, which went through several editions in the nineteenth century.
28. *Brockville Recorder*, 25 April 1833.
29. MacPherson, 148.
30. A.N. Buell to William Buell, 12 December 1833, Public Archives of Canada (PAC), MG 24 B75.
31. A.N. Buell to William Buell, 29 December 1833, PAC, MG 24 B75.
32. A.N. Buell to William Buell, 28 January 1834, PAC, MG 24 B75.

election as a chance to rid the county of Gowan's influence, and they were all too willing to accept the advice of the Beverly magistrate J.K. Hartwell, a friend of the Charles Jones family, that Gowan had recognized that both he and Attorney General Jameson could not win and that by securing Jameson's election Gowan would then be in line to receive a political plum in some other district. Therefore, it was argued, the best thing to do was to ensure Jameson's election and the best way to do this was for all the "magistrates and their loyal Canadian population" to hold back from voting until the Gowanite force was spent and then "plump" (that is, use only one of each elector's two available votes) for Jameson.[33] Whether or not Hartwell intentionally was acting as cat's-paw for Gowan (he probably was), the effect was the same: the old Tory voters decided to hold back their votes.[34]

Then Gowan pounced, swiftly, crudely, and perfectly. The poll, which took place in Beverly, opened with the usual speeches by each candidate and with opposing groups massing around the hustings like teenage gangs in a schoolyard. There were minor scuffles. Most voters hung back, only slightly more than two dozen electors voting on the first day. On the second day of the poll several supporters of the reform ticket of Buell and Howard were hit, kicked, and had their clothes ripped, and some took some small knife wounds as they tried to vote: Gowan's men had surrounded the entrance to the hustings. The reformers tried to have the returning officer, Adiel Sherwood, keep order, but he held that his authority was good only on the hustings proper and not around them (a strange assertion given that he also was sheriff for the county, but his family was strongly anti-reformer). The magistrates present did little or nothing. On the third and fourth days the same tactics continued, with Gowan's Irish supporters intimidating the reformers who wished to vote and the old Tories, because of their ill-conceived theory of hanging back and then plumping against Gowan at the end, stayed away. Buell and Howard became convinced that they could not break through the line of Irish shillelaghs and after the fourth day retired. With the reformers out of

---

33. See quotations of letters from J.K. Hartwell to Charles Jones, 5 May 1834, in Richards, 181. Richards also paraphrases a further letter of approximately the same date from Hartwell to Jones. The dating of this second communication is vexed, but Richard's reasons for dating it close to the 5 May letter are convincing (182 n42).

34. Richards (182) suggests that Hartwell was duped. This is possible, but he was an Orangeman and slightly later came out unambiguously for the Gowan-Jameson candidacy (see MacPherson, 148–9). Hartwell could have been playing either or both sides of the game.

the fight, it was too late for the old Tories to do anything as Gowan and Attorney General Jameson were now far ahead, both over two hundred votes ahead of the nearest rival. Amazingly, Leeds county's seats were held by the attorney general for Upper Canada and by Ogle R. Gowan, Irish demagogue.[35]

35. The fullest reports of the election disturbances are found, not surprisingly, in the *Brockville Recorder*, 10 and 17 October 1834, and 7 November 1834. These accounts obviously were far from disinterested, as the paper was strongly pro-reform. The facts beneath the rhetoric, however, seem to have been accurate and were confirmed by subsequent governmental investigation.

Diary of James Lesslie, March 22–24, 1832

JAMES LESSLIE

22

clear and pleasant—

There are Bills posted up this day all over the Town headed "Great Meeting" to be held in Town tomorrow & calling upon every one who is Loyal to his King & to the Administration of the province to come forward (to put down the "*demagogues*" by an overwhelming Majority.)—Several caucus meetings have been held on this (to them) momentous affair, but no kind of exertion is making by the Reformers—a simple appeal to them in the public papers is all that has been done—

23 March

very fine weather—Spring is evidently at hand.—This day at 12 Oclock the "Great Meeting" assembled, and altho called by the Independants no sooner did the Gun fire at noon than the Sheriff stood up and proposed Dr. D. [William Dunlop][1] as Chairman—the other party nominated Jesse Ketchum as Chairman when a division was called for, & altho' there was not less than 2/3ds of the number present, on the liberal's side yet did the Sheriff decide it to be on the side of the Tories.—Dr. D. then attempted to address the meeting but very justly was not permitted being unfairly chosen.—J. Ketchum then took the Chair in a Waggon (for the Tories would not allow the other party to get access to the Chair on the Court House steps) & moved westward to prevent annoyance from them.—On the Chairs being taken & Mac [W. L. Mackenzie] & a few of his friends having stationed themselves beside the chairman—an attempt was made by the former to address the meeting—but no sooner was the attempt made than Hooting & Yelling from the Tories and their adherents prevented him from being heard.—The utmost good humour was shown

"Diary of James Lesslie, March 22–24, 1832," in *The Town of York 1815–1834: A Further Collection of Documents of Early Toronto*, ed. Edith Firth (Toronto: The Champlain Society, 1966): 134–37. Reprinted with permission of the publisher.

1. Dr. William "Tiger" Dunlop (1792–1848), born at Greenock, Scotland, was an army surgeon. He served in Canada during the War of 1812, and in 1826 returned with John Galt in the service of the Canada Company, eventually settling at Goderich. He represented Huron in the legislature from 1841 to 1846.

them in return:—their disturbance was returned by cheers and when all
attempts to excite angry feelings were found to be in vain—the Tories
tried another expedient—casting Stones—Rotten Eggs &c &c at the
Chairman & persons beside him.—during all these shamefull proceedings
the Authorities were among the disturbers of the peace and if they did not
aid them they did at least give them countenance—but some say they
were among the aggressors themselves. This further outrage against the
friends of Liberty excited not the least retaliation—but all was received
with the most patient Endurance.—Another & brutal expedient was then
resorted to.—A party of Irish Roman Catholics—evidently marshalled for
the purpose—armed with Clubs—made an attack upon the Waggon &
assailed indiscriminately everyone on the Liberal side—the latter prudently & wisely yielded & withdrew aside—The Table & Chairs in the
Waggon were shattered to pieces & used ["by them" interpolated] as
instruments of attack—some persons were severely injured and 1 or 2 it
was feared had their sculls fractured—particularly Shannon a shoemaker—all got out of the Waggon but Mr. Ketchum—& away the Savages
ran with it & were checked before the Court House by running against
one of the Limit Rails—Mac & others then ascended the Waggon a second
time—but these outrages being tolerated—no attempts being made by the
Magistracy to maintain peace & order—it was thought prudent & advisable to withdraw aside until order could be obtained—they did so, and after
the Tories thought they had accomplished their purpose—it was proposed
by the Sheriff that all who were favorable to the Government should walk
up & give his Excellency 3 cheers—a good expedient it was & without it—
doubtless there would have been bloodshed ere long as the Independents
had as yet shown no resistance.—A party—not one third of the meeting—
& composed of Clerks in office—dependent upon Executive favor—and
the very offscourings of Society—went west for that laudable purpose!—
There was then peace & order—the Friends of Liberty & order—assembled upon the ground which the Tories had held—Mac mounted the
chair—addressed the meeting on the blessings of our glorious constitution—the corruptions which existed here—and the necessity of manfully
upholding our rights particularly at this interesting crisis when the
Enemies of Civil & religious freedom were in array against us & evidently
trembled in prospect of the day of their just retribution drawing near.—

A *Resolution* was then passed without a dissentient voice approving of
the sentiments expressed in the petitions & address of July last when after
giving 3 cheers for King William & 3 for his Ministry the meeting
adjourned to Macs house & all who had not signed the address—did so—
and a great accession of numbers was thus obtained.—Just as the party

was returning from the Governors—a few of the Irish Catholics came out from *a very respectable neighbourhood* with an effigy of Mac—paraded up & down the Main St. with it—I saw the Sheriff & his party cheer them as they passed.—In the afternoon the same deluded wretches still under the influence of intoxication—attacked Mac's office & would have destroyed everything had not some defended it & the Magistracy then interfered after a declaration of the state of the Town had been made to the Governor.—In the evening arrangements were made for an attack upon his office & House & his life was to have been sacrificed but his friends well armed guarded the premises & the Magistrates were on duty during the Night—an attempt was about to be made against the office but timely interference prevented.—

The whole proceedings of this day have done more to strengthen the popular Cause and to bring the Authorities into merited unpopularity than any of their previous acts.—Many who were undecided are now alive to the danger they are exposed to under the present system by which reason & argument are not employed as a means of satisfying the popular mind— but the weapons of a pampered superstition are employed to crush those who dare to expose the nature & tendency of their acts as subversive of popular freedom and the best interests of Society.—The strength of their cause they have exposed by this days proceedings in the clearest point of view—& blind must they be who cannot detect the imbecility by which they are surrounded.

24

Clear & mild.—

Expressions having been used by some Roman Catholics to have Macs Life sacrificed before tomorrow—went to Baby & Mosley[2] to aid in his protection—remained to 1/2 past midnight & returned—no attempts having been made altho 40 or 50 had convened at a Tavern & were prepared had no means been taken to guard his premises

---

2. Henry M. Mosley was the son of the auctioneer, Thomas Mosley (1767?–1827), and carried on his father's business on King Street.

FURTHER READINGS FOR TOPIC 8

Michael S. Cross. "The Shiners' War: Social Violence in the Ottawa Valley in the 1830's." *Canadian Historical Review* 54 (1973): 1–26.

Gregory S. Kealey. "Orangemen and the Corporation." in *Forging a Consensus: Historical Essays on Toronto*, ed. Victor L. Russell. Toronto: University of Toronto Press, 1984.

Ian Ross Robertson. "Highlanders, Irishmen, and the Land Question in Nineteenth-century Prince Edward Island." In *Comparative Aspects of Scottish and Irish Economic and Social History 1600–1900*, ed. L. M. Cullen and T. C. Smout. Edinburgh, n.d.: 227–40; reprinted in *Interpreting Canada's Past, Vol. I: Before Confederation*, ed. J. M. Bumsted. Toronto: Oxford University Press, 1986: 360–73.

Scott W. See. "The Orange Order and Social Violence in Mid-Nineteenth Century Saint John." *Acadiensis* 13 (Autumn 1983): 69–92.

TOPIC 9

Rebellion:
In
the
Hearts
and
Minds
of
the
People?

W*hat caused the Rebellions of 1837–38 in Lower Canada? This is one*
of the most controversial issues in Canadian history, attracting the
interest of francophones and anglophones alike. Before 1960, historians
emphasized the political aspects of the conflicts between French and
English in Lower Canada in the years 1800–1837. This approach was
challenged in the late 1960s, when Fernand Ouellet began to stress the
importance of the socioeconomic causes of the rebellions. He argued that
the political conflicts were essentially a reflection of a developing
agricultural crisis after 1802. Economic hardships produced a defensive
nationalism among French-Canadian habitants; they became susceptible to
the arguments of their leaders, drawn from the professional classes, that the
British were responsible for their woes. Thus it was that the habitants
rebelled against the British, rather than against the French-Canadian
priests and landowners whose economic interests were also different from
their own. In the following selection from a brief biography of Louis-Joseph
Papineau, Ouellet highlights the social and economic conservatism, and the
distaste for a genuine social revolution, of that leader of the Lower
Canadian rebellion of 1837.

 William Lyon Mackenzie and Charles Duncombe, leaders of the Upper
Canadian rebellions, had fewer followers and less military success than

their counterparts in Lower Canada. The rebellions in the upper province lacked the bitterness imparted by the racial issue in Lower Canada. Moreover, historians have been unable to find convincing socioeconomic explanations for the rebellions, since supporters of both the government and the rebel leaders were similar in age, economic status, and religion, though it is true that the rebels were more likely to be of American origin. Read argues here that the rebellions in Upper Canada were in fact largely the work of one man, William Lyon Mackenzie, whose earlier career is discussed in Topic 8, and whose manifesto in favour of independence follows.

Papineau

FERNAND OUELLET

Papineau had taken up French Canadian nationalism as he had found it at the time of Bédard. This nationalism was at first pledged to the defence of linguistic rights and traditional institutions, which were in no way liberal and democratic, quite the contrary. In this connection Papineau, when weighing up the principal achievements of the House of Assembly, wrote: "The ecclesiastical institutions of the country would have been reduced to nothing, the notariat debased, not a single Canadien would be at the bar, and landed property would have been taxed to fatten a crowd of tax-collecting Europeans, if the administration had not been checked by the resistance of an elective Assembly." This judgement revealed more than a state of fact, it expressed a permanent element of Papineau's politics and thought.

Papineau had read the *philosophes* of the 18th century and the liberal thinkers of his day, and he declared himself a supporter of their doctrines. By his declamations against medieval feudalism, against nobles and aristocrats of all times, even on occasion against the descendants of the old French Canadian seigneurial families, Papineau might appear a bitter adversary of the old regime. His eulogies of the authors of the American Declaration of Independence and of the Declaration of the Rights of Man in France implied that he was in favour of a conception of property as individual and absolute and opposed to the feudal conception. In reality he remained throughout his life a supporter of the seigneurial regime. He would never admit openly that France had introduced feudal servitudes as well as seigneurial servitudes into Canada, and that the regime served as a support for a hierarchical and aristocratic society. This attitude might be explained by the fact that he was a seigneur himself. But Papineau saw in seigneurial tenure not only a traditional but also a national institution. Indeed in 1855 he wrote to Eugène Guillemot, the former French minister to Brazil: "My father had bought the seigneury he sold to me, being prompted and impelled by the desire to save the remains of our Canadien nationality from being stifled by the English government. Systematically

FERNAND OUELLET, "LOUIS-JOSEPH PAPINEAU," *DICTIONARY OF CANADIAN BIOGRAPHY*, VOL. 10 (1871–80) (TORONTO: UNIVERSITY OF TORONTO PRESS, 1972): 568–76. REPRINTED BY PERMISSION OF UNIVERSITY OF TORONTO PRESS.

the latter denied land to the Canadiens and lavished it upon the men of their own race, but placing it under the operation of English laws, pettifoggers' traps that would have swallowed up our compatriots who were unfamiliar with them." A year earlier he had attacked the Rouges: "The Rouges are hastening their bondage by their anticlericalism and their antiseigneurial attitude, for the clergy and the seigneurs are the country's safeguard." According to him the role of the seigneurial system had been to procure land free for the French Canadians and to protect them against the British, particularly against the merchants, who considered land as property of the capitalist type. Seen in this light the seigneurial system was supposed to act as a brake on the mobility of landed property and on speculation. Instead of concentrating property in a few hands, this system, according to Papineau, tended to divide up the land equally between individuals. The seigneur was not therefore a large landowner to whom a mass of *censitaires* were subject, but the unremunerated architect of equality. If the enormous abuses committed by the seigneurs of Lower Canada were pointed out to him, Papineau replied that the system had deviated from its intentions, and that all that was necessary was to restore its original purity by legislative and judicial means.

After 1830 Papineau became a democrat. Influenced by Thomas Jefferson and by Jacksonian democracy, he considered North America the natural site for the development of a republic of a small landowners. "Canada," he declared in 1833 in one of his speeches, "a country which is impoverished by the harshness of its climate, and in which laws and customs have always favoured the equal division of property, rejects substitutions, condemns the privileges of primogeniture, and should be the last place where such an inept measure should be attempted." Seeking to reconcile his democratic ideas and his attachment to the seigneurial system, Papineau tried to show that the Canadian temperament, the seigneurial system, and democratic ideology all pointed towards the same goal: equality of conditions. This rationalization concerning the seigneurial system and its social intentions was a pure creation of the mind, which was accepted by numerous supporters of the *Patriote* party. But the liberal wing of the party could not but come into conflict with Papineau on this point. The break occurred after the failure of the first insurrection in 1837. Robert Nelson wrote at that time: "Papineau has abandoned us, and has done so for personal and family motives related to the seigneuries and his inveterate love for old French laws." This uncompromising attachment for the seigneurial regime shows that Papineau was not prepared to consider a recasting of civil law. Despite the admiration that he professed for the Code Napoléon, it is clear that he could not accept the conception of property that had served as a basis for this legal revolution. Papineau recognized it himself: he was a liberal and democrat in politics but a conservative in regard to the "sacred right" of property. No better definition of economic and social conservatism can be found. By refusing to interfere with the seigneurial system, he sanctioned the status and economic privileges of the clergy.

Papineau's thought hardly obeys any formal logic. It fluctuates in accordance with his likings and aversions, conscious or unconscious, with his ambitions, his own interests and those of the people he represented. . . . All this tallies indifferently with the claims of Papineau, who posed as a rationalist philosopher and never missed an opportunity to point out the strictness and firmness of his principles. This rigid but poorly connected thought, which might be considered the product of conscious opportunism, reflects the complex personality of the man. His religious ideas in particular reveal his profound uncertainty. Gradually, after leaving the seminary of Quebec, Papineau drew away from Catholicism. While still believing in God, he finally rejected all revealed religions. It is obvious, although this is not the chief explanation for his religious evolution, that the influence of the 18th century *philosophes* and of the La Mennais of *Paroles d'un croyant* was of capital importance. He found in their works, as well as a stimulus to his anticlericalism, the kind of arguments that would confirm his religious, political, and moral attitude. Violently anticlerical, he showed himself to be also a sharp critic of religious education, the privileges of the church and the union of church and state. . . . When he returned from exile, he was to declare himself still more an enemy of nobles, priests, and kings, who were naturally in league against liberty and tolerance in all its forms. The Canadian clergy's attitude towards the Parti Canadien and the *Patriote* movement, and their close association with the state, no doubt helped to increase Papineau's anticlericalism. His religious experience was however accompanied by an authentic questioning of part of the Catholic heritage which had been handed down to every French Canadian of the period. To a certain extent, Papineau, as a political leader, attempted to adjust social institutions to his political and religious beliefs. He certainly envisaged society as a lay society, with churches separate from the state. He put forward and supported several measures with this design in mind. But in this domain he appears to have been surprisingly timid for an avowed liberal. In reality Papineau feared that by modifying the status of the Catholic Church he would play into the hands of the real or supposed enemies of the French Canadian nation.

Papineau saw in Catholicism a national institution, possessing, therefore, the same protective virtues as seigneurial tenure. If he saw the latter as French Canada's buckler against Anglo-Saxon capitalism, the Catholic Church appeared to him as the safeguard of this same nation against the Church of England—"the ally of the persecution that had been contrived against Canadiens"—and against a "Protestant" government. . . .

Papineau was hurt by the incomprehension of the Catholic clergy, who saw in him only a liberal and a democrat dangerous for the church, and he reproached them for equating "sovereignty of the people" with the overthrow of catholicism, for confusing popular sovereignty and national sovereignty without realizing that their real influence must be based upon the support of the French Canadian nation. In a letter to his wife, dated 9 Nov. 1835, he said: "They [the priests] are either knavish or *irresponsible* when they fail to see that there is one maxim the English government will never give up, namely the need to denationalize us in order to anglicize us, and that to accomplish this end they attack our church with no less ardour than they do our *laws, customs, and language*." His obsession with England so obscured Papineau's thinking that he postponed until later, perhaps to the day of independence, the pursuit of his liberal objectives in politico-religious matters. Meanwhile the clergy, under the aegis of Bishop Lartigue, were adjusting their ideology to the new age, without liberalizing it, and undertaking a struggle that in a few decades was to ensure them social supremacy. Papineau did not understand these innovations. Even after his return from exile in 1845, he continued to make similar declarations which, it must be said, were not inspired only by the desire to take back power from La Fontaine. Thus, in 1848, he declared in a public speech: "Our clergy come from the people, live in and for the people, are everything for the people, nothing without the people. Here is an indissoluble alliance. Here is a unity that is strength. . . .Here is a pledge of indissolubility for a nationality. . . .As a politician, I repeat that the agreement and affection between our clergy and our people has been and always will be one of the most powerful elements in the preservation of our nationality." These words throw light on the social conservatism of Papineau, which was incompatible with his religious liberalism. It is here that the contradictions of the man really appear: a deist, he remained nevertheless a prisoner of the social institution, the Catholic Church.

To this social conservatism, of which the seigneur of Montebello, attending church to set a good example to his *censitaires*, was the symbol, was added an economic conservatism. Certainly Papineau had felt the influence of the French physiocrats, who, opposed though they were to the feudal system, had exalted the prime importance of agriculture in the

French economy; but that is not enough to explain his particular emphasis. His economic conceptions were clearly dominated by the idea that the vast majority of French Canadians lived on the land and took a very small part in important commercial activities. For him, agriculture was the predominant economic activity, and any economic policy must proceed from that fact. In a word, the vital objective of French Canadians must be to acquire the land, making use of the framework most suited to its equal distribution and to a humane society: the seigneurial regime. His social ideal was the small farmer, virtuous and, perhaps, enlightened.

Papineau's hostility to commerce was no doubt rooted in tradition, but it also resulted from the fact that large-scale trading was controlled by the British, who were promoters of capitalism in all its forms. He believed that they were endeavouring to build an economy and a society in which the mass of the French Canadian proletariat, both urban and rural, would be dominated by a minority of men of large property of British origin. It was against this eventuality that he fought. It would be pointless to see in him a socialist. When he criticized English tenure and English common law, it was these tendencies that he was condemning. When he objected to the establishment of government registry offices, it was always through fear of the same dangers. Papineau came to the point where he pictured the English business bourgeoisie as an aristocracy of wealth, and therefore an artificial one, which was aspiring to reinstitute in Canada a society founded on inequality. "It seems to me," he said during the debate on the Ninety-two Resolutions in 1834, "that there is nothing baser than the English nobility who come to us in this country, so eager are they to place themselves and to enrich themselves." As his democratic ideas became more deeply rooted, Papineau, the seigneur, saw the merchant classes more and more as the product of an aristocratic plot fomented by England herself. Thus, in objecting to the timber trade, to massive investments in transportation, which was undergoing a total upheaval, and to banks, he had the feeling that he was working against those responsible for the economic bondage of the French Canadians, and he believed also that he was doing away with a developing aristocracy. After recommending to the population that they withdraw their money from the banks, he declared in December 1834, before the electors of Montreal West: "They will call that destroying trade, whereas in reality it will merely be escaping from enemy hands to fall into friendly ones. Producers will continue their habits of work and economy, the only important sources of a country's wealth. Whether there are banks or not, there will not be one acre more farmed, or one acre less. From the moment that there is a surplus of exchangeable produce, the European capitalists, in view of the profit they would derive from it, will have it bought up." This attitude towards banking institutions recalls that of the Jacksonian democrats. In reality the resemblances are only superficial.

This stand is surprising in a man who professed to be the disciple of Adam Smith and Jean-Baptiste Say. In practice, Papineau had retained from his reading of the two economists only their philosophy of free trade. By taking fragments of their thought, he was able, in addition to acquiring allies in England, to combat the protective tariffs on Canadian timber and grain. He needed an effective weapon against the business world, where his chief political opponents were. Finally, even his belief in free trade reveals the ultra-conservatism of his economic thought.

Papineau's nationalism was therefore strongly rooted in his economic and social conservatism. Even on the religious plane, his aims and liberal aspirations were compromised by this dominant attachment to tradition. Seen in this perspective, his political liberalism and his adherence to democratic ideology raise similar questions, for it seems difficult to reconcile fundamental conservatism and doctrinaire liberalism. When we try to determine the roles that these two facets of his thought were called upon to play, the contradiction can be partly resolved. It is clear that in accepting French Canadian nationalism, such as it was at the time of Bédard, Papineau was at the same time endorsing the political strategy which, in order the better to protect the traditional institutional and cultural heritage, aimed at the assumption of power by a "truly national élite." Even if Papineau tended to present himself as the "national leader" and the authorized spokesman of the French-Canadian nation's aspirations and interests, he none the less remained the real representative of a more restricted section of society. His strong ties with the liberal professions, which were aspiring to power and the benefits of patronage, are in this respect most significant. His presentation of himself as a man of principle above factions, as a pure symbol of a will towards national regeneration that was beyond all the pettiness of daily action, came both from his personality and from the image of himself that he wished to project. Papineau, despite a gift for oratory which would have enabled him to put himself on the people's level, was not by inclination a popular speaker. The great majority of his speeches were intended for a more educated group. His political friends even reproached him with not maintaining steady contact with the populace. Thus, when he spoke of the "people" and the "nation," he referred more to a minority that knew the real needs of the worthy masses. His liberalism was therefore in the last analysis bourgeois or even aristocratic. In this sense he belonged to his century.

When Papineau entered politics in 1809, he shared the unbounded admiration of the Lower Canadian élites for British institutions. Montesquieu, Voltaire, and several other eighteenth century *philosophes* had already extolled the merits of the English constitution. The English were moreover the first to see in their political institutions a matchless achievement. Papineau wrote: "My education is more English than French. Indeed it is in the English publicists and in the writings of public men that I have studied the English constitution." He took part in the war of 1812 as a militia captain, for at that period Papineau refused to accept republicanism and democracy after the French or American manner. He remained an ardent monarchist, although he had broken with the absolutist tradition. His attitudes towards the "aristocratic branch" may not be clear; on the other hand his belief in the primacy of the "popular branch" grew stronger over the years. From the beginning of his political involvement, his place was among the Reformers. Certainly one can see here the influence of John Locke in particular, but there were other and more varied influences working upon him. Basically, he looked to the constitutionalists and to active politicians, both in the colonies and in England, for the justification of political choices that he had already made. It is in his nationalism that one must seek the principal source of his reform attitudes. . . .According to him, the constitution of 1791 was supposed to give Canadiens a political instrument destined to ensure the survival of their culture and institutions. On the other hand, according to him, the working of these institutions after 1792 had attributed a kind of supremacy to the governors, the officials of British origin, and the English merchants, who had formed an alliance with the two French Canadian groups least conscious of national objectives: the clergy and the old seigneurial families. In his opinion, the political structures had been manipulated by elements that were hostile to or little aware of the real interests of the French Canadian nation. As to the actual representatives of the nation sitting in the assembly, their influence was almost nil. It was because of this subjective way of looking at the balance of political forces that Papineau accepted the idea of the responsibility of the executive. The aim of those who subscribed to this thesis was to get the real power into the hands of those whom he was to call later "the national representation." After his rise to the leadership of the Parti Canadien in 1815, Papineau, always with this perspective in mind, brought the struggle to bear on the control of public funds. While attacking the French Canadian nation's enemies on all possible fronts, he made the voting of supplies the priority question in his political strategy. Behind the discussions of principles and constitutional theories, Papineau, whose interests were linked to those of the liberal professions, led the fight for the conquest of political power. His movement, which was based on liberal ideas, was in essence primarily nationalist. It was this surface liberalism that won him the cooperation of the English radicals.

Until around 1830, Papineau remained convinced the British institutions constituted a perfect framework for the survival and development of the French Canadian nationality. It was sufficient to model the local constitution on that of England, and allow it to evolve according to the same principles. Moreover, the fact of belonging to the empire was a guarantee against the United States, and in general against American influence. In his mind, the good faith of Britain could not be called in question. The opponents of the French Canadians, he thought, resided in Lower Canada. They were at times the governors, ill counselled by their entourage, but particularly the highly placed officials and the merchants. For him, certain groups within the French Canadian nation, such as clerics and nobles, represented a danger, for they did not understand their true interests. There were also those who, for personal motives, rallied to the side in power. If he thundered against all these types of people, he never questioned the validity of the bonds that united Lower Canada to the mother country. Already in 1823, however, on his trip to England, he was struck by the aristocratic character of English society and the poverty of the urban masses, and began to ask himself questions. In Lower Canada too, economic and social uneasiness was spreading discontent in the rural milieux. The overcrowding in the liberal professions, and the instability of the lower bourgeoisie in country districts and towns, also suggested the need for more radical political action. The influence of the Paris revolution of 1830 was another invitation to take a more extreme stand. Increasing social tensions were having a hardening effect in all sections of society. Papineau let himself be carried along by this prevailing mood, which worked in his favour. It must be said that the growth of his ambitions coincided with his successes. Despite the concessions made by England, the beginning of the 1830s saw the stepping-up of demands. Papineau's thought tended to turn in another direction.

From that time on Papineau believed in the existence of a plot between the mother country herself and the internal enemies of the French Canadians, the object being the complete subjection of the latter by the implantation of an aristocratic society in Lower Canada....Quite obviously, Papineau was seeking to prove that the colonial system was an instrument by which British institutions could be used to ensure economic, political, and social control for an aristocratic minority imported from Great Britain. His rejection of English institutions was only partial, and to the extent that they served his political objectives he was loyal to them. . . .

Papineau's past distrust of the United States now gave place to unstinted admiration for American institutions. In 1832 Papineau declared himself a republican. The influence of Jacksonian democracy on him is not in doubt; that of Jean-Jacques Rousseau and later of Charles-Alexis-Henri Clérel de Tocqueville is also present. American democracy was, according to him, the reflection of a sort of state of nature peculiar to America. . . .

At bottom Papineau, while retaining from the English constitution what served his political strategy, was to draw from the American model a theoretical justification for the radical transformation of the Legislative Council. The latter would need to be elective because of the fundamentally democratic character of the society of Lower Canada. . . . By means of ministerial responsibility, the *Patriote* party and Papineau would have made sure of the control of the executive and the public service; through an elected Legislative Council and the extension of the elective principle to lower levels, the party would have dominated the second legislative branch and the other sources of power. In the light of this naturally democratic society, where the seigneurial regime, the customary law of Paris, and the privileges of the church would still exist, one can understand that Papineau's opponents should question his real objectives. They would certainly not feel that their economic interests and those of the country would be in good hands if Papineau gained his ends.

The idea of instituting by peaceful means a Lower Canadian republic, of which he would naturally be the president, took shape after 1830. By the practice of obstruction, and in particular by the systematic refusal to vote supplies, Papineau proposed to force the British government to bring about radical changes. Nevertheless, in 1834, as is shown by his speech to the electors of Montreal West, he would presumably have been satisfied with a statute allowing a large measure of autonomy, within the empire, for Lower Canada: "A local, responsible, and national government for each part of the Empire, as regards settlement of its local interests, with supervisory authority held by the imperial government, to decide on peace and war and commercial relations with foreign countries: that is what Ireland and British America ask for; that is what within a very few years they will be strong enough to take, if there is not enough justice to give it to them." The Ninety-two Resolutions introduced in the House of Assembly on 17 Feb. 1834 were intended to make clear Papineau's aspirations and political ideas. These resolutions, prepared by a small committee composed of Papineau, Elzéar Bédard, Augustin-Norbert Morin, and Louis Bourdages, contained a summary of the principal grievances of the house and of its most important requests: control of revenue by the legislature, responsibility of the executive, and the election of legislative councillors. In the following year, when a certain number of *Patriotes* contemplated without apprehension the possibility of a violent confrontation, Papineau wrote: "We will not withdraw the requests we have made for the full measure of our political powers and rights.... We hope, but with some unease, that the British government will give us justice. In this hope we will do nothing to hasten our separation from the mother country except to prepare the people and make them ready for an age that will be neither monarchical nor aristocratic." This weakening of the belief in normal political strategies on the part of the Montreal *Patriotes* continued until 1837, when London, by adopting the resolutions of Lord Russell, categorically rejected the *Patriotes'* requests, which it deemed excessive. This formal refusal precipitated a confrontation that rapidly took on the character of a revolutionary movement.

Papineau's behaviour during the 1837 insurrection is not very easy to explain. His conduct appeared more ambiguous than ever, and he also took care to destroy the documents that he knew to be compromising. He warned his subordinates to do likewise. After the event, he maintained the following argument: the *Patriotes* did not intend to revolt; the government, in order to crush them the more effectively, had forced them to defend themselves; and he himself had advised against any recourse to arms. He also declared that he had had no connection with the Banque du Peuple, thereby admitting the justice of the accusations made against that institution. He said that it was only on his way through Saint-Charles that he had gone to the assembly there, and that he had left Saint-Denis at the beginning of the fight only at the express request of Wolfred Nelson. According to his interpretation, he was supposed to keep himself in a safe place in order to be able to act as a negotiator in case of a defeat. It is obvious that, taken as a whole, this explanation does not stand up against a serious examination of the facts.

During the months of April and May 1837 the *Patriotes* put their strategy into shape. Unanimity does not seem to have prevailed among them. The radical wing, dominated by people such as Nelson, Cyrille-Hector-Octave Côté, Édouard-Étienne Rodier, Amury Girod, and Thomas Storrow Brown, certainly opted for openly revolutionary steps. On his side, Papineau represented the more prudent and moderate elements and appears to have favoured more complicated tactics: that while opinion was being prepared for an armed struggle, action should in the first stage be kept within the bounds of "constitutionality." He thought that by stirring up the population and boycotting taxed products, the English government would finally be forced to give way. Under Papineau's direction, the Comité Central et Permanent du district de Montréal, reorganized on 15 May 1837, was to coordinate the action of the *Patriotes* throughout the entire province. If however these methods proved ineffective, he would then agree to the use of force. In this contingency, armed revolt was not to take place until December, after the freeze-up. On 10 May 1837 Papineau drew up two wills. In 1839, Abbé Chartier wrote: "It is unfortunate that Lord Gosford [Acheson] did not put off his attack until after 4 December, the day for which all the leaders received notice to be at Saint-Charles, and when you would have had to sign a declaration of independence: you would not have to defend yourself today against the charge of not wanting a revolution because no contradictory document exists." Abbé Chartier added that he had himself destroyed a note sent by Papineau to the *Patriote* Jean-Joseph Girouard. As well as having been widely known among Lower Canadian *Patriotes* since at least June 1837, this plan had also been communicated to the revolutionaries of Upper Canada. . . .

Once the series of great assemblies in the six counties got under way, Papineau quickly lost control of a number of the revolutionary leaders, who openly preached revolt and sought to direct the movement towards a revolution of a social character, which no doubt the directors of the Banque du Peuple and Papineau scarcely desired. For his part, Papineau, even if he recommended sticking to legal means, encouraged initiatives of a revolutionary character by what he said. This was how the Association des Fils de la Liberté came into being: divided into two sections, civil and military, it "reproduced the double intention of the plan of resistance" advocated by Papineau. This surge of agitation reached its highest point at the time of the great assembly at Saint-Charles, which on 23 Oct. 1837 issued a declaration of the rights of man. Papineau went to Saint-Charles accompanied by an armed escort. A few days earlier Papineau's wife had told her son Lactance, a student at Saint-Hyacinthe, that his father might visit him after the assembly. This assembly truly marked a turning-point. For the radical elements it constituted a virtual declaration of independence and the beginning of a trial of strength between them and the government. As for Papineau, he still urged the use of peaceful means. Forgetting the revolutionary nature of several resolutions passed on that occasion, he later reproached the radicals for having prompted the government, by their behaviour, to intervene before the moment appointed for the uprising.

After the Saint-Charles assembly, Papineau's behaviour appears more and more ambivalent. Indubitably he was afraid. In particular the way the liberals acted frightened him, but at the same time served his ends. His interviews with Denis-Benjamin Viger, before his forced departure from Montreal, are significant of the conflicts within the man himself. The government's decision to arrest the leaders and intervene militarily forced him to go the Richelieu valley. Once he got to Saint-Denis, he acted both as supreme commander, distributing generalships, and as the leader of the civil section. It was probably at the time when these civil and military sections were set up that arrangements were made, perhaps at the direct or indirect suggestion of Papineau himself, to provide cover, in the event of an emergency of a military nature, for the two promoters of the civil section: Papineau and O'Callaghan. Seen from this angle, the visit, after the arrest of Louis-Michel Viger, of Édouard-Raymond Fabre, who no doubt had important news to transmit, may merely have hastened the departure of the two men. Once in the United States, Papineau travelled under an assumed name. Meanwhile he had forgotten his role as a negotiator.

The months that followed marked the break between Papineau and the extreme radical elements of the movement. The *Patriote* leader had met influential Americans, who were ready to back a retaliatory expedition. This plan was not adopted at the assembly of refugees held at Middlebury, Vermont, because Papineau refused to accept a declaration of independence involving the abolition of seigneurial rights, customary law, and titles. His intransigence, more, than differences over strategy, explains the profound disagreement that gradually divided the refugees. It is possible that the religious question also counted for something in this conflict. Dr Thomas Fortier, of Gentilly, wrote to Duvernay in 1840: "I am neither a Jesuit nor a bigot; but when one wants to revolutionize an ignorant people, one must be acquainted with its spirit and not offend its prejudices, but rather utilize them as a stimulus—your railing against the clergy and the tithes has spread terror among this body, they have taken alarm; they have had the idea that you would follow the course of the French revolutionaries, that you would despoil them; [Robert] Nelson's proclamation did not reassure them." It is obvious that Papineau was linked with those *Patriote* elements, clerical or anticlerical, that closely associated religion and nationality. The attitude of Jean-Philippe Boucher-Belleville, who stated around 1840 that anticlericalism was no longer justifiable, since all the parish priests had become nationalists, is significant. That Papineau should have supported the endeavours of Abbé Chartier, who was seeking to modify the anticlerical fever among the refugees, is also revealing. Thus the gap widened more and more between the two groups.

Papineau consequently kept aloof from any invasion plan, at the same time as he tried to obtain the support of the French, Russian, and American governments. The insurrection of 1838 took place without his participation. He was opposed to the venture, yet he did not protest when the leaders of the second rebellion used his name as rallying cry to stir the population to revolt. . . .

From the spring of 1838 on, the refugees' hostility towards Papineau increased. Not only did they reproach him with having abandoned the cause, but they attributed to him more and more responsibility for the failure of 1837. Several went so far as to talk about his flight from Saint-Denis. Côté spoke of exposing him publicly. But several refugees tried to stop an action that would harm the movement, because of Papineau's extraordinary popularity among the people. In October 1839 Dr. Antoine-Pierre-Louis Consigny wrote to Duvernay: "No one blames Papineau more strongly or detests him more heartily than I do; but for the sake of the cause, I believe it is better to keep silent than to try to lay low the arrant poltroon who is the principal source of all the evils that have weighed so heavily on the country since 1837." After the failure of the second insurrection, the refugees, convinced that Papineau's presence in the United States was a basic obstacle to any revolutionary plan, worked out a plot to get him away to France. Papineau was to win French sympathy for the Lower Canadian cause. On 8 Feb. 1839 he sailed from New York for Paris. . . .

The Rising in Western Upper Canada 1837–8:

The Duncombe Revolt and After

COLIN READ

On 3 November 1838 the Reverend A.N. Bethune, editor of the Anglican newspaper, *The Church*, sought to explain the rebellion in Upper Canada. Since the French Revolution, he argued, there had been unceasing conflict between anarchy and infidelity on the one hand and subordination and true religion on the other. There were 'unquiet spirits in every country,' and it would be 'strange if the moral convulsions of Europe, and the nearer agitations of the American republic should leave these infant Provinces unscathed.' His comments demonstrated the Tory conviction that in a world plagued by revolutionary ferment good citizenship and morality were to be found on the side of constituted authority.

Whatever the merits of his explanation of the causes of the rebellion, Bethune was correct in assuming that 'unquiet spirits' had been instrumental in producing it. Foremost of these was William Lyon Mackenzie, leader of the radical Reformers. Before the elections of 1836 he had been an influential but not necessarily the primary voice decrying the abuses of the existing régime. Though he himself was defeated in 1836, his own position among the Reformers was strengthened, for several leading moderates withdrew from policies in disgust after being defeated or, as they thought, cheated at the polls. Mackenzie and the Radicals subsequently moved to mobilize the rank and file, creating political unions and planning a great Reform convention in Toronto in December. Their cause was aided by the severe economic depression in the province which exacerbated existing grievances. In November 1837 Mackenzie organized his rebellion in Toronto. As we have seen, the first news reaching the west reported Mackenzie victorious, and Charles Duncombe and others raised a second insurrection, a hurriedly organized, ill-coordinated one whose immediate origin lay in the erroneous report from Toronto.

To muster men, Duncombe and his cohorts spread various stories, among them reports that the authorities intended rounding up leading local Radicals and turning the Six Nations warriors loose upon the rest. To John B. Askin the many 'false' representation made were 'most plausible'

Colin Read, *The Rising in Western Upper Canada 1837–8: The Duncombe Revolt and After* (Toronto: University of Toronto Press, 1982): 205–12. Reprinted by permission of University of Toronto Press.

and 'insiduous'[1] and after the suppression of the revolt, both he and Allan McNab[2] argued that such reports had led many astray. After the rebellion many captured rebels offered explanations for having joined Duncombe's force in group petitions begging for clemency. Sixty-eight provided such explanations individually in depositions sworn before examining magistrates. Only five of the latter said they had taken up arms because they had believed false information. If the story of Mackenzie's victory at Toronto is regarded as false information, however, it is reasonable to argue that all the rebels had been deceived, that none would have been in the ranks had they known the real situation. This may explain, in part, why the insurgents who petitioned the government after the rebellion for pardon or leniency characteristically argued that they had been seduced from their allegiance 'by wicked and designing' men.[3]

One report that was effective in persuading men to take up arms was that of the arrest and imprisonment of John G. Parker at Hamilton. Though embellished in successive retellings, the basis of the story was true and lent credibility to the rumour that the authorities intended jailing local Radicals. Fourteen of the sixty-eight rebels who individually explained why they had joined Duncombe declared that it was the report of Parker's confinement which had persuaded them. Most wished either to avoid Parker's fate or to free him from jail or both.

The promise of material rewards had apparently influenced the 103 rebels who petitioned MacNab en masse for clemency in December 1837 at Sodom. They had been led to revolt 'by Charles Duncombe, Eliakim Malcolm, and other wicked and designing leaders, who have induced us by promise of large grants of land and great pay for our services, to take up arms against Her Majesty's Government.'[4] Doyle McKenny, the Malahide justice of the peace, thought that James Malcolm's 'promise of 200 acres of land' had led '30 or 40' Bayham men to rebel.[5] Other Tories had no doubt that the rebels coveted their property. A Burford woman claimed that captured documents revealed that Duncombe's men had intended to 'murder every Tory's wife and child' and take over their farms.[6] One can

---

1. Askin to John Joseph, London, 22 Dec. 1837, C.R. Sanderson, ed., *The Arthur Papers* I (Toronto, 1957): 34
2. Dispatch from MacNab, Sodom, 18 Dec. 1837, *Patriot* (Toronto), 22 Dec. 1837
3. Petition of 103 Norwich inhabitants, *Patriot* (Toronto), 22 Dec. 1837
4. Ibid.
5. McKenny to Edward Ermatinger, 11 Dec. 1837, C.O. Ermatinger, *The Talbot Régime* (St. Thomas, 1904): 357
6. Catherine _____ to 'My Dear Mother,' Burford, 11 June 1838, Mrs. Peter D. Luard, 'Oxen, Candles and Homespun', in *A Glimpse of the Past* (Brantford, 1966): 20–1

imagine that some Tories in the immediate aftermath of the revolt might have believed this report but the rebels were neither as bloodthirsty nor as covetous as it suggests.

It is unlikely that the prospect of financial gain provided the primary motivation for many rebels. Only two of those who individually gave their reasons for taking up arms (sixteen-year-old Augustus Chaple of Yarmouth and a recent newcomer to the province, George Conklin of Norwich) admitted having done so in the hope of receiving material reward.[7] Presumably, if others had similar hopes, they would have been too astute to admit them to examining magistrates. It is unlikely, however, that many rebels shared Chaple's and Conklin's hunger for personal gain. Most were better off than either, being neither as young as the one nor as recently arrived as the other.

In fact, most known to have mustered under Duncombe were relatively mature, well-settled, prosperous members of an agrarian community. This seems to have been true, documentary evidence suggests, of the Duncombe insurgents generally. In the regional society of the west neither clear economic nor social conditions distinguished loyalists from rebels. There is no basis for arguing that the rebels comprised a clearly disadvantaged sector of society and hence were driven to arms by economic despair or the prospect of plunder. Indeed, if the evidence of eleven apprehended Norwich insurgents who jointly petitioned for clemency is to be believed, they had joined Duncombe's men because they feared for their own property: 'most of us have been prevailed upon to take up arms against the country partly by threats used by the leading members of the rebel party, partly under the conviction that the Rebels were by far the most numerous part of the population, and that if we refused to fight for that party our lands and property would be confiscated.'[8]

Nine rebels testified in their depositions that threats against their persons rather than their property had led them to muster with Duncombe. A tenth, Abraham Sackrider of Norwich, swore that he had been dragooned, that his brother-in-law and Duncombe, after fruitlessly trying to persuade him to join their cause, 'took him to the Inn and gave him something to Drink and when Deponent was in liquor they got him into a

---

7. Deposition of Chaple, 15 Dec. 1837, *Upper Canada Sundries* (UCS), 181/99925–6. Deposition of Conklin, 21 Dec. 1837, UCS, 180/99727
8. Petition of Jacob S. Esmond et al., n.d., Public Archives of Canada (PAC), Petitions and Addresses, 9

Baggage Waggon and took him to Oakland' where he was kept under guard.[9]

Doubtless some men were tricked or forced into the rebel ranks but, generally, if a man really wished to avoid service with the insurgent troops he could do so. For example, John Treffry of Norwich, a pacifist, adamantly refused the order of rebel sergeant to shoulder arms.[10] Duncombe himself was perfectly willing to leave the Tories alone, provided they swore not to combine against him or his men.[11]

The closely knit nature of much of western Upper Canada's agricultural society helps to explain the involvement of many men in the western rebellion. The Beamers of Oakland, Burford, and Townsend, the Kellys and Yeighs of Burford, the Bedfords, Dennises, Nicholls, Tuttles, and Thompsons of Norwich, the Cavanaughs and Doans of Yarmouth, the Moores of Yarmouth, Malahide, and Dereham, the Cooks of Bayham, the Hagles of Dereham, and the Spragues and Stewarts of Dumfries all sent two or more men from their families to the Oakland camp as, of course, did the Malcolms. One or two of these families, like the Cavanaughs, were British in origin, but most were American.

The rebels of British descent evidently fell into two broad categories. Some, particularly those from the south of Yarmouth and its area, were young men who were perhaps naturally inclined to rebel against constituted authority and only too anxious to seek a little diversion from the tedium of everyday life. Others generally appear to have lived in the province for a number of years and to have settled among North Americans. Perhaps influenced by their neighbours and the passing of time, they no longer felt the necessity of demonstrating loyalty to the existing government with its bonds to Britain. It is noteworthy that in the west those from Great Britain who had settled among their fellow-nationals, or who had emigrated to the colony in the 1830s when adult, were either neutral in the rebellion or active partisans for the government. They were not members of the rebel force.

The majority of rebels were either American-born or the offspring of American parents and may well have retained or adopted the deep American dislike of Britain and have been more willing to rebel, hoping to

---

9. Deposition of Sackrider, 27 Jan. 1838, PAC, Records of the London District Magistrates (RLDM), II
10. John Treffry to George Treffry, Norwich, 24 June 1838, UWO, Treffry Letters
11. See evidence of Joseph J. Lancaster, Archives of Ontario (PAO), Upper Canada State Papers (U.C.S.P.), 45/146

sever the provincial ties to Great Britain. Indeed, Charles Duncombe told Abraham Sackrider that 'he was going to take the country and make it independent.'[12] William McGuire, a school-teacher, and James and Eliakim Malcolm were reported to have said that the rebels would install in Upper Canada 'an independent Government, without any connection with the Queen or the Mother Country, Great Britain.'[13] Fifteen or twenty rebels apparently vowed, as they marched to join Duncombe, 'that they were determined to overthrow the British government...asserting as their reason that the taxes had been raised and that the governor wanted to put tythes upon them as they did in the Old Country.'[14] Two other rebels, however, David Nicholls, whose family was probably American, and Preserved Thompson, who was an American, claimed that the Oakland revolt was raised merely to 'set up a constitutional' or 'Reform Government.'[15] Whether or not most rebels understood that the revolt was to establish an independent government or just to reform the one they had, their American birth or parentage probably conditioned their response to the rebel call.

Some rebels claimed to be complete political innocents, however. Several told examining magistrates that they had played no part in politics before December 1837. A further eleven alleged that they had been unaware that their actions constituted rebellion. In 1838 barrister John Strachan of Hamilton, representing seven of them, insisted that they were 'obscure Peasants,' who were 'chiefly ignorant men, who had little knowledge of their duty as Subjects and thought little more of the insurrection into which they were seduced, than any common quarrel at a fair or Township Meeting. Few of them Know the nature of allegiance, and having no intention of actual rebellion were as much astonished at being accused of treason, the meaning of which they scarcely yet comprehend, as if they had been accused of Witchcraft.'[16]

Other rebels asserted that Duncombe and others had played on the insurgents' naïveté. Paul Bedford declared that Duncombe had suggested that the rebels in taking up arms were not, in effect, rebelling, for British

---

12. Deposition of Sackrider, 16 Dec. 1837, R.C. Muir, *The Early Political and Military History of Burford* (Quebec, 1913): 14
13. Deposition of Peter Coon, 17 Dec. 1837, in E.C. Guillet, *The Lives and Times of the Patriots* (Toronto, 1963): 250
14. Deposition of John Beard, 10 Dec. 1837, PAO, Snyder Papers
15. Deposition of Nicholls, 17 Dec. 1837, UCS, 180/99400. Deposition of Thompson, 17 Dec. 1837, UCS, 180/99402
16. Strachan to Durham, Hamilton, 30 Aug. 1838, UCS, 204/113343–4

precedent sanctioned an appeal to arms by an outraged and wronged populace.[17] Another insurgent, Malcolm Brown, stated that the rebel leaders told their men that they were 'loyal subjects, and determined to rely upon lawful and constitutional means to effect what they conceived to be necessary and reasonable reforms.'[18] Mahlon Burwell, however, firmly told his regiment: 'Every man of sane mind must have known that in quitting his peaceful home and joining the rebel vagrants with arms in his hands, and putting his loyal and peaceful neighbors in fear of being murdered, and their properties plundered, he was guilty of Treason.'[19]

Detailed lists of those attending the political meetings of the fall of 1837 are not available, but newspaper accounts, depositions, and so forth reveal that no less than eighty of the 197 rebels identified in this study had attended them. Also, twenty-four of the 197 are known to have been politically active prior to September 1837, voting in elections, signing partisan petitions, holding township offices, and so on. It is unlikely, therefore, that the leaders could have duped the majority of the rebels by pretending they were not engaging in rebellion. The leaders were instrumental in persuading men to turn out, however, by the force of their personalities and their positions in the area. In the essentially rural townships affected by the uprising, the local personalities were the ones most often admired and emulated. They were a living presence and example for those about them in a way that more widely known figures in Toronto could not be. Of the sixty-eight insurgents who gave their personal reasons for being involved in the revolt, two claimed to have been led astray by unnamed individuals, while no less than twenty-six identified specific people such as Charles Duncombe, Eliakim or Finlay Malcolm, whose arguments and example had induced them to take up arms.

In sum, the Duncombe rising would never have occurred had the rebels known the true state of affairs at Toronto. Those who answered the call to arms believing Mackenzie's revolt successful were certainly misled. Doubtless some men had their own reasons for turning out, a particular grievance against the government, for example, the loss by executive decree of a disputed lot to another claimant[20] or the confiscation of

---

17. Petition of Bedford, 19 March 1838, UCS, 194/107986
18. Petition of Brown, Hamilton Gaol, 20 March 1838, UCS, 189/105538, 105541
19. Regimental Order of Burwell to the Second Middlesex, *Patriot* (Toronto), 30 Jan. 1838
20. This happened to accused rebel Michael Tripp of West Oxford in 1832. PAO, Township Papers, West Oxford, documents for lot 16, Broken Front, and lots 10 to 16, concession 1

property for non-payment of taxes.[21] Others were driven by the desire for material gain, while others simply did not appreciate the significance of their actions. None the less most rebels turned out for similar reasons and purposes. Most were not members of the Church of England and so had not been exposed to its teachings about the necessity of loyalty to the Crown and the sanctity of the colonial tie. Most were North American in lineage as their local communities were in character. They were thus inclined to welcome change in a government which could be construed as British and colonial. In addition, significant numbers had been Reform partisans. Finally, when prominent men they knew as friends or relatives called them to arms, they responded.

Whatever the rebels expected to achieve for themselves and for Upper Canada, their hopes were disappointed. Their revolt was soon crushed by loyalist forces and they themselves put to flight. Subsequent events have led most historians to assert that the triumphant Tories then instituted a 'reign of terror.' The Tories did perpetrate some abuses, of course, particularly against the rebels who had been captured and confined in the Gore district jail at Hamilton. Most were not even examined on their arrival at the Gore jail, and no regular procedures were established to grant them bail. None the less, the great majority of those with whom the government dealt for their parts in the Duncombe rising were treated leniently, in the context of the times. Those times had witnessed the patriot raids upon the province, which had heightened the fears of the loyalists and contributed to the prevailing air of uncertainty and suspicion. That atmosphere helped to persuade some to leave the province and convinced others that Upper Canada's economic and political future was clouded indeed. Judging by its immediate repercussions, the Duncombe rebellion, like the Mackenzie revolt, produced more harm than good.

Apologists for the Canadian rebellions of 1837 have taken the longer view, arguing that the rebels hastened the advent of responsible government by forcing the Colonial Office to send out Lord Durham, who strongly advocated that principle, thereby transforming it into a great and forceful political cry. This view does not sufficiently weigh the fact that Durham's recommendation was ignored by British officials and responsible government was not achieved until 1848. Rather than hastening the advent of responsible government, it is as likely that the rebellions delayed it by discrediting and discouraging the Reformers, particularly

---

21. In 1831 John Malcolm lost lot 1, concession 14 of Walsingham for non-payment of taxes, PAO, Abstract Index to Deeds for Walsingham, 917

those in Upper Canada. Indeed, in much of the province the Reformers took years to regain their strength.

In western Upper Canada, however, the Reformers and Radicals evidently suffered only temporary reversals by being identified with the revolt. In August 1839 that Reverend Mr Proudfoot noted that the Reformers were active once again and were determined to destroy the Family Compact.[22] That year Thomas Parke and George Hackstaff inaugurated a new Radical newspaper at London[23] and Elisha Hall, one of the leaders of the rebels in West Oxford in 1837, recorded that 'from what I can see the reformers are more noisey than ever in Norwich. I heard they taned the toris in stile, and in Oxford on the fourth of June they ware as dosile and harmless as she doves.'[24] Indeed, the Reformers in Norwich were so 'noisey' in 1839 that a belligerent Tory, John George Bridges, who had settled in the township in the wake of the rebellion, found it politic to flee it.[25] To the south-east of Norwich, in Norfolk, Charles Duncombe's brother, David, retained his influence among the Baptists, who were very 'numerous in that county, and nearly all reformers.'[26] His weight was deemed sufficient in 1840 to 'insure the election of any liberal candidate that he would support.'[27] Such evidence suggests that further detailed research is needed to judge the full effect of the Duncombe revolt on the Reformers of the west.

The long-term effects of the Duncombe rising on the political fortunes of the western Tories need further study as well. The generalization that most citizens of the town of London, which became an imperial garrison, were reinforced in any Tory inclinations is time-worn, and no historian has yet probed more deeply into the fate of the western Tories in the decade or so after the rebellion. The revolt did provide the Tories with a benchmark, however, in that for years to come a man would be asked what he had done during the rebellion. If he had not turned out against the rebels, he must have been disloyal then and, in all probability, was disloyal still. Such was the line of reasoning of an anonymous correspondent to Woodstock's *British American* who impugned Benjamin Van Norman's loyalty. Van Norman, a principal in the Long Point iron works,

---

22. Proudfoot to William Peddie, London, August 1839, UWO, Proudfoot Papers
23. James Hunter to W.L. Mackenzie, 18 Oct. 1839, PAO, Lindsey Collection, Mackenzie Correspondence
24. Hall to W.L. Mackenzie, Lewiston, 10 May [1839?], PAO, Lindsey Collection, Mackenzie Correspondence
25. PAO, Tidey Diary no. 2, 11 May 1839
26. James Durand to Robert Baldwin, Toronto, 26 Feb. 1840, TPL, Robert Baldwin Papers, sec. 1
27. Ibid.

was not considered a loyal subject because he had taken 'no part in the valorous proceedings of certain parties in the London District during the famous years of 1836–37 [sic].'[28]

For such Tories the exploits they had performed in 1837–8 were indeed 'valorous;' they felt they had reaffirmed the allegiance of Upper Canada to Great Britain and saved the colony from republicanism. Peril emanated both from the American settlers of the west whose loyalties remained suspect for years (leading Sir John A. Macdonald to comment in 1856 that they helped form 'the most yeasty and unsafe of populations')[29] and from the Americans themselves, whose designs upon the colony had been revealed once more by the patriot raids. Like the Mackenzie revolt and its aftermath, the Duncombe rising and its repercussions led to a reaffirmation of that part of Tory tradition which insisted that America and Americans be watched with care for both were devious and predatory. This attitude has had an enduring history in Canada, and its reinforcement was one of the most significant results of the Duncombe rising and of the rebellion period generally.

---

28. *Oxford Star and Woodstock Advertiser*, 15 Dec. 1848
29. Fred Landon, *Western Ontario and the American Frontier* (Toronto, 1941): 232

INDEPENDENCE

WILLIAM LYON MACKENZIE

Appeals To The People

Independence

There have been Nineteen Strikes for Independence from European Tyranny, on the Continent of America. They were all successful! The Tories, therefore, by helping us will help themselves.

> The nations are fallen, and thou still art young,
> The sun is but rising when others have set;
> And tho' Slavery's cloud o'er thy morning hath hung,
> The full tide of Freedom shall beam round thee yet.

BRAVE CANADIANS! God has put into the bold and honest hearts of our brethren in Lower Canada to revolt—not against "lawful" but against "unlawful authority." The law says we shall not be taxed without our consent by the voices of the men of our choice, but a wicked and tyrannical government has trampled upon that law—robbed the exchequer—divided the plunder—and declared that, regardless of justice they will continue to roll their splendid carriages, and riot in their palaces, at our expense—that we are poor spiritless ignorant peasants, who were born to toil for our betters. But the peasants are beginning to open their eyes and to feel their strength—too long have they been hoodwinked by Baal's priests—by hired and tampered with preachers, wolves in sheep's clothing, who take the wages of sin, and do the work of iniquity, "each one looking to his gain in his quarter."

CANADIANS! Do you love freedom? I know you do. Do you hate oppression? Who dare deny it? Do you wish perpetual peace, and a government founded upon the eternal heaven-born principle of the Lord Jesus Christ—a government bound to enforce the law to do to each other as you would be done by? Then buckle on your armour, and put down the villains who oppress and enslave our country—put them down in the name of that God who goes forth with the armies of his people, and whose

---

WILLIAM LYON MACKENZIE, "INDEPENDENCE," BROADSIDE DISTRIBUTED ABOUT NOVEMBER 27, 1837. IN *THE SELECTED WRITINGS OF WILLIAM LYON MACKENZIE 1824–1837*, ED. MARGARET FAIRLEY (TORONTO: OXFORD UNIVERSITY PRESS, 1960): 222–25.

bible shows us that it is by the same human means whereby you put to death thieves and murderers, and imprison and banish wicked individuals, that you must put down, in the strength of the Almighty, those governments which, like these bad individuals, trample on the law, and destroy its usefulness. You give a bounty for wolves' scalps. Why? Because wolves harass you. The bounty you must pay for freedom (blessed word) is to give the strength of your arms to put down tyranny at Toronto. One short hour will deliver our country from the oppressor; and freedom in religion, peace and tranquillity, equal laws and an improved country will be the prize. We contend, that in all laws made, or to be made, every person shall be bound alike—neither should any tenure, estate, charter, degree, birth or place, confer any exemption from the ordinary course of legal proceedings and responsibilities whereunto others are subjected.

CANADIANS! God has shown that he is with our brethren, for he has given them the encouragement of success. Captains, Colonels, Volunteers, Artillerymen, Privates, the base, the vile hirelings of our unlawful oppressors have already bit the dust in hundreds in Lower Canada; and although the Roman Catholic and Episcopal Bishops and Archdeacons, are bribed by large sums of money to instruct their flocks that they should be obedient to a government which defies the law, and is therefore unlawful, and ought to be put down, yet God has opened the eyes of the people to the wickedness of these reverend sinners, so that they hold them in derision, just as God's prophet Elijah did the priests of Baal of old and their sacrifices. Is there any one afraid to go to fight for freedom, let him remember, that

> God sees with equal eye, as Lord of all,
> A Hero perish, or a Sparrow fall.

That power that protected ourselves and our forefathers in the deserts of Canada—that preserved from the Cholera those whom He would—that brought us safely to this continent through the dangers of the Atlantic waves—aye, and who watched over us from infancy to manhood, will be in the midst of us in the day of our struggle for our liberties, and for Governors of our free choice, who would not dare to trample on the laws they had sworn to maintain. In the present struggle, we may be sure, that if we do not rise and put down Head and his lawless myrmidons, they will gather all the rogues and villains in the Country together—arm them—and then deliver our farms, our families, and our country to their brutality—to that it has come, we must put them down, or they will utterly destroy this country. If we move now, as one man, to crush the tyrant's power, to establish free institutions founded on God's law, we will prosper, for He who commands the winds and waves will be with us—but if we are cowardly and mean-spirited, a woeful and a dark day is surely before us.

CANADIANS! The struggle will be of short duration in Lower Canada, for the people are united as one man. Out of Montreal and Quebec, they are as 100 to 1—here we reformers are as 10 to 1—and if we rise with one consent to overthrow despotism, we will make quick work of it.

Mark all those who join our enemies—act as spies for them—fight for them—or aid them—these men's properties shall pay the expense of the struggle—they are traitors to Canadian Freedom, and as such we will deal with them.

CANADIANS! It is the design of the Friends of Liberty to give several hundred acres to every Volunteer—to root up the unlawful Canada Company, and give *free deeds* to all settlers who live on their lands—to give free gifts of the Clergy Reserve lots, to good citizens who have settled on them—and the like to settlers on Church of England Glebe Lots, so that the yeomanry may feel independent, and be able to improve the country, instead of sending the fruit of their labour to foreign lands. The fifty-seven Rectories will be at once given to the people, and all public lands used for Education, Internal Improvements and the public good. £ 100,000 drawn from us in payment of the salaries of bad men in office, will be reduced to one quarter, or much less, and the remainder will go to improve bad roads and to "make crooked paths straight;" law will be ten times more cheap and easy—the bickerings of priests will cease with the funds that keep them up—and men of wealth and property from other lands will soon raise our farms to four times their present value. We have given Head and his employees a trial of forty-five years—five years longer than the Israelites were detained in the wilderness. The promised land is now before us—up then and take it—but set not the torch to one house in Toronto, unless we are fired at from the houses, in which case self-preservation will teach us to put down those who would murder us when up in the defence of the laws. There are some rich men now, as there were in Christ's time, who would go with us in prosperity, but who will skulk in the rear, because of their large possessions—mark them! They are those who in after years will seek to corrupt our people, and change free institutions into an aristocracy of wealth, to grind the poor, and make laws to fetter their energies.

MARK MY WORDS, CANADIANS!

The struggle is begun—it might end in freedom—but timidity, cowardice, or tampering on our part will only delay its close. We cannot be reconciled to Britain—we have humbled ourselves to the Pharaoh of England, to the Ministers, and great people, and they will neither rule us justly nor let us go—we are determined never to rest until independence is ours—the prize is a splendid one. A country larger than France or England; natural resources equal to our most boundless wishes—a government of equal laws—religion pure and undefiled—perpetual peace—education to all—millions of acres of lands for revenue—freedom from British tribute— free trade with all the world—but stop—I never could enumerate all the blessings attendant on independence!

Up then, brave Canadians! Get ready your rifles, and make short work of it; a connection with England would involve us in all her wars, undertaken for her own advantage, never for ours; with governors from England, we will have bribery at elections, corruption, villainy and perpetual discord in every township, but Independence would give us the means of enjoying many blessings. Our enemies in Toronto are in terror and dismay—they know their wickedness and dread our vengeance. Fourteen armed men were sent out at the dead hour of night by the traitor Gurnett to drag to a felon's cell, the sons of our worthy and noble minded brother departed, Joseph Sheppard, on a simple and frivolous charge of trespass, brought by a tory fool; and though it ended in smoke, it showed too evidently Head's feelings. Is there to be an end of those things? Aye, and now's the day and the hour! Woe be to those who oppose us, for "In God is our trust."

FURTHER READINGS FOR TOPIC 9

Gerald Craig. *Upper Canada: The Formative Years 1784–1841*. Toronto: McClelland and Stewart, 1963.

Allan Greer. "From Folklore to Revolution: Charivaris and the Lower Canadian Rebellion of 1837." *Social History* 15 (January 1990): 25–42.

J. K. Johnson. *Becoming Prominent: Regional Leadership in Upper Canada, 1791–1841*. Kingston and Montreal: McGill-Queen's University Press, 1989.

Fernand Ouellet. *Lower Canada 1791–1840: Social Change and Nationalism*. Toronto: McClelland and Stewart, 1980.

Colin Read and Ronald J. Stagg. *The Rebellion of 1837 in Upper Canada*. The Champlain Society jointly with Carleton University Press, 1985; distributed by Oxford University Press, Don Mills, Ontario.

Carol Wilton-Siegel. "Administrative Reform: A Conservative Alternative to Responsible Government." *Ontario History* 78 (June 1986): 105–25.

TOPIC 10

Natives and the Environment: The Western Perspective

T*he prairie West has been the primary focus of studies on the fur trade, but the business was important elsewhere as well. The effects of the fur trade on the Maritimes after 1600 were explored in Upton's article in Topic 1; here, Robin Fisher discusses the fur trade on the other coast, which began later and endured well into the nineteenth century. The fur trade west of the Rockies differed considerably from that of the prairies in a number of ways, originating as a sea-based rather than a land-based venture and involving the natives of British Columbia, whose cultures were so different from those of the plains natives. Like Upton, Fisher stresses the extent to which natives could retain their autonomy as long as it was the fur trade which dominated the economy. While the fur trade did not prevent changes in the native way of life, these changes were generally positive and could be controlled by the natives. In Fisher's analysis, the relationships between natives and Europeans in the context of the fur trade were those of mutual dependency, not of domination by one race or the other.*

The fur trade on the prairies, meanwhile, was entering a period of decline. Intense competition in the late eighteenth and early nineteenth centuries between the Hudson's Bay Company and companies based in Montreal depleted the animal population of the prairies. The merger in 1821 of the principal Montreal enterprise, the North West Company, with the Hudson's Bay Company, put an end to cutthroat competition and allowed fur traders to consider how to preserve and increase existing stocks of fur-bearing animals. Hudson's Bay Company strategies for conserving the beaver in the pre-1841 period are detailed in A. J. Ray's article. The excerpt from Daniel Williams Harmon's journal discusses some of the methods prairie natives employed for killing animals.

THE LAND-BASED FUR TRADE

ROBIN FISHER

Although the [Hudson's Bay] Company was moving closer towards the establishment of a trading monopoly, the Indians still formed the second half of a mutually beneficial economic partnership. Contemporary critics of the company often assumed that it had an absolute control over the Indians. Frequently, however, these assertions were based on politics rather than facts and revealed the prejudice of the critic not the realities of the frontier. As a monopoly, the company offended current economic dogma in England, and since monopolies in general were pernicious, critics reasoned, this particular monopoly must have been bad for the Indians. In the United States the company was vilified by those who saw it as a hindrance to settlement. Missionaries and humanitarians also tended to denigrate the influence of the company on the Indians, claiming, for example, that the company held the Indians in slavery.[1] But these views were based, at best, on superficial knowledge of the fur trade west of the Rockies and, at worst, on total ignorance.

Certainly the Indians involved in the trade became dependent on the company for European goods, but no more than the Company was dependent on the Indians for furs. Some forts even had to rely on the Indians for their very sustenance, and were therefore doubly dependent. Indians who were relied on for provisions took every advantage of their position, just as they did in other aspects of the trade.[2] Some company traders appreciated the restrictions that their dependence placed upon them in their dealings with the Indians. Soon after the establishment of Fort Langley, the company traders, irritated by Indian stealing, wanted to demonstrate their "disapprobation of so knavish a behaviour." They

ROBIN FISHER, "THE LAND-BASED FUR TRADE," *CONTACT AND CONFLICT: INDIAN–EUROPEAN RELATIONS IN BRITISH COLUMBIA, 1774–1890* (VANCOUVER: UNIVERSITY OF BRITISH COLUMBIA PRESS, 1977): 35–48. REPRINTED WITH PERMISSION OF THE PUBLISHER.

1. See *The Hudson's Bay Question [from the "Colonial Intelligencer"]* (London: W. Tweedie, 1857), p. 24; Frank E. Ross, "The Retreat of the Hudson's Bay Company in the Pacific North-West," *Canadian Historical Review* 18 (1937): 263; and [Herbert Beaver], "The Natives of the North West Coast of America," *Extracts from the Papers and Proceedings of the Aborigines Protection Society* 2 (1841): 140.
2. William Bean to John Tod, 20 June 1840, Hudson's Bay Company Archives (HBCA), B-37/a.

refused to allow any Indian to land near the fort, yet at the same time they realized that the "want of fresh Provisions will soon compel us to concede a little in regard to this restriction." Naturally, the journals are not littered with such comments, for the admission of dependence was not in accord with the white sense of superiority. But Fort McLoughlin was similarly dependent, and Duncan Finlayson pointed out in a letter to his superiors that their living would be precarious as long as the Indians had to be relied on for food.[3]

Like Europeans, Indians became fur traders because they perceived that there were benefits to be gained, and during the fur trade the Indians still had other options. Some preferred not to be involved in the trade and found it possible to exercise that choice. . . .

When the trading partnership was established, however, the Indian and the fur trader shared certain interests, and the best evidence that both recognized them is the relative lack of hostility between the two groups. . . .The nature of the fur traders' relationship with the Indians restrained any desire for wholesale extermination. Unlike other frontier situations, the fur trade placed no premium on dead Indians. . . .

It was argued, in the context of litigation on the land question in the twentieth century, that the establishment of forts by the Hudson's Bay Company constituted a conquest of the area that became British Columbia.[4] In reality, the Indians accepted the existence of trading posts out of self-interest rather than fear, and therefore they can hardly be described as a conquered people during the fur-trading period.

Another measure of the reciprocity of the traders' dealings with the Indians was the nature of their relationship with their Indian wives. The temporary liaisons that were typical of the maritime fur trade continued, but in addition there were more permanent relationships. There was evidently some concern that Indian women and their children were being deserted by traders, for the Council of the Northern Department passed an order in 1824 requiring all officers and servants to make adequate provision for their Indian women, not only while they were resident in the

---

3. J. MacMillan and A. McDonald, "Fort Langley Journal," 1 and 2 September 1827, ms. Public Archives of British Columbia (PABC); Duncan Finlayson to McLoughlin, 29 September 1836, E.E. Rich, ed. *The Letters of John McLoughlin from Fort Vancouver...*, First Series (London, 1941), p. 324.

4. Canada, Parliament, Senate, *Journals*, 16th Parl., 1st sess., 1926–27, Appendix to the Journals of the Senate. . . .Special Joint Committee of the Senate and House of Commons Appointed to Inquire into the Claims of the Allied Indian Tribes of British Columbia..., *Report and Evidence* (Ottawa: F. A. Acland, King's Printer, 1927), p. vii.

country but also after their departure.[5] Probably there were discrepancies between the ideal of the order and the reality of its execution, but some traders did build lasting relationships based on mutual respect with their Indian wives. The pull of the metropolitan society was still strong, and traders were aware that their frontier marriages might be frowned upon in the "civilized" world. Charles Ross, in a letter to his sister, felt it necessary to deny that he was ashamed of his Indian wife. While she was not exactly fitted to grace a nobleman's table, he said, she suited the sphere in which she had to move.[6] John Work described his wife as "an affectionate partner" who took "good care of my children and myself"; but in his opinion it was out of the question for an Indian wife to join "civilized society."[7] Work's views notwithstanding, some traders did take their Indian wives with them when they left the fur trade.[8] The tedium of much of their existence prompted traders, even those who were initially determined not to do so, to seek the companionship of Indian women. Apart from the personal advantages, such unions were often also good business. Although wives involved the company in additional expenses, even the economy-minded Simpson saw that they were "a useful link between the traders and the savages." In fact, during the Athapaska campaign he had positively urged traders "to form connections" with the daughters of Indian leaders because "connubial alliances are the best security we can have of the goodwill of the Natives."[9]. . .

The company's drive for profit even affected the most personal aspects of the lives of its servants and officers, but for the Indians this same

5. Minutes of the Council of the Northern Department, 10 July 1824, in R. Harvey Fleming, ed., *Minutes of the Council of the Northern Department of Rupert Land, 1821–1831* (London: Hudson's Bay Record Society, 1940), pp. 94–95.

6. Ross to Mrs. Joseph MacDonald, 24 April 1843, W. Kaye Lamb, "Five Letters of Charles Ross," *British Columbia Historical Quarterly* (1943), p. 107.

7. Work to Edward Ermatinger, 15 February 1841 and 1 January 1836, "Letters of Edward Ermatinger from John Work, William Tod, Jane Klyne McDonald, and Archibald McDonald, 2 January 1828-14 November 1856," University of British Columbia Library (UBCL).

8. Ibid.; Daniel Williams Harmon, Journal, 8 May 1819, in W. Kaye Lamb, ed., *Sixteen Years in Indian Country: The Journal of Daniel Williams Harmon, 1800–1816* (Toronto: Macmillan, 1957), pp. 194–95; Ross Cox, *Adventures on the Columbia River*...(New York: J. & J. Harper, 1932), p. 311.

9. Sir George Simpson, *Narrative*, 1 (London, 1847): 231; Simpson to governor, deputy governor and committee, 18 May 1821, in E. E. Rich, ed., *Journal of Occurrences in the Athapaska Department by George Simpson, 1820, and 1821, and Report* (London: Hudson's Bay Record Society, 1938), p. 392.

singlemindedness defined the limits of the traders' impact on their culture. Like those who had come by sea, the land-based fur traders made limited demands on the Indians and did not attempt to initiate major cultural change. On the contrary, the company had a considerable investment and interest in keeping much of the Indian way of life intact. Obviously it did not want to see the kind of radical change that would prevent the Indians from being efficient fur hunters. For this reason there was little intrusion on Indian land during the fur-trading period. The Indians retained their village sites, and their hunting and fishing grounds were unmolested. The company was often chided by humanitarians for its lack of philanthropic concern for the Indians and for doing little to "raise their level of civilization." Although it had moments when it tried to deny these charges, the company really had little interest in making major "improvements" to the Indian way of life. "Philanthropy," wrote Simpson in a pointed understatement, "is not the exclusive object of our visits to these Northern Regions, but to it are coupled interested motives." In short, he concluded, "Beaver is the grand bone of contention."[10]

Their efforts to acquire furs from the Indians did sometimes lead traders to attempt to modify Indian behaviour. They preferred, for instance, to see the Indians gathering furs rather than engaging in internecine warfare. When "War, and not Skins" seemed to occupy the Indians' attention, traders became concerned about returns. The obvious response was to try to settle disruptive intertribal conflicts by negotiation. Although Simpson denied it before the 1857 committee on the Hudson's Bay Company,[11] traders did sometimes try to act as mediators between warring parties of Indians. They wanted the Indians to recognize that the forts were neutral ground where all were free to trade; the Indians were told that their disputes should be settled elsewhere.[12] Traders also tried to act as peacemakers in intertribal conflicts that had no connection with the fur trade. In 1835 John Work was concerned about the effects of continued hostility between the Fort Simpson Tsimshian and the Kaigani Haida. He saw that peaceful relations between the two groups would enable the Haida to come to the fort more frequently, so he took Legaic's son to deliver a message from his father to the Kaigani in the hope that it would

---

10. Simpson to governor, deputy governor and committee, 18 May 1821, Rich, *Journal of Occurrences*, p. 356.

11. Great Britain, Parliament, House of Commons, *Report from the Select Committee on the Hudson's Bay Company; together with the Proceedings of the Committee, Minutes of Evidence, Appendix and Evidence* [London: 1857], p. 92.

12. Fort Simpson, Journal, 25 April 1839, HBCA, B-201/a; Roderick Finlayson to McLoughlin, 11 January 1845, HBCA, B-226/b.

facilitate settlement.[13] In all efforts of this kind, however, the company men could use only moral suasion. They were in no position, and had no desire, to use force. Consequently their peacemaking attempts often met with failure. Sometimes traders were simply told to mind their own business,[14] while on other occasions would-be mediators had to desist because their efforts only excited the Indians' derision.[15]

"Conjuring" (the word that Work used to describe Kwakiutl winter ceremonial) was another activity that the traders thought diverted the Indians' attention from hunting. The existence of slavery in Indian society also disturbed some company men. But these were integral parts of the Indian way of life and could not easily be eliminated, or even modified, particularly as the traders had to move with extreme care in their occasional efforts to bring about change. The need for great caution was explained by Douglas in a letter to the governor and committee of the company. He wrote that "undesirable" practices could be discouraged

> by the exertion of moral influence alone, carefully avoiding direct collision either with their selfish feelings or inveterate prejudices, as I don't feel justified in exposing our interests to the shock of excitement and desperate animosity which more active measures, on our part, might provoke.[16]

As long as the traders had to be so circumspect about interfering with Indian social customs and the Indians were still in a position to reject these efforts, control of their society remained in Indian hands.

There were some changes in Indian culture that were brought about inadvertently by the land-based fur traders. The shift from trading with vessels to trading at forts reduced the wealth of those Indian groups living on the outer fringes of the coast. As the traders moved inland, the groups who had reaped the benefits of the maritime fur trade experienced a declining standard of living. It appears that the Nootka could make no effective response to this experience, and they lapsed into obscurity as far as European traders were concerned.[17] The Queen Charlotte Haida, on the

---

13. Work, Journal, 20 February 1835.
14. Duncan Cameron to Donald Mason, 11 November 1844, quoted in A.G. Morice, *History of the Northern Interior*...(Toronto, 1904), pp. 216–17.
15. Letter of John McLeod [1823], "Journals and Correspondence of John McLeod...1812–1844," PABC.
16. Douglas to governor, deputy governor and committee, 18 October 1838, Rich, *McLoughlin's Letters, First Series*, p. 238.
17. John Scouler, Journal, 31 July and 3 August 1825, "Dr. John Scouler's Journal of a Voyage to N.W. America," *Quarterly of the Oregon Historical Society* 6 (1905): 193–94.

other hand, made definite efforts to accommodate themselves to the changed situation. In 1825 the botanist Dr. John Scouler was on the coast, and later he recorded some perceptive observations of the Indian inhabitants. He noted that when the sea otter had abounded around the Queen Charlottes, the Haida were among the most wealthy Indians on the coast, but that with the depletion of the fur-bearing animals they became poorer. To offset this decline in wealth, the Haida looked for other sources of income. They began to cultivate potatoes and sell them in large quantities both to the mainland Indians and, after it was established, at Fort Simpson. The potato became their staple trading article, but Scouler also reported that the Haida "fabricate most of the curiosities found on the coast," and these too were traded. The Haida were turning the superb artistry of their wood carving to profit. Not only were "curiosities" carved in wood, and later in argillite, produced for export, but also their fine cedar canoes were manufactured for sale.[18] In these ways the Haida supplemented their trade in potatoes and regained some of the wealth they lost by the passing of the fur trade from their shores.

Disease was still a factor which the Indians could not control, and for the historian the difficulties of accurately assessing its impact still remain. Permanent contact with Europeans undoubtedly did little to reduce the incidence of venereal disease among the Indians. Mercury treatment was a frequent necessity at the forts, and there are references to cases of both gonorrhoea and syphilis,[19] both of which were passed on to the Indians. Smallpox was also taking Indian lives. Reports of outbreaks became more frequent in the 1830's, and there are comments about the "dreadful ravages" of smallpox taking "great numbers" of Indians. But the evidence is seldom more specific. Douglas wrote in 1838 that reports indicated that smallpox had killed one-third of the Indian population on the northern coast, but the Reverend Herbert Beaver, writing the following day, claimed that the disease had only taken one in three of those attacked.[20]

18. John Scouler, "Observations of the Indigenous Tribes of N.W. Coast of America," *Journal of the Royal Geographical Society of London* 11 (1841): 219; John Dunn, *History of the Oregon Territory and British North American Fur Trade*...(London: Edwards and Hughes, 1844), pp. 293–94.
19. F. Merk, *Fur Trade and Empire, George Simpson's Journal*...(Cambridge, Mass., 1931), p. 99; Simpson *Narrative*, 1: 207; Joseph McGillivray, "Report of Fort Alexandria," 1827, HBCA, B-5/e; MacMillan and McDonald, "Fort Langley Journal," 7 September 1827.
20. Douglas to Simpson, 18 March 1838, Rich, *McLoughlin's Letters, First Series*, p. 271; Beaver to Benjamin Harrison, 19 March 1838, in Thomas Jessett, ed., *Reports and Letters of Herbert Beaver 1836–1838*...(Portland, Ore.: Champeog Press, 1959), p. 88.

All such estimates have to be treated with caution, particularly when they were based on Indian reports. Dr. William Fraser Tolmie, who by profession took a great interest in the incidence of disease, claimed that experience had taught him to place little faith in Indian accounts of the severity of outbreaks because of their tendency to exaggerate misfortune.[21] By 1838 deaths from smallpox should have been decreasing as a result of a fairly extensive programme of vaccination of Indians by company traders.[22] Besides venereal disease and smallpox, measles and respiratory diseases were also prevalent among the Indians. The combined effect of all these complaints was undoubtedly a quickening of the death rate, but the exact degree of mortality cannot be ascertained.

With the possible exception of loss of trade, and the definite exception of disease, the social change stimulated by the fur trade could be controlled by the Indians. During the period of the land-based fur trade the developments in Indian culture were of two kinds. There were changes that involved the quantitative development of traditional aspects of Indian society, and, secondly, there were qualitative innovations introduced into the culture. There were changes in degree, and there were changes in kind.

Those developments that were an elaboration of existing features of Indian culture after the 1820's were largely a continuation of change begun by the maritime fur trade. Intertribal acculturation was stimulated as more frequent trading contacts between Indian groups provided opportunities for cultural borrowing. Indian art forms continued to flourish, particularly among the tribes of the northern coast, not just because metal tools made wood carving easier but also because new wealth allowed more of the ceremonial that accompanied the erection of a totem pole. There is little doubt that the fur trade produced an increase in the number and size of potlatches among the coastal Indians. It has been suggested that an absence of references to the potlatch in the fur trade literature demands a re-evaluation of its development.[23] In fact, there are numerous contemporary accounts of the ritual to support the equally numerous

---

21. W.F. Tolmie, *Journal*, 18 August 1833 (Vancouver, 1963), p. 227. On the tendency of the Indians to generally exaggerate misfortune see Lewis O. Saum, *The Fur Trader and the Indian* (Seattle and London: University of Washington Press, 1963), p. 159.
22. McLoughlin to governor, deputy governor and committee, 1 August 1838, Rich, *McLoughlin's Letters, First Series*, p. 217; Tod, "History," p. 86.
23. Saum, *The Fur Trader*, p. 11.

scholars who contend that the potlatch flourished during the fur trade.[24] The florescence of art and ceremonial that occurred on the northwest coast was perhaps exceptional among North American Indian reactions to European contact, but there is strong evidence that such a response did occur.[25]

The qualitative changes in Indian society included the rise of new leaders who specialized in dealing with European traders. Leaders like Legaic at Fort Simpson and Kwah among the Carrier assumed this role. It was company policy to deal with these leaders and to enhance their authority by bestowing honours upon them. Because of the special treatment they received from the company traders, these leaders were subject to the jealousies of other Indians,[26] but their enormous wealth helped them to withstand challenges to their leadership. In Indian society an individual's position was related to the amount of goods that passed through his hands, so trading chiefs were well placed to maintain and increase their prestige. Legaic's trade monopoly with the upper Skeena Indians "was a very rich privilege," and the traditions record at least one occasion on which he was able to defeat a threat to his life and position posed by the other Tsimshian tribes simply because his wealth was so much greater than theirs. Legaic's rivals were humiliated when con-

---

24. For an early and very detailed account of a potlatch see Magee, "Log," 9 July 1794, photocopy, UBCL. For other references see J.M. Moziño, *Noticias...*(Toronto and Montreal, 1970), p. 33; "Hoskins' Narrative," January 1792, F.W. Howay, "*Voyages of the* Columbia (Boston, 1941)," p. 265; John R. Jewitt, *A Journal...*(Boston, 1807), 12 November 1803, p. 12; John Dunn, *History of the Oregon Territory...*(London, 1844), p. 282; [Peter Skene Ogden?], *Traits of American-Indian Life and Character, by a Fur Trader* (London: Smith, Elder, 1853), pp. 65–67. This last should have been noticed by Saum as the work is frequently cited by him in other contexts. For more recent accounts of the potlatch see Helen Codere, *Fighting with Property: A Study of Kwakiutl Potlatching and Warfare 1792–1930*, Monographs of the American Ethnological Society, no. 18 (Seattle and London: University of Washington Press, 1966), pp. 89–97; June McCormick Collins, "Growth of Class Distinctions and Political Authority among the Skagit Indians during the Contact Period," *American Anthropologist* 52 (1950): 336; Phillip Drucker, "Rank, Wealth and Kinship in Northwest Coast Society," *American Anthropologist*, n.s. 41 (1939): 63; Homer G. Barnett, *The Coast Salish of British Columbia* (Eugene: University of Oregon Press, 1955), p. 256.

25. Cf. Robert F. Murphy and Julian H. Steward, "Tappers and Trappers: Parallel Process in Acculturation," *Economic Development and Cultural Change* 4 (1956): 353; Innis, *The Fur Trade*, p. 18.

26. Fort McLeod, Journal, 7 January 1823, HBCA, B-11/a.

fronted by his great wealth.[27] While increased wealth consolidated the power of certain leaders, it also increased the possibilities for social mobility in some groups.[28] The establishment of forts often required other social adjustments on the part of the Indians. When the nine Tsimshian tribes moved to Fort Simpson, they all lived at the same place for the first time, and an acceptable order of rank, both for phratries and for individuals, had to be established. Legaic certainly had initial advantages, but his pre-eminence was the result of a continuing process of social reordering.

As well as affecting the social hierarchy within Indian groups, the fur trade produced shifts in the intertribal balance of power. The expansion of the Kwakiutl as far south as Cape Mudge was a post-contact phenomenon,[29] and their new power was partly based on wealth acquired by manipulating the fur trade. Increased concentration on hunting fur-bearing animals brought changes in concepts of land ownership among some groups. The fur trade induced Indians to return to the same trapping territory year after year, and among the Sekani the result was the development of family hunting territories.[30] Simpson may have been describing an intermediate stage in the same development when he noted that around Fort St. James beaver hunting grounds belonged to particular families, while the rights to smaller furs were held in common.[31]

Clearly the fur trade brought change to Indian society, and yet it was change that the Indians directed and therefore their culture remained intact. New wealth was injected into Indian culture but not in a way that was socially disruptive, so the cultures were altered but not destroyed. Fur traders occasionally contemplated modifications of Indian customs, but they lacked the power and, ultimately, the will to effect such changes. The nature of their relationship with the Indians precluded such interference. During the fur-trading period Europeans and Indians were part of a mutually beneficial economic symbiosis, in which neither gained from the

27. Marius Barbeau and William Beynon, unpublished field notes (selections from the "Tsimshian File"), nos. 67 and 89a, in the possession of the Department of Anthropology, University of British Columbia.
28. Collins, "Growth of Class Distinctions...," *American Anthropologist* 52 (1950), p. 331.
29. Herbert C. Taylor, Jr. and Wilson Duff, "A Post Contact Southward Movement of the Kwakiutl," *Research Studies of the State College of Washington* 24 (1956): passim.
30. Diamond Jenness, *The Sekani Indians of British Columbia*, Canada, Department of Mines and Resources Bulletin no. 84 (Ottawa: J. O. Patenaude, 1937): 44.
31. E.E. Rich, ed., *Part of a Despatch from George Simpson...* (London, 1947), p. 19.

hostility of the other. To use a category of acculturation established by Ralph Linton and borrowed by other students of the subject,[32] the Indians were experiencing a period of non-directed cultural change. The situation was sufficiently permissive for the Indians to exercise a large degree of choice about those aspects of European culture that they incorporated into their own. It has been pointed out that acculturation, particularly when it is not forced, can be a creative process.[33] The Indians of the northwest coast and New Caledonia provide a case in point. The impact of the fur-trading frontier on their culture was creative rather than destructive. On the other hand, it could well be that the co-operative relationship between the races during the fur-trading period was poor preparation for the Indians when they had to cope with the new and disruptive elements that came with the settlement frontier. Being used to fur traders who were prepared to accommodate themselves to Indian demands to a considerable extent, the Indians were probably ill-equipped to deal with settlers who were not so accommodating.

---

32. Ralph Linton, ed., *Acculturation in Seven American Indian Tribes* (Gloucester, Mass.: Peter Smith, 1963), pp. 501ff; Edward H. Spicer, ed., *Perspectives in American Indian Culture Change* (Chicago and London: University of Chicago Press, 1961), pp. 518–20.
33. L. Broom et al., "Acculturation...," *American Anthropologist*, n.s. 56 (1954), p. 985.

SOME CONSERVATION SCHEMES OF THE HUDSON'S BAY COMPANY, 1821–50:

An Examination of the Problems of Resource Management in the Fur Trade

ARTHUR J. RAY

Current interests in the plight of many Indian groups, and the concern with ecologically directed conservation efforts, has stimulated a re-examination of the North American fur trade. As part of this re-examination, the record of the attempts by the Hudson's Bay Company to adopt and effect a conservation policy for beaver and other fur-bearers in the early nineteenth century deserves careful consideration.

In this paper attention will be focused upon the beaver conservation schemes which the Hudson's Bay Company tried to introduce in Western Canada between 1821 and 1850 under the direction of Governor George Simpson. For this study the lands which lay within the Company's Northern Department have been chosen. [The Northern Department was a vast area, extending from Hudson Bay to the Rockies, and from the American border to the Arctic Ocean.] The problems which Governor Simpson and the Company faced in their efforts to husband beaver populations in this region were similar to those which they faced in other areas and, or, in the management of other resources. . . .

It is clear that when Governor Simpson assumed control of the Canadian operations of the Hudson's Bay Company in 1821, years of overhunting and trapping had left the trade of many areas on a precarious footing. Yet, he was convinced that effective counter measures could be taken. Reflecting this optimism, in his 1822 report to the Governor and Committee in London he wrote:

> The country is without doubt, in many parts exhausted in valuable furs, yet not to such a low ebb as has been generally supposed and by

ARTHUR J. RAY, "SOME CONSERVATION SCHEMES OF THE HUDSON'S BAY COMPANY, 1821–1850: AN EXAMINATION OF THE PROBLEMS OF RESOURCE MANAGEMENT IN THE FUR TRADE," *JOURNAL OF HISTORICAL GEOGRAPHY* 1, NO. 1 (1975): 49–68. REPRINTED BY PERMISSION OF ACADEMIC PRESS LIMITED, LONDON, ENGLAND.

extending the trade in some parts and nursing others, our prospects are by no means unfavourable.[1]

Since beaver had long been the staple in trade, Simpson focused his efforts on "nursing" them back.

One of the cornerstones of his conservation programme involved the curtailment of trapping operations in overhunted districts while at the same time the Company traders were encouraged to extend the trade into new areas. In the Northern Department this meant that the fur trade was to be vigorously prosecuted in the Mackenzie River District, particularly in the mountainous western and northwestern portions of the district, while in most of the territories lying to the south of the Churchill River a variety of approaches were used in an attempt to ease the trapping pressure on the remaining beaver. Recognising the difficulties of obtaining Indian consent to local moratoriums on beaver hunting...Simpson began to shift trading posts around within the districts in accordance with the fluctuations of fur returns. For example, in 1824 he closed Fort Dauphin and the Swan and Red Deer River posts in the Swan River District and Brandon House in the Upper Red River District. To replace these four posts he opened Fort Pelly which was centrally located to serve both districts, including the Qu'Appelle River valley. Besides cutting the Company's operating costs in these overexploited areas, Simpson believed these actions would "remove the Indians from exhausted tracts of country which will recruit, to parts which have of late been little hunted".[2] The Governor based this assumption on the belief that the Indians would gravitate towards Fort Pelly, giving the other parts of the district a chance to recover. Similar moves were made elsewhere.[3] Generally, these moves did have a positive effect, and in the Swan and Upper Red River areas for instance, fur-bearers, especially beaver, were reported to be rebounding by 1826. In part this rapid recovery was due to the fact that the closing of Brandon House and Fort Qu'Appelle had the unexpected effect of leading many Assiniboine and Plains Cree to discontinue trapping activities altogether. Instead, it encouraged these two groups to

---

1. Simpson, Letters Outward, 31st July 1822, Public Archives of Canada, Hudson's Bay Collection [PAC·HBC] D 4/102, p. 42
2. Simpson, Letters Outward, Report to London, Fort Garry, 5th June 1824, PAC HBC D 4/87
3. *Ibid.*, PAC HBC D 4/87, and Simpson, Report to London, York Factory, 10th August 1824, PAC HBC D 4/87

"follow the Herds of Buffolo wherever they go depending on their Bows and Arrows."[4] Simpson added:

> So many Indians being therefore withdrawn leaves a great portion of that country [Swan River District] to recruit, but the improvement is very slow as of late years it was scarsly[sic] possible to trace a vestige of Beaver on the Assiniboine River in any of its feeders; they now however begin to appear and if left undisturbed for a few years there is no question that important advantages will result.[5]

Besides shifting post locations in response to changing local resource conditions, the traders also attempted to swing the focus of Indian trapping activities from beaver to other fur-bearing species. In doing this, the Hudson's Bay Company traders tried to take advantage of the fact that the populations of all of these animals fluctuated a great deal irrespective of the intensities of hunting pressures. Frequently, the oscillations of population in one species did not parallel those of another, but rather complemented them. Furthermore, there was a considerable variation in the amplitude and duration of these population cycles in the different animal species. Governor Simpson was quick to note this phenomenon and he sought to exploit it by having the Hudson's Bay Company traders encourage the Indians to concentrate their trapping activities on one fur-bearing species as it approached a population peak leaving others, usually beaver, to recoup their losses in the interim.

This practice was particularly well suited to the boundary waters area of Ontario and Minnesota, southern Manitoba and central Saskatchewan. The hydrography of much of this area is characterised by rivers and lakes that have extensive shallow water margins which provide ideal habitats for muskrat and beaver. By the 1820s nearly all of the beaver and other prime fur animals had been trapped-out of this country and the fur trade was heavily dependent on muskrat.[6] Of all of the fur-bearers, this animal exhibited the greatest fluctuations in numbers. Significantly, the oscillations of muskrat populations were closely tied to short-term variations in rainfall and runoff. Living in the shallow waters of lakes and rivers and

---

4. Simpson, Letters Outward, Report to London, York Factory, 20th August 1826, PAC HBC D 4/89
5. *Ibid.*, PAC HBC D 4/89. During this period the Plains Indians became relatively independent of the Company. A. J. Ray, *Indians in the Fur Trade* (University of Toronto Press, Toronto, 1974).
6. *Ibid.*

having no control over local water levels, they were more sensitive to water level changes than were the beaver. High water can limit the growth of aquatic plants which the animal feeds upon, principally rootstocks, cat-tails, bulrushes and arrowhead plants, while low water may cause ponds to freeze to the bottom during winter. Should the latter occur, many muskrat starve to death since, unlike the beaver, they do not store food. Low water was an additional problem since it seems to have favoured the outbreak of disease. For instance, in 1824 Simpson reported that water levels were low in the Cumberland Department and, as a consequence, "produced a disease among the Rats that destroyed them by the thousands as heaps were found dead on opening their houses this spring".[7] As a result of this epidemic the muskrat returns of the Cumberland Department declined from 150,000 skins in 1823 to 70,000 skins in 1824.[8] On many other occasions low water levels were said to have produced epidemics which killed many muskrat. In all probability, the disease which broke out under these circumstances was Tularemia.[9]

While muskrat populations thus frequently suffered heavy losses, they rebounded quickly with more favourable moisture conditions. The female muskrat may have up to five litters a breeding season and may produce as many as eleven offspring in each litter. In contrast, the female beaver mates in February, bears her young in May and usually nurses only four cubs per litter. The higher fertility rates of the muskrat allowed them to recoup their population losses much more rapidly than the beaver.[10]

Since the variations of muskrat populations were closely tied to moisture conditions, the traders often used fluctuations in local water levels to make predictions about their future muskrat returns and to plan short-term management strategies on a district basis. For instance, as noted previously, it was very dry in eastern Saskatchewan and western Mani-

---

7. Simpson, Letters Outward, Report to London, York Factory, 10th August 1824, PAC HBC D 4/87
8. *Ibid.*
9. Tularemia is an epizootic disease which causes hemorrhaging of the heart, lungs and liver of the animal and usually death. Low water levels increase the concentration of Tularemia bacteria and therefore increase the probability that muskrat or beaver will contract the disease. For a discussion of this disease (*Pasteurella tularensis*) see W. L. Jellison *et al.*, Epizootic tularemia in the Beaver, *Castor canadensis*, and the contamination of stream water with *Pasturella tularensis*, *American Journal of Hygiene* 36 (1942) 168–82. For a discussion of its effects on muskrat populations see P. L. Errington, *Muskrat populations* (Iowa State University 1963), and P. L. Errington, *Muskrats and marsh management* (Washington D.C. 1961) 49–53
10. Errington, *Muskrats and marsh management* 35–7

toba in 1824 and low water levels along the lower Saskatchewan River led to a precipitous drop in the muskrat trade of the districts adjoining it, particularly the Cumberland Department. In 1825 more humid conditions returned, ending a two-year drought, and spring flooding along the lower Saskatchewan was extensive that year. This flooding led Simpson to predict that the muskrat would soon reappear in considerable numbers in the Cumberland Department. However, because of the severity of the preceding drought and the intensive trapping pressure which had been exerted on the dwindling muskrat population, he believed that it would not be until 1826 that the recovery would be strongly felt in the returns from the district. Indeed, it was not until 1827 that a marked improvement was reported. By the latter date, higher muskrat returns were being registered throughout eastern Saskatchewan and southern Manitoba.[11]

During this wet phase the Indians were encouraged to turn their attention to muskrat once more in the hope that other fur animals, particularly beaver, would have a chance to recover. For example, when discussing the returns of the Swan River area in 1827, Simpson reported:

> This District has improved more during the past year than any other. . . which is to be accounted for by the excellent hunts made in Rats while the returns of other furs have fallen off materially particularly in the article of Beaver; this reduction. . .is owing to the measures taken by Chief Factor Clarke to protect it, who discovering that the natives could find ample employment in rat hunting since the year 1823/24.[12]

Fortunately for the Hudson's Bay Company, the market for muskrat skins was strong in Eastern Canada and the United States during the 1820s, and in this instance their conservation scheme paid immediate economic dividends.[13]

The principal difficulty of attempting to exploit the oscillations of muskrat populations to give the beaver periodic respites from heavy

---

11. Simpson, Letters Outward, Report to London, York Factory, 1st September 1825, PAC HBC D 4/88. Besides the low ebb of the muskrat population of the Cumberland District Simpson indicated that many of the Indians had scattered and he believed that this would adversely affect the department's returns for a year or two. In one of his reports for 1827, Simpson wrote that muskrat were increasing in the Cumberland, Swan River and Winnipeg Districts. Simpson, Letters Outward, Report to London, York Factory, 25th July 1827, PAC HBC D 4/90.
12. Simpson, Letters Outward, York Factory, 25th July 1827, PAC HBC D 4/90
13. Simpson, Letters Outward, Report to London, York Factory, 8th September 1823, PAC HBC D 4/86

trapping related to the fact that the amplitudes of the muskrat cycles were never of sufficient duration to allow the beaver to make a substantial recovery. Simpson was aware of this problem. In 1827 he wrote that although the Indians of the Cumberland District had begun to focus their trapping operations on muskrat, he doubted that it would prove to be very beneficial to future beaver returns from that area since the beaver population was so depleted that it would take many years to recuperate.[14] Simpson's doubts proved well founded. 1828 was a dry year once again. This led him to write:

> I much fear that there will be a considerable falling off next year on this branch of our Trade [Muskrat] as the present season has been hitherto unusually dry, and the Marshes and pools which they frequent are from that cause become stagnant which will engender disease and in all probability destroy them.[15]

Although Simpson's prediction of poor muskrat returns from eastern Saskatchewan and southern Manitoba in 1829 proved to be wrong, persistent low water levels did result in a substantial decline of this trade throughout the region in 1830.[16]

Besides shifting post locations and attempting to exploit alternative fur resources under favourable conditions, the Hudson's Bay Company employed a number of other strategies to manage the dwindling beaver trade. One of these efforts was directed towards encouraging and cajoling the Indians to stop trapping beaver during the summer season when pelts were of little value. Accordingly, in his 1822 report to London, Governor Simpson wrote, "the Indians have been informed that skins out of season will not be taken off their hands".[17] During the competitive period before 1821 they had been accustomed to bringing in summer beaver to obtain alcohol and other items whenever they required them. Thus, the Indians were not willing to readily accept this abrupt departure from well-established trading practices. Because of this Indian reluctance, many of the company's district heads (called factors) apparently made little effort to enforce the new rule in the 1820s and early 1830s. As late as 1836, the

---

14. Simpson, Letters Outward, York Factory, 25th July 1827, PAC HBC D 4/90
15. Simpson, Letters Outward, Report to London, York Factory, 10th July 1828, PAC HBC D 4/92
16. Simpson, Letters Outward, Report to London, York Factory, 26th August 1830, PAC HBC D 4/97
17. Simpson, Letters Outward, Report to London, York Factory, 10th August 1824, PAC HBC D 4/85

London directors complained to Simpson that too many out-of-season skins were still being sent home from the Bay.[18]

In subsequent years, some of the factors did make a more earnest attempt to obtain Indian compliance with the regulation. Some of them— such as George Gladman who was stationed at Norway House in the mid-1840s—resorted to rather dramatic, and questionable, tactics to demonstrate their resolve on this matter to the Indians. In his letter to Governor Simpson dated 21st June 1844, Gladman wrote, "an Indian brought me a Beaver skin the other day/the animal being recently killed/this being against the rule I slapped his face with it. . . ."[19] There can be little doubt that such demeaning treatment would have left a strong impression upon the minds of the local Indians. However,. . .it is unlikely that the Indians discontinued their summer beaver hunts even if they did stop bringing summer pelts to the posts.

In the hopes of curbing the indiscriminate nature of Indian trapping (with respect to ages of beaver) and reducing the effectiveness of their operations, Simpson believed that the use of steel traps and castoreum bait, a trapping technique which came into general usage in the 1790s, should be discontinued.[20] Concerning this subject, in 1822 he wrote:

> The use of Beaver Traps should have been prohibited long ago, they are the scourge of the Country and none will, in the future, be given out except for new Districts exposed to opposition and frontier establishment.[21]

Thus, the further trade of steel traps in the Northern Department was banned except in areas near the United States border and the Red River Colony where the Indians could obtain them from alternative suppliers.

Most of the conservation schemes outlined thus far had little chance of success unless the local Company traders were committed to the Company's long-term goal of placing the fur trade on a sustained-yield basis. Yet there was always the temptation on the part of individual traders to increase their fur intakes on a short-term basis and therefore "look good" in the Company's eyes in terms of profits. Also, the Indians living in one

---

18. Simpson, Letters Inward, Hudson's Bay House, London, 9th March 1836, PAC HBC D 5/4
19. Simpson, Letters Inward, Norway House, 21st June 1844, PAC HBC D 5/11
20. R. F. Wells, Castoreum and steel traps in Eastern North America, *American Anthropologist* 74 (1973) 479–83
21. Simpson, Letters Outward, Report to London, York Factory, 31st July 1822, PAC HBC D 4/85

district could trade their furs in another near by if the local trader was too zealous in his efforts to implement conservation measures. In order to deal with these problems, Simpson and the governing council for the Northern Department (which was composed of the chief factors of the various districts) decided upon a more coercive plan of action. In 1826 they introduced a quota system for the beaver trade of the Northern Department. Under this scheme, the average annual beaver returns were calculated for each of the fourteen districts of the department for the three-year period between 1823 and 1825. In 1826, each district was allowed to take in a percentage of its annual trade during the base period. In the case of two districts, those of the Lower Red River and Rainy Lake, beaver quotas were not established because of the close proximity of American traders. In other districts, the fur intake was reduced by between one-fifth to one-half of what it had been. Governor Simpson indicated that all of these quotas would be rigidly enforced with the exception of that of the Saskatchewan District.

The quota for the Saskatchewan District was not enforced because the beaver returns of that department came largely from the Piegan Indians who obtained their pelts by trapping, trading and raiding south of the international boundary. Few beaver were taken by the Indians living north of the border because the animal had been nearly trapped out in many sections of the Saskatchewan region, especially in the country to the north of the North Saskatchewan River. Also, the Hudson's Bay Company traders were instructed to discourage the Indians living in the latter areas from taking any more beaver. Thus, by not enforcing the quota, Simpson was hoping to underwrite part of the cost of "nursing" the beaver back in the Saskatchewan District by drawing upon the resources of the American territories to the southward.[22]

In brief, during the 1820s the Hudson's Bay Company undertook a series of initiatives which were intended to place the beaver trade on a sustained-yield basis. Yet, in spite of the fact that a variety of approaches were attempted, beaver populations continued to decline.

---

22. Simpson, Letters Outward, Report to London, York Factory, 20th August 1826, PAC HBC D 4/85

Sixteen Years in the Indian Country:

The Journal of Daniel Williams Harmon 1800–1816

DANIEL WILLIAMS HARMON

From the month of June, until the latter end of September, all animals have but little fur; and therefore, at this season, the Indians do not hunt them much. The greater part of the Indians, on the east side of the Rocky Mountain, now take the beaver in steel traps, which we sell them; frequently they shoot them, with fire arms; and sometimes they make holes through their lodges or huts, and then spear them. Otters they take in the same manner as beavers. The lynx or cat, they take in snares. Foxes, fishers, martins, minks, &c. they take in a spring trap.—The large animals are hunted chiefly for their flesh; and are therefore killed, principally when they are the fattest, which most of them are in the fall, and some of them in the winter. Buffaloes, moose, red deers, bears, &c. are generally killed with fire arms. The Indians, however, in the plains, have other methods of killing the buffaloe.

Sometimes the young men mount their horses, and pursue them and bring them down with their bows and arrows, which they find more convenient for this purpose than fire arms, as they can more easily take an arrow from the quiver, than load a musket, in such a situation. The following, is another method of taking the buffaloe. The Natives look out for a small grove of trees, surrounded by a plain. In this grove they make a yard, by falling small trees, and interweaving them with brush; and they leave an opening into it about twenty feet broad. They select, for this purpose, a rising piece of ground, that the yard may not be seen at a distance. From each side of this opening, they fix two ranges of stakes, at about an angle of ninety degrees from each other, extending about two miles into the plains. These stakes rise about four feet above the ground, and are about forty feet apart. On the top of each stake, they put buffaloe dung, or tie a wisp of hay. After this preparation, when a herd of buffaloes is seen at no great distance off, thirty or forty or more young men mount their racers, which are well trained to this business, and surround them; and little difficulty is found in bringing them, within the range of the

Daniel Williams Harmon, *Sixteen Years in the Indian Country: The Journal of Daniel Williams Harmon 1800–1816* (Toronto: Macmillan, 1957): 209–10.

stakes. Indians are stationed by the side of some of these stakes, to keep them in motion, so that the buffaloes suppose them all to be human beings. The horsemen press forward by the sides of the herd and behind them, until, at length, with their tongues lolling from their mouths, they are brought to the entrance of the yard; and through it they rush without perceiving their danger, until they are shut in, to the number, oftentimes, of two or three hundred. When they find themselves enclosed, the Indians say, and I have frequently seen myself, that they begin to walk around the outside of the yard, in the direction of the apparent revolution of the sun, from east to west. Before any of them are killed, the Indians go into the tent of the chief to smoke, which they denominate making the buffalo smoke. They then go out to the yard, and kill the buffaloes with bows and arrows; and there are Indians, who will send an arrow, entirely through one buffaloe, and kill, at the same time, a second. When the buffaloes are all killed and cut up, the tongues of all of them are taken to the tent of the chief; and with a part of them he makes a feast, and the remainder he allows his neighbours to keep. The meat and skins are then distributed among the people of the whole camp; and whether equally or not, no one will complain. Should any be displeased with their share, they will decamp, and go and join another party.

FURTHER READINGS FOR TOPIC 10

Gerald Friesen. *The Canadian Prairies: A History*. Toronto: University of Toronto Press, 1984.

K. Kelly. "The Changing Attitude of Farmers to Forest in Nineteenth Century Ontario." *Ontario Geography* 8 (1974): 64–77.

Kelly, K. "The Impact of the Nineteenth Century Agricultural Settlement on the Land." In *Perspectives on Landscape and Settlement in Nineteenth Century Ontario*, ed. J. D. Wood. Toronto: McClelland and Stewart, 1975: 64–77.

A. J. Ray, "Diffusion of Diseases in the Western Interior of Canada, 1830–1850." *Geographical Review* 66 (April 1976): 139–57.

TOPIC 11

Work:
Farming
the
Land
and
Organizing
the
Workers

In the mid-nineteenth century, fish and furs were yielding in importance to farming and lumbering in British North America. By 1820, the new frontier of commercial farming was Upper Canada (Ontario), which was flooded with Americans before the War of 1812 and with British immigrants thereafter. They faced the daunting prospect of carving prosperous farms out of the stubborn hardwood forests and producing wheat for the markets of Lower Canada (Quebec) and Great Britain. The difficulties of this undertaking were amply elucidated by Susanna Moodie, whose book Roughing It in the Bush *(1852) avowedly discouraged immigration, at least for British gentlefolk. In the following selection, Peter Russell documents the amount of labour required to clear a farm in the Upper Canadian bush. Arduous though this process may have been, the prospect of independence, if not prosperity, continued to attract settlers to the backwoods of Upper Canada until land became available in the prairie West.*

Pre-Confederation Canada boasted little industry, and large concentrations of workers were rare. Workers often faced a precarious existence, characterized by low wages, seasonal unemployment, and unsafe work practices. Nor was there much protection from employers, for both unions and strikes were illegal. In spite of such restrictions, however, workers sometimes banded together to fight for such causes as better wages or working conditions. One such effort is detailed here in Robert Tremblay's article on the shipworkers' union in 1840.

The life of a farmer, though hard, has been praised since antiquity as one which develops the sober virtues necessary for good citizenship. In contrast to this, lumbering has been widely condemned as a rough and lawless trade, a view which the career of Peter Aylen, explored in Topic 8, would seem to confirm. Moreover, it was widely believed that lumbering interfered with the development of agriculture by luring potential farmers away from their ploughs with the prospect of quick and easy profits. Recent research, however, such as the following article by Graeme Wynn, is now calling into question this supposed dichotomy between farmers and lumberers, indicating that the relationship was complementary rather than antagonistic.

FOREST INTO FARMLAND:

Upper Canadian Clearing Rates, 1822–1839

PETER A. RUSSELL

[In Upper Canada,] the rate of clearing forest from the land was a crucial index of both economic success and social advancement. Contemporaries recognized the intimate connection between the rate of clearing forest from the land and the social ambitions of the pioneers, whether emigrants or natives.[1] George Forbes, son of an Aberdeenshire tenant farmer, emphasized the "hard labour" involved in clearing forest, but he still urged his brothers to join him.

> But we in Canada have this glorious privilege that the ground where on we tread is our own and our children's after us;...No danger of the leases expiring and the laird saying pay me so much more rent, or bundle and go, for here we are laird ourselves. I may thank my stars that I am out of such a place.[2]

He proudly recounted the number of acres that he had cleared and fenced the previous year. "I am determined to have a good farm as I have got first rate land. Patience and perseverance will do the rest."[3] The speed with which a man cleared the forest from his land (provided it was of good quality) was the rate at which he advanced his economic and in large part his social status.

Historians have not been oblivious to the importance of clearing rates as a barometer of economic progress. However, contemporary accounts of the probable clearing rate have misled them. Scholars have assumed as a universal rate one which reflects only a part of the pioneering process. The reports of Britons like E. A. Talbot, John MacGregor, and Patrick Shirreff, and residents of the colony like William Lyon Mackenzie and

PETER A. RUSSELL, "FOREST INTO FARMLAND: UPPER CANADIAN CLEARING RATES, 1822–1839," AGRICULTURAL HISTORY 57 (1983): 326–39. BY PERMISSION OF THE AUTHOR AND THE UNIVERSITY OF CALIFORNIA PRESS.

1. E. A. Talbot, *Five Years' Residence in the Canadas* (London, 1824), 1: 155–56; John Howison, *Sketches of Upper Canada* (Edinburgh, 1825), 208–9; John M'Gregor, *British America* (Edinburgh, 1833), 2: 517–18; John Gemmel to Andrew Gemmel, 17 December 1826; see also Gemmel to Gemmel, 21 May 1823 and 26 August 1830, Gemmel Papers, Scottish Public Record Office, Edinburgh (hereafter SPRO).
2. George Forbes to John Forbes, 19 October 1856, Forbes Papers, SPRO. See also Susanna Moodie, *Roughing It in the Bush* (Toronto: McClelland and Stewart, 1962), 27.
3. Forbes to Forbes, 19 October 1856, Forbes Papers, SPRO.

George Forbes appear to point to a clearing rate per man of between four and seven acres a year.[4] That evidence is reflected in the accounts of Edwin Guillet, Robert L. Jones, and Kenneth Kelly.[5] However, Jones did cite Anna Jameson's account of a backwoodsman she met in her travels who insisted testily that an acre a year was all that a lone man could hope to accomplish.[6] In contrast to most historians, J. J. Talman noted that the common rate of clearing appeared to have been about two acres a year by each head of a family.[7] He based his estimate on several assessment rolls. As will be shown, systematic examination of local tax records shows an average of around one and one-half acres per year per adult male, far below the rate reported by most contemporaries. The explanation of that difference requires an examination of the two chief variables in clearing: the method used and the phase of clearing.

Common sense would indicate there was no universal clearing rate for the whole colony. The rate would have depended upon a number of factors, the most important being the type of clearing done and the amount of time a farmer could devote to it. . . .

The amount of time a farmer could spend chopping down trees [was of crucial importance]. Contemporaries reported. . .an initial, or pioneer clearing rate. When a settler arrived on a forest lot, aside from providing immediate shelter for himself and his dependents, he had little else to do for the first years but cut down trees by whatever method. . . .If a man worked at clearing full-time, a rate of four up to even seven acres a year could have been possible. However, as Samuel Strickland observed after many years experience with the Canada Land Company,

---

4. Talbot, *Five Years' Residence in the Canadas*, 2: 198; *Colonial Advocate* (Queenston, later York), 2 September 1824; M'Gregor, *British America*, 2: 549; and Patrick Shirreff, *A Tour Through North America* (Edinburgh, 1835), 363; George Forbes to John Forbes, 14 October 1853, Forbes Papers, SPRO.

5. Edwin C. Guillet, *The Pioneer Farmer and Backwoodsman* (Toronto: University of Toronto Press, 1963), 312; R. L. Jones, *History of Agriculture in Ontario* (Toronto, 1946), 71–73; Kelly, "Wheat Farming," Canadian Geographer 15:2(1971), 103; see also Kelly, "Agricultural Geography of Simcoe County," (Ph.D. Diss., University of Toronto, 1968), 34–36. See also J. Wagner, "Gentry Perception and Land Utilization in the Peterborough-Kawartha Lakes Region, 1815–1851" (Master's thesis, University of Toronto, n.d.), 55–56. Wagner compares about a dozen gentry farmers (who could afford to hire labor to clear) with a "composite average settler" (whose derivation we are not told) whose clearing rate in the first four years of settlement is just about 5 acres per year, declining somewhat below 5 acres a year thereafter (with fluctuations).

6. Jones, *History of Agriculture in Ontario*, 71–73.

7. Thomas Radcliff, *Authentic Letters from Upper Canada* (Toronto: Macmillan of Canada, 1953), xiv.

The emigrant should endeavour to get as much chopping done as possible during the first three years, because after that time he has so many other things to attend to, such as increase in stock, barn and house-building, thrashing, ploughing, *etc.* which, of course, give him every year less time for chopping, particularly if his family be small.[8]

Furthermore, the forest once cleared did not stay cleared. Kenneth Kelly has pointed out that for decades after the initial clearance an appreciable amount of time had to be spent cutting down secondary forest growth which sought to reclaim it.[9] The consequences of all these farm tasks, Strickland indicated, was that the farmer had less and less time for clearing new land. Thus, in addition to the "pioneer rate" (reported by contemporaries) there appears to have been also a long-term rate (reflected in the empirical measure of clearing rates).

In light of the empirically established relatively low rates one might be tempted to dismiss the high rates reported by contemporaries as mere emigration propaganda. Confirmation of the highest, or "pioneer rate" comes from the various estimates offered by contemporary observers of the cost of having an acre cleared by hired labor. For a full-time employee the approximate time equivalent for clearing an acre would be from one month (using the cheapest method and the highest wage rate) to two months (the costliest method and the lowest wage rate). Allowing for time lost due to bad weather and other contingencies, that approximation tends to support contemporaries' estimates of the "pioneer rate" of clearing forest.[10]

Both the empirical and the reported rates are valid. The first reflects the long-term average in clearing as a social (vs. individual) process. The second reflects the initial phase of pioneer farming when nearly all energies were concentrated upon cutting down the forest. Previous historians erred in taking the latter for the former. . . .

The aggregate township assessments and population returns published irregularly in the Appendix of the Upper Canada House of Assembly *Journal* provide the statistics upon which this study is based.[11] . . .

---

8. Samuel Strickland, *Twenty-Seven Years in Canada West* (Edmonton: M. G. Hurtig, 1970), 167.
9. Kelly, "Wheat Farming," 103–5.
10. For examples of farm labor wage rates for different types of clearing, see M'Gregor, *British America*, 2: 441; Shirreff, *A Tour through North America*, 117–20; Cattermole, *Emigration*; Howison, *Sketches of Upper Canada*, 249; Talbot, *Five Years' Residence in the Canadas*, 2: 188; Rev. Joseph Thomson to Thomas Ridout, 29 December 1819, Upper Canada Sundries, Public Archives of Canada (hereafter PAC).
11. Legislative Assembly of Upper Canada, *Journals*, 1822 to 1839, Appendix, PAC.

Information on the population and aggregate cleared acreage by township between 1822 and 1839 was available for 142 townships in Upper Canada [consolidated into 118 units for the purposes of this study]. These represented almost all the populated shoreline along the Ottawa River (below Arnprior), the St. Lawrence River, Lake Ontario, Lake Erie, and the Niagara frontier.[12] The only significant populated area omitted is the Western District, for which consistent data were not available due to the vagaries of the local assessment officers.[13] The population of the 142 townships included represented 87.5 percent of the total rural population in the colony in 1835.[14]. . .

[The] data. . .allow meaningful statements about the rates at which forest was cleared from the land, [although] the necessary approximations of unit boundaries, the very conservative nature of the estimates for cleared acreage, and the occasional vagaries in population data indicate one should not look for [a] high degree of precision. . . .

Clearing rates were calculated for each of the 118 units for four periods: 1822–1827, 1827–1832, 1832–1835 and 1835–1839. Subtraction of the number of acres cleared in each unit in the earlier year from those cleared in the latter, divided by the number of adult males and the years in the interval produced annual rates. Due to missing data from some townships the number of units varies from 78 in 1827, to 116 in 1832, 118 in 1835, and 117 in 1839. These rates, covering over 87 percent of the rural populated area, can be compared to the rates established in an earlier study of farm-by-farm data for fifteen townships selected from eastern and central Upper Canada.[15]

---

12. The map shows the area in each district covered by the 142 townships. District boundaries changed somewhat over time. To keep constant units for comparison, districts retain their 1836 configuration throughout the study. This requires hyphenated names occasionally to show that a unit has been held constant, e.g., London-Talbot includes all the townships covered in the old London district before the 1837 division. See W. G. Dean et al., *Economic Atlas of Ontario* (Toronto: University of Toronto Press, 1969), pl. 98.

13. The person responsible for the Western District periodically gave only *district* aggregates of assessment rather than township aggregates. For comparison with table 2, it may be noted that in 1832–1835, the Western *District's* clearing rate was 0.84 acres per year per adult male.

14. The total rural population of the province in 1835 (excluding the centers of Cornwall, Kingston, Toronto, Hamilton, Niagara, and London) was 310,522 of whom 271,575 (87.5 percent) lived in the 142 townships covered by this study. Upper Canada House of Assembly, *Journals*, 2 sess, 12 Parl., 1836, vol. 1, report 46, PAC.

15. P. A. Russell, "Upper Canada: A Poor Man's Country? Some Statistical Evidence, 1812–1842," in Donald H. Akenson, ed., *Canadian Papers in Rural History*, vol. 3 (Gananoque, 1982), 129–47. On somewhat comparable American work, see Martin L. Primack, "Land

The results, calculated from aggregate assessment data, reflect a low long-term rate of clearing. For 1822–1827, the average (or mean) rate was 1.25 acres per year per adult male for 78 units (the Eastern, Johnson, and Niagara Districts had insufficient data for the earliest period) with a range from 5.1 to 0.15 acres per year per adult male. Five years later the rate had risen to 1.41 acres for 116 units and a range of rates from 5.8 to 0.01 acres. Within two years however it dropped to 0.96 acres (for 118 units) while the range narrowed to 3.1 acres down to 0.03 acres. By 1839 the rate rose again to 1.02 acres for 117 units with the range of rates widening to 0.09 up to 6.9 acres.

Allowing for the fact that there were more adult males on average than farms, these figures fall within the range to be expected from the results of the earlier study. The clearing rates in that case, calculated as acres cleared per year per *farm*, were 1.23 (1812–1822), 1.47 (1822–1832) and 1.55 (1832–1842).[16] While that study focused on 15 well-settled townships, the 118 units represent a much broader cross-section of the colony. Thus, the larger group includes many newly opened townships with a high proportion of pioneers. This can be seen in the greater upward range of some rates—reflecting figures closer to the "pioneer rate." While in the 15 settled townships the highest rates were 3.03 and 3.18 acres cleared per year per farm (for Augusta in 1832 and 1842), every period but one in the larger group had rates over five acres per year per adult male. . . .

The long-term clearing rate empirically established was much lower than almost all previous accounts led one to expect. The social implications of that fact are clear. The promise of the "poor man's country" was first of all a change in *social* status. Every immigrant could be a "proprietor," and landowner.

> Can you place before the farmer who is a lease-holder in England a more powerful motive to emigration than that one year's rent of a farm going to his landlord would purchase him a freehold of the same extent in Canada? Every motive is placed before him to improve his estate, and, further the interest of the province—The cultivator is at once the cultivator and the owner of the soil; every improvement which he makes is exclusively his own.[17]

Clearing Under Nineteenth-Century Techniques: Some Preliminary Calculations," *Journal of Economic History* 22:4 (1962): 484–97.
16. Russell, "Upper Canada: A Poor Man's Country?" 137.
17. *Patriot* (Kingston, later York), 29 November 1836.

But the promise of a life of ease within a few years, from pioneer farming, was false.[18] The *economic* status of the would-be yeoman farmer could remain at the subsistence level for a considerable length of time. The Church of Scotland magazine in Upper Canada spoke more truly of

> ...thousands upon thousands in this vast uncultivated territory, struggling with the hardships and penury of new settlements, and with whom years of constant toil must pass away, ere they can hope to attain any thing beyond the merest necessaries of life.[19]

Unquestionably, Upper Canada drew a large number of immigrants, many of whom, to judge from the surviving correspondence, remained enthusiastic about the colony after their arrival.[20] Yet one needs to be careful about exactly what was considered to have been promised by "the poor man's country." It was an advance in social status through landownership first of all, with the expectation of eventual economic success. Five years after their settlement at Peterborough, the Irish there were described as having been removed

> ...from scenes where they were lingering under distressing despondency and gloomy despair, to those, where they now breathe the air of comfort, and comparative ease, and look forward with a cheering certainty to approaching independence....[21]

The promise Upper Canada offered to the poor emigrants was a start on the road to prosperity. The long-term clearing rates offer an effective measure of just how lengthy that road was.

---

18. *Canadian Emigrant* (Sandwich), 13 July 1833; *York Weekly Post*, 25 January 1820.
19. *Canadian Christian Examiner* (Niagara-on-the-Lake), April 1838, p. 115
20. Mary McNicol and John Tolmie to James McNicol, 2 August 1831, "Emigrant Manuscripts," National Library of Scotland, Edinburgh; Arthur Stock to John Colquhoun, 10 December 1823, Stock Papers, SPRO; John Scott to Andrew Redford, 29 August 1835, Redford Papers, SPRO; Adam Hope to Robert Hope, 30 July 1837, Hope Papers, SPRO; John Gemmel to Andrew Gemmel, 8 November 1824, Gemmel Papers, SPRO; George Forbes to John Forbes, 18 January 1846, Forbes Papers, SPRO.
21. *Upper Canada Herald* (Kingston), 29 September 1830.

The Strike of Workers in the Quebec Shipyards (1840)

Robert Tremblay

"For the worker, life can easily be summed up in these three words: you are born, you suffer and you die. Want is with you from the moment of your birth. It is, with very few exceptions, your constant companion until your death."

—*L'Echo de la fabrique* (*The Echo of the Factory*), Lyon, France, February 17, 1833.

The sentiment expressed by a worker in the silk factories of Lyon during the famous strike of 1833 could apply equally well to the workers in the Quebec shipyards who, at the same time, stopped work for a period of 18 days in an effort to change the equation that capitalist accumulation means want for the worker.

Why should we analyze the 1840 strike of ship's carpenters in the Quebec shipyards?...A study of this conflict challenges the version of Quebec historiography which claims that after the *patriote* rebellion of 1837–38, the popular movement no longer had the heart to act. If we examine certain events of this time, we can observe the strength of a developing workers' movement. This was manifested, for example, in the canallers' strike of 1839[1] at the Chambly canal, the strike of 1,200 shipworkers and the creation of a union in Quebec (1840), the coalition of painters in Quebec (1842)[2] and a strike involving 4,000 canallers in the Lachine and Beauharnois canals (1843).[3] It would not be surprising that these crucial struggles of the 1840s are the culmination of the process that Marx described, the passage from the existence of the working class as a distinct entity to the emergence of a working-class consciousness.[4]

Robert Tremblay, "La Grève des Ouvriers de la Construction Navale à Québec (1840)," *Revue Historique d'Amérique Française* 37, no. 2 (September 1983): 227–39. Translated here for the first time.

1. Province of Canada. Legislative Assembly. *Journal*, 1843, appendix to Vol. 3.
2. Eugene Forsey, *Trade Unions in Canada, 1812–1902* (Toronto: University of Toronto Press, 1982): 15.
3. H. C. Pentland, "The Lachine Strike of 1843," *Canadian Historical Review* (1948): 255–77; Raymond Boily, *Les Irlandais et le Canal de Lachine: La Grève de 1843* (Montreal: Leméac, 1980).
4. K. Marx, *Misère de la philosophie* (Paris: UGE, 1965): 490.

The Shipbuilding Industry in the First Half of the Nineteenth Century

In the first half of the nineteenth century, Quebec City was an important shipbuilding centre for British North America. From 1760 to 1825, 52 percent of the entire tonnage of ships built in Lower Canada came from the Quebec shipyards. . . .

The shipbuilding industry worked in two ways: subcontracting or direct manufacture. In the former case, the shipbuilder was under contract to the seller and was responsible for all the equipment and material necessary to build the ship. In the second case, the shipbuilder himself was solely responsible for supervising the work and financing the operation. It is not clear why, but the second method of direct manufacture became predominant in the 1820s in Quebec's shipyards. Though freed from the yoke of the merchants, the master builders were not for all that free of their troubles. From 1830 to 1840, the tightening of the British market and the high rates charged by insurance companies[5] caused the selling price of a Canadian ship to fall. In spite of this, by reducing wages, the shipyard owners were able to show 13 percent gross profits,[6] some of which were paid in commission to agents in London, England.[7] In 1834, 16 ships worth $84,037 were built in Quebec. Only $29,446 was paid in wages to the workers; $43,615 was used to buy raw materials imported from England (copper, iron, rope, sails, etc.) and to supply wood to the colony.[8] The result of the uncertainties of this stage of capitalist accumulation resulted in pressure to keep workers' wages down.

---

5. Adam Shortt and A. G. Doughty, *Canada and Its Provinces* (23 vols.; Toronto, 1913–17), X: 577.
6. This figure was arrived at from statistics, found in *La Gazette de Quebec* of February 12, 1834, on the costs and value of production in naval construction. Pierre Dufour, "La construction navale à Québec, 1760–1825," *Revue d'histoire de l'Amérique française* [RHAF] 35, no. 2 (September 1981): 244 ff.
7. The commissions paid to agents represent about 5 percent of the sale price of a ship; agents were usually employed to find markets for the production of naval shipyards or simply to obtain a loan in London's financial market.
8. *La Gazette de Quebec*, February 12, 1834, and January 18, 1837. These sources indicate that it cost 35 percent more for materials to construct a ship at Quebec than in the well-known shipyards of the river Clyde in Scotland; this was because of the high price in the colony of wood suitable for construction and because of tariff duties on products imported into England. See J. S. MacMillan and A. J. H. Richardson, "James Dunlop," *Dictionary of Canadian Biography*, Vol. 5 (1983); and Lower Canada, Assembly, *Journals*, January 28 and March 9, 1825.

An equally structured system governed work in the shipyards. Over the years, a method of work had been devised that would reconcile the complexity of the tasks involved in building a ship with the collective nature of this work.[9] The work crews were the keystone of this method of production.[10] They were organized in a hierarchy, with the foreman in command. The foreman was responsible for the hiring and supervision of the workers. Beneath him were the skilled workers (carpenters, joiners, caulkers, blacksmiths, painters, etc.) who were responsible for the construction and finishing of the ships. At the bottom of the ladder were apprentices and labourers reduced to being under the direction of one of the skilled workers. Obviously, from 1820 to 1840, the number of unskilled workers increased greatly at the expense of the carpenters whose wages were much higher.[11] As the historian Richard Rice has said, in the first half of the nineteenth century, the naval yards were far in advance of other colonial enterprises in terms of capital, production, division of labour, and discipline.

Working Conditions

Nineteenth-century studies often depict the shipyard workers as outdoor workers able to escape the monotony of the indoor workshops.[12] It is true that their work was seasonal and, since they owned their own tools, they were somewhat independent. However, can one conclude that these workers were able, even partially, to escape proletarian status? Not at all. They never knew what the day would bring. Life was often difficult and accidents and the fear of unemployment were their daily lot. It is

---

9. It was impossible to measure at exactly what point the work process was transformed by the impact of the introduction of steam machinery or of mechanical winches by the shipyard owners, such as John Goudie and John Bell, between 1810 and 1820.
10. For more details on the work crews, see D. T. Ruddell, "Quebec City, 1765–1831: The Evolution of a Colonial Town" (Ph.D. Thesis, Université Laval, 1981).
11. This type of worker was generally recruited from among the peasant community in the regions near Quebec, although sometimes immigrants just off the boat were recruited for the purpose. Thus, between 1821 and 1822, more than 700 Irish immigrants found temporary work in shipbuilding at the Quebec shipyards. On this subject see Fernand Ouellet, *Le Bas-Canada, 1791–1840: Changements structuraux et crise* (Ottawa, 1976): 220.
12. This idyllic vision of the shipbuilding workers was also prevalent in France during the nineteenth century. The work of Michelle Perrot, *Les ouvriers en grève, France, 1871–1890*, 2 vols. (Paris: Mouton, 1974): 377–79, is eloquently informative on this.

significant that the 2,860 shipyard workers[13] in the eleven Quebec shipyards during the winter of 1840–41 supported 10,000 people, more than
20 percent of the population of Quebec at the time. The meagre wages
given at the end of 1840[14] and the increasing cost of food were bitterly
resented by the working community that depended on the shipbuilding
industry, reviving the familiar spectre of food shortages. . . .

It is estimated that in 1840, on the eve of the strike, a ship's carpenter
needed more than half of his wages of 3 shillings a day to keep his family
fed.[15] Wood to heat his house, at 12 shillings a cord, would eat up 20
percent of his salary during the winter months. It was difficult for the
worker to budget for the times when he would be out of work due to the
weather, accidents, or extended periods of unemployment. Many families
suffered hardships and were reduced to begging. Most workplace
accidents occurred at the beginning of the winter, when large pieces of
wood had to be moved during dangerous weather conditions,[16] or when
work was speeded up and hours lengthened to compensate for a delay in
delivery. Unemployment was especially high during the 1840s when the
contraction of the British market created slowdowns in the shipyards. For
shipyard workers living through this difficult period, the problem of
layoffs was extremely serious, as they could not even count on work as

---

13. *Quebec Mercury* April 10, 1841; the same newspaper on February 11, 1840, provided an
    estimate of the numbers of workers in the shipyards of Quebec from 1818 to 1840.
14. It is worth noting that the average salary of a shipyard carpenter and of a caulker went
    from 7 shillings a day in the summer of 1839 to 3 shillings a day at the end of 1840. See
    Narcisse Rosa, *La construction de navires à Québec et ses environs* (Quebec, 1897): 10. In
    addition, throughout the nineteenth century, there was a tradition in British North
    America of lowering wages by one quarter or even one half in winter. In an article called
    "The Seasonal Contours of Pre-Industrial Poverty in British North America, 1815–1860,"
    Canada Historical Association, *Historical Papers* (1974), historian Judith Fingard indicates
    that this custom continued long enough that the Commission of inquiry on the relations
    between capital and labour mentioned it in 1889 as one of the principal sources of
    seasonal poverty among workers.
15. This figure was arrived at on the basis of the price of foodstuffs contained in the *Annual
    Reports of the Quebec Board of Trade, 1832–1842*, deposited in the National Archives of
    Quebec at Quebec City (hereafter ANQ-Q). This same source shows that naval carpenters
    at Quebec were among the least well paid workers in 1840. Most skilled workers
    (blacksmiths, bricklayers, carpenters in construction, etc.) of Quebec made more than 5
    shillings per day at this time.
16. The newspaper *Le Canadien* (Quebec) for December 4, 1840, contains an account of an
    accident which took place at the timberyard of Mr. Oliver in the suburb of Saint-Roch:
    "Thomas Rostevin, 18 years, apprentice-carpenter, was killed by a piece of wood which
    fell on him from a considerable height. He was so badly crushed that by the time he was
    reached, he was already dead."

stevedores, since the sailors were kept on board to unload the cargo.[17] Isolated and trapped in the suburb of Saint-Roch, the working population lived in the worst conditions in all the city of Quebec (lack of sanitation, famine, etc.).[18] Despite some bourgeois philanthropy—offered essentially to minimize worker transiency because of the future needs of capital—this separation by class within the city developed the seeds of a class consciousness among workers.

The Mobilization of the Naval Construction Workers in December 1840; or the Scenario of a Strike

Because of the slow development of capitalist production in Lower Canada before 1840, labour resistance was often quite primitive and scattered.[19] Moreover, the makeup of the working class changed too quickly, because of internal migrations resulting from seasonal unemployment, to permit the organization of a real movement against social inequality in the cities. In 1840, all of this changed when the shipworkers of Quebec began one of the first general strikes.[20] What led up to this strike? In early December 1840, the major shipbuilders in Quebec, anticipating new orders for the winter, had made an agreement to lower wages from 4 to 3 shillings a day. In defence, 1,200 workers, mainly carpenters, woodcutters, and labourers from different shipyards in Quebec, began an

---

17. Fernand Ouellet, *Histoire économique et sociale du Québec, 1760–1850* (2 vols.; Montreal: Fides, 1971), II: 504. This striking situation with regard to employment encouraged the establishment of new systems for exploiting the workforce. In 1842, John Munn suggested opening his shipyards for the construction of "barges" required by canalling businesses in Lower and Upper Canada; always, the workers who were interested were supposed to agree voluntarily to work, lured by more or less vague promises of an eventual sharing of the profits. See *Quebec Mercury*, December 27, 1842. At the end of the 1840s, numerous naval construction workers found employment constructing the aqueducts or acting as labourers in the stone quarries after being laid off.

18. For a detailed description of these social conditions, see the newspaper *L'Artisan* (Quebec), December 12, 1842, and the *Quebec Mercury*, December 10 and 27, 1842.

19. By "primitive" labour resistance, we mean individual and spontaneous actions (theft, absenteeism, insubordination, sabotage, etc.) which indicate a questioning of the employers' authority. These isolated initiatives show the combative spirit that is typical of workers in the first stages of capitalist industrialization.

20. In 1741, there was a strike in the royal shipyards of Quebec. The intendant, Hocquart, quickly crushed this "mutiny" by imprisoning the leaders and replacing them with workers brought from Rochefort, in France. See on this subject: S. B. Ryerson, *The Founding of Canada* (Toronto, 1960): 154.

immediate strike to protest what they rightly termed "the famine pact."[21] On December 3, the shipyards were closed down and the carpenters organized a meeting of all striking workers in the Saint-Roch school in order to decide on the action they should take and agree on their demands. They agreed to continue the strike all winter if necessary until the salaries returned to 4 shillings a day. Despite the illegality of the action, they decided to collect funds (more than £50 in 24 hours) to support the most needy strikers. A strike committee of 21 was formed to inform the shipbuilders of the strikers' complaints. As the strike progressed, the strikers attempted to find support among various groups in Quebec, such as other trade groups, small businessmen, and intellectuals like the journalist Napoléon Aubin.[22]

Despite the organized nature of the strike, the irritation of the strikers was so strong that some individual action and violence could not be prevented. On December 8, a riot broke out in the Munn shipyards, and the next day, there was theft and looting in the Edward Oliver shipyards in Saint-Roch.[23] Finally, on December 12, 1840, after 18 days of conflict, the strikers managed to break the shipbuilders' monopoly on wages, and wages were reinstated at 4 shillings a day. During a demonstration in Quebec that day, more than 800 shipworkers presented an address to George Black, for having been the first shipbuilder to reopen his yard at the salary demanded.[24]

Although this was essentially a defensive strike, it allowed a whole first generation of workers to realize their strength and their importance, as evidenced in this comment from the newspaper *Le Fantasque*: "The benefits this temporary alliance has brought the class of ship's carpenters should show them the necessity of forming a permanent association."[25]

The Birth of the Ship's Carpenters' Union

One of the most important steps in the development of the workers' consciousness was, without doubt, the founding of the "Société amicale et bienveillante des charpentiers de vaisseaux de Québec" (The Friendly and

---

21. *Le Canadien* (Quebec), December 4, 1840; *Le Fantasque* (Quebec), December 10, 1840.
22. *Le Canadien* (Quebec), December 4 and 7, 1840; *Quebec Mercury*, December 10, 1840; *Le Fantasque* (Quebec), December 10, 1840.
23. ANQ-Q, Prison Registers of Quebec, criminal files, 1840–41.
24. *Le Canadien* (Quebec), December 21 and 28, 1840; *Montreal Gazette*, December 26, 1840.
25. S. B. Ryerson, *Le Capitalisme et la Confédération* (Montreal: Parti pris, 1972): 234.

Benevolent Society of Quebec Ship's Carpenters) in the wake of the 1840 strike. Although this purported to be a friendly society, it was essentially a union for collective action.[26] Some ship's carpenters and labourers in the Saint-Roch shipyard were reminded that they should support the strike (of 1840) or they would be "expelled from the Society or judged unworthy of admittance to it."[27]

The idea of forming a "workers' union" was first considered in a December 12 meeting of ship's carpenters in the Saint-Roch area, shortly after the start of the 1840 strike. People spoke of the importance of "maintaining the influence of this trade association on society."[28] At this time, a committee of 12 was elected, with François Giffard as president, to establish the society's rules and aims. One of the first aims of the committee was to establish a common workers' league to oppose on a permanent basis the employers' coalitions. In order to do this, they opened membership to all categories of worker in the shipbuilding industry provided they were residents of Lower Canada and between the ages of 15 and 50.[29] However, since carpenters made up 75 percent[30] of the 255 members of this society in January 1841, a second aim of fighting the competition of immigrant workers and unskilled labour was considered equally important.[31] The duality of both proletarian and artisanal viewpoints was a characteristic of the Society from its inception. This duality was typical of industries where capitalist production had not totally transformed the old artisanal working practices.

Once united under the union banner, the shipworkers consulted a legal professional to advise them on their demands. On December 18, 1840, they nominated the notary Joseph Laurin[32] as secretary of the Society and asked him to put the society on a legal footing. He was also to keep the

---

26. Under common law, workers' coalitions were considered conspiracies. For this reason, the first unions acted in secret, hiding behind the name of friendly society. The money supposedly set aside to help members in cases of sickness or accident was often, in reality, a strike fund.
27. *Le Canadien* (Quebec), December 21, 1840.
28. *Ibid.*, December 16, 1840.
29. See the act which officially created the Society, preserved at the ANQ-Q in the minutes of notary Joseph Laurin, dated January 5, 1841.
30. *Ibid.*
31. Forsey, *Trade Unions in Canada, 1812–1902*: 15; Ouellet, *Histoire économique et sociale du Québec*, II: 501.
32. For a better understanding of this forerunner of legal advisors to unions, see Lucie Bouffard and Robert Tremblay, "Joseph Laurin," *Dictionary of Canadian Biography*, vol. 11 (Quebec), 1982): 549 ff.

minutes of committee meetings and inform the members of their legal rights, especially in the case of a strike. Laurin declared that he was ready to fight the shipbuilders' monopoly and that "their determination would eventually conquer the disgusting greed of these Quebec speculators."[33]

The Society was to be fully self-governing. Resolutions were adopted by majority vote; in the case of a tie, the president of the Society could cast the deciding vote. The regulations governing the Society were advanced for the time, since they were based on the principle of the executive committee's responsibility to the members at large. For example, the members could remove an "officer" at any time for malpractice.[34] As Médéric Lanctôt said several years later, the first unions were amazingly democratic for the time.[35] The formation of the ship's carpenters' society shows us how well the workers could look after their own interests, but we must realize that the governing rules and the democratic principles of this organization were the product of an outsider, the notary Laurin, who was responsible for the legal incorporation of the Society and its rules and regulations. Recent studies of the working class in France in the period 1830–48 have shown that the ideology of the common people was influenced by internal forces such as the feeling of being exploited and by external forces such as religion and the idea of popular sovereignty.[36]

The State as Policeman and the Working Class

Apart from economic grievances and the desire for a fair wage, the shipworkers' strike was also an act of resistance, a defiance of the laws of the bourgeoisie. By refusing to work without fair remuneration, these striking workers were challenging the bourgeois idea of a "free individual contract"—which hides inequality in the employer–employee relationship—and implicitly stating that a contract has no legal value unless it is made with the workers as a collectivity.[37] The creation of the Society

---

33. *Le Canadien*, December 21, 1840.
34. ANQ-Q, Minutes, Joseph Laurin, January 5, 1841.
35. Margaret Heap, "La Grève des Charretiers à Montréal," *RHAF* 31, no. 3 (December 1977): 385.
36. Note that the ship's carpenters' society survived the crisis of the 1840s in the shipbuilding industry. In 1850 it was incorporated, and in 1867 it was responsible for another strike in this sector.
37. The question of the existence of a "workers' legality" is thoroughly discussed in the thesis of J. Chamard, "Discours d'émancipation et discours de pouvoir: étude de la

defied bourgeois law relating to the right of association. According to the "Combination Acts," passed in the British Parliament in 1800 and adopted in the colony shortly thereafter, any person meeting with others for the purpose of protesting for higher wages or shorter working hours could be found guilty of criminal conspiracy.[38] Taking up collections and meeting to organize collections were also considered crimes according to the law. Like many other strikes in the nineteenth century, the conflict of December 1840 in the shipbuilding industry implicitly illustrates two opposite ideas of rights and freedom. The state would be called upon to decide whose concept was the correct one.

Social unrest in Quebec forced the state to intervene. It used its political and legal powers selectively against the working class. After the shipyard riots on December 8 and 9, five of the "alleged leaders"[39] were arrested and sentenced by Quebec district magistrates to sentences ranging from 10 days in jail to 4 months of forced labour.[40] The judges also nominated John Munn, a shipbuilder, as head of a Quebec police watchdog committee with 140 members.[41] Lobbying by Quebec shipbuilders and merchants was probably the cause of a law passed in 1841 by the newly reformed Legislative Assembly "governing malicious damage to property."[42] This law, with sentences of life imprisonment or exile, was intended to punish acts of sabotage, particularly sabotage of vessels under construction. Article 25 of this law makes the intention perfectly clear. Guilt could be established on grounds of malicious intent; thus any group action, and most particularly strike action, could be considered intent to destroy the employer's ownership of capital.[43] Obviously, even at this early date, the power of the state was the bastion of the bourgeoisie when they felt themselves even slightly threatened by labour unrest. . . .

---

pensée des maîtres-tisserands de Lyon" (M.A. Thesis, Department of History, University of Quebec at Montreal, 1980), 113-16.

38. Robert Tremblay, "Un aspect de la consolidation du pouvoir d'État de la bourgeoisie coloniale: La legislation anti-ouvrière dans le Bas-Canada, 1800–1850," *Labour/Le Travailleur* 8/9 (Fall/Spring 1981–1982): 247 ff.

39. The defendants were Jacques Bezeau, Jacques Lévesque, Olivier Lévesque, Jean-Baptiste Marcoux, and Élie Simard, all labourers working in the naval construction industry.

40. ANQ-Q, Magistrates' court, Quebec District, January 16, 1841.

41. Quebec City Archives, Council Series and minutes, December 14, 1840.

42. Province of Canada, Legislative Assembly, *Statutes*, 1841, c. 26.

43. Tremblay, "Un aspect de la consolidation du pouvoir d'État de la bourgeoisie coloniale. . .": 250.

Conclusion

Despite its collective nature, the shipbuilders' strike remains, first and foremost, a defensive action, by means of which the workers' resistance attempted to curtail the overall powers of the employers and thus place limits on their ability to exploit and overwork the employees. One can explain this stand in light of the prospect of a slowing down of production. This prospect forced the shipyard workers to postpone pressing the owners of capital for their main demands, such as the ten-hour work day. This decision to wait for a favourable moment to launch an offensive action is typical of what has now become known as the "workers' awareness of circumstances." Nevertheless, the mere use of the strike tactic could not help but augment the little experience accumulated in this area by the working class.

More than just a footnote to the strike movement, the inception of the Society of ship's carpenters should be interpreted as the emergence of the leadership abilities of the working class, at a non-governmental level. In that respect the birth of the first unions prefigures, according to Gramsci, a new workers' power base in society. But this new power base was destined to be stifled for many years to come, since, let's not forget, the act of striking, through its social reverberations, brings with it its own counterpart: the fear of the strike, which pushes the state to adopt measures in order to dissuade the working class, and which exhorts the employers to address the masses in such a way as to indoctrinate them in a spirit which runs contrary to their own interests.

Whatever else it may be, the strike of workers in the shipyards, which took place in Quebec in 1840, reveals the desire for emancipation of a group of men who, in the words of the poet Paul Chamberland, were at the mercy of the sovereign whim of Capital.

DEPLORABLY DARK AND DEMORALIZED LUMBERERS?

Rhetoric and Reality in Early Nineteenth Century New Brunswick

G. WYNN

Reality—Lumbering and Farming in Early New Brunswick

Despite the importance of the timber trade in the provincial economy, New Brunswick was far from the extensive lumber camp that some have envisaged.[1] Rural dwellers formed the majority of its steadily increasing population, which rose from some 25,000 early in the century to almost 200,000 by 1851. At mid-century approximately 30,000 people lived in the port city of Saint John; Fredericton, the capital, had fewer than 5,000 residents; clusters of two or three thousand people lived in small urban centers along the lower reaches of the St. Croix and Miramichi valleys. Elsewhere, villages served a population dispersed about the coasts and along the major river valleys of the province. A thin line of settlement along the Southwest Miramichi River linked the peripheral population of the gulf shore to the more densely occupied ribbon of land flanking the St. John River. Following the main overland route to Nova Scotia, and the fertile valleys of the Kennebecasis and the upper Petitcodiac rivers, an arm of settlement linked Saint John to the densely settled agricultural district at the head of the Bay of Fundy.[2]

In this essentially preindustrial environment, individual family farms were the setting of most New Brunswick lives.[3] Fifty or a hundred forested acres, available even at mid-century for as little as £ 15, met basic immigrant aspirations to independence. With perhaps thirty acres

---

G. WYNN, "DEPLORABLY DARK AND DEMORALIZED LUMBERERS? RHETORIC AND REALITY IN EARLY NINETEENTH CENTURY NEW BRUNSWICK," *JOURNAL OF FOREST HISTORY* 24 (1980): 176–87.

1. Some have claimed, for example, that 85 percent of the provincial population was dependent on lumbering. See W. S. MacNutt, "Politics of the Timber Trade in Colonial New Brunswick, 1825–1840," *Canadian Historical Review* 30 (March 1949): 47.
2. "Population and other statistics of the Province of New Brunswick, 1851" *Journal of the House of Assembly*, 1852, Appendix.
3. The history of New Brunswick agriculture remains to be written. This section is largely dependent upon my ongoing work on the province, some of which is included in a forthcoming study of the New Brunswick lumber industry.

cleared, a property of this size could be the foundation of moderate comfort. Mixed farming yielded many of the necessities of existence; small surpluses might be exchanged at the nearest general store for imported items, such as sugar, rum, and fancy cloth. At the census of 1851, approximately 60 percent of those listing their occupations, in a cluster of sample parishes in the St. John Valley, described themselves as farmers. Craftsmen and "mechanics"—among whom carpenters and shoemakers were perhaps the most common—made up a further 10 to 15 percent of the total. Laborers formed a slightly larger group. By comparison, those who designated themselves "lumberman" were a small proportion of the whole.[4]

Yet these statistics mislead. By rigid classification, they obscure a widespread pattern of occupational pluralism in early nineteenth-century New Brunswick. With few exceptions labor was irregular and unspecialized. Families gave their time to a variety of tasks as needs, inclinations, and weather dictated. On the coasts, fishermen farmed and farmers fished. In cities and towns, laboring men turned to almost any manual toil available. The seasons imposed their rhythms upon existence. For those settled upon the land, short winter days marked a respite from the seemingly endless round of agricultural chores culminating with the harvest. And in many parts of the province, farmers and their sons occupied a proportion of their relatively slack days between Christmas and Easter at work in the forests.

Small-scale enterprises were the backbone of the provincial lumbering industry before 1850.[5] To be sure, physiographic and hydrological conditions, settlement patterns, and permissive regulations fostered oligopsony and entrepreneurial dominance of the industry in the northeast of the province during the 1840s—a circumstance that did not go unremarked by those sensitive to the constriction of individual opportunities in the trade this entailed.[6] But for the most part, and especially in the first quarter of the century, temporary partnerships of three or four men and slightly

---

4. The published census of 1851 includes a tabulation of "Occupations." This broadly confirms the pattern, but the seven-class breakdown is too gross to be really useful here. These comments are based upon the enumerators' returns for Hampton, Upham, and Norton parishes in Kings County and Kingsclear in York County.
5. G. C. Wynn, "The Assault on the New Brunswick Forest, 1780-1850," (Ph.D. thesis, University of Toronto, 1974), chapter 5.
6. Report of speech by Assemblyman A. S. Carman, *Gleaner and Northumberland Schediasma*, April 20, 1847.

larger ventures contracting work to individuals were typical. Examples best illustrate the scale and variety of these organizational arrangements.

With the rapid rise in the market for ton-timber after 1805, many families and friends entered the trade. At first perhaps little more than extensions of the regular winter work of cutting wood for domestic fires, their ventures could be conducted close to home. In the St. John Valley in particular, an extended line of settlement backed onto extensive, pine-rich forests. Cutting was essentially unregulated before 1817; thereafter licenses were readily and cheaply available to those unwilling to risk trespass upon the Crown domain. The river provided a magnificent artery by which the cut could be brought to market.[7]

Above Fredericton, near the little town of Woodstock, the sons of Frederick Dibblee, a Loyalist clergyman and farmer, combined timber-making with work on the family farm for twenty years after 1805. The two activities were closely intertwined. In three April and May weeks of 1818, for example, the Dibblee boys cleared new land, began their spring plowing, and sold their rafts of timber in the capital. In the following fall, Jack Dibblee had the help of a friend at the harvest, so (his father recorded), "they may tomorrow go a Timber Hunting."[8] By the mid-1820s William Dibblee had increased his commitment to lumbering. In the winter of 1823–1824, he hired at least five men to assist in cutting and hauling his timber. Yet still he combined lumbering and farming. Similar ventures were legion. Country storekeepers in many parts of the province collected small parcels of timber—twenty or thirty tons, fifteen sticks—from settlers in their hinterland. Agents directed the winter's cut of three- and four-man lumbering ventures to wholesale traders in the province's ports.[9] As the trade expanded and accessible pine became scarcer, opportunities for part-time timber-making declined, but the rising market for sawlogs offered an alternative market for those who worked farm and forest.

Contract labor allowed more circumscribed participation in the lumbering industry. Hewing thirty or forty tons of timber for the organizer of a lumbering venture could yield an individual £ 10 or £ 12 in cash or,

7. Wynn, "New Brunswick Forest," pp. 180–269.
8. Diary of the Reverend Frederick Dibblee of Woodstock, New Brunswick, October 9, 1818, New Brunswick Museum, Saint John.
9. See for examples: the Buckingham-Camp Correspondence and the Robertson Family Papers, New Brunswick Museum; the William and George Harper Papers, MG 24 D58, Public Archives of Canada; and the Letterbook of W. J. Bedell, 1837–1838, in the Archives of the University of New Brunswick, Fredericton.

more commonly, credit with a local storekeeper.[10] A man with an oxteam and time might haul logs from stump to brow for a week or two for similar returns. The frequency of such arrangements and the returns available from them are reflected in the fragmentary business records of early storekeepers. Among them, for example, the ledgers of Crane and Allison of Westmorland County document payments to one George Barnes of £ 3 for "12 days Cutting timber" and £ 4/o/3d for "Hauling 8 tons & 1 foot Timber." Similarly, James Hicks received £ 1 for "2 days with Team in the Camp," £ 5 for 28 1/2 days "Work in the Woods" by him and his sons, and £ 13/5/o for "Drawing 26 1/2 Tons Timber."[11]

Here, in outline, are sketched some important features of countless New Brunswick lives. Time and again, settlers in this premodern domain, where existence was still heavily dependent upon the strength and energy of man and beast, turned diverse but relatively simple skills to account as circumstances allowed and needs required. There is no way of knowing just how widely this flexible pattern of occupational pluralism involved men in the timber trade. Indeed, patterns differed regionally within the province and varied with fluctuations of the New Brunswick economy. Yet overall it is clear that lumbering provided an important, available, and oft-utilized source of employment for common men. For some it was their source of livelihood; for many—perhaps most—its returns were a vital supplement to the produce of small family farms.

Despite the importance of the family farm in early New Brunswick, agriculture certainly provided no easy and assured route to prosperity and independence. Clearing the forest and establishing a productive farm was hard work enough in the best of nineteenth-century circumstances. In New Brunswick inferior soils compounded the settlers' difficulties. Beyond Chignecto (at the head of the Bay of Fundy) and the narrow valleys of the St. John River and its lower tributaries, fertile land is scarce. Dauntingly often, the initial fertility of humus-rich new cleared land was belied by the poverty of stony, leached soils beneath.[12]

An unreliable climate, marginal for the cultivation of available strains of

---

10. Testimony of Solomon Tracy, October 17, 1842, REX/Pa, Surveyor General, 29, 1842, Land Matters, and Statement of Ebin Grant, January 27, 1840, REX/Pa, Surveyor General, 23, 1840, Miscellaneous, both in the Provincial Archives of New Brunswick.

11. Crane and Allison Ledger, 1818–1827, MG3, Vol. 300, Public Archives of Nova Scotia, Halifax.

12. The reports of the *New Brunswick Soil Survey* (e.g., No. 1, P. C. Stobbe, Fredericton-Georgetown area) and soil-capability maps (ARDA, Canada Land Inventory [Ottawa: Queens Printer, various dates]) provide evidence of soil quality in much of the province.

wheat, further limited the province's agricultural prospects. Inclement summers and bad harvests were a recurring difficulty for New Brunswick farmers in the nineteenth century. A crop failure in the St. John Valley in 1798 left many settlers indebted to the merchants who had supplied them.[13] The seasons of 1815 and 1816 were particularly unfavorable for agriculture. On June 7, 1816, snow fell in many southern parts of the province, and bleak harvest prospects led men to consider abandoning their land. From Charlotte County at the end of this "year without a summer" came a brief report eloquently summarizing conditions in the province: "Crops of hay and potatoes are very slim, Cattle are very cheap, Men is plenty and Money was never known to be so scarce."[14] A "great failure of the crops" produced similar consequences in the St. John Valley in 1825, and the province's farmers suffered a further series of bad summers in the 1830s.[15]

Yet land clearance continued, and at a rate considerably in advance of the rate of population increase in the colony. No data are available for the first quarter of the century, but if we represent both the population (74,000) and the estimated cleared area (200,000 acres) in 1824 by an index base of 100, the comparable indices for 1851 are 262 and 320.[16] This is much as we would expect if older farms were extended as new ones were opened up by incoming settlers. Indeed, the ongoing extension of the arable area is apparent from the records of bounties paid for the cultivation of grain on newly cleared land after 1817.[17] In 1825 between 15.5 and 18 percent of family heads in the counties of Kings, Westmorland, and

---

13. Stephen Jarvis to Munson Jarvis, July 12, 1798, and John Bedell to Munson Jarvis, July 6, 1798, both in Jarvis Papers, 1791–1800, New Brunswick Museum.

14. Joel Hill to G. S. Hill, October 19, 1816, Hill Family Papers, MHI/1/32, Provincial Archives of New Brunswick. See also *Royal Gazette*, June 11, 1816; P. Fisher, *Notitia of New Brunswick* (Saint John, 1836), p. 20; and H. Steeves, *The Story of Moncton's First Store and Storekeeper* (Saint John: Macmillan, 1924).

15. Henry and Elizabeth White to John C. Robertson, September 23, 1825, Robertson Family Papers, New Brunswick Museum: Robert Crookshank to John and Robert Crookshank, March 15, 1838, Crookshank Family Papers, Box 3, PKT 9, New Brunswick Museum.

16. Census of New Brunswick, 1824, *Journal of the House of Assembly*, 1825, Appendix; Census of New Brunswick, 1851, *ibid.*, 1852, Appendix; Wynn, "New Brunswick Forest," p. 76.

17. The bounties were instituted in 1817 and were payable on grains raised on land "within two years from the time when the wood growing thereon was cut down, burned or cleared off...and which were the first and only crops raised on such land." Extant returns are not complete; most are in REX/Pa, Bounties, Provincial Archives of New Brunswick, but see also MNO/7/1 in the same repository.

York received the bounty. Of the recipients in York, almost one-third had received bounties between 1817 and 1821.

At this scale, too, the links between farming and lumbering are evident. Many of those who claimed grain bounties for the summers between 1817 and 1825 participated in the timber trade during one or more of the intervening winters. Nineteen of the 353 recipients of the grain bounty in the county of York in 1825 held timber licenses during the previous winter.[18] More, almost certainly, worked on the licenses of others, sold timber cut from their own land, or otherwise derived cash or credit from involvement with the timber trade. Some of them, perhaps, were among those who reported a quarter century later that "almost all farmers in this neighbourhood were lumberers before they were farmers, and it was by lumbering they got their farms stocked, etc."[19]

Lumbering and farming were closely interconnected and to a considerable degree interdependent industries in New Brunswick. Lumbering parties provided a market for many a farmer's surplus hay. "Work in the woods" offered newly arrived immigrants the best prospect of accumulating the capital necessary to buy and stock a farm in this still underdeveloped colony where urban labor was highly seasonal and agricultural employment was relatively scarce. For those already on the land, participation in the timber trade could provide the additional £ 10 to £ 15 necessary to hire labor in the summer, to purchase stock, to build a barn, or to acquire farm implements. Visiting agricultural chemist J. F. W. Johnston discovered in 1849 that many of the province's successful farmers had built their independence by judicious participation in the timber trade. Although his inquiry about the success of "industrious agricultural settlers in past years" brought a number of adverse comments about the impact of lumbering on farming, Johnston also heard of poor migrants from Britain "compelled occasionally to hire out and get lumber until their land was sufficiently cleared to live on" and of prosperous farmers who occasionally did "something in the lumber way."[20] . . .

---

18. The timber license records of the Crown Lands Office reveal the names but not the residences of license holders. This figure is a minimum. No definitive count of bounty claimants who held timber licenses from 1818 to 1825 is possible. See RNA/C/10 and Timber Petitions, in boxes by year, Provincial Archives of New Brunswick.

19. J. F. W. Johnston, *Report on the Agricultural Capabilities. . .of New Brunswick* (Fredericton, 1850), pp. 84–85.

20. *Ibid.*

Toward Reinterpretation

The critiques considered in this essay have offered a ready source of judgment to twentieth century commentators on nineteenth-century New Brunswick. Reinforced by the braggadocio of the lumberer's camp songs (most of which originated after 1850), the colorful rhetoric of these criticisms has echoed through many accounts of provincial development. From the literature of the last half century, we learn that New Brunswick agriculture languished while the population worked in the forest; that lumbering was "a gambling trade"; that New Brunswick's early nineteenth-century development resembled a gold rush; and that the lumberers were a "wild intemperate and unstable" crew, "made so by the conditions" of their lives. In the province, as elsewhere in North America, "the sack of the largest and wealthiest of medieval cities could have been but a bagatelle compared with the sack of the...forest, and no medieval ravisher could have been more fierce and unscrupulous than the lumberman." The industry held out "illusory promises." Generally, those who tried to combine farming and lumbering fell between two stools and sank into destitution. "Unfortunately the course of the sturdy young fellows who were attracted by the wild, free life of the woods, was too often steadily downward, and they found themselves with youth ebbing, health perhaps broken, and no recourse but to keep on in the rocky path they had chosen."[21] Here New Brunswick appears as a land of underutilized agricultural potential, of indebted lumberers, and of decaying farms abandoned for all or part of the year by settlers lured into lumbering by the illusions of quick profit and an unrestricted life.

Now it is clear that this interpretation is overdrawn. The early nineteenth-century provincial economy was as complex as the critiques of lumbering were derivative. Lumbering and farming were intricately interconnected through most of the province before 1850. Together they were the essential supports of a developing society. Undoubtedly in New Brunswick, as elsewhere, a protracted and heavy commitment to lumber-

---

21. See A. R. M. Lower, *The North American Assault on the Canadian Forest* (Toronto: Ryerson Press, 1938), pp. 26, 65, 79; Lower, *Settlement and the Forest Frontier in Eastern Canada* (Toronto: Macmillan, 1936), pp. 31–37; and Michael S. Cross, "The Dark Druidical Groves: The Lumber Community and the Commercial Frontier in British North America, to 1854" (Ph.D. dissertation, University of Toronto, 1968), pp. 82–117. Also see Franz L. Rickaby, ed., *Ballads and Songs of the Shanty-Boy* (Cambridge: Harvard University Press, 1926), and Edith Fowke, *Lumbering Songs from the Northern Woods* (Austin: University of Texas Press, 1970).

ing was incompatible with successful farming. No one has revealed this better than the English traveler, Sir James Alexander. At a boarding-house in the St. John Valley in the 1840s, he remarked upon the proximity of the landlady's bed to the stove. The reason, he was informed, was that "her husband was lumbering in the woods for ten months in the year during all of which time she never saw him."[22] But this pattern was the exception in the early nineteenth century. Countless New Brunswickers benefited from the part-time, off-farm work that lumbering provided in an unaccommodating agricultural environment. The seasonal demands of part-time lumbering and subsistence farming were almost diametrical; thus the two pursuits could be complementary. They were often combined with success.

Undoubtedly, the cyclic fluctuation and commercial uncertainty of the timber trade were causes of economic hardship and anxiety in the province. Whereas conventional arguments in praise of agriculture were voiced quite regularly, criticisms of the timber industry were at their most strident in the wake of market downturns. As an anonymous contributor to the *New Brunswick Courier* recognized, "the minds of some men are like the elastic ball thrown against the wall: when they are suddenly checked they rebound in the opposite direction."[23] Faced in the 1840s with reduction of the British tariff preference afforded colonial wood, "many persons who formerly built their hopes upon [New Brunswick's] lofty groves of pine" turned to "decry all commerce in. . .native timber as injurious to the Colony." Yet such consternation was often unduly pessimistic. Tariff adjustments rarely proved as crippling as anticipated. And the evidence of lean years should not lead us to ignore the timber trade's contribution to provincial development and individual prosperity in more expansive times.

Further, we should recognize that—origins of the critical rhetoric aside—contemporary indictments of lumbering and lumbermen in New Brunswick were often erected upon the most slender of foundations. Most commonly, condemnations of lumbering were supported by accounts of individual indebtedness or by tales of the springtime debauchery of an itinerant raftsman; similarly, justifications of the farmer's life were found in the success and happiness of a single settler. But such arguments are prey to what historian David Hackett Fischer has called "the fallacy of the

---

22. Sir James Alexander, *L'Acadie, or Seven Years Exploration in British North America*, 2 vols. (London, 1849), 2: 85.
23. "Resources of New Brunswick," cited in *Royal Gazette*, October 6, 1841.

lonely fact."[24] They have not always been treated with the caution they deserve. Interpretations have been built by extrapolation from the particular rather than upon generalizations describing a number of known and specified cases.

Ultimately, the caliber of information required for sound generalization may be wanting. But fuller consideration of the context in which particular cases were set is warranted. It can be sketched but briefly here. There is no doubt that many New Brunswick settlers failed; abandoned clearings along the province's rivers and public announcements of absconding debtors and bankrupts were ready reminders of pioneer disappointment and of the incidence of financial hardship.[25] Similarly, drunkenness and unruly behavior were common enough; the province imported extremely large quantities of rum in the early nineteenth century. As yet, we know little about transiency and population turnover in early New Brunswick.[26] But scant evidence suggests that before 1850, at least, the flux of population in the province was not exceptional. Neither were bankruptcy and debt evasion the prerogative of lumbermen. Farmers, laborers, merchants, and mechanics were among those—and overall they were but a fraction of New Brunswick's population—whose failures were recorded before mid-century. Inebriation and lawlessness were probably no more frequent in New Brunswick than in many other areas of the continent at a comparable stage of development. Settlers on numerous North American frontiers warmed their souls with imported spirits during the long months of winter. And certainly New Brunswick did not have the annual brawling, drinking springtime of lawless terror that the Irish "Shiners" brought to Ottawa in the 1830s, when they challenged both upper-class representatives of the established order and French Canadian rivals for jobs in the timber trade.[27] Occasional skirmishes between competitors for timber berths; a certain amount of head bashing among rival camps at election time; July conflicts between Orange and Green; evasion and defiance of

---

24. Fischer, *Historians' Fallacies: Toward a Logic of Historical Thought* (New York: Harper and Row, 1970), pp. 109–10.
25. Notices of absconding debtors are to be found in many issues of the *Royal Gazette*. For some treatment of mercantile bankruptcy, see Wynn, "New Brunswick Timber Trade."
26. T. W. Acheson, "A Study in the Historical Geography of a Loyalist County," *Histoire Sociale/Social History* 1 (1968: 53–64, offers a beginning.
27. Michael S. Cross, "The Shiners' War: Social Violence in the Ottawa Valley in the 1830s," *Canadian Historical Review* 54 (March 1973): 1–26.

timber license regulations; all these New Brunswick knew.[28] But their incidence was sporadic. This violence was "recreational" or "communal"—the incidental, essentially unorganized conflict of interacting groups; in this it differed little from prevalent patterns elsewhere in North America.[29]

In sum, then, twentieth-century judgments of New Brunswick's early nineteenth-century lumbering industry have been harsh. Contemporary criticisms of the "rising crusade against the forest" (on which these judgments have been based) were frequently exaggerated.[30] Engaged in the arduous and closely connected tasks of establishing themselves and their communities, many early New Brunswickers, in common with their pioneering counterparts in most regions of recent European settlement, found comfort in the puritanical ideals of hard work and self-denial.[31] Extravagance and intemperance they regarded with suspicion; frugality and industry they esteemed. And these were the values reinforced in the didactic literature of the day. But this literature was the product of visitors to, and the elite of, the province. It was structured by convention and cast around stereotypes. Eighteenth and early nineteenth-century convictions that social isolation (of employer from employee, of laboring men from the "middle classes") led to the depravity of the working man—which had limited relevance to conditions in the provincial lumber industry—ran through this writing.[32] So, too, did the traditional rhetoric of agrarianism. Those who embraced pastoral values found a clear focus for their enthusiasms in opposition to the timber trade, without troubling themselves to understand circumstances in the developing colony. Similarly,

---

28. W. S. MacNutt, *New Brunswick, A History: 1784–1867* (Toronto: Macmillan, 1963), pp. 276, 347–49, and Graeme Wynn, "Administration in Adversity: The Deputy Surveyors and Control of the New Brunswick Crown Forest before 1844," *Acadiensis* 7 (Autumn 1977): 49–65, offer brief treatment of these matters.

29. See Charles Tilly, "Collective Violence in European Perspective," and Richard Maxwell Brown, "Historical Patterns of Violence in America," in H. D. Graham and T. R. Gurr, eds., *Violence in America: Historical and Comparative Perspectives* (New York: Praeger, 1969), pp. 4–84; and K. McNaught, "Violence in Canadian History," in John S. Moir, ed., *Character and Circumstance: Essays in Honour of Donald Grant Creighton* (Toronto: Macmillan, 1970), pp. 66–86.

30. The phrase is from R. Cooney, *A Compendious History of the Northern Part of New Brunswick* (Halifax, 1832), p. 68.

31. R. Cole Harris, et al., "The Settlement of Mono Township," *Canadian Geographer* 19 (1975): 1–17; Robert Chapman, "Fiction and the Social Pattern," in Wystan Curnow, ed., *Essays on New Zealand Literature* (Auckland: Heinemann Educational Books, 1973), pp. 80–81.

32. Reinhard Bendix, *Work and Authority in Industry: Ideologies of Management in the Course of Industrialization* (New York: John Wiley and Sons, 1956), pp. 69–70.

declamations against the idleness and intemperance of the poor (common in contemporary Britain) were reiterated in New Brunswick with lumbermen their target, although drunkenness there as in Britain was "not confined...to any particular class of men."[33]

In short, New Brunswick lumbering provided a convenient point of convergence for contemporary commentary on the shape of society in the province during the early nineteenth century. That this commentary was derivative, and that it reflected a limited perspective, is not surprising. But recognition of the clichéd terms in which the failings of New Brunswick lumberers were described is crucial to our understanding of both provincial development and the North American lumber industry. At other times and in other places, sailors, city dwellers, soldiers, gypsies, cowboys, and coureurs de bois have been the butt of criticisms essentially analogous to those directed at lumbermen. This fact reminds us once again that, however vigorous, contemporary descriptions of the lumber industry and those engaged in it cannot be understood apart from the context of ideas and beliefs in which they were articulated. Full consideration of this context must lead to reconsideration of the view that lumbering was the debilitating and reckless occupation revealed in the writing of many contemporary commentators.

FURTHER READINGS FOR TOPIC 11

Ruth Bleasdale. "Class Conflict on the Canals of Upper Canada in the 1840's." *Labour/le travailleur* 7 (1981), 9–39.

Douglas McCalla. "Forest Products and Upper Canadian Development 1815–46." *Canadian Historical Review* 68 (1987): 159–98.

Kenneth Norrie and Douglas Owram. *A History of the Canadian Economy*. Toronto: Harcourt Brace Jovanovich, 1991.

Graeme Wynn. *Timber Colony: A Historical Geography of Early Nineteenth Century New Brunswick*. Toronto: University of Toronto Press, 1981.

---

33. Cited in *ibid.*, p. 70.

P A R T

4

Conflict and Change in a Shrinking World: 1841–67

Topic 12

Responsible Government

R esponsible government was one of the most important steps on the road from colony to nation for British North America. It meant that colonial governments no longer required the approval of the British government for matters of purely colonial concern. The centre of power within the colonies therefore shifted away from the Governor, a British official, to the cabinet, composed of members of the legislative assembly who had to answer to the legislature. In order to achieve and maintain power, local leaders worked hard to establish political parties both within the legislatures and among the voting public. These three changes—local autonomy, cabinet government, and party government—constituted the essence of responsible government.

Responsible government did not mean, however, that the colonies were altogether free from British control. On the contrary, the British government retained the final say on matters affecting the Empire as a whole, including defence, trade, and foreign relations. This continuation of British control was not objectionable to the moderate Reformers of Upper Canada and Canada West who fought for responsible government. Quite the reverse. They argued, as the article by Carol Wilton shows, that the new constitutional arrangements would cement the bonds of Empire by reducing colonial discontent. Beyond that, Reformers believed that responsible government, far from leading to Americanization as the conservatives maintained, would instead entrench the British system of government, a belief echoed by Joseph Howe, the leading Nova Scotian promoter of responsible government.

While British political philosophies and practices shaped colonial politics, French cultural influences also had a powerful effect. Jacques Monet's article shows how the rise in France of ultramontanism—the belief that the state should be subordinate to the church—was mirrored in

Canada East (Quebec). The result was a growing movement in the direction of conservatism among the French-speaking population and their politicians. This movement helped pave the way for the absorption of the LaFontaine moderates, known as Bleus in Canada East, into the Conservative party in 1854.

French-Canadian Nationalism and the Challenge of Ultramontanism

JACQUES MONET

A funny thing happened to French-Canadian nationalism on its way to responsible government. It became ultramontane.

At the end of the 1830s French Canada was in ferment. Under British domination for some 75 years, the French had succeeded in surviving, but not in developing by themselves a full, normal, national life. They had kept the essentials: their ancestral land, their French language, their Catholic Faith, their time-honoured and peculiar jurisprudence, and their long family traditions. But they needed a new life. The seigneurial system could no longer hold the growing population, the economy lagged, the problems of education had reached such an impasse that the schools were closed, and the old civil code no longer applied to modern circumstances. Above all, the upward thrust of the growing professional middle class created a serious social situation of which the rebellions of 1837–38 were only one expression. Clearly, if the struggle for national survival were to hold any meaning for the future, French-Canadian nationalists needed new solutions.

They were divided, however. Inspired by the ideology of Louis-Joseph Papineau some considered *la survivance* could be assured only by political isolation in a territory over which French-Canadians would be undisputed masters. Militant idealists, they were led by John Neilson and Denis-Benjamin Viger until Papineau returned to politics in 1847. Others, broader minded and more practical, held to a doctrine of which the Quebec editor Etienne Parent was the clearest exponent, and which Louis-Hippolyte LaFontaine translated into politics. They reasoned that it was the flexibility of the British constitutional system that could best assure not only their acquired rights, but also (by means of self-government) the certain hope of a broadening future for their language, their institutions, and their nationality.

Before achieving responsible government, however, LaFontaine needed to accomplish two things. He had to forge the unity of his people in favour of British parliamentary democracy and, along with this, form a

Jacques Monet, "French-Canadian Nationalism and the Challenge of Ultramontanism," Canadian Historical Association, *Historical Paper* (1966): 41–52. By permission of Canadian Historical Association and Jacques Monet.

united political party with the Upper Canadians. Neither was easy. In the years immediately following the rebellion French Canada's strongest sympathies belonged to the leaders of the Viger-Neilson group, believers neither in responsible government nor in Union with Upper Canada. After the election of 1841, for instance, out of some 29 members elected by French-Canadian ridings, LaFontaine could count on only six or seven to be sympathetic to his views. By 1844, he had succeeded in persuading many more—at least he could then count on some two dozen. But not before the end of the decade could he be certain of victory, for until then Papineau, his followers, and especially his legend remained one of the strongest forces in the country. Still, after a decade of fistfights on electoral platforms, scandals, riots, and racial fury; after a brilliant, dynamic, and flexible partnership with Robert Baldwin, LaFontaine became in 1848 the first Canadian Prime Minister in the modern sense and, by means of the British Constitution, the first French-Canadian to actually express and direct the aspirations of his people.

He had also gradually, and all unwittingly perhaps, presided over the marriage of ultramontanism with the practical politics and the nationalist ideology of his party. At the beginning of the decade, the hierarchy and priests of the Roman Catholic Church in French Canada hardly conceived that practical party politics could be their concern, nor did they think of adding significantly to the nationalist theme. They worked behind the scenes: and, in 1838, for instance, after deciding to oppose the Union, they composed and signed an unpublicized petition which they sent directly to London to be presented to the Queen. But in 1848, during the crisis which consecrated the practice of responsible government, they openly took sides with LaFontaine's party, and allowed their newspapers to give approval to his administration. Likewise, at the time of the rebellions, most of the priests, and especially those among the hierarchy, had officially disassociated themselves from what seemed to be the main preoccupations of the leading French-Canadian nationalists. . . . Within a decade later, however, they openly wrote and talked of the doctrine that the Catholic Faith and French Canada's nationality depended one upon the other. . . . Of course, much happened between 1838 and 1848 to change the thinking of both nationalists and Catholic clerics.

One very important thing was the advent of Ignace Bourget. A short time after succeeding to the See of Montreal in 1840, this earnest and authoritarian Bishop made it clear how much he intended to renew the face of Catholicism in French Canada. During his first year—incidentally, after successfully reasserting in an interesting conflict with Poulett Thomson the doctrine of Papal supremacy and of episcopal independence of civil authority—he had organized a great mission throughout his diocese, preached by Bishop Forbin-Janson, one of France's foremost orators. Between September 1840 and December 1841, the French Bishop travelled across Lower Canada, visiting some sixty villages and preaching rousing sermons—two of which Lord Sydenham attended in state at Notre-Dame—before crowds sometimes estimated at ten thousand. Bishop Bourget thus initiated close and large-scale religious contacts with France.

Indeed, while Forbin-Janson was still in Canada, the new Bishop of Montreal left on the first of some five voyages to France and Rome, a trip from which he would return carrying with him the reawakened energies of the Catholic revival. While in Europe, he held discussions with a cluster of interesting and influential Catholic ultramontane leaders. At this time, European ultramontanes—whose intellectual roots reached as far back as the quarrels between Philippe LeBel and Boniface VIII, the pope "beyond the mountains"—...urged the subservience of civil government to the papacy, of State to Church. They had not understood that there was a difference between the surrender of all men to God's will, and the obedience of civil society to the Pope. They were mistaken—but they were, perhaps because of this, all the more dogmatic, energetic, aflame with zeal: they directed newspapers, notably Louis Veuillot's *L'Univers*, entertained crucial political polemics over education, censorship, and "secret organizations"; by the 1840s, they had founded hundreds of pious societies for desirable ends, collected a multiplication of relics from the Roman catacombs, covered Europe with imitation Gothic and filled their churches and parlours with Roman papier-maché statuary....

Back in Montreal, Mgr Bourget began injecting into the Canadien mood the full fever of his Roman creed. With a crusader's singleness of purpose, he arranged for the immigration from France of the Oblate and Jesuit Orders of the Dames du Sacré-Coeur and the Sisters of the Good Shepherd; he founded two Canadian religious congregations of his own, established the Saint Vincent de Paul Society; carried out an extensive canonical visitation of his diocese, and pressed Rome to establish an ecclesiastical Province that extended within a few years to new dioceses in Toronto, Ottawa, British Columbia, and Oregon....He also organized a whole series of Parish revivals and religious ceremonies superbly managed to stir the emotion of all classes. At Varennes on July 26, 1842, for example, before a huge crowd of several thousand, surrounded by some sixty priests and in the full pontifical splendour of his office, he presided over the crowning of a holy picture of Saint Anne, according to

"le cérémonial usité à Rome pour de semblables solennités".[1]...Through-
out the 1840s, he ordered many more such occasions....

The new Orders naturally aided Mgr Bourget with his ultramontanism—especially the Jesuits who began in 1843 to lay the foundation of
Collège Sainte-Marie, an institution that would train so many energetic
young nationalist Catholics. The *Mélanges Religieux* also helped. In this
bi-weekly newspaper, the priests from the bishopric published over and
over again long articles of praise for the papal states, and copious excerpts
from the works of leading ultramontanists....[2] They also issued vibrant
appeals to Canadian youth to join their movement....They also gave
news of Catholicism throughout the world, concentrating especially on
the independence of the Papal States and the University Question in
France....In a word, the *Mélanges* opened a window on the Catholic
world. And through it there blew in the high winds of ultramontanism,
which, for the Canadiens, felt so much like their own aggressive and
assertive nationalism.

Through it there also came for the clergy a novel regard for the layman.
Since the Restoration in Europe, the Catholic Bishops and priests had
achieved some success there in reintegrating the Church into educational
life and social services. Very often they had done this with the assistance
of influential laymen. Through the *Mélanges* publication of articles and
speeches by these European ultramontane politicians, the Canadien
priests gradually developed a fresh respect for their own lay politicians.
They began to think of new ideas on how they could work with them. In
fact, with the coming of responsible government the old ways which the
priests had grown accustomed to were passing into history forever. The
Union had marked the end of the courteous and courtly style which the
Bishops and the British governors had so carefully devised over the years
to fuse the good of the throne with the good of the altar. Now, effective
political power was passing from the hands of Governors-General to those
of the Canadien electors. And if the Church was to exercise the influence
which the priests felt in conscience it must, then the clergy must begin to
deal directly with the politicians and the people.

Besides, they were finding nationalist politicians whom they liked.
Indeed, by the middle of the decade, it was becoming obvious how much
LaFontaine's followers and the priests seemed made to understand each

---

1. *Mélanges Religieux (MR)*, 28 juillet 1842.
2. *MR*, 20 novembre 1849.

other. The debate on the Union, during which they had been on opposite sides, was settled. And since then, they had forged new personal friendships. In Quebec, politicians such as René-Édouard Caron, Étienne-Pascal Taché, and specially Joseph-Édouard Cauchon, the editor of the influential *Journal de Québec*, enjoyed frequent hospitality at the Séminaire. Taché and Cauchon were also close correspondents of the Archbishop's secretary, the talented and ubiquitous abbé Charles-Félix Cazeau. In Montreal, LaFontaine's close friend, Augustin-Norbert Morin, also received a cordial welcome at the bishopric, especially from Mgr Bourget's *Grand-Vicaire*, Mgr Hyacinthe Hudon. So did other partisans like Lewis Thomas Drummond and Joseph Coursol. Indeed, as these priests and politicians grew to admire each other, a new esteem was also developing between their leaders, between the new Bishop of Montreal and the man who in 1842 had become French Canada's Attorney-General. Despite initial suspicion on both their parts, Bourget and LaFontaine were by temperament made to understand each other. Both were heroes to duty, strong-willed leaders, unyielding in their principles, and expert at manoeuvring within the letter of the law. Especially they had this in common that each one thought in absolute terms that he was in total possession of the truth. Neither could accept from an adversary anything but complete conversion.

Thus it was that slowly within the womb of LaFontaine's party, despite appearances, the pulse of the clerico-nationalist spirit began, faintly, to beat.

None of these things—Bishop Bourget's trip to Europe and its effects in Montreal, the historical turn in Canadian politics caused by responsible government, the new intimacy between ultramontanes and nationalists— none could weigh enough to bring the priests officially into LaFontaine's party. But they did prepare the way. Then, in 1846, the public discussion over a new Education Bill and over the funds from the Jesuit Estates revealed to the clergy which politicians were its natural allies and which were not. The Education Bill of 1845, proposed by Denis-Benjamin Papineau, the great tribune's brother, who was Commissioner of Crown Lands in the Viger-Draper administration, did not satisfy the clergy. Although it provided for the Curés being *ex officio* "visitors" to the schools, it did not give them the control they wished. They therefore began a campaign to have the project amended in their favour. . . .

From his seat on the Opposition benches, with the aid of his colleagues Taché, Drummond, and Cauchon, A.-N. Morin proposed amendment after amendment to bring about a system which would happily unite clerical authority on the local level with centralized control by the Superintendent at the Education Department. . . .Finally, in mid-1846, Dennis-Benjamin Papineau bowed to the pressure, and accepted the Morin amendments.

If the Bishops accordingly felt happy about the Act in its final form, they owed it in great part to the support of politicians like Morin and his friends. At the same time, they were receiving support from LaFontaine's friends on another critical issue: the Jesuit Estates.

The problem of these lands which had been granted by a succession of French Kings and nobles to serve as an endowment for education, had definitely passed to the British Crown in 1800 at the death of the last Jesuit. Their revenues were used by the Colonial Office for any number of Government sinecures until 1832 when as a gesture of conciliation it agreed that they be administered by the Lower Canadian Assembly. Then there began another struggle with the Catholic Bishops who claimed that they and not the Assembly were the true heirs of the Jesuits. By 1846 the controversy had reached the floor of the House, and the Provincial Government, led by Denis-Benjamin Viger, refused the Bishops' claim. As in the debate over Papineau's Education Bill, LaFontaine and his party supported the priests. LaFontaine, Morin (who had been acting as confidential advisor to the clergy on the question), Drummond, and Taché each delivered an impassioned speech against the "spoliation" of French Canada's heritage; Morin himself proposing that the funds be transferred entirely to the Church. Viger defended the Government's action on the grounds of precedent and Parliamentary supremacy. He won the vote. But in appealing to Parliamentary supremacy, he began a disagreeable discussion which continued in the press for over three months. At the end, it was clear how wide a division had taken place among French-Canadian nationalists: a division as explicit as the opposing doctrines of liberalism and ultramontanism.

While traditionally nationalist papers such as *Le Canadien*, and *L'Aurore des Canadas*, defending Viger, assailed the Church's position, *La Minerve*, *Le Journal de Québec*, and *La Revue Canadienne*, all LaFontaine papers, became like the *Mélanges* defenders of the Faith. . . .

This was not the first difference of opinion that had brought Viger's party and the *Mélanges* into conflict. Back in 1842 they had measured paragraphs against each other over the interpretation of Bishop Lartigue's famous *Mandement* against rebellion in 1837; and at that time also they had been quarrelling from the viewpoint of opposing ultramontane and liberal doctrines.[3] Yet somehow that discussion had not caused any overt

---

3. Cf. F. Ouellet, "Le Mandement de Mgr Lartigue de 1837 et la Réaction libérale", *Bulletin des Recherches historiques*, 1952 (58), pp. 97–104.

split. The 1846 one did—and soon with the reemergence of Louis-Joseph Papineau into political life, all bridges were broken between his party and the clergy. By 1849, the priests had become one of the great forces on the side of responsible government in Canada.

Having returned from his exile in liberal, anticlerical France, the great rebel found little to encourage him in Canada. He was disgusted by LaFontaine's politics, repelled by the growing power of the priests. Especially he suffered at being forced to witness his people's growing commitment to the British Connection. In the late fall of 1847 he issued what Lord Elgin called "a pretty frank declaration of republicanism",[4] reviving his dreams of the 1830s for a national republic of French Canada. Around himself he rallied Viger's followers and a group of enthusiastic young separatists who edited the radical newspaper *L'Avenir*. They shared the rebel leader's philosophy: if it only depended on them they would win through the sharpness of their minds what he had not by sharpness of sword.

What struck the ultramontanes about Papineau and *L'Avenir* was of course not so much the attacks against LaFontaine and responsible government. It was their anticlericalism. As things turned out the republicans would hurt their own cause more than they would the Church: on the subject of responsible government, Papineau might conceivably weaken LaFontaine, especially if he concentrated on nationality and the defects of the Union. But by challenging the Church, the *rouges* merely helped to cement the alliance between LaFontaine and the priests. . . .

In return, of course, the priests supported LaFontaine. At the time of Papineau's Manifesto at the end of 1847, during the general election that swept LaFontaine to the final achievement of responsible government, reports from different parts of Lower Canada came to Montreal that "certains prêtres, même à Montréal, ont prononcé en chaire des discours presqu'exclusivement politiques".[5] But more important still than such electoral advice was the increasing involvement in party politics of the *Mélanges Religieux* and its junior associate in Quebec, the weekly *Ami de la Religion et de la Patrie*. Edited by Jacques Crémazie, *L'Ami* first appeared in early 1848 under the interesting motto: "Le trône chancelle quand l'honneur, la religion, la bonne foi ne l'environnent pas." It endorsed LaFontaine's ideas so unequivocally that Cauchon was glad to

---

4. *Elgin-Grey Papers* I, 102. Elgin to Grey, December 24, 1847.
5. *MR* 14 décembre 1847.

recommend it to his party leader for patronage. . . .[6]As for the *Mélanges*, since mid-1847 it had practically become a LaFontaine political sheet. In July 1847, the clergy had handed over the editorship to a twenty-one-year-old law student who was articling in the offices of A.-N. Morin: Hector Langevin, whose religious orthodoxy they felt well guaranteed by his two brothers (and frequent correspondents) in Quebec: Jean, a priest professor at the Séminaire, and Edmond who in September 1847 became secretary to the Archbishop's *Grand-Vicaire* Cazeau.

With mentors like Morin, the youthful editor soon threw his paper into the thick of the political fight. In fact he became so involved that at last the priests at the Bishopric felt they had to warn him (they did so several times) to tone down his enthusiasm for LaFontaine. He did not, however. His greatest service was perhaps the publicizing of the clergy's support for LaFontaine at the time of the trouble over Rebellion Losses. . . .

Perhaps it was inevitable that during the closing years of the decade the French-Canadian clergy would come to play an increasingly political role. For with responsible government the Canadians had, for the first time in their long national life, taken over the direction of their own destiny. And as the Catholic Church had long played an important part in fashioning their thought, it was natural for most of those on the political stage to welcome the support of the priests. Yet, would it have happened as effortlessly if Bishop Bourget had not fallen in with the *Veuillotistes*? If LaFontaine and Morin had not supported clerical schools in 1846? If Hector Langevin had not articled in Morin's office? If *L'Avenir* had not attacked the Papal States? Would it have happened at all if Denis-Benjamin Viger had won the election of 1844? If the Papineau legend had persisted? Be that as it may, the *bleu* alliance of priest and politician (since we can now give it its name) radically transformed LaFontaine's party and French-Canadian nationalism.

Except when the rights of the Church were in question, ultramontanes tended to consider politics as secondary. They concentrated rather on Church-State problems, thus gradually moving away from areas of cooperation with Upper Canada—especially at a time when the "voluntary principle" was converting Baldwin's party as ultramontanism was LaFontaine's. Gradually they came to appeal almost exclusively to ideas and feelings which were proper only to French Canada. When he began in the

---

6. Public Archives of Canada, MG 24, B-14. *LaFontaine Papers*. Joseph Cauchon à LaFontaine, 24 octobre 1849.

late 1830s LaFontaine aimed at political and economic reforms in which both Canadas would share. In his famous *Adresse aux Électeurs de Terrebonne*, he described the problems of French Canada in political and economic terms alone. As the decade moved on, however, under pressure from his opponents and his followers, he found himself becoming more and more involved with ultramontanism and a narrower nationalism. Reluctantly, it seems. . . .LaFontaine had wanted to break with Papineau's particularist and republican nationalism. He appealed to a more general, open point of view, founding his hopes on cooperation with Upper Canada and in the British political system. Yet, in the end, he found himself the head of a party which tended to be as particularist as Papineau's (although for different reasons).

His party also turned out to be one which did not understand Parliamentary institutions. The ultramontanes were not rigid republicans like Papineau, but they were rigid Catholics, used to "refuting the errors of our time", with a doctrine which they proudly wanted as "toujours une, toujours sublime, toujours la même".[7] They were accustomed to think in an atmosphere rarified by unchanging principles. Instinctively they reacted in dogmatic terms, pushing ideas to their limits—and students of the absolute make poor parliamentarians. The ultramontanes could not really understand parliamentary practice as LaFontaine and Parent had. They lacked political flair and skill in manoeuvring. They could not adapt to the gropings and costs of conciliation. To them, "rights" were an objective reality which could not be negotiated, only acknowledged. "Toleration" could not mean respect for an opposing opinion; at best it was a necessary evil. Applied to theology, their attitude might have had some validity (although not for ecumenism!) but transferred to politics and nationalism—as inevitably it was—it could not but extinguish LaFontaine's hopes for a broadening democracy of the British type.

For years the *bleus* and their Upper Canadian colleagues supported the same men, but as the French party gradually concentrated so dogmatically on Faith and Nationality, there could be no true meeting of minds. Outwardly, LaFontaine's and Parent's wider nationalism seemed to have prevailed: responsible government and British Parliamentary institutions were secured. Also, a political party uniting Upper and Lower Canadians continued to govern the country for over a generation. But this was external appearance only: in reality, the party from which LaFontaine resigned in 1851 was assiduously becoming less concerned with the larger

---

7. *MR*, 15 décembre 1843.

perspective than with the particular Church-State problems of French Canada; it was becoming decreasingly parliamentarian, increasingly authoritarian.

A funny thing indeed had happened to French-Canadian nationalism on its way to responsible government.

BRITISH TO THE CORE:

Responsible Government in Canada West

CAROL WILTON

In retrospect, responsible government seems such a logical solution to the difficulties that bedevilled the relationship between the British North American colonies and Great Britain. It did not seem so obvious at the time. Indeed, many contemporaries expressed great consternation when Lord Durham's Report in 1839 recommended the granting of responsible government in British North America. For those who liked their constitutions to be clear and simple, responsible government seemed only to muddy the waters. Take, for example, the problem of local autonomy. What made any given issue a matter of local concern, as opposed to one that British officials must approve? Then there was the Cabinet, whose members were to make decisions on matters of local concern (as long as they could command a majority in the Assembly). What if the Cabinet members recommended one course of action to the Governor and the British government another? What would the Governor do then? Both problems, sceptics thought, could produce divisions between colonial politicians and the mother country that could lead only to separation from the Empire.

A third drawback of responsible government in the eyes of its critics was that it required political parties. Cabinets stay in power because they have a majority in the Assembly, and political party ties are what binds the majority together. Yet political parties seemed to be institutions that would promote political divisions instead of healing them; they thus appeared to be a dangerous innovation. In conservative quarters, of course, the Reform party was especially suspect, particularly in Upper Canada/Canada West, for it was Reformers who had fomented the rebellion, and the Reform program of responsible government was widely believed to be a front for the cause of separation from the Empire. Responsible government in general and party government in particular were alike tarred with the brush of disloyalty to the mother country.

The cause of responsible government was supported by most Reformers in Upper Canada/Canada West, but those who were its most ardent

CAROL WILTON, "BRITISH TO THE CORE: RESPONSIBLE GOVERNMENT IN CANADA WEST." PUBLISHED HERE FOR THE FIRST TIME.

proponents were the Baldwins and Francis Hincks. Their public careers in the 1830s and 1840s were in large measure devoted to defending responsible government as the essence of the British constitution, and political parties as necessary to a free society. In this they were utterly sincere, for British political values were part and parcel of their own thinking about the constitution.

Robert Baldwin and his father, Dr. William Warren Baldwin, did not "invent" responsible government. Its origins have been traced to the views of Irish Whigs in the late eighteenth century, whence they were borrowed by Lower Canadian reform leaders.[1] The Baldwins have, however, generally been given credit for being its foremost promoters in Upper Canada. Their championship of the doctrine dated back at least to the 1820s. Dr. Baldwin's letter to the Duke of Wellington, dated January 3, 1829, is usually taken as the opening salvo in the Baldwins' campaign.[2] Although Dr. Baldwin was a member of the House of Assembly during much of the 1820s, his son Robert sat only from 1829 to 1830. Thereafter, both dropped out of active politics, until the younger Baldwin agreed to join the Executive Council under Bond Head in 1836. This experiment lasted only three weeks. While Dr. Baldwin took an active part in protesting the corrupt methods by which the election of 1836 was won by the Tories, Robert was travelling in Europe, trying to recover from the tragic death of his wife earlier that year.

The younger Baldwin's return to active politics was marked by another call to office, this time as Solicitor General of Upper Canada under Lord Sydenham in 1840. Robert was elevated to the Executive Council in February 1841, but resigned four months later, when Parliament opened. When he took office again, in the fall of 1842, it was for the first time as part of a cabinet whose members were essentially agreed on the issues of the day, and who were responsible to the Assembly. The first Baldwin–LaFontaine Ministry resigned after little more than a year in office, when the Governor, Lord Metcalfe, refused to accept the advice of Reformers on a number of issues, including patronage.

Baldwin and the Reformers were defeated in the general election of 1844, but they were victorious in the contest of early 1848. Baldwin served

1. W. L. Morton, "The Local Executive in the British Empire 1763–1828," *English Historical Review* 70 (July 1963): 436–57.
2. Paul Romney, however, has indicated that as early as 1823, Dr. Baldwin was asserting that Upper Canada had the right of calling ministers to account, though this was not being put into practice. Paul Martin Romney, "A Man out of Place: The Life of Charles Fothergill; Naturalist, Businessman, Journalist, Politician, 1782–1840" (Ph.D. thesis, University of Toronto, 1981): 462.

as leader of the Western section of the Ministry and as Attorney General until his precipitous resignation in 1851, after an adverse vote by the Canada West MLAs on the question of the reorganization of the Court of Chancery. Although L.-H. Lafontaine, his counterpart in Canada East, also resigned later in the year, the party carried on in office until 1854 under the leadership of Francis Hincks and A.-N. Morin, though it became increasingly the victim of internal tensions. Baldwin lived out the remainder of his days in quiet retirement in Toronto, dying in 1858 at the relatively early age of fifty-four.

Baldwin's close associate, Francis Hincks, was another leading proponent of responsible government and the party system. Hincks was an aspiring businessman who arrived in Toronto from Ireland in 1831. A tenant of the Baldwins, he quickly exhibited Reform sympathies. By 1835, he was cashier (general manager) of the Bank of the People, an institution established by Reformers. Two years later, he became Secretary of the newly formed Toronto Political Union, a moderate body dedicated to protesting the corrupt methods by which the election of 1836 had been carried.[3] Like the other leaders of the post-Rebellion party, Hincks had not been implicated in the Rebellion. In 1838, encouraged by the appointment of Lord Durham, he took the lead in reviving Reform fortunes in Upper Canada by establishing the *Examiner* in Toronto, with a banner which read "Responsible Government and the Voluntary Principle."[4] Although Hincks took his journalism very seriously indeed, it was always secondary to his political career. Thus, he sold the *Examiner* when he entered the government in 1842, and resumed his career in journalism by starting the *Pilot* in Montreal in 1844, some months after the resignation of the Reform Ministry. After the Reform victory at the polls in 1848, Hincks in turn sold the *Pilot* to become Inspector-General in the new Ministry.[5] Hincks lacked Baldwin's reputation as a man of unswerving integrity; his nickname was "The Hyena," and, as Lord Elgin reported, he was able and energetic, but his colleagues never fully trusted him.[6] This mistrust proved justified; Hincks's career was derailed in the mid-1850s by a

---

3. *The Constitution*, October 12, 1836.

4. Sir Francis Hincks, *Reminiscences of His Public Life* (Montreal, 1884): 22.

5. William G. Ormsby, "Hincks, Sir Francis," *Dictionary of Canadian Biography* Vol. 11 (Toronto and Montréal: University of Toronto Press and les Presses de l'université Laval, 1976): 410.

6. Sir Arthur G. Doughty, ed., *The Elgin–Grey Papers, 1846–1852*, Vol. 2 (Ottawa: King's Printer, 1937): 651, 823. For a more recent assessment, see Paul Romney, "The Ten Thousand Pound Job," in *Essays in the History of Canadian Law*, Vol. 2, ed. David H. Flaherty (Toronto: University of Toronto Press and Osgoode Society, 1983): 143–99.

financial scandal which propelled him for a time into honourable Caribbean exile.

It was Robert Baldwin's proud boast that his understanding of responsible government had been "imbibed from my father."[7] Whatever the precise process, it is clear that by 1836, the younger Baldwin had a very thoroughly developed understanding of how the principle ought to operate. By that date, he was articulating his interpretation of responsible government, which featured a party system in which the Executive Council (Cabinet) was dependent on a majority in the Assembly, and a distinctly subordinate role in local affairs was assigned to the Governor. The purpose of introducing responsible government, however, was not to loosen the tie to Britain, but to confirm the allegiance of the colony to the mother country. Baldwin made his position clear on this in a letter to Lord Glenelg, the Colonial Secretary, in 1836:

> ...educated in the warmest attachment to the monarchical form of Government, believing it to be best adapted to secure the happiness of the people, and fully sensible that it can be maintained in Upper Canada only by means of the connexion with the Mother Country, I have always been most earnestly anxious for the continuation of the Connexion. ...[8]

Responsible government would also "give satisfaction, and, at least most probably, insure good government in the management of the internal affairs of the Colony."[9] Once their legitimate grievances had been addressed by the granting of responsible government, the colonists would be satisfied and more firmly attached than ever to the British connection.

In the aftermath of the Rebellion, Hincks found it doubly necessary to stress the loyalty of Reformers to British values and institutions. In the opening number of the *Examiner*, he proclaimed:

> When we say reformers, we mean the whole body that has for several years been seeking an improved government of this country,—distinguishing them from the impatient and violent band that has ruined themselves, and distracted the empire by revolt and war. The reformers properly so called are the men who would generally sympathize with the politics of Lord Durham and Her Majesty's Ministers, and who

---

7. National Archives (hereafter NA). Pamphlet #1–1536. Upper Canada, House of Assembly. "Select Committee to which was referred the Answer to the Lieutenant Governor." Report (Toronto, 1836), Appendix C: 10.
8. Letter to Glenelg, July 13, 1836, in *Statutes, Treaties and Documents of the Canadian Constitution, 1713–1929*, 2nd ed., ed. W. P. M. Kennedy (Toronto: Oxford University Press, 1930): 335. See also Doughty, *Elgin–Grey Papers*, Vol. 2: 610.
9. Letter to Glenelg, July 13, 1836, in Kennedy, *Documents*, 338–39.

desire to see in Canada...the British Constitution in its free and perfect operation.[10]

Reformers, then, did not seek the overthrow of the government, but wished to perfect British institutions by peaceful means.

Reformers frequently stated publicly that responsible government was nothing more nor less than the British constitution. As Hincks observed in an article entitled "What Is Responsible Government?" it was "the British system of Government."[11] This contention was forcibly argued in the very first number of the *Pilot*, where the editorial began with a quotation from Lord Durham's Report which endorsed responsible government as the essence of British government.[12] It went on to state that the journal would support responsible government, and "maintain the principles of Lord Durham's Report—the principles of the British Constitution—the principles established by our ancestors."

This emphasis on Durham's Report, which was typical of Hincks's writing on responsible government throughout the 1840s, illustrates the importance of a related point—that responsible government was approved in Britain. As Hincks argued in later years, responsible government by the 1840s had become the avowed policy of the British government, and it was repeatedly announced in the dispatches of the Colonial Ministers.[13] Thus, there was nothing unconstitutional or un-British about Reformers' demands for responsible government: "the true Constitutional party in Canada is that one which is guided in all its proceedings by English practice, and which limits its demands to what is consistent with the principles and practice of the British Constitution."[14]

In the face of charges that political parties were American institutions which would, by promoting the selfish ambitions of a designing few, wreak havoc with the body politic, the Baldwins frequently emphasized the British origins of responsible institutions. As Dr. Baldwin told Lieutenant Governor Francis Bond Head in 1836:

—that as the Government of England has, so must every free government and especially these Provinces, have two parties; a Governing

---

10. Ontario Archives. Mackenzie–Lindsey Papers, Series A–2, Clippings, #340 A, *Examiner*, July 3, 1838.
11. *Pilot*, February 9, 1847.
12. *Ibid.*, March 5, 1844.
13. *Ibid.*, February 5, 1847.
14. *Ibid.*, July 17, 1844.

party and a party in check; it was no matter what the parties were called, whig or tory—parties will be, and must be....[15]

When Bond Head objected that party government would make the Lieutenant-Governor a "cipher," Baldwin tartly responded that this official would have as much power over the internal administration of the province as the King had in the affairs of the Empire, "which appeared... to be all that he could desire, and at all events all that the Constitution had given him."[16]

In an effort to disprove or discredit charges of disloyalty, Reformers— with some degree of subtlety—asserted their innocence by associating their cause with that of the British Whigs. Hincks frequently invoked the voices of the *Edinburgh Review*, a British Whig journal, and such Whig luminaries as Edmund Burke, Lord Durham, Lord John Russell (the Colonial Secretary), and the historian Thomas Babington Macaulay.[17] He also attempted to associate the Reform party of Upper Canada with the Whig party in Britain. Like the party which in Britain opposed monopolies under Elizabeth I and secured Habeas Corpus under Charles II, the Reformers of Upper Canada, he said, were responsible for "all that has been done for human liberty and human happiness in this province."[18]

The appeal to British tradition, however, went well beyond invoking the names of Whig luminaries. Indeed, Whiggish attitudes were funda- mental to Reformers' concepts of how politics functioned. In particular, the traditional Whig suspicions of an over-mighty executive had been staples of Reform politics in the 1820s and 1830s, when the opposition had crusaded against the undue influence of the Executive in the government of Upper Canada. Hincks, too, was clearly influenced by Whig attitudes to executive power. The *Pilot*'s efforts to demonstrate the parallels between the early years of the reign of George III and the administration of Sir Charles Metcalfe was clearly derivative of eighteenth-century British Whiggism.

Whig lore, particularly as expounded by Edmund Burke, theorist of the Rockingham Whigs, held that George III had come to the throne in 1760 determined to overthrow the party system and to restore personal monar-

---

15. Metro Toronto Public Library, Baldwin Room, Robert Baldwin Papers (hereafter BP), A 83–2, William Warren Baldwin to Robert Baldwin, April 27, 1836.
16. NA, Pamphlet #1–1536, Appendix C, p. 11.
17. *Examiner*, September 9, 1840; *Pilot* March 8, May 13, 1844.
18. *Examiner*, September 9, 1840.

chy. To this end, he undermined the principle of ministerial responsibility by relying on the advice of an "inner cabinet" rather than on his responsible ministers, the most important "advisor behind the curtain" being Lord Bute, who finally resigned government office in 1763 after being the target of much Whig abuse. Another of the King's alleged objects was to loosen party ties and cripple parliamentary management.[19] The parallels to Metcalfe's period in officer were irresistible, and the *Pilot* spent a great deal of time in 1844 and 1845 casting Metcalfe as George III, his Secretary Higginson as Lord Bute, and various Tories as secret advisers "behind the curtain."[20] Like the British Whigs, Hincks used the Bute story to justify the development of political parties.

The administration of Lord Metcalfe provided Reformers with further arguments on behalf of the British character of responsible government. The term "responsible government" had many advantages as a slogan, not the least of which was the implication that the alternative was irresponsible or absolute government.[21] Reformers took full advantage of this, and defended themselves against charges of being un-British by retorting that it was their opponents who promoted a type of arbitrary government quite unlike that which could be found in Britain. Governor Metcalfe provided a particularly vulnerable target in this respect: his insistence on controlling patronage appointments, his rejection of legislation passed by both branches of the legislature (such as the Secret Societies Bill), his close personal identification with the Tory party, and his interference in the 1844 election—all were denounced as unconstitutional.[22] If government were to be carried on in such a fashion, the *Pilot* declaimed, "it would be infinitely better that the mockery of representative institutions was abolished." It went on to insist, "The Prerogatives of the British Crown are so extensive that without Responsible Government, it would be preferable to live under the government of a Russian or

19. B. W. Hill, "Executive Monarchy and the Challenge of the Parties," *Historical Journal* 13 (1970): 391–92; Henry R. Winkler, "Sir Lewis Namier," *Journal of Modern History* 35 (March 1963): 4; and Herbert Butterfield, *George III and the Historians* (London: Collins, 1957): 151–55.
20. For example, see "From our London Correspondent," *Pilot*, April 26, 1844; January 10 and 15, and March 15, 1845.
21. See also Graeme Patterson, "The Myths of Responsible Government and the Family Compact," *Journal of Canadian Studies* 12 (Spring 1977): 10.
22. *Pilot* March 5 and 12, April 9, 1844; January 3, September 23, 1845.

Austrian despot."[23] It did not escape notice that Metcalfe's previous experience as Governor in India and Jamaica, where he had functioned in a most authoritarian fashion, had minimized his exposure to popular government and responsible institutions.[24]

The Baldwins and Francis Hincks were tireless publicists on behalf of responsible government and the party system. Their efforts helped ensure that by the time the British granted responsible government in the late 1840s, the people of the Canadas would understand how to use it. Some Upper Canadians were fearful that responsible government would lead to the Americanization of their province. They needed to be convinced that the new system of government, and the institution of political parties, were compatible with their own British traditions, and with maintaining a political culture distinct from that of the Americans. It was assurance of this that the Reformers provided.

23. *Ibid.*, March 5, 1844.
24. Ibid., March 12, 1844.

LETTER TO LORD JOHN RUSSELL

JOSEPH HOWE

Halifax, Nova Scotia [Sept. 18, 1839].

My Lord,—

...I have ever held, my Lord, and still hold to the belief, that the population of British North America are sincerely attached to the parent State; that they are proud of their origin, deeply interested in the integrity of the empire and not anxious for the establishment of any other form of government here than that which you enjoy at home; which, while it has stood the test of ages and purified itself by successive peaceful revolutions, has so developed the intellectual, moral, and natural resources of two small Islands, as to enable a people, once comparatively far behind their neighbours in influence and improvement, to combine and wield the energies of a dominion more vast in extent and complicated in all its relations than any other in ancient or modern times. Why should we desire a severance of old ties that are more honourable than any new ones we can form? Why should we covet institutions more perfect than those which have worked so well and produced such admirable results? Until it can be shown that there are forms of government, combining stronger executive power with more of individual liberty; offering nobler incitements to honourable ambition, and more security to unaspiring ease and humble industry; why should it be taken for granted, either by our friends in England, or our enemies elsewhere, that we are panting for new experiments; or are disposed to repudiate and cast aside the principles of that excellent Constitution, cemented by the blood and the long experience of our fathers and upon which the vigorous energies of our brethren, driven to apply new principles to a field of boundless resources, have failed to improve? This suspicion is a libel upon the colonist and upon the Constitution he claims as his inheritance; and the principles of which he believes to be as applicable to all the exigencies of the country where he resides, as they have proved to be to those of the fortunate Islands in which they were first developed.

If the conviction of this fact were at once acknowledged by the intelligent and influential men of all parties in Britain, colonial misrule

JOSEPH HOWE, "LETTERS TO LORD JOHN RUSSELL," IN *DOCUMENTS OF THE CANADIAN CONSTITUTION, 1759–1915*, ED. W. P. M. KENNEDY (TORONTO: OXFORD UNIVERSITY PRESS, 1928): 482, 487.

would speedily end and the reign of order indeed commence. This is not a party question. I can readily understand how the Duke of Wellington and Sir Robert Peel may differ from your Lordship or the Earl of Durham as to whether measures should be carried, which they believe would impair, and you feel will renovate, the Constitution; but surely none of these distinguished men would wish to deny the Constitution itself to large bodies of British subjects on this side of the water, who have not got it, who are anxious to secure its advantages to themselves and their children; who, while they have no ulterior designs that can by any possibility make the concession dangerous, can never be expected to be contented with a system the very reverse of that they admire; and in view of the proud satisfaction with which, amidst all their manly struggles for power, their brethren at home survey the simple machinery of a government, which we believe to be, like the unerring principles of science, as applicable to one side of the Atlantic as to the other, but which we are nevertheless denied. . . .

The planets that encircle the sun, warmed by its heat and rejoicing in its effulgence, are moved and sustained, each in its bright but subordinate career, by the same laws as the sun itself. Why should this beautiful example be lost upon us? Why should we run counter to the whole stream of British experience; and seek, for no object worthy of the sacrifice, to govern on one side of the Atlantic by principles the very reverse of those found to work so admirably on the other. The employment of steamers will soon bring Halifax within a ten days' voyage of England. Nova Scotia will then not be more distant from London than the north of Scotland and the west of Ireland were a few years ago. No time should be lost, therefore, in giving us the rights and guards to which we are entitled; for depend upon it the nearer we approach the mother country, the more we shall admire its excellent constitution, and the more intense will be the sorrow and disgust with which we must turn to contemplate our own.

FURTHER READINGS FOR TOPIC 12

J. M. Beck. *Joseph Howe, Vol. I: Conservative Reformer 1804–1848*. Kingston and Montreal: McGill-Queen's University Press, 1982.

J. M. S. Careless. *The Union of the Canadas, 1841–1857*. Toronto: McClelland and Stewart, 1967.

Jacques Monet. *The Last Cannon Shot: A Study of French Canadian Nationalism, 1837–1850*. Toronto: University of Toronto Press, 1969.

Graeme Patterson. "An Enduring Canadian Myth: Responsible Government and the Family Compact." *Journal of Canadian Studies* 12 (Spring 1977): 3–16.

TOPIC 13

*Popular
Politics
in
the
Age
of
Responsible
Government*

Responsible government resulted in greater self-government, but it did
not mean democracy or universal suffrage. Many British North
Americans who lacked the opportunity to express their views at the polls
nevertheless continued in the mid-nineteenth century to make their
opinions on public questions known in other ways. Most striking, perhaps,
was the resistance to the sleighing laws in Canada East during the early
1840s, a period when most of the Québécois were still smarting from the
suppression of the Rebellion of 1837–38 and the subsequent suspension of
their constitution. Most had viewed the union of the Canadas in 1841 with
grave misgivings, fearing that it was a prelude to assimilation. Stephen
Kenny's article shows how the residents of Canada East effectively
expressed disaffection from the government by passive resistance to
regulations that were at once arbitrary and silly.

Like other disfranchised people, women in the nineteenth century have
generally been considered as operating outside of and apart from public
affairs. Yet even when they lacked the vote, women were not without a role
in the political process. For example, one of the avenues open to them was
to petition the government, as the women of New Brunswick did on the
issue of prohibition of alcohol in the 1850s; this movement is detailed in the
following selection by Gail Campbell. Such involvement in politics, however
limited, was important as a forerunner to the much greater participation of

women in public life in the late nineteenth century, and to their ultimate obtaining of the franchise.

Popular protest was not always sparked by the activities of the government, as the excerpt from J. M. S. Careless's description of the Gavazzi riots indicates. In this case, it was the visit of an anti-Catholic former priest to Canada East in the highly charged religious atmosphere of 1853 which provided the occasion for the expression of popular outrage. A counterpart to this was the Clergy Reserves riots in Toronto in 1851. In neither case did the authorities act impartially, and their evident sympathy for one side over the other demonstrates an important link between popular protest and high politics in the mid-nineteenth century, as we have also seen in Topic 8.

"Cahots" and Catcalls:

An Episode of Popular Resistance in Lower Canada at the Outset of the Union

STEPHEN KENNY

The years between the suppression of the rebellions and implementation of the Union in 1841 have invariably been described by French- and English-speaking historians as bleak and menacing for French Canada.[1] The heavy hand of the imperial government finally turned to colonial affairs and designed a solution predicated on the assimilation of the French Canadians for whom, it seemed, there was no alternative but to submit. Indeed, political leaders who remained in the colony were powerless to act otherwise. In accepting new British policy, Louis Hippolyte LaFontaine apologized for his co-operation and defended his participation by claiming he would never agree with the ultimate goals of the Union.[2] By working within the system, he hoped to transform it. Bitterness toward La Fontaine and other French Canadians willing to collaborate with the British tyrant was profound. From his exile in the United States, Amédée Papineau, the son of Louis-Joseph Papineau, claimed to be scandalized and ashamed that compatriots and former friends would grovel to the conqueror....

However, within Canada such resentment and despair could neither publicly nor safely be expressed. In fact, one immediate result of the rebellions of 1837 was that newspapers were obliged to be extremely cautious in their political criticism....Leaders were obliged to be circum-

---

STEPHEN KENNY, " 'CAHOTS' AND CATCALLS: AN EPISODE OF POPULAR RESISTANCE IN LOWER CANADA AT THE OUTSET OF THE UNION," *CANADIAN HISTORICAL REVIEW* 65, NO. 2 (JUNE 1984): 184–208. REPRINTED BY PERMISSION OF UNIVERSITY OF TORONTO PRESS.

1. The danger of the political conjuncture is universally remarked upon by historians, many of whom express amazement at the unexpected evolution of the Union and at the inventive and effective participation of French Canadians in it. See, for example, Jean Paul Bernard, *Les Rouges, libéralisme, nationalisme, anticléricalisme au milieu du XIXème siècle* (Montreal 1971), 21: Denis Vaugeois, *L'Union des deux Canadas: nouvelle conquête, 1791–1840* (Trois Rivières 1962), 194; Georges Vincenthier, *Une Idéologie québécoise: de Louis-Joseph Papineau à Pierre Vallières* (Lasalle, Que 1979), 17; J.M.S. Careless, *The Union of the Canadas: The Growth of Canadian Institutions, 1841–1857* (Toronto 1967), 7; Jacques Monet, *The Last Cannon Shot: A Study of French Canadian Nationalism, 1837–1850* (Toronto 1969), 41; Mason Wade, *The French Canadians 1760–1967* rev. ed. (Toronto 1968), I, 220.

2. Adresse aux électeurs du Terrebonne, *Le Canadien*, 31 August 1840

spect in their public expressions on important contemporary issues. . . .If élite views of the theoretical, constitutional, and political issues of the day are less than obvious, it is probably impossible to know what the majority of the population thought. . . .At this time, Lower Canada was essentially a rural and illiterate society. And even if one would like to believe that most of the people reflected negatively on the obvious injustices of the proposed new Union, on its unbalanced system of representation, on the unfair sharing of the public debt, on the choice of Kingston as capital, or on the fact that English was to be the only official language, such propositions cannot be demonstrated in any concrete way.[3]. . .

If direct questions cannot be asked, then they must be posed indirectly. One way to understand popular sentiments is to examine how people reacted to laws which affected immediate and personal interests. Fortunately for the historian, the colonial authorities were not solely interested in the larger constitutional and political issues and the imposition of the Union. Afforded an uncommon latitude for executive action between 1838 and 1841, they also attempted to regulate society in direct and sometimes extraordinarily picayune ways. When this happened people sometimes refused to comply and popular opposition continued even after proclamation of the Union. One well-known example was the resistance to schools in Lower Canada. The operation of an 1841 statute establishing schools depended upon the municipal authorities created by Charles Poulett Thomson in 1840.[4] So fundamental was the hostility that the school legislation never worked.[5] A less familiar example was the failure

---

3. Historians have often confronted their inability to measure popular reactions in Lower Canada. For example, in his discussion of an earlier effort to unite Upper and Lower Canada in 1822, Donald Creighton mentioned the number of petitions against it in Lower Canada and referred sarcastically to the enormous number of crosses serving as signatures as an indicator of the lack of political sophistication of this community. See *The Commercial Empire of the St Lawrence* (Toronto 1956), 216. In a recent more objective and dispassionate article, Allan Greer has suggested that at the end of the 1830s only about 12 per cent of rural French speakers could be considered literate, and this at an uncertain and elementary level. See 'The Pattern of Literacy in Quebec, 1745–1899,' in *Histoire Sociale/Social History*, XI (Nov. 1978), 315.

4. *Ordinances*, 4 Vict., cap. 4, 1840. An Ordinance to Provide for the Better Internal Government of This Province by the Establishment of Local or Municipal Authorities Therein

5. See Thomas Chapais, 'La Guerre des éteignoirs,' *Proceedings and Transactions of the Royal Society of Canada*, 3rd Series, XXII (May 1928). See also J.-B. Meilleur, *Mémorial de l'Education du Bas Canada*, 1615–1865, 2nd ed. (Quebec 1876). Meilleur claimed there was a more fundamental objection than direct taxes for the schools. Thomson, the anglifier and instigator of the schools, intended to use them for the purposes of assimilation. Consequently the people opposed them (189–91).

of census legislation passed by the first Union parliament in 1841.[6] It provided for an enumeration in 1842 and every five years thereafter, but gathering statistics in Lower Canada proved impossible. As for schools, the collection of information depended upon the mechanisms of Thomson's municipal ordinance. Eventually, in 1843, a second census law was specifically designed for Lower Canada.[7] Commenting on the first, the Governor General, Sir Charles Metcalfe, attributed failure to the fact that it was directly linked in the popular mind to the detested Thomson administration.[8] The reactions to the school and census legislation were but two instances of effective popular opposition. Laws associated with the hiatus after the rebellions and prior to the Union continued to be the cause of distrust well into the 1840s.

One of the most remarkable and concrete indicators of the general attitude of the Canadiens in these years was their refusal to build and use sleighs as required in a series of executive ordinances of the Special Council dictated first by Sir John Colborne and then even more enthusiastically by Thomson. Sleighs and the winter roads over which they passed were the subject of detailed, intricate, and absurd regulations.

The sleigh ordinances were rather like an unwelcome spring snowfall of a couple of centimetres after most of it has already melted, undeniably there, definitely bothersome, but, it is hoped, soon to disappear. At first glance, these laws do not appear particularly extensive or abusive. Indeed, the entire statutory condition governing winter roads and vehicles in Lower Canada was comprised of only three ordinances with a total of twenty-two clauses promulgated between 1839 and 1841. However, their stipulations were specific and minute, and, contrary to the intentions of the lawmakers, confusing. Significantly, all three were proclaimed by means of arbitrary executive ordinance in a period when normal civil government was suspended in the colony....

Even as far removed as the contemporary observer is from horse-drawn vehicles, the implications of these laws are obvious. Elementary reflection on their details suggests their absurdity. Why would the authorities believe that instead of the traditional sled, an elevated sleigh placed upon runners and a frame nine or ten inches above the ground would run more

---

6. *Statutes of Canada*, 4 & 5 Vict., cap. 42, 1841. An Act to Repeal Certain Parts of an Act Therein Mentioned, and to Provide for Taking a Periodical Census of the Inhabitants of This Province, and for Obtaining the Other Statistical Information Therein Mentioned
7. *Statutes of Canada*, 7 Vict., cap. 24, 1843. An Act for Taking the Census of the Inhabitants of Lower Canada and for Obtaining Certain Statistical Information Therein Mentioned
8. Public Archives of Canada (PAC), RG7 G12, no. 26, Metcalfe to Stanley, 27 Jan. 1844

efficiently through deep or drifted snow of twice that depth? Why would anyone believe that a single horse, or draught animal, hitched to the left would pull better than one hitched to the centre? In addition to these problems and despite their detail, the regulations did leave room for interpretation and confusion. This is particularly noticeable in comparing the French and English versions. Technical sleigh vocabulary was obviously not the forte of the translator of the Thomson ordinance. Words such as 'rave' and 'bobsled' were untranslatable. More importantly and mistakenly, the French version required that the distance between the runners be two and a half feet and no more.[9] If the law had been obeyed rigorously, the colony would have had nothing but extremely narrow sleighs. . . .

The sleigh ordinances and the [model sleighs promoted by the government] were badly received and universally detested. Indeed, an examination of the popular reaction is as important as the investigation of the laws themselves. Certainly the prevailing mood in Lower Canada in the late 1830s and early 1840s was far from happy. In the doldrums of poverty, agricultural crisis, economic dislocation, and political repression episodes of extraordinary bitterness and incidents of violence underscored the continuing popular alienation in society. Surprisingly, several contemporary English-speaking observers described the Canadiens as happy and peaceloving.[10] The truth was otherwise. Put bluntly, no ambience of

---

9. The French version of the Thomson ordinance was entitled 'Ordonnance pour pourvoir à l'amélioration des Grands Chemins de la Reine, dans cette Province, en hiver, et pour d'autres objets.' The language of sleigh components was technical and not easily rendered into French. Terms such as 'bobsled' and 'rave' were not translated. The word 'rave' has disappeared from most modern dictionaries but is defined in *Webster's American Dictionary of the English Language* (1858) as the upper side-piece of timber of the body of a cart.

   More importantly, it appears the French version is a literal translation of the English. In describing the distance between the runners and the raves the language of the English version is quite clear, 'such sleigh or sled to have an open space between the runners and the raves on which the body rests.' The French version was far more complex: 'telle voiture devant avoir un vide entre le dessus du bas du patin et le dessous du haut sur lequel repose le corps de la voiture.'

   At least one serious translation error radically altered the specific dimensions of a legal sleigh. In defining the distance between the runners the English ordinance demanded 'a clear distance of at least two and a half English feet between the inside of the runners at the bottom thereof.' The French went 'il y aura aussi un espace franc de deux pieds et demi anglais, entre les patins, en dedans, à leur partie inférieure...'

10. If the observations of several contemporary English speakers are to be believed, French Canadians were often perceived as harmless, happy, unenthusiastic rural bumpkins. See, for example, a letter to the editor, *Quebec Gazette*, 28 Dec. 1838. See also Sir Richard

harmless insouciance existed. Were it so, one might logically wonder why, at the constitutional and political level, the imperial government and colonial authorities were so determined to undermine such a tranquil and placid people? Or one might wonder why, for three years, they felt obliged to govern so callously and arbitrarily? In fact, the society which the British supposedly ruled in Lower Canada was powerful and menacing and their fear of it was palpable.

Mutual hatreds which partly inspired the rebellions and which were strengthened by the brutal suppression of the disorder continued unabated.[11] The ferocity of these sentiments poisoned the normal functioning of society and reinforced fears. For example, the unrestrained burning and pillaging of the British troops and local militia to the south of Montreal in late 1838, unchecked by Colborne, illustrated the intensity of feeling which existed in the colony. The rhetorical extremity of the English-speaking press in Montreal in commenting on these same events was a further indication. Rejoicing at the severity and effectiveness of the treatment meted out to the rebels in this second rising, the *Montreal Herald* suggested the time had come to chase all French Canadians into the woods to perish of cold and hunger for this was the only way to guarantee British supremacy in Canada.[12] Indeed the English minority believed itself to be surrounded by a savage and bloody-minded population. . . .

Such mutual hatred and fear were common sentiments in Canada during these years. Every colonial governor of the period, Durham, Colborne, Thomson, and Bagot, admitted and acknowledge these conditions. Durham believed nothing could be improved or changed in Canada until such hatred was somehow resolved and in his report on colonial affairs he repeatedly used phrases like 'deadly animosity,' 'bitter and irreconcilable hatred,' and 'invincible hostility.'[13] The situation only

Bonnycastle, *The Canadians in 1841* (London 1841), 76–7, and Charles Dickens, *American Notes for General Circulation* (New York 1842), 76.

11. In reflecting upon attitudes prior to and during the rebellions, which he characterizes as a truly popular phenomenon, Fernand Ouellet claims that the motives of the leadership and the people were distinct. The vague and rather fuzzy ideology of the leadership was not transmitted to the people, but they did share one very important attitude, namely hatred for the English, who were held responsible for all society's ills. See 'Les Insurrections de 1837–1838: un phénomène social,' *Histoire Sociale/Social History*, II (Nov. 1968), 67.

12. The *Montreal Herald* was quoted verbatim by *Mackenzie's Gazette*, 24 Nov. 1838 and these remarks were commented upon by the *Courrier des Etats-Unis*, 29 Dec. 1838.

13. *Lord Durham's Report*, Gerald M. Craig, ed. (Toronto 1963), 23, 26, 40.

worsened as a result of Colborne's administration. Shortly after his arrival in Canada in the fall of 1839, Colborne's successor, Thomson, claimed that things remained very bad. He was convinced that only the French Canadians' own sense of powerlessness and the corresponding strong and arbitrary government of the executive preserved calm.[14] Likewise, Sir Charles Bagot, who arrived in early 1842, understood the situation in Canada perfectly. The continuing alienation and resentment he partly blamed on his predecessors' unrestrained methods. Perhaps their approach had been too arbitrary. In Bagot's opinion, too many laws, and the Act of Union itself, had been implemented without any regard for the interests of the French Canadians and only enraged them more.... Whatever the nature of their administration, provocative or conciliatory, all the governors understood the disturbed and unbalanced condition of society.

It is in this context of sullen resentment and smouldering bitterness that the sleigh ordinances were proclaimed in Lower Canada. Even if their purpose was commendable, the nature of their imposition was definitely provocative. The real impracticability of the new vehicles only increased the anger surrounding their introduction. Reaction to these laws provides a concrete illustration of the true sentiments of the people toward the government. When examining these years could there be conceived anything more innocuous, more innocent than laws regulating winter vehicles? Yet they too would be the occasion for popular resistance and violent episodes so typical of the period. Describing these days as dark and dangerous, the historian Jacques Monet wrote, 'Mercifully, however, the Canadiens had a chance to laugh.'[15] 'Poulet' Thomson and all his works would become the target of ridicule and sarcasm. As for the sleighs, not only would people laugh heartily, their reactions would range from mirth to derision to popular outrage. The laws would never work and the force of popular opposition would stop the colonial government in its proverbial tracks....

Could anyone fault editors for criticizing sleighs? For so they did, with gusto. It was a wonderful opportunity to reflect upon the stupidity and obtuseness of the government and an exhilarating release for opposition which they could not otherwise express. It was also an occasion to excoriate the man who imposed them, Charles Poulett Thomson. His

14. PAC, RG7 G12, vol. 54, no. 4, Thomson to Russell, 31 Oct. 1839
15. Monet, *The Last Cannon Shot* 41

sleighs came to be known as 'des sleighs Thomson'[16] or 'des sleighs de travers.'[17] His 'ordonnance de cahots'[18] was characterized as 'monstre,'[19] 'tracassière,'[20] 'tyrannique,'[21] and 'Algérienne,'[22] Algeria being the only place such contraptions would work since there was no snow. . . .

Despite the hopes of the colonial government, few were the rapid and graceful cutters slipping over flat and even winter roads. Travel upon them continued to be a bruising and bone-breaking proposition. The idea of sleighs hitched 'à la Thomson' was considered absurd. After a recent snowfall, the streets of Montreal were described as filled with all sorts of vehicles, carriages, carts, wagons, gigs, but not a single legal sleigh.[23] Despite the universal refusal to comply, Thomson and the authorities continued to attempt to enforce the law. His agents came to be called spies who acted as 'vrais valets du diable,'[24] their exaggerated zeal attributed to their avaricious hopes of collecting half the fines.[25]. . .

Hostility to this law and the sleighs continued unabated. As for the winter of 1841, so too for that of 1842, the province continued to be plagued by 'cahots.'[26] Public meetings were held all over the colony which expressed discontent with Thomson and all his works. Resolutions derided his municipal ordinances and school laws which depended upon them, the legitimacy of the authority of the Special Council, and even that of the Governor himself. And invariably, the people complained of the sleighs. Ringing phrases like 'point de taxes sans réprésentation' mixed with resolutions against the 'ordonnance de cahots.' In early 1842, such meetings were held in Quebec,[27] in the districts of Saguenay, Lotbinière,

---

16. *Le Canadien*, 2 Dec. 1840
17. *Gazette de Québec*, 1 Dec. 1840
18. *Le Canadien*, 18 May 1840
19. *La Canadienne*, 7 Sept. 1840
20. *Gazette de Québec*, 12 Dec. 1840
21. *Ibid.*, 17 Dec. 1840
22. *Aurore de Montréal*, quoted by *Le Canadien*, 4 Jan. 1841. Even newspapers in Vermont commented sarcastically. The *Burlington Sentinel*, reporting on a smashed model sleigh, claimed the 'grannies' of the Special Council were up to no good, noting that in Canada, 'It is said the government intend to issue an order that no Canadian shall smoke with a pipe having a stem less than half an inch long.' Quoted in the *Swanton North American*, 9 Dec. 1980
23. *Aurore de Montréal*, quoted in the *Quebec Gazette*, 1 Dec. 1840
24. *Gazette de Quebec*, 17 Dec. 1840
25. *Ibid.*, 12 Dec. 1840
26. *Le Canadien*, 4 Mar. 1842
27. *Ibid.*, 25 Feb. 1842

and Portneuf,[28] and in towns like Maskinongé,[29] St Thomas de Montmagny,[30] Ste Anne de la Pocatière,[31] and Ste Geneviève de Batiscan.[32] In February, nearly 2,000 people met at L'Islet.[33] . . .

The disrespect of the people for the government was apparent. Could the 'petrified brains' which invented the sleigh laws be expected to provide good government? The answer appears to have been a resounding no. Reaction to the ordinances indicated the true nature of popular attitudes to the authorities who governed between 1838 and 1842. The people resisted in their fashion, as their political leaders claimed they would in theirs. Is it any wonder that the biographer and brother-in-law of the unlamented and recently enobled Thomson, Lord Sydenham, could not find a single obtituary in all of French-speaking Canada worth printing?[34]

As Parent had promised in the spring of 1840, once things returned to normal, the two great issues would be repeal of the 'ordonnance de cahots' and the 'acte d'union.' Thomson hardly cold in his grave, the newly elected legislators of the first Union parliament at Kingston focused its attention on the sleigh laws. The widespread failure of the regulations was evident. The member of the assembly for Champlain referred to them as 'a species of tyranny that gave universal dissatisfaction.' The represent-ative of Berthier called them 'a complete failure' and 'a dead letter.' The assemblyman from Bonaventure, in the Gaspé, used the same words and, discussing the plowing ordinance, claimed that the very idea of clearing winter roads in a region so sparsely inhabited was utterly ridiculous. Etienne Parent, himself elected for Saguenay, described the laws as 'an abominable tyranny.'[35] Thomson's plowing ordinance of February 1841 never saw its first snowfall and was repealed in September the same year.[36] In 1842, his earlier sleigh ordinance was amended and revised. The

---

28. *Ibid.*, 4, 9 Mar. 1842
29. *Le Canadien*, 21 Feb. 1842
30. *Ibid.*, 25 Feb. 1842
31. *Ibid.*, 4 Mar. 1842
32. *Gazette de Québec*, 19 Apr. 1842
33. *Le Canadien*, 21 Feb. 1842
34. G. Poulett Scrope, Esq., *Memoir of the Life of the Rt Hon. Charles Lord Sydenham with a Narrative of His Administration in Canada* (London 1843)
35. *Debates of the Legislative Assembly*, 21 Sept. 1841
36. *Statutes of Canada*, 4 & 5 Vict., cap. 30, 1841. An Act to Amend a Certain Ordinance Therein Mentioned, Relative to Winter Roads, in that part of the Province Formerly Called Lower Canada

lopsided hitching clauses were repealed outright and many regions were completely exempted from any part of the law.[37] Such exemptions continued to be legislated in the coming years.[38] In effect, almost immediately, the sleigh laws disappeared as one source of popular resentment. And so one of the two great injustices foisted upon Lower Canadians was put to rest. The second, the Act of Union, would take a bit longer to rearrange.

When the government imposed sleighs, the people of Lower Canada refused to obey. Perhaps they could not resist the fundamental political and constitutional reconstruction in which the British were engaged, or the policy of assimilation and anglification which it implied, but they could resist sleighs. And so they did. The innate absurdity of the laws, the insensitivity of the authorities, and an already keenly developed resentment for everything English explain why. Everywhere the model sleigh went it was attacked and ridiculed. Significant events of rural violence followed its progression. Everywhere enforcement was attempted the ordinance was disobeyed. The public meetings of these years illustrate the popular disregard and disdain for the authorities and their laws. Certainly, the widespread indignation and opposition were sufficient to guarantee that the sleigh laws would not work. The popular response also shows that the people and their leaders were of one mind on the issue. The force of such solidarity explains the quick and effective nullification of at least this one injustice. Such strength may also explain the later, but equally effective and more fundamental revision of the unjust system imposed arbitrarily on the colony on 10 February 1841.

Examination of the reaction to the sleighs does help to explain the true nature of the attitudes of the community toward the government which quite cavalierly was about to set out to assimilate the Canadiens and thus settle the problem once and for all. Given the real relationship of the government and the governed, such a policy seemed doomed to failure. The events surrounding the imposition of sleighs illustrate that colonial officials not only misunderstood the physical and climatic conditions of the colony, but more importantly, they also seriously miscalculated the dynamism and energy of the community which they so ineptly attempted to regulate. This episode of popular resistance demonstrates the true frame of mind of Lower Canadians. When it came to sleighs, the Cana-

---

37. *Ibid.*, 6 Vict., cap. 12, 1842. An Act to Amend Two Certain Ordinances Therein Mentioned, Relative to Winter Roads in that Part of the Province formerly Called Lower Canada
38. *Ibid.*, see the subsequent statutes regarding winter roads. For example, 8 Vict., cap. 52, 1845; 9 Vict., cap. 53, 1846; 10 Vict., cap. 40, 1847; and 12 Vict., cap. 59, 1849

diens refused to be subjugated by stupid and inappropriate laws. Contrary to the common notion that in these years there was no choice but to submit, the sleighs prove the opposite.

DISFRANCHISED BUT NOT QUIESCENT:

Women Petitioners in New Brunswick in the Mid-19th Century

GAIL G. CAMPBELL

Canadian women's participation in the political life of their society is usually dated from their struggle for and achievement of the vote.[1] Yet denial of the franchise had not prevented women from being actively involved in the political life of their communities. Indeed, from the earliest times, women had found ways to influence their government.[2] In the

GAIL CAMPBELL, "DISENFRANCHISED BUT NOT QUIESCENT: WOMEN PETITIONERS IN NEW BRUNSWICK IN THE MID-NINETEENTH CENTURY," ACADIENSIS 18, NO. 2 (SPRING 1989): 22–54. BY PERMISSION OF ACADIENSIS AND THE AUTHOR.

This paper builds on a data base that was created while I was a post-doctoral fellow at the University of New Brunswick. This particular study is part of a much broader project dealing with political culture in mid-19th century New Brunswick.

1. Although New Brunswick women were not disfranchised by statute until 1843, historians have found no record of even propertied women in the colony voting before that time. John Garner, *The Franchise and Politics in British North America, 1755–1867* (Toronto, 1969), pp. 156–6. While it is true that in debates on franchise extension in later years politicians claimed that women of the province had voted before their specific exclusion in 1843, the only evidence that has been found to support their claims is a single letter to the editor that appeared in the *Gleaner and Northumberland Shediasma* in 1830, cited in Elspeth Tulloch, *We, the undersigned: A Historical Overview of New Brunswick Women's Political and Legal Status, 1784–1984* (Moncton, 1985), pp. 3–4. Garner argues that exclusion by statute did not represent a new restraint on the franchise. For centuries, women in Great Britain had not exercised the franchise despite the lack of a formal legal restraint, having, as one judge argued, "always been considered legally incapable of voting for members of Parliament". This exclusion by convention had been accepted by the colonies as part of their legal heritage. Garner, *The Franchise and Politics*, p. 156. Indeed, evidence from extant newspapers suggests that the purpose of the 1843 statute was mainly to clarify the law in order to "promote the public peace at elections". By giving convention the weight of law, the revised statute provided county sheriffs with clear guidance in deciding whether a demanded scrutiny should be carried out. The disfranchisement of women was quite incidental to the amendments and went unnoticed by the newspapers of the day and, apparently, by their readers as well. See "The Election Law—The Loan Bill—And the Legislative Council in a Ferment", *The Standard or Frontier Gazette* (St. Andrews), 6 April 1843; "Prorogation of the Legislature", *ibid.*, 20 April 1843; *Weekly Chronicle* (Saint John), 31 March 1843 and "House of Assembly", *ibid.*, 14 April 1843; "Provincial Legislature", *The Gleaner and Northumberland, Kent, Gloucester and Restigouche Commercial and Agricultural Journal* (Miramichi), 14 February 1843, and "Editor's Department", *ibid.*, 13 March 1843; "The New Election Law", *The Loyalist* (Saint John), 23 March 1843; and "Parliamentary", *St. John Morning News and General Advertising Newspaper*, 31 March 1843.

2. For example, following a long-established European tradition, the women of New France took to the streets during the late 1750s to protest food shortages. Terence Crowley,

period prior to the introduction of manhood suffrage—a period characterized by deferential politics—distinctions between men's and women's
political behaviour were often blurred. Women, as well as men, regularly
participated in politics by petitioning legislatures to achieve specific
political goals.[3] Women, like men, were involved in creating the political
culture of their society.... [T]his paper will focus on women's direct
political participation by analysing the nature and extent of political
lobbying by women from three New Brunswick counties, as measured by
the number and content of their petitions to the Legislative Assembly
during the mid-19th century. In political terms, the decade selected for
analysis—1846 through 1857—was a highly significant one. Political
parties emerged during this period. Those great moral questions, temperance, and then prohibition, became, for a time at least, the major political
issue. And it was on the moral issue that women began to petition the
Legislature in numbers during the decade....

[F]or those who wish to analyse the nature and significance of women's
political role in the 19th century, petitions provide the key. Only through
the medium of petition could a woman gain official access to her government or express her views about policy to the legislators. Thus, the
petition provides a useful measure of the signatory's knowledge of the
way government worked, her degree of interest in the issues of the day,
and her attitudes concerning those issues.

Petitions and petitioners can be divided into two discrete categories.
The first category includes petitioners seeking to use the law in some way:
to apply for a government subsidy to which they were legally entitled, to
redress a grievance, to appeal for aid at a time of personal distress, or to
request a grant from public monies to carry out a worthy public project.

"Thunder Gusts: Popular Disturbances in Early French Canada", Canadian Historical
Association, *Historical Papers* (1979), pp. 19–20. And evidence from the pre-history period
strongly suggests that Iroquois women, at least, had enormous political influence in their
society. See especially Judith K. Brown, "Economic Organization and the Position of
Women Among the Iroquois", *Ethnohistory*, 17 (1970), pp. 153–6.

3. In an article discussing the role of women in American political society, Paula Baker has
made this argument very effectively. Of course, the political transition which separated
male and female politics occurred much earlier in the United States where the introduction of manhood suffrage (demonstrating definitively to women that their disfranchisement was based solely on sex) and the rise of mass political parties dated from the early
19th century. Paula Baker, "The Domestication of Politics: Women and American Political
Society, 1780–1920", *American Historical Review*, 89 (1984), pp. 620–47. For a review of
the literature concerning the role of deference in male political behaviour during the
antebellum period, see Ronald P. Formisano, "Deferential-Participant Politics: The Early
Republic's Political Culture", *American Political Science Review*, 68 (1974), pp. 473–87.

Individual petitioners normally fall into this first category, and while such petitions do not reveal the petitioner's opinions on the issues of the day, they do suggest the extent to which she both understood the system and was able to use it to her advantage. The second category includes petitioners seeking to change the law in some way. Through the medium of the petition, they sought to influence their government, to persuade the legislators to accept their view. Occasionally such people petitioned as individuals, but usually they petitioned in concert with others. Legislators would, after all, be more inclined to take a petition seriously if they could be persuaded that a majority of their constituents supported it. Regardless of the success or failure of the petition, such documents can provide important insights concerning societal attitudes. Whether the signatories were members of an organized group with a specific platform and goals, or a group of unorganized individuals who coalesced around a specific issue, an analysis of the demographic characteristics of the supporters of the issue can enhance our understanding of political attitudes and political culture. . . .

This study is concerned with the women petitioners of the counties of Charlotte, Sunbury and Albert in the mid-19th century. All three counties are in the southern half of the province. Charlotte is a large, economically diverse county in the south-west corner. Sunbury is an agricultural county in the central region, just east of Fredericton; and Albert is in the south-east region between Saint John and Moncton, on the Bay of Fundy. Although originally selected because of the richness of their sources for the study of political history, Albert, Charlotte and Sunbury proved typical in many ways. Thus, while these three counties cannot be considered a microcosm of the province as a whole, they did encompass a broad spectrum of 19th century anglophone New Brunswick society, including areas of pre-Loyalist, Loyalist and post-Loyalist settlement and encompassing rural communities, villages and even large towns. Moreover one fifth of New Brunswick's petitioners came from one of these three counties.[4] . . .

[Single women dominated the ranks of female petitioners concerned

---

4. Of the 5,081 petitions considered, 1,029 originated in one of the three counties. This suggests that the people of Albert, Charlotte, and Sunbury were slightly over-represented among the colony's petitioners, comprising 20.25 per cent of petitioners as compared to 16.3 per cent of the total population of the province. (The discrepancy is not statistically significant, however, as differences of plus or minus five per cent could occur entirely by chance.)

with individual and family matters; they included the widows of soldiers and school teachers requesting the provincial school allowance.].... Custom—and perhaps some husbands—prevented married women from signing more petitions dealing with individual and family affairs, but one should not assume either a lack of knowledge about or a lack of interest in the political system and the way it worked, on the part of such women. Moreover, starting in 1853, married women began to sign petitions in numbers. The petitions they signed were qualitatively different from the petitions women had signed up to that time. Such women fell into the second category of petitioners: those who sought to change the law. The issue that finally mobilized them to take up their pens was, not surprisingly, a reform issue. By the final decades of the century it would be an issue closely associated with the organized women's movement. The issue was temperance....

For many years temperance advocates sought to achieve their goals by moral suasion, but by the late 1840s some had become convinced that moral suasion alone was not enough. For a time, they focussed their efforts on gaining control of liquor consumption within their own communities through attempts to secure limitations on the number of tavern licenses issued by county and city councils.[5] But such efforts proved unsuccessful. In Maine, temperance crusaders facing a similar failure had appealed to a higher authority. By 1851 they had gained enough support in the Legislature there to achieve an effective prohibition law. The 'Maine Law', which was the first prohibitory liquor law in North America, had a significant effect on the New Brunswick temperance movement. In 1852, a so-called 'monster petition' calling for the prohibition of the importation of alcoholic beverages was presented to the House of Assembly.[6] The 9000 signatures on the petition so impressed the province's legislators that they were persuaded to pass "An Act to Prevent the Traffic in Intoxicating Liquors". This act "forbade the manufacture within New Brunswick of any alcoholic or intoxicating liquors except for religious, medicinal or chemical purposes. Beer, ale, porter and cider were excepted".[7]...

---

5. T. W. Acheson, *Saint John* (Toronto, 1985), p. 141. Similar attempts were made in New England to control licensing at the local level. Ian R. Tyrell, Sobering Up (Westport, 1979), pp. 91, 242–3.

6. Petitions to the New Brunswick Legislature are located in Record Group 4, Record Series 24, 1846–57/Petitions [RG4, RS24, 1846–57/Pe], Provincial Archives of New Brunswick [PANB]. RGA, RS24, 1852/Pe 406, PANB. The Maine Law also had a significant impact in England and within the United States. See Brian Harrison, *Drink and the Victorians* (Pittsburg, 1971), p. 196; Tyrell, *Sobering Up.*, p. 260.

7. J. K. Chapman, "The Mid-Nineteenth Century Temperance Movement", *Canadian Historical Review*, 35 (1954), p. 53.

The new law was to come into force on 1 June 1853. In fact, it never came into effect. No sooner had it passed into law than the lobby against it began. Petitions calling for the repeal of the new law flooded in from nearly every county in the province. And the legislators were disposed to listen. Perhaps they had, after all, been just a little too hasty. The Legislative Assembly depended mainly on customs duties for its disposable revenue and duties on rum alone represented over one third of that revenue.[8] It was at this stage that the women of New Brunswick mobilized for action. Women who had never before signed a petition took up their pens. They begged their legislators not to repeal the new law. Men had achieved the law; the women were determined to keep it.[9]

After the election of 1854, temperance advocates, many of them women, redoubled their efforts. Through the medium of petitions, they urged their newly elected Assembly to enact yet another law "to prevent the importation, manufacture and sale of all intoxicating liquors within this province". Sunbury prohibitionists, for example, addressed three separate petitions to their legislators in 1854. Those petitions contained no less than 915 signatures and 488 of those names were female.[10] Three hundred and seventy-five (77 per cent) of these women were living in the county when the census was taken in 1851.[11] They represented well over 30 percent of the county's 846 families. One hundred and fifty-five of these women (just over 40 per cent) were married and the majority of them (95) petitioned with their husbands and children. Thus, fathers and sons signed the petition from "the male inhabitants of Sunbury County" while mothers and daughters were signing the petition from "the female inhabitants of Sunbury County". Often fathers signed on behalf of their sons, and mothers on behalf of their daughters. Occasionally parents included the names of very young children on the petition: 16 of the daughters listed were under ten years of age in 1854. In very rare cases, one parent signed both petitions on behalf of the entire family, but these amounted to less than five per cent of the total signatures. . . .

On the whole. . .the women who signed the Sunbury petitions of 1854

---

8. Chapman, "The Mid-Nineteenth Century Temperance Movement", p. 44.

9. Women from both Charlotte and Sunbury participated in the 1853 campaign against the repeal of the Act. See the index of the *Journal of the New Brunswick House of Assembly*, 1853, which refers to: Petition 366, Lucinda Garcelon, Clara A. McAllister, Margaret Robinson and 300 others, female inhabitants of Charlotte, and Petition 386, Israel Smith, Thomas H. Smith, Esq. and 996 others of Sunbury and York. Other petitions for Charlotte which might well have numbered women among their signatories include: Petition 318 from Charlotte County, Petition 354 from St. Andrews and Petition 355 from St. George. None of the above has survived in the PANB.

10. RG4, RS24, 1854/Pe 394, 1854/Pe 395, 1854/Pe 404, PANB.

11. Manuscript Census for Sunbury County, N.B., 1851, PANB.

were very ordinary women, unremarkable within their community. The average signatory was relatively young, between 20 and 29 years of age, and was likely to sign with some other member of her family. Like the majority of her contemporaries, she was probably part of a farm family and attended either a Baptist or Methodist Church. Although she had never before signed a petition, she was prepared to stand up and be counted in support of her beliefs or those of her parents or friends. She may not have been either sophisticated or worldly, yet her interests and knowledge extended beyond the domestic sphere. The action she took was a decidedly political one and it would be difficult to argue, at least in the case of any of the 109 women over the age of 20 who signed the petition independent of any husband or parent, that she did not understand the principle behind that action. And, for one brief moment, her action had the desired effect, for in 1855, the Legislature did pass yet another prohibitory liquor act.

Of course, the women of Sunbury did not achieve their goal single handed. In 1854, at about the same time as the people of Sunbury were presenting their petitions, a second 'monster petition' was presented to the House of Assembly. It was far longer than the petition that had so impressed the legislators back in 1852; this petition included over 20,000 signatures. Moreover, it suggested more broadly based support. Whereas the signatories of the earlier 'monster petition' had been drawn largely from Saint John City and County, this time they came from at least half of the 14 counties of New Brunswick, although not from Sunbury. Well over half of the 20,000 signatories were women, including 143 women from Hillsborough in Albert County, and 198 women from Charlotte County, 93 from St. Stephen Parish and 105 from the parish of St. Andrews.[12]. . .

The patterns that emerged in Sunbury were repeated in Hillsborough. Eighty per cent of Hillsborough's women signatories were living in the parish when the census was taken in 1851.[13] They included representatives of more than one quarter of the parish's families. Forty-eight were married women, while a further six were widows. The husbands of 28 of these women could be identified as having signed temperance petitions in the past. . . .

Of the 61 single women who signed, 48 were the daughters of temperance advocates. . . .Only 13 of the 61 single women signatories identified could claim to have taken a stance independent of their parents. As was the case in Sunbury, the wives and daughters of the farmers of Hillsbor-

---

12. RG4, RS24, 1854/Pe 465, PANB.
13. Manuscript Census for Albert County, N.B., 1851, PANB.

ough were over-represented among the signatories: although only 59 per cent of the parish's families were headed by farmers, 72 per cent of the women signatories came from farm families. The Baptists were again significantly over-represented.[14] While Baptists comprised 76 per cent of the parish population, fully 92 per cent of the Hillsborough women who signed the 'monster petition' of 1854 were Baptists. Many were descendants of the original German settlers who had begun immigrating to the parish from Pennsylvania as early as 1765. On the whole, then, the Hillsborough women were a more cohesive group than the Sunbury women, although their demographic profile is very similar.[15]

The Charlotte County signatories, drawn mainly from the two major towns in the county, were a more diverse group of women. . . .

The typical Charlotte County woman signatory was married or widowed and was between 30 and 50 years of age. She lived in one of the two major towns in the county and was solidly middle class, the wife of a relatively prosperous merchant or artisan. Her daughters were likely to sign with her. She might be a Congregationalist, a Presbyterian, a Methodist or possibly an Episcopalian, but whatever her religious faith, she would be joined in the temperance crusade by other members of her local congregation.

As significant and impressive as the petition campaign was, the petitioners did not comprise a majority of the adult population of the province. And the 1853 act had not proved popular. Thus, it is scarcely surprising that the newly elected government proved reluctant to act. Early in November, however, a vote in the House of Assembly went against the government and the government of the day resigned. The Lieutenant-Governor called upon the Liberal opposition to form a government; and among the leaders of this new government was Samuel Leonard Tilley, a man who had recently been chosen Most Worthy Patriarch of the Sons of Temperance in North America.[16] Shortly thereafter, in the parlia-

---

14. Religious affiliation was drawn from the 1861 Manuscript Census for Albert County, PANB. Fully 72 per cent of Hillsborough's female signatories were located in the 1861 census. In this case, marriage records were used to trace those women who may have removed to another parish within the county. This, coupled with the tendency to greater geographical stability within Albert County as a whole, accounts for the high rate of record linkage for Hillsborough.

15. It should be noted, however, that the Hillsborough Baptists were quite different from the Sunbury Baptists. While the Hillsborough Baptists traced their roots back to the religious traditions carried as part of their cultural baggage by the original Pennsylvania German immigrants, Sunbury Baptists had been strongly influenced by the New Light movement of the late 18th century.

16. Chapman, "The Mid-Nineteenth Century Temperance Movement", p. 53.

mentary session of 1855, Tilley put forward, as a private member, a new prohibitory liquor bill, which passed narrowly in the House of Assembly and in the Legislative Council. Despite personal reservations, the Lieutenant-Governor, John Manners-Sutton, gave his assent on the advice of his Executive Council and the act was scheduled to become law on 1 January 1856.

For a brief moment it seemed as if the fight had been won. But, as was the case in 1853, agitation for repeal began almost immediately. Petitions opposing the new law poured in. No women were among the signatories of these petitions.[17] After a brief, ineffectual attempt to enforce the act, the legislators gave up. Yet they did not repeal the act. The Lieutenant-Governor demanded that they either repeal it or enforce it and the entire issue became so controversial that the Lieutenant-Governor forced a dissolution of the House and yet another election was called. Shortly after that election, which was held in 1856, the act was repealed. The temperance fight, for the moment at least, was over.

Even though the fight was ultimately lost, the role women played in it is highly significant. The very fact that two prohibitory liquor acts were passed demonstrates the power of the petition as a political tool in mid-19th century New Brunswick. Petitions and petitioners were taken seriously. Nor was it suggested that women had less right than men to petition their Legislature. There is no evidence to suggest that women's signatures carried any less weight than men's.[18] By analyzing the women signatories,

17. This is not so surprising as it might appear. Women were not involved in repeal campaigns in the United States, either. In general, 19th century women saw drinking as a male vice and sought to reform men. B. L. Epstein, *The Politics of Domesticity* (Middletown CT, 1981), pp. 1, 110; Tyrrell, *Sobering Up*, p. 181.

18. In discussing women signatories of the 'monster petition' of 1852, Mr. Hatheway, the Representative for York County, argued that women's signatures on petitions were "a sufficient reason" for passing the Liquor Bill then before the House. He believed a politician needed "the good opinion of the fair portion of the community" and declared that he "would always rather have one lady canvasser than a dozen men". *Reports of the Debates and Proceedings of the House of Assembly of the Province of New Brunswick* (Fredericton, 1852), p. 101. In the 1854 debates, while some members questioned the signatures of "children in schools", the right of women to sign was generally accepted. Indeed, the majority of those who rose in the House to comment on the 1854 Bill argued that 30,000 signatures in favour of the Bill, as opposed to 4,000 against, was strong evidence of the public feeling. *Reports of the Debates and Proceedings* (1854), pp. 70–3. Similarly, American and British legislators attacked the validity of children's signatures on temperance petitions but did not question the signatures of non-voting women for, as the women themselves argued, "although they did not themselves vote, their husbands did, and their husbands would be heeding the advice of their spouses". Harrison, *Drink and the Victorians*, p. 229; Tyrrell, *Sobering Up*, pp. 279–80.

we can gain new insights concerning 19th century politics and political culture. It is true that wives and daughters of men who signed repeal petitions are rarely to be found among the signatories calling for prohibition. At the same time, almost half of the married women who signed petitions were not joined by their husbands in their fight for the cause. Moreover, there is some indication that mothers were more influential than fathers, for sons proved twice as likely to follow their mothers in signing temperance petitions as they were to follow their fathers in signing repeal petitions. But daughters were even more likely to follow their mothers' lead than were sons. More important than any of these considerations, the women's decisions to take up their pens in the cause of temperance when they did, demonstrates that women had followed the political progress of the temperance legislation and were prepared to take a public political stand on an issue they believed to be important. And in many cases their stand was quite independent from that of their husbands.

Of those inhabitants who petitioned the Legislative Assembly during the 12 years covered by this study, women represented only a very small minority.[19] Thus, while female petitioners from each of the three counties numbered in the hundreds, male petitioners numbered in the thousands. Nonetheless, in Sunbury, the county for which the most complete records are available, women from over 30 per cent of the families listed in the 1851 census signed at least one petition to their Legislature during the period. Petition signatories included women of all ages, all classes, all ethnic and religious groups. But no matter what their age, ethnicity, religious denomination or economic status, the very fact that significant numbers of women signed petitions is historically important. Women did not have the right to vote in the mid-19th century. Yet, in New Brunswick, at least, women were not passive and they were not silent. Many understood the law and were determined to make it work for them. They petitioned for pensions and subsidies to which they were legally entitled and, from time to time, they petitioned for redress of personal grievances. Most were successful in achieving their ends. Many more women became politically active during the decade, seeking, through the medium of petitions, to influence their government to change the law. Working in concert with others of like mind, they effectively demonstrated their power to persuade, although ultimately they failed to achieve their goal.

---

19. This refers to all petitions; in the case of temperance petitions, like these discussed here, however, there were as many women signatories as men.

Whether they petitioned as individuals or in association with others, whether they were seeking to change the law or merely to use it, whether they succeeded or failed, these 19th century New Brunswick women had stepped outside the domestic sphere and into the world of politics. Their lives had a political dimension and, by exercising their rights as subjects under the crown, they helped to shape the political culture of their province.

The Gavazzi Riots

J. M. S. CARELESS

[T]he imposing, fervid and theatrical Father Alessandro Gavazzi...was an Italian patriot and ex-military chaplain of '48, who had broken with Rome when it set its face against Italy's Liberals in that revolution: a renegade monk or an evangelical crusader, depending on where one's own face was set.[1] Now [1853] he was engaged on a North American mission of preaching the evils of Popery; and when he swept northward into Canada, late in May, he came as a burning brand of passionate conviction, who aroused vehement response from Protestant and Roman Catholic alike. In Toronto his lectures at St. Lawrence Hall were a public sensation, as he poured scorn on the "blindness" of the popish system, and dramatically thundered, "No peace with Rome!"[2] But then, with this sort of record behind him, he boldly, or foolishly, moved on to the heart of thoroughly Catholic French Canada, to the capital city of Quebec, which was already deeply stirred by the excited religious disputations that were going on almost daily in its legislative halls.

It was on the electric evening of June 6 that Gavazzi addressed an audience in Quebec's Free Presbyterian Church on St. Ursule Street. Not long after 9:30, as the tall, black-frocked figure was blasting away at Cardinal Wiseman's activities in England, someone yelled—"That's a lie!"—and, as if at a signal, a shower of stones crashed through the windows. A mob burst headlong into the chapel and poured down the aisle, intent on dragging Gavazzi down from the pulpit. He defended himself manfully, both with fists and a stool, but was finally tumbled fifteen feet into a struggling mass of friends and foes below; from there his supporters managed to rescue him before he incurred serious injury. Others of the audience were less fortunate, for the whole church was now a chaos of battering fists, sticks, howls, and the shrieks of women. Nor was the violence checked till troops arrived about ten o'clock to scatter the mob.[3] Disturbances had not ended, however. A strongly Irish crowd of

---

From J. M. S. Careless, *Brown of the Globe: The Voice of Upper Canada*, Vol. 1 (Toronto: Macmillan, 1959): 173–75. By permission of the author.
1. J. C. Dent, *Last Forty Years*, Vol. 2 (Toronto, 1881), p. 274.
2. *Globe*, June 4, 1853.
3. *Ibid.*, June 9, 1853.

several hundred re-formed, and marched off fiercely to the Parliament Buildings to seek the politician whom more than anyone else they identified with anti-Catholicism. They massed about the doors. "Brown, Brown [George Brown, anti-Catholic editor of the Toronto *Globe*]," they roared, "We'll treat you like Gavazzi!"[4] But he was not there. He had not yet come in for a late night session. Frustrated, the throng at last dispersed. It was an anti-climax; but the Gavazzi troubles had still to reach their peak.

The next day in parliament Drummond, the Attorney-General East, deplored the outbreak, explaining somewhat lamely that although he had asked for adequate police protection around the chapel the magistrate in charge had been too ill to act.[5] Brown tried to speak, but was ruled out of order. Drummond, however, did advise the proprietor of the Russell Hotel, where Gavazzi was staying, to post armed men at the windows with instructions to shoot if necessary. That day, in fact, Russell's was in a state of siege; and when the inflammatory Italian left for Montreal by boat in the evening, guards lined the streets leading to the docks.[6] On June 9 he spoke at Zion Church in Montreal. It was there that the disastrous climax came.[7]

Another ugly riot broke out, a spatter of shots was exchanged between Protestant and Catholic participants, and troops, this time ready to hand, were hastily ordered in. Someone gave a detachment orders to fire—who, it was never settled—and a volley struck into the dispersing Protestant congregation. Nine were killed, one died later, over a dozen were wounded.[8] Those responsible for the tragedy of military confusion were never effectively prosecuted. But far from shocking Montreal into order, for days afterwards anti-Protestant bands continued to attack evangelical churches and molest their ministers. This without restraint from either civic or provincial authorities, as the most turbulent Roman Catholic elements worked off their spleen and the more moderate, apparently, let them do so.[9]

Of course, in Upper Canada, the disorders produced almost as strong a reaction. There was a wave of furious indignation, wild talk about St. Bartholomew's Eve and Protestant martyrdom. For better or worse, it

---

4. *Ibid.*, June 14, 1853.
5. *Ibid.*, June 9, 1853.
6. *Ibid.*, June 9, 16, 1853.
7. *Dent, op. cit.*, p. 277.
8. *Globe*, June 14, 1853.
9. Brown Papers, William Workman to Brown, July 26, 1853.

served to enhance the stature of George Brown. The very fact that he had been chief villain, next to Gavazzi, in Catholic Quebec made him a hero in the Protestant West. His refusal to be overawed by the disturbances at the capital, where he ploughed straight on in attacking the power of priest-craft embodied in religious corporations, brought him vigorous approval from angry Upper Canadians. He was the one man in parliament, they warmly agreed, who stood unbowed by Lower Canadian Catholic violence, who upheld the principle of religious freedom before a spineless ministry that even condoned the suppression of liberty by lawlessness. Harassed Lower Canadian Protestants, too, were ready to endorse the judgement.[10] Parliament finally adjourned a few days later, still in the bitter, strained aftermath of the Gavazzi riots. They had left Brown a far more influential figure than he had been when the session began.

FURTHER READINGS FOR TOPIC 13

Kathryn M. Bindon. "Hudson's Bay Company Law: Adam Thom and the Institution of Order in Rupert's Land 1834–54." In *Essays in the History of Canadian Law*, Vol. 1, ed. David H. Flaherty. Toronto: The Osgoode Society, 1981: 43–87.

Gregory S. Kealey. "Orangemen and the Corporation." In *Forging a Consensus: Historical Essays on Toronto*, ed. Victor L. Russell. Toronto: University of Toronto Press, 1984.

Alison Prentice, Paula Bourne, Gail Cuthbert Brandt, Beth Light, Wendy Mitchinson, and Naomi Black. *Canadian Women: A History*. Toronto: Harcourt Brace Jovanovich, 1988.

Peter Waite, Sandra Oxner, and Thomas Barnes, eds. *Law in a Colonial Society: The Nova Scotia Experience*. Toronto: Carswell, 1984.

10. *Globe*, July 5, 1853.

TOPIC 14

The
Railways:
Engines
of
Progress

It was during the 1850s that railways made a sudden appearance in the Canadas. In 1850 the United Province boasted only 66 miles of track; a decade later, the total had soared to 2,000 miles. It was American competition which stimulated this outburst of construction, just as the completion of the Erie Canal in 1825 had inspired the canal building on the St. Lawrence in the 1840s. That same commitment to canals had, however, tied up money which might otherwise have been devoted to railways, delaying railroad construction until the Americans had already undertaken an extensive building program. Once again, the Canadians had to play catch-up. The most important railroad, the Grand Trunk, was completed from Sarnia to Portland, Maine, by 1860. The section from Sarnia to Montreal ran essentially parallel to the Great Lakes–St. Lawrence waterways, confirming that some trade would still travel on an east–west axis in spite of the boost to north–south trade provided by the Reciprocity Treaty of 1854 with the United States. But while the railroads have been justly celebrated for their role in promoting trade, it is less often realized that they were among the largest manufacturers in the colony, a subject explored in the following article by Paul Craven and Tom Traves.

The railways transformed not just transportation and manufacturing, but politics as well. The government had an important role in railway development, not only because it granted charters, but because it provided much of the funding, directly or indirectly, for railway construction. This provided an obvious opportunity for unscrupulous politicians to feather their own nests by using their political influence to promote pet railway projects, *unimpeded by any conflict of interest legislation. Sometimes these politicians were themselves officers and directors of railroads, as was Sir Allan ("all my politics are railways") MacNab. On other occasions, politicians acted on behalf of lobbyists like the unsavoury contractor Samuel Zimmerman, whose career is detailed in the following excerpt by Keith Johnson. This close cooperation between government and business was part of a pattern established on a much smaller scale in the 1820s with the Welland Canal promotion, and it would continue in the late-nineteenth-century collaboration between the Macdonald Conservatives and Canadian Pacific Railway interests. In spite of their deleterious effects on Canadian politics, however, railways could still inspire great hopes for economic progress and improvement, an attitude reflected in the following excerpt from T. C. Keefer's* Philosophy of Railroads *(1850).*

"One Bold Operator":

Samuel Zimmerman, Niagara Entrepreneur, 1843–1857

J. K. JOHNSON

Hamilton, March 12, 1857. In the growing darkness of the late afternoon, the Great Western train from Toronto, due at the Hamilton Station at 5:45, slowed down before crossing the swing bridge over the Desjardins canal. Without warning, just as the engine reached the bridge, it left the tracks, crashed through the wooden side railings and plunged fifty feet into the frozen canal, taking with it the tender, baggage car and two passenger cars. Within seconds a terrible railway disaster had happened. Fifty-nine people died instantly, eighteen others were badly injured.[1] Among the dead was the most famous Canadian railway contractor of his time, Samuel Zimmerman. A spectacular career spent in building railways had come to a swift, tragic and ironic end on the "train which did not stop".[2]

Zimmerman's funeral, held a few days later, was described by the Hamilton *Spectator* as the largest ever seen in Canada.[3]...Long flattering obituaries soon followed, mourning his early death, at age forty-two, noting his many accomplishments; Welland Canal contractor, builder of half a dozen railways, owner of hotels, foundries, mills, utilities, real estate and of his own bank....Canada, it was plain, had lost one of her great men.

But there can sometimes be a difference between reality and glowing eulogies of the recently dead. The truth is that while Zimmerman had certainly done the things that he was said to have done, he had often achieved his results using means which must be called, at best, unscrupulous. He had given and accepted bribes. He had grossly overcharged companies for whom he had done work. He had operated a bank using funds that were not his. He had built badly constructed railways and badly

---

J. K. Johnson, " 'One Bold Operator': Samuel Zimmerman, Niagara Entrepreneur, 1843–57," *Ontario History* Vol. LXXIV, no. 1 (March 1982): 26–44. By permission of the Ontario Historical Society.

1. Hamilton *Spectator* (Extra) Mar. 13, 1857.
2. T.C. Keefer, "Travel and Transportation," in H.Y. Hind *et al., Eighty Years; Progress of British North America* (Toronto, 1865), p. 224.
3. Hamilton *Spectator*, Mar. 18, 1857.

constructed bridges. He had been, in T.C. Keefer's phrase, a "bold operator"[4] who was prepared to use any means to get what he wanted.

Zimmerman's career presents a problem—a problem in the nature of ethical standards. To many of his contemporaries, during his lifetime as well as after his death, he was a great man, a builder, an important contributor to national growth and national pride. To a twentieth century observer he may look more like a greedy unprincipled opportunist. Were ethical standards so different 130 years ago? Or is it simply that we now know more about the actual situation than people at the time did? Was Zimmerman's conduct exceptional or typical of his time? To try to answer these questions it is necessary to go back, back from the end of Zimmerman's career to its beginning, to look more closely at his enterprises and his methods and those of his contemporaries and at the extent of public awareness of the nature of nineteenth century business practices.

Samuel Zimmerman was a self-made man. Born in Pennsylvania in humble circumstances, he left school early and went to work as a labourer. By the time he was twenty-eight he was a labourer no longer but a contractor. By the time he was thirty-five he was a wealthy man.[5]

He came to Canada, to the Niagara Peninsula, in 1842 or 1843 because he saw an opportunity. The provincial Board of Works was in the process of rebuilding the Welland Canal. Zimmerman was hired as a contractor, replacing the old wooden locks with large stone structures.[6] His employers were pleased with his work. The Honourable Francis Hincks, who first became friendly with Zimmerman at this time, described him as "one of the best and most successful contractors that had ever been employed by the government."[7] When the canal contracts ended he saw new opportunities ahead, especially among the many railway schemes then being floated. He decided to stay. He married a local girl, Mary Ann Woodruff, daughter of a well-to-do miller of St. Davids in 1848,[8] and set up housekeeping near a village then called Elgin, later part of Clifton, now

---

4. Keefer, *op. cit.*, p. 222.
5. *Canadian Merchants Magazine and Commercial Review*, Vol. 1 (1857); H.S. Morgan, *Sketches of Celebrated Canadians* (Quebec, 1862), p. 735; F.N. Walker, *Daylight Through the Mountain: Letters and Labours of Civil Engineers Walter and Francis Shanly* (Montreal, 1957), p. 82.
6. Hamilton *Spectator*, Mar. 19, 1857; P.A.C., RG 11 (Public Works) Vol. 94. Subject Register, 1839–47, p. 321; RG 43 (Railways and Canals) B447, Vol. 301. p. 367.
7. Toronto *Weekly Leader*, Nov. 7, 1855.
8. Walker, *op. cit.*, p. 214.

Niagara Falls, on a choice location overlooking the Falls, in what is now Victoria Park. From there he began to build a business empire.

A characteristic common to many Upper Canadian entrepreneurs of the mid-nineteenth century era was their inability to set any limits on the range of their business activities, or on the extent to which they were prepared to spread their own and other people's talents and capital.[9] Because Zimmerman fits this pattern perfectly, it is difficult to summarize in logical order the progress of his fortunes, because he did almost everything at once.

As a railway contractor, Zimmerman's firm was involved in building the eastern section of the Great Western Railway and the Erie and Ontario (Zimmerman's own privately-financed railroad) from Niagara-on-the-Lake to Chippawa. He helped to build the first Niagara Suspension Bridge connecting the Great Western with the New York Central Railroad, and he built all of the Woodstock and Lake Erie Railroad that ever got built. A bit farther afield his firm was the contractor for two competing railroads, the Port Hope, Lindsay and Beaverton and the Cobourg and Peterborough. Much of this work was carried on simultaneously through the use of sub-contractors. Out of his railway work grew, also simultaneously, a variety of side lines. The Niagara Harbour and Dock Company was acquired by Zimmerman in 1853, with a view to building railway cars and engines there for the Erie and Ontario and other railways, though he also continued to have ships built, including the *Canada* and the *America*, the largest lake steamers to be built up to that time,[10] and his own "opulently appointed sidewheeler",[11] aptly named the *Zimmerman*. These lake boats were intended to run in conjunction with the Great Western and Erie and Ontario railroads and to connect with a number of points on lakes Erie and Ontario.[12] Railways and boats are transporters of goods, some of which was provided by another Zimmerman acquisition, the large flour mills at Thorold formerly owned by George Keefer, obtained by foreclosure of a mortgage in 1855.[13]

At the eastern terminus of the Great Western Zimmerman found not

9. P.B. Baskerville, *The Boardroom and Beyond: A Study of the Upper Canadian Railroad Community*. Unpublished Ph.D. thesis, Queen's University, 1973, p. 360.
10. B. Parker, "The Niagara Harbour and Dock Company". *Ontario History* LXXII, No. 2 (June, 1980), pp. 114–117.
11. B. Dyster, "Duncan Milloy", *Dictionary of Canadian Biography* Vol. X (Toronto, 1972), p. 515.
12. Parker, *op. cit.*, p. 117.
13. W.G. Ormsby, "Jacob Keefer", *Dictionary of Canadian Biography* Vol. X (Toronto, 1972), p. 394.

only a location for his home but a place to take advantage of urban growth and tourism. Niagara Falls had always attracted sightseers and the first railway suspension bridge added a man-made marvel to the natural wonder. By 1854 two Zimmerman-built railways, the Great Western and the Erie and Ontario, brought traffic to the Canadian side of the Falls and he hoped to add a third. Even in advance of the coming of railways to the Falls, Zimmerman had bought more than a hundred acres of land south and west of the Canadian end of the bridge and also bought two Niagara Falls hotels, one of them the well known landmark, the Clifton House,[14] which he renovated and enlarged so that he could get 1000 guests into the ballroom and 300 into the dining room.[15] Meanwhile he was busy subdividing his Niagara Falls land, selling lots, in the area now bounded by Bridge Street, Zimmerman Avenue, Morrison Street and Victoria Avenue, putting up commercial buildings and building gas and water works.[16] Since such a sizeable business operation required working capital, in 1854 he founded at the Falls, his own bank, modestly named the Zimmerman Bank.[17] Finally, like so many other businessmen of the time he bought, mostly as a speculation, a lot of land in a lot of places. . . .In addition to actual property Zimmerman's assets also included "sundry mortgages" valued at over $99,000.[18]

Samuel Zimmerman is reported to have said that when he came to Canada he had "nothing but a gray horse and a buggy".[19] By 1857 he was believed to be a millionaire. How was this rags-to-riches success achieved? Obviously by hard work, shrewdness and a willingness to take risks. But there is more to it than that. To anyone interested in nineteenth-century business and nineteenth-century morality, Zimmerman's methods of operation are worth examination in detail. First, in a general way, he had more than a little help from his friends. He had quite a wide collection of business partners. A man named James Oswald was his most frequent collaborator on railway and real estate schemes[20] but at various times he also worked in partnership with people like Milton Courtwright,

---

14. Morgan, *op. cit.*, p. 736
15. Toronto *Weekly Leader*, Nov. 7, 1855.
16. *The History of Welland County*, Ontario (Welland, 1887), pp. 342–343.
17. J.A., Haxby, "The History and Notes of the Zimmerman Bank" *Canadian Paper Money Journal* XIII (July, 1977), p. 84.
18. Financial and Departmental Commission, *op. cit.*
19. Morgan, *op. cit.* p. 735.
20. Ormsby, *op. cit.*, p. 394; Canada, Legislative Assembly, *Journals* 1849. Appendix QQQ. Oswald had also been a contractor on the Welland Canal in the 1840's (P.A.C. RG 43, B447, Vo. 300, p. 56) before working with Zimmerman on the Great Western contract. *The Canada Directory* for 1857–8 lists him as proprietor of the Welland Mills, Thorold.

an American railwayman from Erie, Pa., and with the Honourable Luther Holton of Montreal.[21] Zimmerman was president of his own bank but also on the board of directors were Oswald and Holton, a couple of his Woodruff in-laws and the Honourable John Hillyard Cameron.[22] Zimmerman liked to have people on whom he could rely to share the financial risks or at least to add a touch of class to his business image. His use of friendship though went much further. He was an affable, gregarious man known for his "suavity and equanimity of manners"[23] who liked to entertain. He gave dinners, he bought drinks, he gave free rides on railroads. Most of all he liked to entertain prominent people, especially politicians. When he gave a party to bid farewell to his friend Francis Hincks in 1855 the head table guests included the then Premier, Sir Allan MacNab, cabinet members William Cayley, John A. Macdonald and Robert Spence plus members of the legislature, J.G. Bowes, George Macbeth, J.C. Morrison and his brother Angus Morrison, and other notables like Thomas Clark Street (another Niagara entrepreneur) and T.G. Ridout, Cashier of the Bank of Upper Canada.[24]

He was an early, persistent and successful political lobbyist. If he could not always win friends he was prepared to try to buy them. It was his practice to keep a suite of rooms at the provincial capital, where it was alleged that "the choicest brands of champagne and cigars were free to all the people's representatives, from the town councillor to the cabinet minister."[25] Some of the property he accumulated no doubt came from purchases he made in such surroundings, from grateful owners glad to rid themselves of unpromising land. Beginning in the late 1840's he began to acquire a reputation as a man who could get things done, especially as a man who could get governments to introduce, and members to support, the "right" railway legislation. Until about 1853 while Zimmerman was still mainly concerned with building it, the "right" legislation was Great Western legislation, in opposition especially to a proposed "Southern" or "Great Southern" railway, parallel to but south of the Great Western, which found its efforts to obtain a charter consistently blocked.[26] By the

---

21. W. Neutel, *From "Southern" Concept to Canada Southern Railway, 1835–1873.* Unpublished M.A. Thesis, University of Western Ontario, 1968, p. 37.
22. Haxby, *op. cit.*, p. 85.
23. Hamilton *Spectator*, Mar. 19, 1857.
24. Toronto *Weekly Leader*, Nov. 7, 1855.
25. Keefer, *op. cit.*, p. 222.
26. Neutel, *op. cit.*, p. 20–26.

time the Great Western and its principal branches were nearly finished however, Zimmerman reversed his field. An apparently unlikely railroad, The Woodstock and Lake Erie Railroad and Harbour Company, became a means of constructing the eastern half of a "Southern" railroad which Zimmerman now intended to build and control.[27] This railroad began successfully to secure necessary amendments to its charter to change it from a railroad which had been chartered to run north and south to one which ran east and west.[28] Precisely how much influence Zimmerman had on such parliamentary events of course cannot be exactly determined. Undoubtedly T.C. Keefer's claim that he was "virtually ruler of the province for several years"[29] is an exaggeration, but there are some indications of the extent of his influence. When the Toronto and Hamilton Railroad (an extension of the Great Western) applied for a charter of incorporation in 1852, Zimmerman "took an active interest in obtaining support from the members."[30] His lobbying must have been worth something, for he was paid at least $40,000 for it.[31] In 1855 when the Vice-President and the Managing Director of the Great Western went to Quebec to lobby for the passage of a Great Western amendment they were told by those two wily and experienced railway politicians, Francis Hincks and Sir Allan MacNab, that "the only sure way"[32] of getting what they wanted was to see Zimmerman. Zimmerman was seen and the bill passed, but at a price. Zimmerman's commission for these parliamentary services was a contract to double the Great Western tracks as far as London, on his own financial terms.[33]

Zimmerman's power as a political lobbyist rested on a reputation for being able to get things done and also for being able to block railway initiatives which he opposed. Public belief in his influence worked for him

---

27. *Ibid.*, pp. 40–41.
28. Canada, *Statutes*, 10 & 11 Vic. Cap. 117, 16 Vic. Cap. 234, 18 Vic. Caps. 179, 183. The original charter provided for a line from Woodstock to Lake Erie at Port Dover or Port Burwell or any point in between. The amendments permitted the railway to build extensions east and west from Simcoe to St. Thomas and to Dunnville (where the railway would join the Buffalo and Brantford Railroad).
29. Keefer, *op. cit.*, p. 222.
30. P.A.C., M.G. 24, D16 (Buchanan Papers) Vol. 48, p. 39178, J.C. Morrison to Isaac Buchanan, Jan. 12, 1853.
31. *Ibid.*, Vol. 14, p. 2146, P. Buchanan to R.W. Harris, Jan. 24, 1854, Vol. 56, pp. 44793-96, J.C. Street to I. Buchanan, May 8, 1861.
32. *Ibid.*, Vol. 39, p. 32311, W. Longsdon to R.W. Harris, Apr. 17, 1855.
33. *Loc. cit.*

not only in the legislature but also at the level of municipal politics. This was largely due to the fact that most nineteenth-century railroads, especially short railroads, were built at public expense. The Municipal Loan Fund Act, introduced by Hincks in 1852 as part of an overall strategy to promote provincial economic growth, encouraged municipalities to borrow money for investment in roads and railways. Towns, counties and townships, if their ratepayers could be persuaded to take on the debt, were often only too eager to advance money to railroad companies so long as the railway ran through their municipalities, thereby, it was assumed, bringing automatic prosperity. Railway promoters and railway contractors saw in this arrangement a golden opportunity. Local governments– that is the people–would pay. Promoters—and especially contractors– would take the money.[34]

Zimmerman worked this system on three short railways, the Cobourg and Peterborough, the Port Hope, Lindsay and Beaverton and the Woodstock and Lake Erie. The pattern was much the same in each case, with some interesting variations. First the municipalities had to be persuaded to subscribe as heavily as possible. For the Port Hope, Lindsay and Beaverton for instance, the town of Port Hope alone provided $680,000 out of a total of $920,000.[35] At this money-raising stage Zimmerman's reputation was useful for municipalities were told that with the great Zimmerman as contractor the line was sure to be built and to pay a profit, or if they were reluctant, that he would throw his weight behind a rival railroad, leaving them in hopeless backwardness. Sometimes the process had to be helped along in less subtle ways. A local reeve developed "scruples" about the honesty and solidity of the directors of the Woodstock and Lake Erie and refused to turn over municipal bonds to the company. He was visited by one of Zimmerman's subcontractors who removed his "scruples" with two plain envelopes, one before and one after the bonds were handed over, the first containing $500 and the second $400. The subcontractor kept $100 for his trouble.[36]

Only with this "up front" money from the municipalities in hand, could construction of a railroad begin (for the amount invested by the actual

---

34. Good case studies of how this system was worked are provided in L.A. Johnson, *History of the County of Ontario 1615–1875* (Whitby, 1973) chapters 12, 14 and L.A. Johnson, *History of Guelph, 1827–1927* (Guelph, 1977), chap. 7.
35. J.M. and E. Trout, *The Railways of Canada* (Toronto, 1871) p. 167.
36. Canada, Legislative Assembly, *Journal* 1857, Appendices 4–6 Vol. XV, No. 2 (Report of the "Foley" committee).

promoters, directors and shareholders was inevitably very small).[37] The construction phase presented new chances to turn a profit. Here the role of the engineer became important. An engineer was hired first, before the contract was let, to survey the route and prepare an estimate of costs. The engineer also usually advised on the selection of a contractor and on the nature of the contract entered into.[38] Zimmerman was remarkably lucky in the choice of engineers with whom he worked—lucky because they were close friends of his. This was especially true of two men, Roswell G. Benedict and Ira Spaulding, expatriate Americans like himself, with whom he was associated on the Great Western, the Cobourg and Peterborough and the Woodstock and Lake Erie, and incidentally on some other business ventures.[39] Benedict was probably instrumental in getting Zimmerman his first big railway contract with the Great Western.[40] He continued to be helpful by approving "extra" contractor's charges above the original contract price and by recommending a bonus for "early completion" of more than $44,000,[41] even though the work was in fact completed well after the deadline and was even then in such an unfinished state that the engine of the opening-day ceremonial train on its way to Zimmerman's home at Niagara Falls fell off the tracks when loose rails gave way.[42]

There were other tricks of the trade which could be profitable with the cooperation of the engineer. On a contract which stipulated a certain price per mile, the mileage could be increased by going around hills rather than cutting through them (which also lowered the amount of excavation necessary) and where grades could not be avoided, by making them the maximum height allowed under the contract (on level ground embankments could be made the minimum height).[43] Perhaps the most notoriously badly built railroad constructed by Zimmerman as general contrac-

---

37. A group of Toronto railway promoters once explained that private investors could not invest heavily in railways because "the sudden abstraction of such a large amount from the active capital of the country would inevitably produce a most injurious effect in our financial position and probably terminate in a panic bankruptcy and general distress" Cited in L.A. Johnson, *History of Guelph*, p. 153.
38. Baskerville, *op. cit.*, pp. 217–221; T.C. Keefer, "A Sequel to the Philosophy of Railroads," in H.V. Nelles, ed., *Philosophy of Railroads* (Toronto, 1972), p. 102.
39. They were involved in real estate speculation at Niagara Falls on land bought from Zimmerman. Hamilton *Spectator*, Mar 19, 1857.
40. Baskerville, *op. cit.*, pp. 213–215.
41. *Ibid.*, p. 222.
42. Toronto *Examiner*, Nov. 9, 1853.
43. Keefer, *op. cit.*, p. 102.

tor was the Cobourg and Peterborough, on which Ira Spaulding was the engineer. This line had to cope with two natural obstacles. Between Cobourg and Peterborough there is a steep height of land running along the north shore of Lake Ontario, known as the South Slope, which peaks about eight miles north of Cobourg.[44] The gradient on the railway built there by Zimmerman had a rise of one-in-thirty, which meant that in operation a railway engine could move only one-tenth the load up the slope that it could on level ground.[45] The second obstacle proved even more troublesome. Between the ridge and Peterborough lies Rice Lake. Zimmerman's friend Ira Spaulding, the engineer, decided that a bridge could be built across it and Zimmerman undertook to build it. One of the longest bridges in existence at the time, almost three miles in length, was built across the shallow, soft-bottomed lake, resting on piles and on wooden cribs filled with stone. The bridge was opened for traffic at Christmas, 1854. On January 1, 1855, part of the bridge shifted four feet off its base crushing the south end into the shore, splintering timbers twelve inches by eighteen inches and bending iron rails double. Spring breakup did even greater damage. Piles which had not been driven deeply enough rose out of the lake. Thawing and refreezing caused constant cracking and shifting of the structure. The bridge had simply not been built strongly enough for its purpose. As a result it was closed more often than it was open. Six years after it was built it had to be abandoned.[46]

It might be supposed that given the unsatisfactory nature of the work performed, Zimmerman's company would have had to compensate the railway company, or make extensive and expensive repairs, and even lose money on the contract. In fact the opposite was the case. Out of the Cobourg and Peterborough contract, and the Woodstock and Lake Erie and Port Hope, Lindsay and Beaverton contracts as well, Zimmerman emerged a financial winner. How was it done? The answer is that it was done "according to contract"[47]—that is, done in a manner to meet legally the minimum standards of performance set out but also according to a contract mutually agreed upon in advance by the engineer and the contractor, approved by a board of directors composed partly of inexperienced local businessmen but also usually including some of the contrac-

---

44. L.J. Chapman and D.F. Putnam, *The Physiography of Southern Ontario* (Toronto, 1966), pp. 287–289.
45. A.W. Currie, *The Grand Trunk Railway of Canada* (Toronto, 1957), p. 284.
46. Trout and Trout, *op. cit.*, p. 118.
47. Keefer, *op. cit.*, p. 102.

tor's "friends". "According to contract" the contractor, on the approval of the engineer, imposed additional, unforeseen charges pushing the costs much above original estimates. "According to contract" the contractor got paid when his work was finished. If not he simply refused to turn over the tracks, engines and rolling stock until he was paid.[48] This meant that the railway companies themselves began their operations without funds. The money raised by the municipalities was inevitably used up in the construction phase. As well Zimmerman customarily took his payment half in cash and half in company bonds, so that he not only got all of the railway's ready cash but also became a major bondholder—in effect a part owner— and he collected interest, when the railway could afford to pay it, on his bonds.[49] The Cobourg and Peterborough was in fact relatively lucky in this regard. Though they protested that Zimmerman's bill for his work was "exorbitant and unreasonable"[50] they managed to pay it. The Port Hope, Lindsay and Beaverton wound up not only broke but mortgaged to Zimmerman for $100,000.[51] When the Woodstock and Lake Erie ran out of money after paying Zimmerman $348,000 for work done to that point, he lent the company money with which to pay himself for finishing a section of the route.[52] He had taken their available funds and they were in his debt until they could raise some more.

The use that Zimmerman made of his "friends" on the boards of directors of railways can be well illustrated by the case of the Woodstock and Lake Erie. The president of this railway in 1852–3 was Zimmerman's friend Francis Hincks. Hincks recommended R.G. Benedict as engineer.[53] In his written recommendation to the directors Benedict didn't actually name Zimmerman but urged that the directors choose a contractor who was known to have the "practical knowledge" and the means to finish the work.[54] Zimmerman got the contract in preference to three other bidders. When this contract had to be annulled because the railway company hadn't managed to get their finances sorted out in time, tenders were again called for in 1854. Two firms bid for this contract, Zimmerman and

48. Currie, *op. cit.*, p. 284.
49. Keefer, *op. cit.*, p. 102.
50. Trout and Trout, *op. cit.*, p. 117.
51. Currie, *op. cit.*, p. 282.
52. Buchanan Papers, vol. 100, pp. 67791, 67803–809.
53. *Ibid.*, Vol. 31, pp. 25789–91. Hincks to A.A. Farmer, May 13, 1853.
54. *Ibid.*, Vol. 3, p. 1592.

Company and Hall, Valentine and Company. One of the directors of the Woodstock and Lake Erie, Henry DeBlaquiere, secretly advised Hall, Valentine and Company as to the price they should quote in order to get the contract. Unknown to Hall, Valentine and Company, DeBlaquiere was actually working for Zimmerman. Their bid turned out to be higher than Zimmerman's and Zimmerman got the contract. Henry DeBlaquiere got a $50,000 bribe.[55]. . .

What lessons, if any, are to be learnt from the career of Samuel Zimmerman, entrepreneur? Was he a heroic builder of railways and communities, a public benefactor, or just a "bold operator"? Was he perhaps a symptom of an unfortunate period of public and private morality? Certainly a number of business historians have agreed that during the first great railway building era of the 1850's morality took a sharp downward turn. The late Max Magill wrote that "if one were to be asked to select a period when commercial and political morality were at their lowest in this country the ten years between 1850 and 1860 would be a good choice".[56] Professor Peter Baskerville, in his admirable thesis on the Upper Canadian Railway Community, goes even farther and argues that not just businessmen and politicians, but also lawyers, journalists, bankers, even the judiciary and the clergy mostly shared in and condoned "railway morality".[57] Obviously Samuel Zimmerman was a prime example of "railway morality". Nor is it difficult to find examples of politicians, businessmen, journalists, bankers and others aiding and abetting his activities. Zimmerman was a man of the times, and the times were not characterized by a strict moral code. Yet there may be room for at least some qualification of this gloomy picture of general depravity. There were, even at the time, signs of dissent from the apparently prevailing ethical standards.

Shortly after Zimmerman's death a parliamentary committee under the chairmanship of Michael Foley investigating the tangled affairs of the Woodstock and Lake Erie railroad found and bluntly stated that it was "distinctly proved" that Zimmerman had offered bribes and made exhor-

---

55. Canada, Legislative Assembly, *Journal* 1857, Appendices 4–6, Vol. XV, No. 2.
56. M.L. Magill, "James Morton of Kingston-Brewer" *Historic Kingston* no. 21, 1972, pp. 30–31.
57. Baskerville, *op. cit.*, p. 370.

bitant profits.[58] A government commission established a few years later to look into, among other matters, the workings of the Receiver-General's department, was equally harsh in its judgment of "great laxity of practice" in the department's dealings with the Zimmerman Bank and also with the way in which this transaction "was veiled from the public eye".[59] In 1865 the engineer and author, T.C. Keefer, went out of his way to include a bitter attack on Zimmerman and his methods in an article supposedly devoted to the progress of transportation in Canada.[60] It is true that these strong criticisms of Zimmerman, his friends and his moral standards were made when he was safely dead, but even while he was alive there were some who had misgivings. Keefer had already in 1855 and 1856 made speeches, later published in pamphlet form, which precisely described Zimmerman's railway business methods (though without naming him) and condemned them in the strongest terms.[61] A number of newspapers, among them the Hamilton *Gazette* and the St. Catharines *Post*, frequently were critical of Zimmerman's methods and worried about the extent of his influence.[62] During the many public railway meetings at which Zimmerman was generally praised by local politicians and businessmen for his "ability...perseverance and integrity", sometimes "deprecatory remarks" were also reported to have been made.[63] Finally, there is evidence to suggest that while Zimmerman's standards may well have been acceptable to or identical with those of the majority of the elite of the time, they were not necessarily those of society as a whole. In the election of 1857 after the revelations of the "Foley Committee" had been made public, Zimmerman's two closest political allies, The Honourable J.C. Morrison and Arthur Rankin, ran for re-election. Morrison didn't even try for renomination in Niagara, was rebuffed by his party in Peel and Grey and wound up running in South Ontario.[64] He was soundly defeated and indeed never managed to win elected office again. Arthur Rankin also went down to defeat, to none other than his local railway rival, John

---

58. Canada Legislative Assembly, *Journal* 1857, Appendices 4–6, Vol. XV, No. 2.
59. Canada, Financial and Departmental Commission, *First Report*, 1863, p. 46.
60. T.C. Keefer, "Travel and Transportation" in H.Y. Hind, *et. al., Eighty Years' Progress of British North America* (Toronto, 1865), pp. 222–224.
61. Keefer, *op. cit.*, pp. 101–103.
62. J.J. Talman, "The Impact of the Railway on a Pioneer Community" Canadian Historical Association *Annual Report*, 1955, p. 8.
63. Windsor *Herald*, Nov. 28, 1856.
64. Toronto *Globe*, Dec. 2, 14, 16, 29, 1857.

McLeod. The people (for whatever reasons) had spoken.[65] It is possible, at least for an optimist, to interpret these political results to mean that though much of the leadership of government and society was quite prepared to accept and to profit from "railway morality", the people as a whole had not been so easily nor so deeply infected by it. Perhaps, after all, you really can't fool all of the people, all of the time.

---

65. It must be admitted however, that neither Rankin nor Morrison was denied a chance to serve the public for long. Rankin was again M.P.P. for Essex, 1861–1867 and Morrison although again defeated in a by-election in 1861, was made a judge (by John A. Macdonald) in 1862.

Canadian Railways as Manufacturers, 1850–1880

PAUL CRAVEN AND TOM TRAVES

Most accounts of Canadian industrialization in the mid-nineteenth century attribute a dual role to the railways. First, by breaking down the old "tariff of bad roads" that protected small local markets for artisanal producers, they laid the groundwork for the concentration of industrial production in a handful of metropolitan centres. Second, it is often recognized that the railway companies were themselves important markets for a wide range of commodities, and so helped to create the opportunity structure for new investment in manufacturing. While the significance of the railways in the development of the market is indisputable, however, it is less frequently recognized that the railways were important industrial *producers* as well. Indeed the well-worn argument that railways represented commercial, as *opposed* to industrial, capital becomes quaintly irrelevant once it is realized that these companies owned and operated some of the largest and most sophisticated manufacturing plants in the Canadian economy from the early 1850s on.[1]

Railways were not just simple transportation companies. To understand their operations and management from their inception in the 1850s it is necessary first to appreciate the range of functions they performed in the daily course of business. In some respects they operated almost like states unto themselves; their company rules had the force of law, they

---

PAUL CRAVEN AND TOM TRAVES, "CANADIAN RAILWAYS AS MANUFACTURERS, 1850–1880," CANADIAN HISTORICAL ASSOCIATION, *HISTORICAL PAPERS* (1983): 254–81. REPRODUCED WITH PERMISSION OF THE AUTHORS.

Research for this paper, and for the larger Canadian Railways Industrial Relations History Project of which it forms a part, has had the generous support of the Social Sciences and Humanities Research Council of Canada. We gratefully acknowledge the research assistance of David Sobel and Rose Hutchens.

1. In December 1862, the Great Western's Inside Locomotive Department (i.e. shops as distinct from running trades) employed 255 men at Hamilton, and the Car Department 265; see Hamilton Public Library, GWR Mechanical Dept. Paysheets. In early 1860 the company held a dinner for six hundred men to celebrate the completion of the first locomotive built entirely in its shops; see Hamilton *Spectator*, 10 February 1860. The Grand Trunk published a breakdown of employment and wages in its locomotive department in its *Report* for the half-year ending 31 June 1859, showing 684 men employed in its locomotive shops alone.

employed their own police, and their executives, as the Grand Trunk's goods manager put it, were "as important as generals in an army or Ministers of State".[2] By 1860 the typical large railway, like the Grand Trunk or the Great Western, had the capacity to rebuild its line and repair its tracks, to manufacture its own cars and locomotives and even a good part of the machinery and equipment used in these manufacturing processes, to communicate telegraphically, to store and forward freight, to operate grain elevators and steamships, and to maintain large depots and complex administrative offices, all in support of its basic service as a common carrier. In short, the railways were Canada's first large-scale integrated industrial corporations.

This essay focuses on one aspect of integrated railway operations, the manufacturing activities of the railways' locomotive and car departments. By describing the nature and scope of these activities, and some features of the plant, organization and technology that sustained them, it is intended to contribute towards a reassessment of the railways' place in the history of Canadian industrialization.

The Scope of Manufacturing

The Grand Trunk and the Great Western, in common with some smaller roads, built extensive car shops as part of their original construction programme in the early 1850s, but at the outset they leased these structures to private contractors who equipped them to supply large orders for cars. Although they had to cope with eager competition from British and American car builders, and had to import such crucial parts as wheels and axles, independent Canadian car manufacturers were able to realize their considerable transportation cost advantage to dominate the local market. Dissatisfaction with the quality of the product, and even more pressing difficulties with financing large purchases, soon brought the railway companies to the view that it would be both cheaper and more efficient to build some of their cars themselves. In March 1855, the cash-poor Great Western attempted to cover its debts by foisting GWR bonds on its principal suppliers; shortly thereafter the company cancelled outstanding contracts and began building its own cars. "It is believed that a considerable saving, both in first cost and repairs, may be effected," its

---

2. Myles Pennington, *Railways and Other Ways* (Toronto, 1894), p. 119.

president explained, "by the company building cars in their own workshops, besides insuring the use of none but the best materials, which is the greatest safeguard against accidents. . . ."[3]

The Grand Trunk entered the car business for exactly the same reasons. After its major supplier refused to do any more work on credit, the GTR board accepted its chief engineer's proposal to operate the company's Point St. Charles workshops on its own account. By July 1857 the GTR car works were supplying half the road's requirements, and the board was so impressed with this success that it decided to construct an iron foundry, rolling mills and machinery to produce its own rails as well.[4]

The more complicated task of building locomotives was not undertaken until a little later. Independent Canadian suppliers certainly were active in this market as in cars, but at first the bulk of the orders went to large producers in Britain and the United States. . . .

Both the Grand Trunk and the Great Western began to consider building locomotives in their own shops, not only for the familiar reason, that it would "doubtless effect a considerable saving in expense", but also because it could furnish slack-time employment for skilled shopworkers in whose recruitment and retention the railways had a large investment. Grand Trunk shops turned out the *Trevithick* in May 1859, and the Great Western's *George Stephenson* was put to work a few months later.[5]

Between January 1864 and December 1873, the Grand Trunk shops built forty-nine new locomotives, or five per year on average. In the same period, they produced 1224 new freight cars (122 per year) and rebuilt, thoroughly renovated or converted substantial proportions of their existing stock. Over the ten years, the Grand Trunk built 172 new passenger cars (seventeen per year), and converted, thoroughly renovated or rebuilt 573 more (fifty-seven per year). In 1880, when the pattern of shopwork characteristic of the early 1870s had been reestablished after the disrup-

---

3. Public Archives of Canada (hereafter PAC), RG 30, Canadian National Railways Papers (henceforth *CNR*), vol. 1, 24 August 1855, Report of G.L. Reid, Chief Engineer, to the Shareholders; *ibid.*, 4 June 1853; *CNR* 1000, 11 December 1856; PAC, John Young Papers, 20 April 1852; *CNR* 2, 2 September 1853; 2 February 1855; 2 March 1855; 30 March 1855; Hamilton *Spectator*, 15 September 1855.
4. *CNR* 1000, 11 December 1856; Montreal *Pilot*, 1 August 1857.
5. Hamilton *Spectator*, 25 January 1861. See Paul Craven and Tom Traves, "Dimensions of Paternalism: Discipline and Culture in Canadian Railway Operations in the 1850s", in C. Heron and R. Storey, eds., *On the Job* (forthcoming). Hamilton *Spectator*, 10 February 1860; Hamilton *Times*, 12 May 1859; Toronto *Globe*, 17 May 1859.

tions occasioned by the change of gauge, the Grand Trunk built eighteen locomotives, thirty-one new passenger cars and 550 new freight cars, as well as converting, rebuilding or thoroughly renovating fifty-two passenger and 1414 freight cars. The shops also manufactured or remanufactured substantial quantities of parts to be used in repair; in the early 1870s, for example, the GTR car shops were turning out approximately six hundred new and renewed trucks per year, as well as between a thousand and fifteen hundred additional new and renewed axles.[6]

Similarly, the Great Western's locomotive shop manufactured or rebuilt sixty-eight engines—four a year on average—between 1860 and 1876. Like the Grand Trunk's it also produced parts and components used in locomotive manufacture and repair. For example, in the year ending 31 January 1871 the GWR turned out five crank axles (four steel, one iron), eleven straight engine axles, eleven truck axles, twenty-two tender axles, sixty-four axle boxes, twenty-six pistons, eight eccentric pulleys, four eccentric straps, twenty-one crank pins, three cross heads, nine driving wheels (eight cast iron, one unspecified), 389 chilled wheels, forty-five engine springs, sixty tender springs, eleven engine bells, 118 steel tyres, two tender trucks, one connecting rod, four valve spindles, two tender frames, and two flue-sheets (one copper, one steel), as well as completing three new boilers to be used in rebuilding locomotives and beginning work on three others. The Great Western's car shops were equally busy with new construction and rebuilding.[7]

Figures like these seriously underestimate the extent of manufacturing activity in the car and locomotive departments of the major railways, however. First, the published reports provide little or no systematic information about the production of all sorts of parts and components, although we know from various sources that a wide range of such things, such as iron bridge castings, locomotive boilers, springs, cast iron and wrought iron wheels, and lamps of various descriptions, were made in

---

6. The data in this paragraph are calculated from mechanical (or locomotive) superintendent's reports and associated tables published in the Grand Trunk's half-yearly *Reports* (varying titles) for the appropriate dates. We have so far been unable to compile a wholly unbroken run of these reports from mid-1854 (when the first one appeared) to mid-1863. The December 1873 cut-off date is used here because the Grand Trunk's change of gauge substantially altered the pattern of shopwork in the years immediately following.

7. For details on locomotive components and construction see, for example, Matthias N. Forney, *Catechism of the Locomotive* (New York, 1883). The figures in this paragraph are calculated from the Great Western's *Reports* for the appropriate dates.

quantity by the shops, as well as such items of operating equipment as semaphore signals.[8]

Second, there is a dearth of systematic quantitative information about the manufacture of tools and machinery for use by the railway shops themselves. Again, we know that they produced a wide range of such equipment, from the machinery for turntables and grain elevators to such sophisticated machine tools as the "powerful drilling machine with six drills. . .for drilling the iron skeletons for our new trucks, and a similar machine with fine drills. . .for boring the wood-work of the same trucks", which the Grand Trunk built in 1869; "by the use of these and other labour-saving machinery we are enabled to build trucks at a much lower cost than in former years."[9]

Third, and perhaps most important, it is necessary to consider the extent to which shopwork characterized as "repair" really amounted to manufacturing activity. On the Great Western, it was said that "a first-class car. . .only lasts nine years, or, in other words, at the close of a nine years' servitude, the repairs will have been so numerous and extensive that not one atom of the original car remains in use." The Grand Trunk's mechanical superintendent said that much of the "general repairs" consisted in "actual rebuilding of cars", and warned not to take the construction figures as a "measure of the actual work done towards maintenance inasmuch as a very large number of cars receive from one half to four fifths of new material into their construction, none of which are reckoned as new cars".[10]

The work of the railways' car and locomotive shops might be classified under five headings: maintenance, repair, renewal, replacement, and capital construction. Replacement and capital construction involved essentially the same sorts of activity—building cars or locomotives "from scratch"—but for the most part they were reported differently in the

---

8. *CNR*, #1597, 27 August 1861; #1643, 15 January 1862; GTR *Report*, half-year ending 30 June 1869, p. 11; GWR *Report*, half-year ending 31 January 1861, p. 27; Hamilton *Spectator*, 9 August 1860; *CNR* 1042, 28 November 1879; *CNR* 6, #1649, 26 February 1864.

9. *CNR* 7, #1380, 20 May 1859; *ibid.*, #s1651–2, 11 March 1862; GTR *Report*, half-year ending 30 June 1869, p. 11.

10. Hamilton *Spectator*, 4 March 1857; GTR *Report* for half-year to 30 June 1864; *ibid.*, half-year to 30 June 1865. "Maintenance" here meant keeping the car stock up to numerical strength.

railways' accounts.[11] Great Western (subsequently Grand Trunk) locomotive superintendent Richard Eaton defined renewals as "that class of work which adds new and additional life to the Engine, beyond its average term of fifteen years. Consequently new fire boxes, Tubes, Tyres or Wheels, supplied to Engines under the ordinary heavy repairs cannot be considered as renewals, as these, and other articles, are necessary to the life of fifteen years alone."[12] At the other extreme maintenance might be distinguished from light repairs by limiting it to routine cleaning, lubricating, and so forth.

Expenditure on Manufacturing

...Manufacturing activity in locomotive and car departments appears in both the capital and revenue accounts. Railway accounting practices were inconsistent in this period (especially in the earlier years), and one suspects that the assignment of an item to one or the other frequently depended on a political assessment of the shareholders' collective frame of mind rather than on any theory of industrial finance....About all that can be said of the capital account data is that the railway shops evidently produced a substantial annual volume of rolling stock over and above the expenditure shown in the revenue accounts.

The locomotive and car repair schedules in the revenue accounts supply a more satisfactory basis for estimating the value of manufacturing activity in the railway mechanical departments....

[I]t is conservative claim that the Great Western mechanical departments expended a quarter of a million dollars on manufacturing activity in 1859, and over three-quarters of a million in 1874; or that the Grand Trunk spent over $600,000 a year on mechanical department manufacturing in the early 1860s and about $1.5 million annually in the later 1870s. Manufacturing expenditure on revenue account grew steadily over the period as a proportion (approximately 20 per cent) of total ordinary working expenses.

It should be noted that these expenditure figures are not equivalent to census value-added statistics, in that they include no profit component and, so far as we can ascertain, no market price adjustment for materials

---

11. It was not until well into the 1860s that the larger railway companies worked out even a moderately consistent accounting response to the problem of depreciation; previously new equipment had frequently been charged to revenue account, and renewals to capital.
12. *CNR*, #1643, 15 January 1862.

and components manufactured by the railway companies themselves. But even on a straight comparison of mechanical department expenditures to census value-added figures for other manufacturers, it appears plain that the railways were among the largest manufacturing firms in Canada in the period, and quite possibly the largest bar none....It is clear that the central car and locomotive shops on the two largest railways—the Grand Trunk's at Brantford and Montreal, and the Great Western's at Hamilton—were as big as the largest independent establishments in those industries, and that as *integrated*, multiplant manufacturers the larger railways were bigger by far—in terms just of *manufacturing* employment, consumption of materials, and output—than any of the independent firms. The exclusion of the railway company facilities from the aggregate tables published in the 1871 census reports resulted in a grossly distorted picture of the scale and organization of the Canadian railway supply and heavy engineering industries.[13]

---

13. "Engine builders" included manufacturers of all manner of steam engines, not merely locomotives. A detailed systematic examination of the industrial schedules for locations other than those surveyed here might well turn up other misclassified and/or omitted establishments. The published report should be used with the greatest caution: Canada, *Census (1870–1)* (Ottawa, 1875), v. 3.

Philosophy of Railroads

T. C. KEEFER

Speed, economy, regularity, safety, and convenience—an array of advantages unequalled—are combined in the Railway System. These we will notice separately. . . .

Speed

The importance of speed in the transport of goods is annually increasing; even now the more valuable descriptions of merchandize take the rail in preference to the slower and cheaper route by canal; and since the cost of transport upon a Railway varies in an inverse proportion with the business of the board, it is annually becoming less, so that economy of time and economy of transport are becoming less and less antagonistical, and are approaching each other so rapidly, as to render the establishment of any line of demarcation exceedingly difficult if not impossible.

Economy

Compared with all other land communications, their freighting capabilities may be inferred from the consideration that a horse usually draws from fifteen to thirty hundred weight on a good turnpike or macadamised road (exclusive of vehicle), four to six tons on a plate rail tram road, and fifteen to twenty tons on an edge rail including the waggons;—the friction on a level Railway being only from one-tenth to one-seventh of that upon the roads above mentioned. If this be the effect of the rail alone, it is needless to enlarge upon its power when travelled by an iron horse, with which hunger and thirst are but metaphorical terms, which knows no disease nor fatigue, and to which a thousand miles is but the beginning of a journey, and a thousand tons but an ordinary burthen.

But it is in a more extended sense than the mere *cost* of transport that the economy of the Railway is vindicated. While upon the best roads

T. C. Keefer, *Philosophy of Railroads*, ed. H. V. Nelles (originally published 1850; reprinted Toronto: University of Toronto Press, 1972): 3, 12–14. By permission of University of Toronto Press.

travelled by horses, the cost and time of transportation increases rapidly with the distance, it is clear that there is a point from whence the transport of certain articles becomes unprofitable or impracticable. Milk, fruits, and vegetables, for immediate use, will not bear ten or twelve hours jolting over fifty miles of the best turnpike to reach a market; while fresh meats, fish eggs, cattle, pigs, and poultry, lumber, staves, shingles, and firewood, and many other necessaries of life, either could not afford the time or the cost of a hundred miles transport by horse-power. The production of these articles, therefore, is very limited in certain districts; but wherever a Railway takes its track their extensive production becomes at once a new element of wealth, and the Locomotive a public benefactor—making 'two blades of grass grow where only one grew before.' Thus the essence of a Railway system is *to increase its own traffic*, adding twenty-five per cent to the value of every farm within fifty miles of the track, doubling that of those near it, and quadrupling the value of timbered lands through which they pass. Railroads are in one respect more economical carriers than canals, in as much as they are both freight and toll receivers, and are therefore content with one profit.

Regularity

The superior speed and safety of Railway travel over the most expeditious water communications are scarcely more important than its extraordinary regularity; to which latter circumstance it is chiefly owing that in every country the Railway has been selected for the transportation of the mails. This monopoly of mails and passengers enables them to transport goods proportionally cheaper—thus becoming powerful rivals to the most favourable water communications. From this principle of regularity, Railways in the winter season have no competitors; and working the whole year round, without delay of lockage, wind or tide, fog, frost, or rain, they, with a full business and fair 'grades,' can compete with ordinary canals in price, while they can make two trips, to one on the canal, in less than half the time.

Safety

The comparative safety of Railway travel with that upon steamboats is best appreciated by the reflection, that the causes which endanger human life upon the former are limited to collisions or leaving the track—both to be avoided by ordinary care: whereas in the latter, explosion, fire, collision, or wrecking, are attended with imminent risk to all, the only choice often being—the *mode* of death. Explosion of a locomotive boiler, besides being exceedingly rare, is scarcely ever attended with any danger to the lives of the passengers. The remarkable safety of well managed Railways may be further illustrated by the statement of Baron Von Reden, that upon the Railways of Germany only one person in every twelve and a quarter millions of passengers was killed or wounded from defective arrangements of the road, one in every nine millions from his own misconduct, and one in every twenty-five millions from his own negligence. The Germans are undoubtedly a prudent people.

Convenience

The convenience of the Railway System lies chiefly in its adaptation to its peculiar traffic:—artificial navigation is restricted to favourable ground and supplies of water, but modern improvements have enabled the Locomotive to clamber over mountains and penetrate the most remote corners of the land; there is therefore no limit to the number of its auxiliary branches, which can be multiplied and extended until their ramifications give the required facilities to every wharf and every warehouse—to the solitary mill or factory, or to the most neglected districts as an outlet to otherwise worthless products.

FURTHER READINGS FOR TOPIC 14

W. T. Easterbrook and Hugh G. Aitken. *Canadian Economic History*. Toronto: Macmillan, 1956; reprinted 1963.

Kenneth Norrie and Douglas Owram. *A History of the Canadian Economy*. Toronto: Harcourt Brace Jovanovich, 1991.

Paul Romney. " 'The Ten Thousand Pound Job': Political Corruption, Equitable Jurisdiction, and the Public Interest in Upper Canada 1852–6." In *Essays in the History of Canadian Law*, Vol. 2, ed. David H. Flaherty. Toronto: The Osgoode Society, 1983: 143–99.

Jacob Spelt. *Urban Development in South-Central Ontario*. Toronto: McClelland and Stewart, 1972.

Gerald Tulchinsky. *The River Barons: Montreal Businessmen and the Growth of Industry and Transportation, 1837–1853*. Toronto: University of Toronto Press, 1977.

TOPIC 15

Middle-Class Work

In the generation before Confederation, population growth and the spread of settlement brought new job opportunities for immigrants and residents alike. One of those who sought to take advantage of these new frontiers was John Boles Gaggin, a genteel Irishman who arrived in 1859 in the newly established colony of British Columbia. Gaggin was fortunate indeed to find work in the colonial service; there seem always to have been fewer such places available than job-seekers anxious to fill them. On the other hand, Gaggin's physique and character were ill-suited to the niche he was destined to fill, and he came to a sad end. Yet Gaggin's career is of lasting significance because it illustrates some important themes in the history of middle-class work. The pattern of multiple office-holding which characterized his work was typical of the pioneer civil service in most jurisdictions. Moreover, this pattern was not confined to government work. Lawyers, for example, also commonly acted as businessmen and politicians, and as we have seen in Topic 11, farmers often found employment in lumbering. Indeed, working at several occupations simultaneously may well have been the norm rather than the exception in mid-nineteenth-century British North America.

Women had access to new opportunities as a result of social and economic changes during this period. Whereas their horizons outside the home had once been largely confined to domestic service and prostitution, and to the convent if they were Roman Catholic, the expansion of formal education after 1850 encouraged them to enter the profession of teaching. The ensuing process of the "feminization of teaching" cannot, however, be regarded as an entirely benign development, as the following article by Alison Prentice reveals.

The third selection is an anecdotal account of an incident in the career of J. R. Gowan, an Irish immigrant who was admitted to the bar of Upper

*Canada in 1839. When the Simcoe District was established in 1843,
Gowan became its first Judge of the District Court, as well as Surrogate
Court Judge. The following excerpt from his biography not only highlights
the multiple duties performed by judicial officers on the frontier, but casts
an interesting light on the practice of frontier justice.*

"Poor Gaggin":

Irish Misfit in the Colonial Service

DOROTHY BLAKEY SMITH

In December 1858 John Boles Gaggin resigned his commission as first lieutenant in the Royal Cork Artillery Militia, and, armed with an introduction from the Secretary of State for the Colonies to Governor James Douglas, prepared to seek his fortune in the newly established gold colony of British Columbia.[1] He was one of a group of Anglo-Irish gentlemen recommended to Sir Edward Bulwer Lytton by that "intellectual, picturesque, and friendly Irishman" Chichester Fortescue, who served as Parliamentary Undersecretary at the Colonial Office during most of the period 1857–1865. At this time the Colonial Secretaryship itself was held by members of the nobility, and affairs abroad were consequently much under the influence of the "swarm of Under Secretaries [who] had to meet the House of Commons." Gilbert Malcolm Sproat, from whose fragmentary but illuminating "History of British Columbia"[2] the foregoing quotations are taken, admits that Chichester Fortescue's recommendations for the Colonial Service of British Columbia, "though over-numerous and followed by expectants, were, generally, men of a good character." Most of them, it appears, made a success of their new career.[3] J. Boles Gaggin (as he usually signed himself) most emphatically did not. . . .

It would appear that John Boles Gaggin was born in the early 1830s[4] [and]. . .[o]n 10 April 1859 he arrived at Victoria. . .[5]

<hr />

DOROTHY BLAKEY SMITH, " 'POOR GAGGIN": IRISH MISFIT IN THE COLONIAL CIVIL SERVICE," *B.C. STUDIES* NO. 32 (WINTER 1976–1977): 41–64. BY PERMISSION OF THE PUBLISHER.

This article constitutes an expansion of a short biography of John Boles Gaggin commissioned for a forthcoming volume of the *Dictionary of Canadian Biography*, and is printed here by permission of the general editor of *DCB*.

1. The original commission, the letter of introduction, and the testimonials cited in the following paragraph are all in the J. B. Gaggin Correspondence, Colonial Correspondence, the Provincial Archives of British Columbia (hereafter cited as PABC).

2. MS, PABC.

3. See Margaret A. Ormsby, "Some Irish Figures in Colonial Days," *British Columbia Historical Quarterly* XIV (1950), pp. 61–82.

4. In his "Confidential report" on his officers in 1863 Governor Douglas gave Gaggin's age as "about 28" (Douglas to the Duke of Newcastle, 13 February 1863. PRO microfilm CO 60/18, PABC). But A. T. Bushby, probably on the basis of the marker on Gaggin's grave, which he visited in 1874, says that he died (in 1867) "aetat 36." (Journal, 1874, MS, PABC).

5. See the diary of Peter O'Reilly, *passim*, March-April 1859, MS, PABC. O'Reilly himself sailed from Galway for New York on the *Prince Albert* on 5 February 1859 and on the *Illinois* for Aspinwall on 7 March; but it is not until 22 March 1859 that the name of Gaggin

Gaggin was appointed chief constable at Yale in June 1859.[6] At the beginning of October he became stipendiary magistrate and assistant gold commissioner at Port Douglas,[7] the settlement at the southern terminus of the Harrison-Lillooet route to the gold mines of the Fraser River, a road which had been commenced by the miners themselves, under the supervision of the government, in October 1858 and then improved by the Royal Engineers. Like the other assistant gold commissioners in the British Columbia service, he also served as justice of the peace, county court judge, deputy collector of customs, deputy sheriff, head of the postal service, and sub-commissioner of lands and works.[8] In this latter capacity he was responsible for inspecting and keeping in repair the two perennially troublesome portages along the chain of lakes between Port Douglas and Pemberton. From time to time during his first years at Port Douglas he received the Governor's "entire approval for his promptitude and judgment in keeping the communications open for traffic."[9]. . .

Like most of the other assistant gold commissioners, Gaggin had no legal training, and he wrote frequently, on an informal basis, to Attorney-General Henry P. Pellew Crease for advice. "What am I best do?" he asks, in the matter of four Indians he has just committed for trial at the assizes for stealing a barrel of whiskey:

> Tis the deuce keeping the fellows in and giving them. . .free quarters when tried. Don't you think it wd be better, if practicable, and advise, for me to give them what I may think proper, thereby saving cost to

---

occurs in his diary. See also *Victoria Gazette* 12 April 1859. Stewart returned to England on 28 August 1859 (O'Reilly, diary).

6. W. A. G. Young to Chartres Brew, 8 June 1859, and to E. H. Sanders, 16 June 1859. These two letters, and all other letters signed by the Colonial Secretary, will be found, unless otherwise indicated, in British Columbia, Colonial Secretary, Correspondence outward, 1859–1867 (Letter-books Nos. 2–7).

7. The British Columbia *Blue Books*, 1860–1867, give the date of this appointment as 4 October 1859.

8. For the multifarious duties of the assistant gold commissioners see Margaret A. Ormsby, *British Columbia: A History* (Toronto, 1958), p. 180. On 1 October 1859 Gaggin wrote from Yale that he had been "appointed by His Excellency the Governor Justice of the Peace at Port Douglas." Douglas was himself in Yale on 1 October and gave Gaggin a letter to C. S. Nicol, whom he was replacing, authorizing him to act as J.P. (see Gaggin to Colonial Secretary, 7 November 1869). His official commission as J.P. was not forwarded until 19 November 1859. He was appointed County Court Judge on 10 January 1860 and deputy collector of customs on 6 November 1860. On 19 March 1860 he was made responsible for the postal service at Port Douglas.

9. Minute by J.D. on Gaggin to Colonial Secretary, 28 January 1862; and cf. minutes of Gaggin to Colonial Secretary 3 April and 30 November 1861.

Government, and punishing the beggars by making them work during Summer?[10]

...If Gaggin had confined himself to seeking private advice from his friends among "the Bloaks"[11] at government headquarters in New Westminster, his public image might not have suffered. But being, as he said himself, "a stupid hound naturally,"[12] he was apt to refer to higher officials, even to the Governor himself, local problems he should have settled on the spot.... When charges were made against the constable at Port Douglas, Gaggin referred them to Chief Constable Chartres Brew, who commented: "I do not see any reason why Mr. Gaggin should not hold this enquiry himself."[13]...

[Gaggin more than once incurred the wrath of Governor Douglas. In 1862 he was severely reprimanded when he failed as a magistrate to keep order on the steamboat *Henrietta* after it was boarded by a group of unruly miners.] The following year Gaggin was rapped on the knuckles again. He had requested the appointment of a constable at Pemberton, which he declared to be "from my knowledge...one of the most depraved, rowdy, and bla'guard places in the Colony."[14] The Governor refused the request, ostensibly because of "the expense attendant," but seized the occasion to admonish Gaggin that

> the Magistrate is to endeavour by all means in his power—by his advice to the better disposed—by the weight of his influence and example among the evil doers—to remedy the state of things. Much in such a case can be done by a Magistrate, who by the exercise of firmness, moderation, judgment & the force of good example has earned for himself the respect of his district.

The emphasis here on "the force of good example" invites speculation that by this time rumours of some of Gaggin's less desirable social habits had reached the Governor, and the Governor was not amused.

It will be observed that in his reply to Gaggin's defence in the *Henrietta* affair the Governor completely ignored the excuse that he "was ill at the

---

10. Gaggin to Crease, 28 April 1863. Crease Correspondence inward, Crease Collection, PABC.
11. Gaggin to Crease, 1 December 1862. *Ibid.*
12. Gaggin to Crease, 24 April 1863. *Ibid.*
13. Brew to Colonial Secretary, 31 December 1862. C. Brew Correspondence, Colonial Correspondence, PABC.
14. Gaggin to Colonial Secretary, 19 August 1863.

time."[15] Indeed, this particular excuse for failure in duty was hardly likely to get much sympathy from James Douglas, himself endowed with a rugged constitution and an iron will. In Gaggin's correspondence illness is a recurring theme, for Port Douglas did not agree with him. In the rush to begin construction of the trail to the mines in 1858, the site of the settlement had been hastily chosen on Little Harrison Lake. Four years later Dr. Cheadle called it "a vile hole in a hollow formed by continuation of lake basin up to hill beyond lake."[16] The house provided for the magistrate was far from comfortable. It had no "waterproof office"[17] and it was very cold, for the upper storey had no ceiling and the chimney was a fire hazard.[18] By the summer of 1861 these defects had been remedied. Gaggin had also had all the trees endangering his dwellings cut down by prisoners and was now permitted to "render this at present insecure building more safe from storms" by adding a verandah on two sides.[19] During the next two years he spent out of his own pocket "a very large amount of money on improvements about this house [and] made it one of the best-looking pieces of ground attached to any Magistrate's house in the Colony."[20] But despite these improvements to his quarters, Gaggin often reported himself unwell. . . .

[In the *Henrietta* affair and on other occasions, Gaggin's conduct left him vulnerable to the critics:] In that incident, as in other dealings with his fellow men. . .he was too kind and generous for his own good. Full of sympathy for those who appeared to him "wretched creatures" returning penniless from the mines, he had neglected what the Governor saw as his first duty: to enforce the law. Indians as well as white men were encompassed by his compassion, and here again his warm-heartedness stood in the way of his own advancement in the public service. In the winter of 1861 he reported to the Colonial Secretary that the Indians at Port Douglas, because they could not get employment as packers, were "actually starving," and asked for funds to relieve them.[21] The Governor's

---

15. Reply, 26 August 1863, written on the application form.
16. Walter B. Cheadle, *Cheadle's Journal of Trip across Canada 1862–1863*, ed. A. G. Doughty and Gustave Lanctot (Ottawa, 1931). Entry for 2 October 1863.
17. Gaggin to Colonial Secretary, 30 November 1859.
18. Gaggin to Colonial Secretary, 7 and 30 November 1859; Colonial Secretary to Gaggin, 19 November 1859.
19. Colonial Secretary to Gaggin, 16 January 1861; Gaggin to Colonial Secretary, 20 June 1861; and Colonial Secretary to Gaggin, 2 July 1861.
20. Gaggin to H. M. Ball, Acting Colonial Secretary, 30 November 1865.
21. Gaggin to Colonial Secretary, 11 January 1861.

minute on the letter reads: "Mr. Gaggin's application has no precedent—in this colony—and if granted might for a temporary good, give rise to permanent evils, by encouraging improvidence, and encouraging a belief that Government had the means of providing for every case of distress—which should be relieved by the hand of private charity." Obviously, Douglas wanted no part of the welfare state. In justice it must be said that his own charity was considerable, as his private account books show, and that in this particular instance he did authorize the sending of $100 for the "relieving of real objects of distress" among the Port Douglas Indians. In acknowledging this sum, Gaggin assured the Colonial Secretary that many *had* been relieved by private charity, and that the "severe lesson" of this winter would teach the natives to attend more closely to fishing instead of relying too much on packing. Upon which Douglas authorized another $100 "if it is absolutely necessary for the preservation of life," and if the sum previously granted had been spent.[22] It is clear, however, that in this instance too, as well as in the *Henrietta* affair, Gaggin's generosity of spirit had run counter to the system, and that he had, at least by implication, criticized the Governor's policy.

But however much one may applaud Gaggin's humanity to man, both Indian and white, it must be admitted that his expansive good nature, besides creating a certain distrust of his judgment in the mind of Governor Douglas, sometimes led to social behaviour of a style quite likely to interfere with the performance of his official duties. His friend Crease once admonished him: "Try and keep out of good companye, you old 'father of the fatherless' as we all [christen] you."[23] In the autumn of 1863 Lord Milton and Dr. Cheadle arrived at Port Douglas on their way to Lillooet and found that the stage was not due to leave for another two days. Cheadle's journal then gives a vivid little sketch of the warm-hearted, convivial, and somewhat irresponsible Gaggin in action:

Saturday, October 3rd.—...Walk up to inquire of Mr. Gaggin the Judge if there are any other means of getting forward. Regular jolly Irishman from Cork; kindly promises to lend Milton a horse if I can find another. Agree to start on horseback tomorrow....

---

22. Gaggin to Colonial Secretary, 4 February 1861; Colonial Secretary to Gaggin, 19 February 1861.
23. Crease to Gaggin, 24 October 1864. H. P. P. Crease, Private Miscellaneous Letters, 1864–1865, Crease Collection, PABC.

Sunday, October 4th.—After sundry beers & procrastinations we set out, Gaggin having found a mule for me for which I had to pay $10 for the 29 miles. The Judge accompanied us on a grey horse which had been left behind by a Mr. Flinn gone down to Victoria. "The Judge" turned out a "whale for drink," & we pulled up at every wayside house to refresh... we trotted on to the 16-mile house...& finding it late, we resolved to stay the night & ride forward in time for the steamer in the morning. Gaggin & I had two jugs of mulled claret which made us sleep like tops.

Monday, October 5th.—Off at 7 to catch the steamer at 12....My mule "Yank" falling lame, I rode on, leaving Milton & Gaggin at the 24-mile house refreshing. Arrived at foot of the little lake (29-mile house) an hour before the steamer started, dined & waited in vain for Milton & Gaggin; the steamer at last starting & leaving us in the lurch.... Presently stage came in from Douglas, bringing only one passenger, Mr. Flinn whose horse Gaggin had impressed to ride along with us....About 4 o'clock Milton & "The Judge" arrived, the latter having met some friends at the last house & gone through 1/2 doz. of stout!...Gaggin & the landlady (an Irishwoman) had chaff all the evening....

Tuesday, October 6th.—Over Little Lillooet Lake in tiny steamer...& then in fine steamer "Prince of Wales" over Great Lillooet Lake to Pemberton....Gaggin accompanied us. Continual liquorings up, which Milton & I shirked as well as could....

Wednesday, October 7th.—Bid a kind adieu to Gaggin....

It is clear from this little episode that besides being a "whale for drink," Gaggin needed little inducement to absent himself from his headquarters. From 1860 on, there are frequent references in the Colonial Secretary's letters to this fact, and in August 1863 Gaggin had been plainly told that "His Excellency would prefer your remaining in Douglas as much as is compatible with the requirements of the public service," and, furthermore, that he must make formal application for any leave of absence before taking it.[24] Undoubtedly Gaggin's superiors realized by this time that he would use any pretext to get away from Port Douglas for even a brief respite and had chosen this method of trying to curtail his travels. And yet perhaps Gaggin can hardly be blamed too severely for feeling somewhat aggrieved by this blanket decree. After all, he was responsible for keeping open the trail to Pemberton so that thousands of men and their

---

24. See, for example, Colonial Secretary to Gaggin, 30 April and 22 May 1860; 31 August 1863.

supplies could reach the gold mines on the upper Fraser. Hastily surveyed and constructed in 1858 through difficult terrain, the trail was extremely vulnerable to slides and washouts, and Gaggin must have repairs made as quickly as possible and in a satisfactory manner. It is rather difficult to see how he could be expected to carry out this duty if he must wait to receive formal permission before leaving his headquarters—especially considering the state of postal communication at the time, when a letter from Victoria might take nearly four weeks to reach Port Douglas, and a letter from Lillooet to Port Douglas had to be sent via New Westminster.[25] In his own defence Gaggin pointed out that

> at no time this season did my absence on duty exceed a week. I have the entire charge of fifty-six miles of road, which extends over a distance of eighty miles from Douglas. . . .My absence was on duties connected with my office of Assistant Commissioner of Lands, and that, unless I thought it absolutely necessary I would not have gone during the worst time of the mosquitos, besides being considerably out of pocket, having to pay from 8 to 12 shillings a day for feed for my horse.[26]

But the rock on which Gaggin's civil service career finally foundered was his inability to cope with the paper work required, especially in the matter of accounts. His reports were late, incomplete in detail, and not always sent in duplicate. Some letters he never answered; sometimes he failed to keep copies of his own; and he made payments without proper authority. As the Colonial Secretary complained on 27 August 1863: ". . .great inconvenience is occasioned in this Department, and the transaction of business is greatly impeded, through the neglect of officers, of the simple rules laid down for their guidance. . . ." Gaggin was admonished that he must "take care that established forms are, for the future, complied with.". . .

In November 1866 the mainland colony of British Columbia was united with the colony of Vancouver Island, and the perennial problem of Gaggin was solved. In the necessary reduction of the civil list his sinecure at Wild Horse Creek could with justification be abolished, and on 16 December 1866 he was dismissed, with practically no hope of further employment in the public service. Birch wrote to him that if he wished to return to

---

25. Nind to Colonial Secretary, 12 December 1863. P. H. Nind Correspondence, Colonial Correspondence, PABC.
26. Gaggin to Colonial Secretary, 4 September 1863.

England, he would be given a free passage and three months' salary. If he preferred to remain in British Columbia, his claims for further employment would be considered "when the occasion offered."

Gaggin stayed on at Wild Horse Creek, but not for long. The "first rate health" of which he had boasted soon after his arrival rapidly declined and he had been confined to his bed for some time before, on 27 May 1867, he died.[27] On that same day, Constable John R. Lawson of Kootenay was shot to death by a horse thief. O'Reilly's successor in the Columbia District, W. G. Cox, was ordered at once to Wild Horse Creek, and on his arrival reported that it was thought Gaggin's death had been brought on by "the shock which he sustained on hearing of Lawson's death."[28] Magistrate and constable were buried side by side in the cemetery at Wild Horse Creek, and O'Reilly, when he visited the "grave of poor Gaggin & Lawson" later that summer, had "a wall built round it up to the fence.[29] The grave can no longer be identified. In 1953 a group of volunteer citizens undertook to restore the old burial ground at White Horse Creek. They found only one wooden marker remaining in the whole cemetery, and the inscription on that could not be deciphered.[30] The obituary of J. Boles Gaggin in the Victoria *Colonist*, 4 July 1867, spoke of him as "a favourite with all classes on the mainland." To his friends in the civil service of British Columbia—Ker, Nind, O'Reilly, Arthur Bushby (who visited his grave in 1874 and remarked that he was only thirty-six when he died)—he would always be "Poor Gaggin."

---

27. W. G. Cox to Colonial Secretary, 27 June 1867. W. G. Cox Correspondence, Colonial Correspondence, PABC; Barkerville *Cariboo Sentinel*, 28 July 1867.
28. W. G. Cox to Colonial Secretary, 27 June 1867.
29. O'Reilly, diary, 7 August 1867.
30. W. A. Burton, "Old Burying Ground Link with Days of '64," *Cranbrook Courier*, 4 December 1942; *Cranbrook Courier*, 30 June 1965.

The Feminization of Teaching

Alison Prentice

I

According to Solomon Denton, the local school inspector for the county of York in New Brunswick, many districts in his area were having trouble keeping schools open in 1856. There were many reasons, but a striking and not uncommon one mentioned by Denton was the failure in certain places to agree "as to what Teacher to employ." The problem, the inspector said, was that "one party wishes for a female, while the other insists upon a male Teacher; the end is, that they engage neither."[1]

While most such disputes probably ended less drastically, it is nevertheless clear that the same debate was taking place in many parts of British North America in the middle years of the nineteenth century. Yet, by the end of the century, the question of whether to employ a male or a female teacher had become academic, for in most places in Canada, almost the only elementary school teachers available for hire were women. What had happened between 1856 and 1900 to bring about this significant change?

The answer, as in most historical questions, is a complex one, which goes beyond either the history of women or the history of education alone, to a consideration of a series of interrelated developments in the roles played by schools, teachers and women, and in the ideology concerning them during this period. Perhaps the first point that has to be made by way of introduction is the negative one that the "feminization of teaching" does not refer to the entry of women into a role that they had never occupied before. Women did teach school before the middle of the nineteenth century in British North America; what they did not do, in most regions, is teach publicly to any great extent, that is, in large schools outside the home. The first thing to consider, then, is the making of elementary school teaching into an occupation that was conducted chiefly in non-domestic surroundings.

While this may seem an obvious point, it requires some discussion, largely because the movement of elementary instruction out of the home

---

Alison Prentice, "The Feminization of Teaching." in *The Neglected Majority: Essays in Canadian Women's History*, ed. Susan Mann Trofimenkoff and Alison Prentice (Toronto: McClelland and Stewart, 1977): 49–65. Reprinted with permission.

1. Report of the Superintendent of Education for New Brunswick for the Year 1856, p. 71.

and into the larger environment of the school has been misunderstood by historians in the past. Students of educational history are now becoming increasingly aware, however, of both how momentous the movement was in the totality of western social history,[2] and how rapidly the alteration sometimes occurred in particular places during times of intense economic and social change.[3] Equally important too is the growing recognition that the movement of formal elementary instruction into institutions known in Canada as public schools, its extension to greater numbers of children, and to more years of their lives, does not mean that, prior to this movement, most children went totally uninstructed. Many, on the contrary, we believe, were exposed to considerable "schooling" in the earlier decades of the century, and many of their teachers, furthermore, were women. How many, in both cases, it is probably impossible to know, for useful statistics did not begin to be gathered before the creation of centralized educational administrations, which, in central and eastern British North America, took place at mid-century. But we do know that before the 1840s there were, in the populated regions, a great many small "private" schools, schools located in the households of both men and women, and sometimes of married couples.[4] Male teachers were no doubt in the majority in most provinces before the 1840s, and they probably also conducted most "public" schools of that era, the schools that were too large to accommodate in households. The feminization of teaching which took place in the second half of the nineteenth century was thus, in the first place, a movement of women into *public* school teaching, at a time when elementary education itself was gradually moving out of the household and into the ever growing public institutions that would eventually almost monopolize the name of "schools."[5]

---

2. Although part of his thesis have been challenged, the most dramatic general account of this change remains that of Philippe Ariès, *Centuries of Childhood: A Social History of Family Life* (New York: Random House, Vintage Books, 1962) trans. by Robert Baldick.

3. For a Canadian example of a sudden increase in the average ages and number of children attending school in a particular locality, see Michael B. Katz, "Who Went to School?" *History of Education Quarterly* 12 (Fall 1972); reprinted in Paul H. Mattingly and Michael B. Katz, eds., *Education and Social Change* (New York: New York University Press, 1975), pp. 271–93.

4. The variety of schooling in early Upper Canada is described in R.D. Gidney, "Elementary Education in Upper Canada: A Reassessment," *Ontario History* 65 (September 1973); reprinted in *Education and Social Change*, pp. 3–27.

5. In the absence of statistics it is impossible to estimate the number of women teaching in non-domestic schools before the mid 1840's. Early official encouragement to the idea of employing females may be found in Dr. Charles Duncombe's Report on Education to the Legislature of Upper Canada (1836) and in the Nova Scotia Board of Education's "Rules and Regulations for the guidance and government of the several Boards of Commissioners..." (1841). J. Donald Wilson, "The Teacher in Early Ontario," in F. H. Armstrong, H.

The second and better known aspect of the feminization of teaching is the fact that in the third quarter of the century in most of British North America and Canada, women became a majority among common or elementary school teachers. Less well known is the fact that this change was closely related to two contemporary educational movements: the first, a campaign to promote the grading of school children, and, as a result, to promote the consolidation of small schools into larger schools and school systems, especially in urban areas; and the second, a passionate campaign to raise the status of teaching as a profession.

The first of these movements, the physical separation of children into classes or grades within each school or school system, was undertaken largely in the name of efficiency. The chief goal was an efficient division of labour, with the more experienced teachers taking the advanced grades and the less well trained, engaged at lower rates of pay, taking the younger children or beginners. The end result of organizing schools in this way, it was claimed, was that larger numbers of pupils could thus be more cheaply and effectively taught.[6] At the same time, however, higher salaries were energetically pursued by schoolmen of the same era, as an essential part of their campaign to make the teaching profession respectable and to induce well qualified people to remain in it as a lifetime career.[7] Clearly the two goals were to some extent incompatible, as cheapness was promoted on the one hand and higher salaries and respectable careers were touted on the other. The gradual introduction of more and more female teachers at least partially solved the problem, for the employment of growing numbers of women in the lower ranks of expanded teaching staffs made it possible for school administrators to pursue both goals at once. Relatively higher salaries could be made available for male superintendents, inspectors, principal teachers and headmasters, yet money could be saved at the same time by engaging women at low salaries to teach the lower grades.[8]

As the dilemma reported by school inspector Denton illustrates, all of this could not have taken place without considerable discussion of the pros and cons of admitting women to public school teaching in the first place. Was it respectable for women to teach outside the home? More

---

A. Stevenson and J. D. Wilson, eds., *Aspects of Nineteenth Century Ontario* (Toronto: University of Toronto Press, 1974) pp. 223 and 229; and School Papers, Halifax City 1808–1845, RG 14, No. 30, Public Archives of Nova Scotia.

6. This point examined more fully in my doctoral dissertation, "The School Promoters: Education and Social Class in Mid-Nineteenth Century Upper Canada," (University of Toronto, 1974).

7. "The School Promoters," chapter 8.

8. Ibid, pp. 298–310.

pertinent to school authorities was the question of female ability. Were women capable of governing large numbers of pupils in the not always comfortable environment of the public school? These questions were raised again and again among educators and laymen. The idea of a predominantly female elementary teaching force was one which only gradually gained acceptance in British North America.

The feminization of teaching was made possible by three conditions. One was the eventual acceptance and promotion of the idea by leading educational administrators and propagandists of the day. Another and probably more basic condition was the growing tendency on the part of money-conscious school trustees to see women as having a vital economic role to play in their rapidly expanding schools and school systems.[9] Between 1845 and 1875, more and more women were hired, and by the latter date they had become the majority among common or elementary school teachers in most provinces. Equally basic to all of this was, of course, the interest in and acceptance of their changing role by the women themselves, and by the society that financed and used the schools.

II

...Thus in the three decades between 1845 and 1875, chief superintendents in at least three provinces had joined J. B. Meilleur of Quebec in accepting female teachers in public schools. Their acceptance, however, was clearly qualified by the tendency, in at least two cases, to stress woman's special suitability to instruct the very young. And in Nova Scotia, J. B. Calkin still refused to adopt the new stance....

If the provincial superintendents were accepting a trend, there were also a number of ways in which they were promoting it. The first and most obvious encouragement given to female teachers was the opening of normal schools to women. In Upper Canada, male students were in the majority when women were first admitted to the provincial Normal School soon after it opened in the 1840s, and remained in this position

---

9. In "Trends in Female School Attendance in Mid-Nineteenth Century Ontario," *Social History/Histoire sociale* 8 (November, 1975) Ian Davey notes the extent to which the expansion of schooling was associated in that province with an increase in the enrollment of girls. But I have found no evidence of school authorities relating the hiring of more female teachers to this trend. On the other hand, the two factors were associated in early rural schools in the common practice of hiring women to replace the male teachers during the summer, when there were undoubtedly fewer male students at school, and in a reference to the need for female teachers if girls were to be educated in separate classrooms or separate schools from boys. On the latter point, see *Remarks on the State of Education in Canada* by "L" (Montreal, 1848) pp. 129–30.

throughout the 1850s, but by the end of the 60s female students became numerically dominant, reflecting their position in the profession as a whole.[10] In Quebec too, sex ratios among normal school students seemed to reflect the provincial situation, with women in the majority at McGill Normal School when it opened in 1857, and becoming the majority provincially as soon as Laval opened its new normal school to women in the session of 1857/58.[11] In some cases, prospective women teachers received special consideration. In Upper Canada, for example, they continued to be admitted to the normal school at the age of sixteen when the minimum age for men was raised to eighteen. According to the instructions of the Chief Superintendent of Schools in that province, also, restrictions on the employment of aliens in the 1840s were not, after 1847, to be applied to women teachers. Finally, regulations of the Upper Canadian Council of Public Instruction for 1850 exempted women who were applying for first and second class teaching certificates from examination in a small number of specified areas.[12] In Lower Canada, in 1852, female teachers were to be examined by School Inspectors, but were excused from the usual examinations before Boards of Examiners.[13]

The insidious feature of such concessions of course was that they helped to ensure both the lower pay and status of many female teachers. Yet it is also true, as has been suggested, that low pay and status were probably a condition of female employment in the first place. In New Brunswick, the Chief Superintendent associated the introduction of increasing numbers of women teachers into the schools, in 1865, with two factors: the low wages offered by rural trustees on the one hand, and the classifying and grading of schools in villages and towns on the other. In the latter case, he judged, "nearly three-fourths of all the teaching could be most economically and satisfactorily performed by females."[14]...

In 1850 a trustee from Hamilton, Upper Canada, listed the benefits of centralized graded school systems as follows: (1) the attraction of more

10. *Report of the Superintendent of Education for Ontario for the Year 1869*, Part II, Table K.
11. *Report of the Superintendent of Education for Lower Canada for the Year 1858*, Normal School Reports. On the interest of women in the McGill Normal School, see Donna Ronish, "The Development of Higher Education for Women at McGill University from 1857 to 1899 with Special Reference to the Role of Sir John William Dawson" (M.A. Thesis, McGill University, 1972) pp. 15–19.
12. "The School Promoters," pp. 301 and 305.
13. Province of Canada, *Journals of the Legislative Assembly, 1852–53*, Volume 2 No. 4, Appendix J. J., "Report of the Superintendent of Education for Lower Canada for 1852."
14. *Report of the Superintendent of Education for New Brunswick for the year 1865*, p. 9.

children into the school system because higher classes could be provided; (2) an improvement in the status of teachers; and (3) provision for the instruction of larger numbers of children at less cost.[15] The trustee did not elaborate further, but as has already been suggested in a general way, the second and third goals could only be achieved at the same time through the creation of hierarchies based on sex, with male teachers receiving higher salaries as principals and teachers of the upper grades, while females taught the lower grades at lower rates of pay.

In Toronto between 1851 and 1861, the relative salaries of female teachers, compared to those of their male colleagues, declined and the decline was dramatic, from 69.9% to 41.4%. In the province of Upper Canada as a whole, where hierarchical patterns had not yet made as great an impact, relative female salaries also dropped, but only from 60.3% to 50.1%. It is interesting to observe that during this decade the relative salaries of female teachers who boarded with their employers, or "boarded around" as the expression went, actually went up from 67% to 71.4% of the salaries of male teachers who boarded around. Only salaries "without board" worsened in comparison with men's salaries, suggesting that in Upper Canada traditional rural communities where the teacher was an itinerant who boarded with the local inhabitants, treated male and female teachers more equally than the urban centres that were coming into being.[16]. . .

In the light of these differences, why were women willing to take on the job of teaching in city schools? Part of the answer to this question is of course the shortage of employment available to women other than domestic work. But one must add to this, first of all, the very desire to work outside the home, as the household became less and less the centre of industry and as the domestic employment which had for so long claimed large numbers of women clearly began to lose whatever attraction it may have had. Evidence from Upper Canada in the 1840s suggests,

---

15. D. Legge to Egerton Ryerson, 31 October, 1850, Education Records, (RG2) C-6-C, Public Archives of Ontario.

16. "The School Promoters," pp. 304–05. This did not hold true for New Brunswick, however, where in 1855, at least, male teachers were paid an average, semi-annually of £ 26.16.2 without board; compared to the £ 20.19.18 1/2 paid to women. Their salaries were thus closer, with women earning about 78% on the average of what was earned by men, than were the salaries of male and female teachers who boarded around, at £ 17.8.3 1/2 and £ 10.13.5 1/4 respectively, for in the latter case women earned only 61% of what was earned by men. *Report of the Superintendent of Education for New Brunswick for the Year 1855.*

indeed, that to some observers there was little to choose between domestic service and teaching in the early years, from the point of view of either status or wages. The two occupations were frequently compared, and in tones of considerable disparagement, with some holding that female teachers were on the same (low) social and educational level as "spinsters and household servants," while others noted that teachers in general were no better than the "lowest menials."[17] It was not surprising, such critics felt, that the wages of the two occupations were similar.

If domestic work and teaching commanded similar wages in the 1840s, any improvement, however little, in the salaries or status of the latter would be bound to make teaching seem an attractive possibility. The salaries of female teachers in Halifax and Toronto, furthermore, were so much higher than the provincial averages for teachers in Nova Scotia and Upper Canada, that they must have held a special allure for women coming from outside these cities, in spite of the fact that they compared so poorly with the salaries of urban male teachers. For many women, then, even the lowest ranks of city school hierarchies may have provided opportunities for respectable employment, and, as time went on, both a higher status and higher wages than had been available to them in the past. . . .

If elementary school teaching, even at comparatively low rates of pay, nevertheless opened up opportunities to work outside the home for women who, before, had largely devoted their lives to the domestic sphere, and if the propaganda and discussion of the period also helped to steer women into subordinate positions in urban school systems, a third force helped to ensure that they would remain in the lower ranks. This was the reputation, deserved or otherwise, that women had for retiring from the profession after a few years, just as experience was "beginning to make them really efficient" as the Superintendent of Schools for New Brunswick put it. The problem, in this administrator's view, was that their places were then filled by "younger and less experienced recruits from the Training School," the ultimate effect of which was to lower the reputation of all female teachers, whether they were experienced or not.[18] Men too, however, were accused of treating the profession as temporary employ-

---

17. W. H. Landon, *Report of the Superintendent of Schools for the Brock District* (Woodstock: 1848), pp. 3–4; The Colborne Memorial, 1848, RG 2 C-6-C, pp. 3–4, Public Archives of Ontario.

18. *Report of the Superintendent of Education for New Brunswick for the Year 1867*, pp. 8–9.

ment, undertaken only for quick money during bad times, and there seems, at this stage of the research, no way of knowing whether or not the tendency was really more pronounced among women. It remains sufficient, perhaps, to know that at least one influential superintendent thought this to be the case, for, once again, the spread of such opinions was bound to suggest to women as well as to their male colleagues that the lower salaries for female teachers were justified. . . .

The entry of large numbers of women into public school teaching was thus accepted because their position in the schools was generally a subordinate one. Their move into public teaching facilitated—and was facilitated by—the emergence of the public school systems, in which hierarchical professional patterns were feasible. To the extent that school children absorbed messages from the organization of the institutions in which they were educated, Canadian children were exposed to a powerful image of woman's inferior position in society. One must not discount, moreover, the impact on the women themselves. The experience of public school teaching, the experience of its discipline and of its hierarchical organization, became the experience of large numbers of Canadian women by the end of the nineteenth century.

LIFE OF HON. SIR JAMES ROBERT GOWAN

HENRY H. ARDAGH

[In Upper Canada,] for many years the resident Judge [in a Pioneer District] was an all important factor in progress; besides discharging the duties of Judge of all the Courts, Civil and Criminal, and of selection and appointment of officers thereto, as a rule he voluntarily aided in the establishment and development of municipal and educational institutions, and indeed in all that made for the well-being and progress of the people—then his Court circuits involved long and perilous journeys, on horseback in the summer and by sleigh in the winter. This round of duties—"Single Seated Justice"—and general supervision over an immense territory, needed courage and discretion as well as physical ability, and a thorough knowledge of the people. . . .

On a glorious Indian Summer day, [probably in the 1840s,] Judge [J. R. Gowan,] in a new district, was riding through a long stretch of woods. The road was cut through a primeval forest, a vast avenue of colored foliage brightened in the light of the "red summer sun." He was alone. . . . He was a good horseman and rode rapidly along, his thoroughbred horse as active as a cat in picking his steps over the bits of "Corduroy," and in jumping trees that here and there had fallen across the "line." He came upon two men seated on a log by the roadside, who stood up and uncovered as he approached. One of them then advanced, saying: "You'll be our Judge; we heard you were coming to hold Court to-morrow at ——— and have been waiting to catch your Honour; we have a dispute and we want your word what is right between us." The other said "Yes, we want that."

Both men were well advanced in life, and probably double the age of the Judge, respectably dressed, men grave and earnest in demeanor, their faces showing much strength of character—both good types of the grand race they were of, for they were Highland Scotsmen. "I never saw you before; how did you know I was the Judge?" said that official. "We thought we knew you fine, you and your horse, a mile off. Your man, whom we met, told us you were coming, and when you leaped over the fallen tree instead of going round it, we were sure it was your Honour," said the chief spokesman. Their request somewhat surprised the Judge,

HENRY HATTON ARDAGH, *LIFE OF HON. SIR JAMES ROBERT GOWAN* (TORONTO: UNIVERSITY OF TORONTO PRESS, 1911): 249–54. REPRINTED BY PERMISSION OF DR. JOHN RUSSELL ARDAGH.

for it was the first of many such appeals to him, and he said, "Yes, I am the Judge, but matters of controversy must come before me in Court in the regular way." "We want no law," said the spokesman, "We are friends and neighbors and have talked over and prayed over our dispute and cannot agree, so we concluded to leave the matter to your Honour's say;" to this the Judge replied, "You can arbitrate the matter, making two of your neighbors judges between you." "No, no! we won't do that," both said; "You are the Queen's Judge, we want you to settle the matter this day and this hour, we won't be denied—you will do the right thing between us and here we are all before God, you must help us." The Judge, touched with the solemn earnestness of the men and their common desire for a peaceable adjustment of their difficulties, said: "But you may not agree on the facts, and if I did hear you as you desire and declared what I thought right between you, one or both of you might be dissatisfied, and my decision thus given would not be binding on either."

With one accord, each lifted his right hand, saying: "Our oath to it," and together in a solemn voice said, "In the presence of God, and as we shall answer to God at the great day of judgment, we will accept and abide by our Judge's decision." They had evidently talked over the matter, and determined on what they would do and probably thought out the form they used; their grave, solemn earnestness bore down the Judge's scruples, and he said as he dismounted, "In God's name I will at least hear you." The situation was intensely dramatic, the red light of the evening sun shone full upon the solemn and earnest faces of the men, the horse stood motionless, as if conscious of having part in a serious matter; the great forest trees on each side like ramparts, every leaf at rest, an unclouded sky above, all nature in repose as it were.

When the Judge dismounted, he seated himself on the log the men had been sitting upon, they then each told his story without interruption from the other; indeed, the one whose English was not as good as the other was occasionally helped with an English word, and rightly aided, as the Judge, who had some knowledge of the Gaelic, gladly noticed, and they answered every question the Judge thought it necessary to put to them promptly and fully; there was really no controversy as to the facts and the Judge was enabled to obtain a full view of the case.

The dispute was as to the ownership of a small strip of land between their farms, and grew out of different surveys of "the line" between them—neither survey, probably, being exactly correct—land at that time (in the forties) was cheap, and the Judge thought that under all the circumstances an equal division between them of the strip of land in dispute would be a fair and wise solution of the dispute between them, the fence that had been erected by one of the men to be re-erected by the other on the compromise line.

It was what might be termed rough and ready justice, but both men were entirely satisfied and subsequently carried out the decision fairly and fully. It was well, for litigation would have been expensive and plunged both in debt, possibly ending in one of them losing his whole farm.

The proceeding was novel in the annals of justice and no doubt irregular and without precedent; but who will say the Judge was wrong in acting the part of a peacemaker between men who in simple confidence appealed to him as a Minister of Justice and the Queen's representative.

The Judge at all events experienced no mental discomfort because of his part in the incident, the suffering was in his right hand, which he had offered the men in parting and which they had gratefully wrung with Highland energy.

FURTHER READINGS FOR TOPIC 15

Dictionary of Canadian Biography, Vols. 7–9.

J. K. Johnson. *Becoming Prominent: Regional Leadership in Upper Canada, 1791–1841*. Kingston and Montreal: McGill-Queen's University Press, 1989.

J. K. Johnson. "John A. Macdonald, The Young Non-Politician." Canadian Historical Association, *Historical Papers* 1971: 138–53.

Susan E. Houston and Alison Prentice. *Schooling and Scholars in Nineteenth-Century Ontario*. Toronto: University of Toronto Press, 1988.

Carol Wilton. "Beyond the Law: Lawyers and Business in Canada, 1830–1930." In *Beyond the Law: Lawyers and Business in Canada, 1830–1930: Essays in the History of Canadian Law Vol. IV*, ed. Carol Wilton. Toronto: The Osgoode Society, 1990.

Topic 16

Confederation: Nationalism, Expansionism, Imperialism

*C*onfederation was achieved about a generation after the
implementation of responsible government, and represented a further
step in the direction of colonial autonomy. The British government, in
particular, was anxious for British North Americans to assume more
responsibility for themselves, especially in the area of defence. Nevertheless,
the new Dominion of Canada remained closely tied to the mother country.
Though the new constitution was written almost entirely by British North
American politicians, it was passed as an act of the British parliament, the
British North America Act. Even after Confederation, the British
government retained, among other functions, the power to amend the
constitution, and to conduct foreign relations on behalf of the new
Dominion of Canada.

The prospect of Confederation prompted many to express their views on
British North America's place in a world that was being transformed by the
rise of American power and the unification of Germany on the
international scene, and by concerns about social disorder at home. Three
different views of this question are highlighted in the selections which
follow. George Brown, a perennial Canadian nationalist, was leader of the
Reformers of Canada West and editor of the Toronto Globe. He made
Confederation possible by joining a coalition with the Conservatives of both
sections of the province in 1864 to push for a federal union. As his
biographer J.M.S. Careless shows, Brown had close links with the farmers
of the southwestern part of the province, whose concern about the
impending unavailability of frontier farmland is reflected in Brown's
expansionist attitude toward the Hudson's Bay Company territories to the

west. *George-Etienne Cartier, a Montreal lawyer with close ties to some big businesses of the era, was the leader of the Conservatives of Canada East at the time of Confederation. Brian Young suggests that Cartier's acceptance of the British institutions entrenched at the time of Confederation sprang from his concern to maintain the existing social order. Joseph Howe, author of the "Botheration Letters," was a leading anti-Confederate in Nova Scotia. Murray Beck's assessment of Howe's career suggests that Howe was another kind of nationalist, one to whom the future of the British Empire was of far more concern than the union of the British North American colonies.*

BROWN OF THE GLOBE

J. M. S. CARELESS

In the previous summer (1863) a group of British financiers had bought control of the Hudson's Bay Company for a million and a half pounds, and Watkin, the aggressive president of the Grand Trunk, had figured prominently in the transaction. Its hopeful significance, as Brown could clearly see, was that the title to the North West had now been transferred from old, unchanging fur monopolists to a powerful group of business men particularly concerned to open up the territory and develop a transit route to the Pacific.[1] Watkin still had his starry vision of building the bankrupt Grand Trunk into a huge all-British transcontinental system, which would require both the Intercolonial railway to the Maritimes and communications across the western plains to British Columbia—the first phase here to be by wagon road and a telegraph line. Indeed, in 1862 Brown had had three meetings to discuss British North American development with the grandiose promoter in London—and they had disagreed on practically everything, "except on the subject of opening up the North West territories".[2]

Since then, Watkin had been in Canada to pursue that very subject, and had found that Sandfield Macdonald, Cartier, and John A. Macdonald all shared his own view that a separate Crown Colony could be erected in the territory. Yet Brown, of course, held out for its annexation to Canada. He and Watkin had had another stiff interview; for each of them had formed a thoroughly low opinion of the other—the narrow, intransigent Clear Grit, to Watkin; the brash embodiment of Grand Trunk waste, to Brown.[3] Nevertheless the Reform politician could at least expect new developments in the North West under a reorganized Hudson's Bay Company, especially when he was sure that Newcastle, the Colonial Secretary, was himself strongly interested in opening the territory.[4] Here, then, was another item on the agenda for 1864, and all the more reason to urge that

J. M. S. Careless, *Brown of the Globe: The Voice of Upper Canada*, Vol. 2 (Toronto: Macmillan, 1963): 107–12. Reprinted by permission of the author.
1. *Globe*, July 27, 1863.
2. *Ibid.*, May 23, 1863.
3. E.W. Watkin, *Canada and the United States* (London, 1887), p. 173.
4. Mackenzie Papers, Brown to Holton, September 3, 1862; *Globe*, July 3, 1863.

Canada should press her own claims to the North West, lest British capitalists, if not Americans, develop that vast region purely in their private interests and leave Canadians virtually as poor relations cut off from their natural inheritance.

As for the Americans, their threat to the North West was all too evident. "Cooped up as Canada is between lake, river and the frozen North," the *Globe* declared, "should all the rest of the continent fall into the possession of the Americans, she will become of the smallest importance."[5] Brown heard of alarming plans for the extension of the St. Paul and Anoka Railway northward into British territory, right to Fort Garry: "Once let the railway be built, and the whole country, cut off from any but a roundabout and costly communication with Canada, will speedily become Americanized. . . . We believe that the movement which has now been instituted for the purpose of facilitating communication between the Red River and the State of Minnesota is nothing more or less than the handing over of the vast North West Territory, not only commercially but politically, to the United States."[6] The issue was one of basic continental strategy: the competition between north-south and east-west designs for the communications and control of western British North America.

And yet this issue, like the others that were forcing themselves on Brown, could still not be considered central to his thinking. His primary concern remained what it had always been: reform of the existing Canadian union through settling the representation question; it was just over ten years since he had first moved representation by population in parliament. No, these broader and external questions acted, rather, on his mind from the periphery. In consequence, however, they worked to expand its horizons, leading him increasingly to view reform of the Canadian union in the full context of the development of British North America. They served to stimulate that wider sense of statesmanship already revealed in his proposal for a select committee to examine every aspect of the constitutional question. In a very real way Brown was what he had always been: a leader of Upper Canadian sectionalism, pre-eminently devoted to the "rights of Upper Canada". Yet, in no less real a fashion, he was prepared by this time to integrate that sectionalism into a design for a great new national structure. And since any new British North

---

5. *Globe*, January 27, 1864.
6. *Ibid.*

American state must rest on the integration of disparate regions, sections, and cultures, his position was itself a thoroughly realistic one.

One necessary aspect of this realism was a clear recognition that the French-Canadian community had as much right to maintain sectional interests in a new union as Upper Canada had. Brown had now abandoned his earlier presumption that French Canadians would be assimilated; in fact, he had abandoned the belief that at first had underlain his advocacy of rep by pop: that there was no reason to have a sectional line dividing Canada in two, or to regard the inhabitants of the East as in any way requiring different institutions from those of the West.[7] It would be wrong to say that he had come to understand the French Canadians or even to appreciate their devotion to customs, faith, and culture, which to him still appeared unprogressive and priest-ridden. Nevertheless (and this was highly important), he was prepared at the least to let the French-speaking community go its own way, to concede the cultural duality of Canada, and, at the most, to see valuable attributes in the French Canadians that made possible a constructive future partnership of peoples.

This change in his thinking, increasingly in evidence since his marriage and return from Britain, was best exemplified in the *Globe*, which, as always, reflected George Brown's leading opinions and set them before the country. It ran a number of articles, some probably by Brown himself, on the relations of the two communities in Canada. No doubt the aim was partly to calm Lower Canadian fears of rep by pop. But the articles constituted a public commitment to a line of policy for Brown, often couched in language so forthright that it would be hard to say that he was merely wooing French Canada with soft blandishments. His recognition of facts was rather the significant thing.

"For all we care," the *Globe* now announced, "the French Canadians may retain their language, laws and institutions till the end of the world. The employment of their language in parliamentary proceedings may involve some expense, but no one would think of giving deep offence to the French people in order to save a few thousand dollars or pounds per annum. The laws of Lower Canada are very good laws, as far as we can judge, and nobody desires to change them. The institutions, so long as they please the people of Lower Canada, will remain unchanged, for no one in Upper Canada takes any interest in them."[8] As for any complaint against the Roman Catholic hierarchy, it was not at all that they had

---

7. *Brown of the Globe*, vol. 1, pp. 167–8.
8. *Globe*, April 7, 1863.

worked ill in Lower Canada, but that they had sought to interfere with the institutions of Upper Canada—an interference that had to be resisted.

Furthermore, the frequent charge that the *Globe* considered French Canadians an inferior race that must inevitably succumb was sheer political libel, a device employed to weaken Brown's allies in the East in the same way as the "No looking to Washington" cry had been used against the western Grits. Quite bluntly, the journal reversed the accusation. It was the French Canadians who thought they were superior. "They attribute all to jealousy of their superior institutions, and behind this impassable barrier entrench themselves against the assaults of reason and experience."[9] But, in any case, the real question at issue was not the superiority or inferiority of the French, but their power—their power to dominate the union, which had to be removed without any subsequent domination being imposed on them instead.

"By their bond of a common nationality," the *Globe* declared, "the French Canadians will always possess power in Canada greater in proportion to their numbers than the British population. We do not object to that. Let them make all they can out of it. But let them not expect to govern us by a minority. As to the merely sectional and commercial differences between Upper and Lower Canada, there is not one which cannot be fought out in the legislative arena without an atom of bitterness....Upper Canada has not the slightest objection to allowing Lower Canada to manage her own affairs. If she will consent to leave us alone we have no desire to interfere between priest and people in Lower Canada....But let us endeavour in carrying on the affairs of our common country to arrive at some basis on which we all may stand in peace and contentment. We see no insuperable difficulty in the way of this result, and shall not cease to strive for its accomplishment."[10]

Going further, Brown's journal set forth the qualities of the French Canadians that could make them worthy partners in the development of this common country—"naturally industrious, frugal, temperate, handy, ingenious, and under favorable circumstances, enterprising". Indeed, "the French Canadian has penetrated every part of the American continent. In the West as well as the Eastern States you find him, and he is beloved and respected wherever he goes."[11] Not so energetic or ambitious as the Anglo-Saxon, he was more uniformly successful. If at home his

---

9. *Ibid.*, January 29, 1863, See also January 12, 1863.
10. *Ibid.*, July 11, 1863.
11. *Ibid.*, February 3, 1863.

agriculture was deficient, his technical skills and education limited, it was only because of his self-imposed isolation. "The pride of race is strong in the French Canadian, but it is a false pride when it leads him not to deeds which show his superiority over his neighbours, but on the contrary compels him to shut himself up in a cold and barren corner of a vast and fertile continent, afraid lest if he venture forth, some portion of his individuality may be lost in the vigorous life around him."[12] The *Globe* eagerly urged him forth instead. "We ask the opening of a vast territory, from which will flow a great stream of traffic through the St. Lawrence, fertilizing its exhausted shores, and affording the French race an opportunity for developing the rare qualities which they possess, such as even the early pioneers of New France never imagined."[13]

As the Grit organ saw it, it was precisely because of this bright prospect that the great majority of Upper Canadians desired "to see Upper Canada not only united with Lower Canada, but with all the other British American territories adjacent".[14] And French Canadians had no reason to fear being swamped in such a combination: "No one will dream of one government for the Gut of Canso and the Saskatchewan River, or even for the St. Lawrence and Lake Winnipeg."[15] The *Globe*, in short, was recognizing the need for a general federal scheme of government.

But how would representation by population fit into such a scheme? It would be a basic requirement in any federal union, the first ingredient of its general government—the essential prerequisite to settle the wrongs done Upper Canada. "Before entering into new alliances," affirmed the *Globe*, "it should be the effort of Upper Canadians to regulate the affairs of their own province, to obtain representation by population, to open the North West territory so that, when federation of all the British American provinces does come, it may be formed with Upper Canada as the central figure of the group of states, with western adjuncts as well as eastern."[16] Here, accordingly, sectional and national aspirations were again combined in Brownite thinking; yet once more this was a not unrealistic forecast of the Canadian federal structure that would actually emerge.

Such was the position George Brown had reached by 1864. Still seeking the reform of the Canadian union, he was prepared to accept the dualism

---

12. *Ibid.*
13. *Ibid.*
14. *Ibid.*, July 24, 1863.
15. *Ibid.*
16. *Ibid.*, January 6, 1863.

of French- and English-speaking communities, and to comprehend it through the federal principle. He was willing to see that principle extended to bring all the British provinces together. He was concerned with the underlying economic problem, heedful of American reactions, keenly anxious to gain the West. In sum, Brown was ready for his greatest role: as the initiator of British North American union.

George-Etienne Cartier:

Montreal Bourgeois

BRIAN YOUNG

The annexation movement of 1849, the debate over the choice of a capital, and Confederation provided three opportunities for the exercise of Cartier's political conservatism and his use of British institutions as a guarantee of the status quo and as a bulwark against popular unrest. . . .

Confederation resulted from chronic political stalemate. By 1859 the assembly had voted over 200 times on the seat-of-government issue and every session was poisoned by interminable debates over the question and over various schemes to introduce representation by population.[1] Political paralysis was everywhere evident. Cartier's own political career stalled and after seven years in power he spent two years in opposition, 1862–64. In addition, the economy was sluggish, the United States was bellicose, and Britain's changing colonial policy had made her increasingly reluctant to meet heavy Canadian costs.

Federalism was one solution for politicians seeking economic expansion, social stability, and a resolution of the political crisis. It was also a logical extension of political and administrative forms developed under the Union Act. Cartier, however, accepted the judgment of his peers only slowly.[2] Well before his acceptance of the principle of federal union, fellow Lower Canadian politicians like Joseph-Charles Taché, Joseph Cauchon, A. A. Dorion, D'Arcy McGee, and Alexander Morris had begun to legitimize the idea. A sarcastic critic of Alexander Galt's federal union proposals before the summer of 1858, Cartier did an about-face with the collapse of the short-lived Brown-Dorion government.[3] Named prime minister in August 1858, Cartier brought Galt into the cabinet by accepting the principle of federation. Two months later he was in London with Galt and John Ross to discuss federation at the Colonial Office, and

Brian Young, *George-Etienne Cartier: Montreal Bourgeois* (Kingston and Montreal: McGill-Queen's University Press, 1981): 75–85. Reprinted by permission of the publisher.

1. David Knight, *Choosing Canada's Capital* (Toronto: McClelland and Stewart, 1977), p.x.
2. W. L. Morton, *The Critical Years: The Union of British North America, 1857–73* (Toronto: McClelland and Stewart, 1964), p. 65.
3. P. B. Waite, *John A. Macdonald: His Life and World* (Toronto: McGraw-Hill, Ryerson, 1975), p.62.

although the document was apparently Galt's work, Cartier's name was prominently attached to the federation proposal.[4]

In 1864, following George Brown's initiative before the constitutional committee and the emotional meetings on the floor of the assembly and in Quebec City's Hotel Saint-Louis, Cartier joined the coalition cabinet committed to federalism and representation by population. Although it was George Brown who made the significant gesture, it may have been Cartier's region that made the more important concessions. The application of proportional representation in the all-important House of Commons as opposed to an ongoing structure of equal provincial representation or a double-majority system facilitated the integration of Quebec francophones into a larger English-speaking state. For their part, the province's anglophones were relegated to a minority position within Quebec by the implementation of a federal system.

On several occasions Cartier explained why he had accepted representation by population and minority status for French Canadians—principles which he had fought for years. He had, of course, other explanations than George Brown's interpretation that Cartier had been cornered "by the compulsion of circumstances" and "driven into the necessity of taking up the representation question openly and vigorously."[5] Whereas Brown predicted to his wife that French Canadianism would be "entirely extinguished," Cartier argued that French Canada would be protected by representation by population in a federal state.[6] *La Minerve* discerned a difference between its application under the existing union and in the proposed federation. Under the former it would bring "servitude and degradation" but applied in a larger federal union, representation by population would be "a safeguard and guarantee of independence."[7] The difference would result from the addition of the Maritimes which, according to Cartier, would offset any threat from Upper Canada:

> In a struggle between two—one a weak, and the other a strong party—
> the weaker could not but be overcome; but if three parties were
> concerned, the stronger would not have the same advantage; as when it
> was seen by the third that there was too much strength on one side, the

---

4. O. D. Skelton, *The Life and Times of Sir Alexander Tilloch Galt* (Toronto: Oxford University Press, 1920), p. 96.

5. Public Archives of Canada, Brown Papers, no. 953, Brown to wife, June 20, 1864.

6. Ibid., October 27, 1864.

7. *La Minerve*, July 16, 1864, quoted in J. C. Bonenfant, *French Canadians and the Birth of Confederation* (Ottawa: Canadian Historical Association, 1966), p. 14.

third would club with the weaker combatant to resist the big fighter. He did not oppose the principle of representation by population from an unwillingness to do justice to Upper Canada. He took this ground, however, that when justice was done to Upper Canada, it was his duty to see that no injustice was done to Lower Canada. He did not entertain the slightest apprehension that Lower Canada's rights were in the least jeopardized by the provision that in the General Legislature the French Canadians of Lower Canada would have a smaller number of representatives than all the other origins combined.[8]

Usually a tenacious *quid pro quo* bargainer, Cartier apparently demanded little in the federation negotiations at Charlottetown and Quebec City in the autumn of 1864; unlike Galt and other defenders of special-interest groups he did not fight hard on specific issues.[9] Protection of sectional interests was largely delegated to an upper house that did not exercise financial control and whose members were named for life by the central government. According to Cartier this upper house, the Senate, would be "our security."[10] Provincial autonomy was also compromised by the granting of the appointment of the lieutenant governor to the central government. Even more threatening to many francophones and defenders of provincial rights was the federal power of disallowance. However, as a centralist Cartier accepted a broad and vague definition of disallowance envisaging its use in cases of what he called "unjust or unwise legislation."

Outside Quebec, Cartier's behaviour in 1864 was interpreted as a symbol of ethnic cooperation. He received standing ovations before English-speaking audiences when he sang "God Save the Queen" in French, visitors to the Quebec Conference praised his graciousness, and his gallic charm was welcome in London drawing-rooms. Observers were particularly impressed by his call for ethnic harmony and a new "political nationality":

Now, when we were united together, if union were attained, we would form a political nationality with which neither the national origin, nor the religion of any individual, would interfere. . . . We were of different

---

8. Cartier in Legislative Assembly, February 7, 1865, quoted in P. B. Waite, ed., *The Confederation Debates in the Province of Canada*, 1865 (Toronto: McClelland and Stewart, 1963).
9. In the final conference in London in the spring of 1867 Cartier apparently did block Macdonald's attempts to increase centralization. See J. C. Bonenfant, *La naissance de la Confédération* (Montreal: Leméac, 1969), p. 107.
10. Waite, *Confederation Debates*, p. 115.

races, not for the purpose of warring against each other, but in order to compete and emulate for the general welfare. We could not do away with the distinctions of race. We could not legislate for the disappearance of the French Canadians from American soil, but British and French Canadians alike could appreciate and understand their position relative to each other. They were placed like great families beside each other, and their contact produced a healthy spirit of emulation.[11]

Speaking throughout the Maritimes after the Charlottetown Conference Cartier expressed fears common to many British North Americans. Reiterating his distrust of American democracy, he argued that Confederation would give Canada a distinctive "monarchical element." The alternatives were simple: "either we must obtain British American Confederation or be absorbed in an American Confederation."[12] Cartier also regularly reminded audiences of their common commercial interests. "Prosperity" was the word he repeated in his Maritimes speeches.[13] Federation would lead to the abolition of customs barriers and to the building of the Intercolonial Railway joining Quebec to the Maritimes.

Within Quebec, critics focused more on provincial autonomy and minority rights than on ethnic cooperation. Christopher Dunkin and A. A. Dorion pointed out the possibility of indiscriminate disallowance and the potential tyranny of an overlapping party system. Dunkin felt that French Canadians—given the lopsided nature of Confederation—would be able to retain power only by being aggressive. Dorion spoke in favour of what he called a "real Confederation" in which the important powers were put in sole jurisdiction of the provinces. Identifying Cartier as a conservative who wanted to strengthen the power of the crown and diminish the influence of the people, Dorion described the proposed federation as "the most illiberal constitution ever heard of in any country where constitutional government prevails."[14] His outspoken brother was even blunter. Accusing French Canadians of being "fast asleep," he charged that Confederation would be simply "Legislative Union in disguise" and provincial legislation "nothing but a farce."[15]

---

11. Cartier in Legislative Assembly, February 7, 1865, Waite, *Confederation Debates*, pp. 50–51.
12. Ibid., p. 50.
13. Cartier Collection, McCord Museum, Montreal, clipping from *Canadian News*, April 27, 1865.
14. Waite, *Confederation Debates*, pp. 88, 95.
15. Ibid., pp. 88, 148–49.

Angry opponents of Confederation in Quebec derided Cartier as a tyrant, monarchist, spokesman for railway interests, and the dupe of Upper Canadians who would "throw him aside like a worn-out towel":

> To attain this eminence, he has crushed the weak, cajoled the strong, deceived the credulous, bought up the venal, and exalted the ambitious; by turns he has called in the accents of religion and stimulated the clamor of interest—he has gained his end. . . . When his scheme of Confederation became public, a feeling of uneasiness pervaded all minds; that instinct forewarned them of the danger which impended. He has hushed that feeling to a sleep of profound security. I shall compare him to a man who has gained the unbounded confidence of the public, who takes advantage of it to set up a Savings Bank. . . . When that man has gathered all into his strong box, he finds an opportunity to purchase at the cost of all he holds in trust, the article on which he has long set his ambitious eye; and he buys it, unhesitatingly, without a thought of the wretches who are doomed to ruin by his conduct. The deposit committed to the keeping of the Attorney General is the fortune of the French Canadians—their nationality.[16]

To overwhelm these opponents and to win approval of the Quebec Resolutions, Cartier used several tactics. One useful asset was the absence of the Rouges from the federation negotiations. Whereas Ontario was represented by both Brown and Macdonald, the Rouges were excluded from the coalition and the conferences in Charlottetown and Quebec City. French-Canadian Conservatives—Cartier, E. P. Taché, Hector Langevin, Jean-Charles Chapais, and Joseph Cauchon—spoke for French Canada. Only Cartier and Taché had more than regional stature; Taché was ninety years old, was absent from the Charlottetown Conference, and died in 1866. Only four of the thirty-three delegates to the Quebec Conference were French Canadian. The conference negotiations were held *in camera* and no official minutes were kept.

Since the federation debate in Quebec took place in a "politics as usual" atmosphere, Cartier was able to exploit the vulnerability of the Rouges and his own image as *chef*. Moderate, respectable, and intelligent men favoured federation; its opponents, according to Cartier, were "extreme men," "socialists, democrats and annexationists."[17] *La Minerve* had another argument. Quebec faced "ruin" if it became obstructive: "When a general movement towards Confederation develops and when this move-

---

16. H.G. Joly speech in Legislative Assembly, February 7, 1865, ibid., p. 96.
17. Cartier in Legislative Assembly, February 7, 1865, ibid., p. 51.

ment is perfectly motivated, can we allow ourselves to stand in the way like an insuperable barrier, at the risk of bringing about their ruin and our own?"[18]

The Roman Catholic hierarchy's silence on the Confederation proposals allowed Cartier to claim clerical support. Since the conquest, the church in Quebec had supported established authority in the face of American invasions, the rebellions of 1837, and the annexation movement. During the Union period, conservative politicians—led by La Fontaine and Cartier—had cooperated with the Catholic hierarchy to impose social controls and to shape educational institutions and national societies.[19] Wealthy religious communities had supported government economic policy by sponsoring and investing in railways. Religious authorities had approved the judicial and landholding reforms accomplished in Quebec in the 1850s and 1860s, and federation, which created a conservative political structure with guarantees for Catholic rights, was a logical political extension.

Cartier publicly stated that Catholic clergy at all levels of the hierarchy supported federation because it protected their rights and limited political dissent: "I will say that the opinion of the clergy is favorable to Confederation. . . . In general, the clergy are the enemy of all political dissension and if they support this project, it is because they see in Confederation a solution to the difficulties which have existed for so long."[20] Although one of Bishop Bourget's spokesmen privately disputed Cartier's claim, his younger ultramontane colleague, Louis-François Laflèche, privately expressed strong support for Confederation.[21] Bourget himself was in Rome and quarrelling with Cartier and the Sulpicians over the division of the parish of Montreal. Other important Quebec clerics, particularly Bishops Baillargeon and Larocque, agreed that Confederation, if not desirable, was at least inevitable. *La Minerve* assured its readers that the Pope himself approved Confederation.[22]

In contrast to the ease with which he neutralized his Rouge critics,

---

18. *La Minerve*, n.d., quoted in Bonenfant, *French Canadians and the Birth of Confederation*, p. 14.
19. See chap. 4.
20. Quoted in Bonenfant, *French Canadians and the Birth of Confederation*, p. 15; see also Cartier speech in Waite, *Confederation Debates*, p. 52, and Walter Ullmann, "The Quebec Bishops and Confederation," in Ramsay Cook, ed., *Confederation* (Toronto: University of Toronto Press, 1967), pp. 48–69.
21. Vicar General Truteau to Vicar General Cazeau, February 20, 1865, quoted in Ullmann, "The Quebec Bishops," p. 56.
22. *La Minerve*, May 30, 1866, cited in Ullmann, "The Quebec Bishops," p. 57.

Cartier was extremely prudent with what John Rose described as "the undefined dread" towards Confederation shown by Quebec's English-speaking minority.[23] That community had long been favourably impressed by Cartier's conservatism, his pro-British views, his appointment to key civil service posts of anglophiles like P.J.O. Chauveau, his expansive economic policy, and his educational, civil code, and land-tenure reforms. As John Rose confidently expressed it, "We had the guarantee of the past to justify us in setting aside our fears. Whatever we desired our French-Canadian brethren at once gave us".[24]

Powerful Conservatives pushed hard for specific political, religious, and educational guarantees and Cartier acceded to demands concerning Protestant schools, the division of school taxes, and the granting of a fixed number of Eastern Township ridings. He further promised to use the federal government's veto in the case of a provincial act "hostile or destructive" to the English-speaking minority.[25] When a French-Canadian member received assurances in the assembly that the French language would be protected in the House of Commons, Cartier jumped up amidst cheers to promise that a similar provision would be made to protect English in the Quebec legislature.[26] These concessions and published statements that Cartier had given Galt a private, written pledge concerning English-speaking minority rights offended French-Canadian nationalists.[27] Even Conservative colleagues like Langevin protested against Cartier's compromises. In 1866 Cartier refused to name a French Canadian as chief justice of the Superior Court, telling Langevin that Galt and McGee agreed with him that ["justice must be rendered to the British professional element."][28]...These efforts were appreciated: a month before Confederation, Galt publicly "rendered homage" to Cartier, noting the English-speaking community's "debt of gratitude" for the "elevated views" of Cartier and his colleagues.[29]

Since the government's majority in the united assembly easily approved the federation resolutions, Cartier did not have to call on direct support from the church and commercial élite until 1867. The federal

---

23. Quebec *Morning Chronicle*, February 23, 1865.
24. John Rose quoted in Quebec *Morning Chronicle*, February 23, 1865.
25. McCord, Cartier to John Rose, February 21, 1867.
26. Quebec *Morning Chronicle*, March 11, 1865.
27. Ibid., March 20, August 10, 1865.
28. National Archives of Quebec (ANQ), Chapais Collection, Box 8, Cartier to Langevin, April 17, 1866; Langevin to Cartier, April 19, 1866.
29. J. Boyd, *Sir George Etienne Cartier* (Toronto, 1914), p. 399.

elections of that year in Montreal-East demonstrated both the political potential of the city's working class and the élite's ability to channel and control dissatisfaction. Cartier was at the peak of his prestige, a minister of the crown, a lawyer for international concerns, and a recent house-guest of the Queen. His opponent, Médéric Lanctôt, was a young liberal-nationalist and local alderman.[30] A volatile lawyer and former partner of Wilfrid Laurier, Lanctôt had been associated with the Institut Canadien and a secret anti-Confederation society, le club Saint-Jean Baptiste (not to be confused with the St. Jean Baptiste Society). However, instead of forming an alliance of liberal moderates and campaigning against Confederation, Lanctôt made a direct appeal to working-class sentiment. His newspaper, *L'Union Nationale*, concentrated on basic issues like wages....[31]

In the spring of 1867 Lanctôt formed the Great Association of Workers. Incorporating European socialist principles, the association's program demanded Prudhomme-type councils to settle wage disputes, equality before the law, tariff protection for industry, and improved wages and working conditions.[32] It won support from twenty-five labour groups in Montreal and participated in two strikes. To force lower prices, Lanctôt opened food cooperatives. Three months before the election 15,000 workers and their families attended a workers' rally.

Faced with evident social unrest, the Montreal élite rallied quickly. The Conservative press made much of Cartier's triumphant visit to England and Rome. In his speeches Cartier defended Confederation although he never made it a central issue. Instead, he emphasized local issues, taking credit for the Victoria Bridge and noting the government's achievements in the construction of railroads, the abolition of seigneurial tenure, and the codification of Quebec civil law. The Grand Trunk Railway, the Allan Steamship Company, the Richelieu Navigation Company, the Montreal City Gas Company, the banks, and the manufacturers supported him; William Molson nominated him. Cartier had full control over government patronage in Quebec and had ample funds to distribute to the faithful.

Another substantial asset, despite his battle with Bishop Bourget, was support from important elements in the church. Even Bourget—while

---

30. A full description of the campaign of 1867 is contained in Gaetan Gervais, "Médéric Lanctôt et *L'Union Nationale*" (M.A. thesis, University of Ottawa, 1968).
31. *L'Union Nationale*, March 20, 1867.
32. Ibid., March 30, 1867.

showing his displeasure with Cartier's newspaper by approving a new ultramontane paper, *Le Nouveau Monde* —issued two pastoral letters, May 23 and July 25, 1867, in which he urged voters to submit to authority and to respect the *status quo*.[33] Given his strength with the gallicans Cartier did not have to depend on Bourget's statements for evidence of clerical support. Other bishops, notably Larocque of St. Hyacinthe, publicized their support for the Conservatives. The clergy of St. Hyacinthe received Cartier with great ceremony during the election campaign; moreover, Cartier's managers used an election pamphlet, *Contre-poison*, to give wide distribution to Larocque's attack on radicalism.

Despite this support from the élite and the lukewarm help Lanctôt received from Liberals like Dorion, Cartier's winning margin was small. Although he won all three wards, the opposition's vote was impressive. Cartier defeated Lanctôt 2,433 to 2,085 and Ludger Labelle, his provincial opponent in the riding, 2,408 to 2,051. The opposition increased its share of the vote from 39 per cent in 1863 to 46 per cent in the 1867 federal election.[34]

---

33. For the politics of this newspaper, see Gérard Bouchard, "Apogée et déclin de l'idéologie ultramontaine à travers le journal *Le Nouveau Monde*, 1867–1900," *Recherches Sociographiques* 10, nos. 2–3 (1969):261–91.
34. Norman Séguin, "L'Opposition canadienne-française aux élections de 1867 dans la grande région de Montréal" (M.A. thesis, University of Ottawa, 1968), p. 119.

Joseph Howe, Anti Confederate

J. MURRAY BECK

In their essence the accounts of Principal Grant, E. M. Saunders, W. L. Grant, and Donald Creighton are all highly questionable. At the outset they accept, with practically no evidence, the contention that an egotistical Howe instinctively rejected union because Tupper rather than himself had helped to devise it; they then gloss over Howe's own arguments, even though they were thoroughly consonant with his past activities and statements. Howe's conduct is understandable and even predictable, apart from any consideration of egotism or jealousy. The possibility of putting Tupper in his place may have appeared attractive to him, but there is no real evidence that it governed his actions.

Howe feared, most of all, that the discussion of union would take the minds of both Britons and colonials away from what he deemed was the most vital question of the time, the organization of the Empire, and that the implementation of union would prevent such an organization from being effected for many years to come, if at all. Thus he was not being inconsistent with his basic nature in opposing the Quebec Resolutions. He already had a far-reaching project to which he had committed himself and he could not be enthusiastic about anything which might stand in its way.

The organization of the Empire was not a new theme for Howe. Even before responsible government had been conceded, he was already arguing that colonials ought to have some say in determining the Empire's policies. British subjects everywhere, he maintained, had "a common right to share in much that our ancestors have bequeathed," including that of helping to make the decisions which affected them. He thought, too, that the leading colonial minds should be able to aspire to colonial governorships and senior positions at the Colonial Office, or, as he put it, "to have a fair field of competition on which to illustrate, side by side, with the other branches of the family the heroic or intellectual qualities which 'run in the blood'." A stout autonomist like Professor Lower might wonder whether Howe, "despite his earlier work for Responsible Government was [any] more than a colonial who preferred the crumbs that fell

J. Murray Beck, "Joseph Howe, Anti Confederate" (Ottawa: Canadian Historical Association, Booklet 17, 1963): 14–19. By permission of the Canadian Historical Association.

from the rich man's table in England to the promise of North American nationhood." But actually Howe's proposals indicated anything but subservience; in his mind they were simply the logical outcome of responsible government.

Professor Creighton calls Howe a liberal imperial federationist born out of his time. "Even Whigs like Russell and Palmerston," he says, "would have thought him comically old-fashioned. Hard-eyed, cost-accounting Liberals like Cardwell and Gladstone would have regarded his imperial dreams as stupid and dangerous. There was not the slightest chance that the Empire for which he hoped could ever come into existence during his lifetime." Creighton seems to imply a much more complex organization of the Empire than Howe had intended. But in any case Howe could not be expected to possess the hindsight of modern historians. Perhaps he was obtuse; certainly he had not yet realized that none of the British statesmen cared nearly as much for the Empire as he did. That disillusioning experience was to come later. In 1865–66 Howe was not the worn-out, lack-lustre, despairing individual whom Roy portrays, but no less energetic and ebullient than before. And with the same enthusiasm for the Empire. "Do we want to be part of a great nationality?," he asked the people of Yarmouth in May, 1866. "We are already a portion of the greatest empire on which the sun has ever shone." A little later he told the people of Barrington:

> When the Apostle [Paul] claimed his Roman citizenship, he knew what it embraced—the protection of the eagles, the majesty and power of Rome. I am a British subject, and for me that term includes free trade and a common interest with fifty Provinces and two hundred and fifty millions of people, forming an Empire too grand and too extensive for Paul's imagination to conceive. You go down to the sea in ships, and a flag of old renown floats above them, and the Consuls and Ministers of the Empire are prompt to protect your property and your sons in every part of the world.

Howe had no doubts about the direction in which Nova Scotians ought to look, and it was not westward to the backwoods of Canada. None gloried more than he in the Nova Scotian mercantile marine and the doings of his compatriots upon the high seas. Should they not continue, therefore, to work out their own destiny along these lines "without running away, above tide-water, after the will-of-the-wisp at Ottawa, which will land us in a Slough of Despond?" What could Ottawa ever be anyway? It was as close to the North Pole as almost any city in the world, and had no attractions other than a waterfall. "Take a Nova Scotian to Ottawa, away above tidewater, freeze him up for five months, where he cannot view the Atlantic, smell salt water, or see the sail of a ship, and the man will pine and die."

A union, he admitted, might sometime be practicable. But it had to come by stages, "by Railroads first, social and commercial intercourse afterwards, and then, when we were prepared for it by a natural development of our system on the model we admire at Home." To union in general he put forward the same objections as in 1840,—the defenceless state of the frontier of Canada, the mixed and hostile character of the population, and so on. Had the French Canadians, by sticking together, not controlled the government of Canada since the Act of Union? "They will do the same thing in a larger Union. . .But should a chance combination thwart them, then they will back their Local Legislature against the United Parliament, and, in less than five years, will as assuredly separate from the Confederacy as Belgium did from Holland."

Of the Quebec scheme in particular Howe was equally critical. The United Kingdom, for its own safety, had repudiated the local legislatures which Scotland and Ireland had once possessed. Yet it would now foist five Parliaments upon four millions of people who had no foreign affairs to manage or colonists to govern. If the Dominion Parliament was to be completely paramount, as it was apparently intended, why have provincial legislatures at all? Would they not be useless, mischievous, perhaps even dangerous? Not only had the Nova Scotian delegates permitted the provincial Assembly to be "shorn of all dignity and authority," but in accepting representation by population they had been "done Brown." As a result, the Canadians would "appoint our governors, judges and senators. They are to 'tax us by any and every mode' and spend the money. They are to regulate our trade, control our Post Office, command the militia, fix the salaries, do what they like with our shipping and navigation, with our sea-coast and river fisheries, regulate the currency and the rate of interest, and seize upon our savings banks." All in all, he concluded, that "where there are no cohesive qualities in the material, no skill in the design, no prudence in the management, unite what you will and there is no strength."

Howe's case suffered somewhat because he resorted to too many arguments, some good, some bad, some mutually inconsistent. The contention that union would put the colonies in an even more indefensible position than before seems way off the mark. So was the assumption that the Nova Scotian members of Parliament could exercise little or no influence in the new House of Commons. But Professor Creighton is unduly severe in suggesting that "The Botheration Letters" seldom rise above their lame title; after all, they were not state papers prepared for Lord John Russell's perusal. Nor were all of his arguments "thin," as Professor Lower would have us believe. Indeed, some of his insights were unusually prophetic. His prediction that tariffs would be doubled and that Nova Scotian commerce would be seriously burdened as a result came true with a vengeance. In fact, it turned out to be the province's greatest grievance under the new order. It now appears, too, that Howe was more than right when he prophesied that it would take the wisdom of Solomon and the energy and strategy of Frederick the Great to weld a people with such few cohesive qualities into "a new nationality."

But it was none of these factors which propelled Howe once more into active politics; what did it was Tupper's determination to implement union without putting it before the electorate. The man who had fought governors and battled with bigwigs about lesser denials of the people's rights could not, as George Johnson points out, accept what he regarded as coercion in a matter of such magnitude.

> It was reversing all the principles for which he had fought. This firm, fixed, strong passion for the people's rights was at the bottom of all Mr. Howe's opposition to the Union of the Provinces under the Quebec scheme and had more to do with settling him into the position of opponent than all the facts his powerful mind, during months of thought, had massed into consecutive arguments and flung with such intensity of feeling at the Imperial Government, the Confederate Party and the Legislatures concerned.

The Grants, Roy, and Creighton present Howe as a middle-aged man who, despite his earlier triumphs, felt he had not realized his full possibilities and who, like a desperate gambler, threw caution to the winds and tried a last desperate fling on the question of union. Perhaps a more accurate picture is that of a man who had got almost everything he wanted, who still hoped for an Imperial office if he could secure one, but who appeared not to be unhappy with the second-best appointment which he had just accepted, the editorship of the New York *Albion*. Above all, the record is conclusive that it was a man who did not relish the thought of getting back into active politics.

The decision not to consult the people led to Howe's return to Halifax late in March, 1866. Neither Lieutenant-Governor Williams nor Adams Archibald would do anything to accommodate him. It was the refusal of Archibald, says Professor Chester Martin, which "brought Howe into the field, horse, foot and artillery." Was it not true in England, he asked, that "no important change in the machinery of Government is made without an appeal to the country?" To McCully, who said that Parliament could do anything but change a man into a woman, he replied: "Mr. McCully may have the power to knock out his mother's brains, but the act, if done, would be murder, nevertheless."

In Howe's mind the struggle to prevent Confederation and later to secure its repeal did not differ in essence from that for responsible government. George Johnson considered he was more eloquent during this agitation than in any previous one because he felt more indignant. This indignation was directed against the "marauders outside and enemies within" who thought only of themselves and cared little for Nova Scotia. Within were the Assemblymen who had reversed themselves for the sake of preferment and the Confederate leaders who had bought them and who refused to let the people decide. Outside were the Canadians who sought to overthrow the constitution of a free province simply because they chose to make representative government unworkable. Apparently they did not mind drawing Nova Scotia into their own peculiar brand of political turmoil with its ever recurring crises and deadlocks. But surely they should realize that "even French girls who would have no objections to being married don't like to be ravished." Outside, too, were the British financial interests who, through union, hoped to ensure greater security for their present and future investments in British North America, and the British politicians who wanted to reduce their own burden by shifting part of it onto the new federal government, perhaps as a preliminary step to getting rid of the colonies altogether. "But," asked Howe, "who, if anybody, thought of Nova Scotia?"

This booklet is an attempt to understand Howe, not to judge him. But if he is to be judged, it ought to be on proper grounds. Just because Confederation appears to have been successful, or just because historians feel that by its very nature it was ordained to be a good thing, it cannot be assumed—as some historians have done—that anyone who opposed it was guilty of bad judgment or suffered from a deficiency of character. Historians, like everyone else, have the right to make value judgments but not to impute bad motives or attribute faulty judgment to others simply because they adopted different premises.

As to using success for measuring the soundness of political action, there is, in Professor Trotter's words, "no justice in that sort of *ex post facto* verdict on political opinions." Certainly it would lead to an uncertain, erratic type of history. For if Quebec separatism were now to succeed the historian of the future might regard Howe as the true prophet, Tupper and Macdonald as the false ones. It would also mean that a public man who was anxious to have his activities recorded favourably in the history books would have to make a careful calculation of the probabilities and then pursue a line of conduct in accord with the likely outcome rather than his own principles. But could even a coldly calculating Howe have forecast the probable success of the union in April, 1866? This kind of criterion for making judgments would "downgrade a person of unimpeachable motives who makes a strong fight against impossible odds and at the same time tend to enthrone Machiavellianism as a cardinal virtue of politics."

Has something like this not actually occurred in the case of Howe? Is it not strange that the same historians who psychoanalyzed him and ferreted out bad motives for which there is little direct evidence passed over in silence the conduct of the Confederate leaders, who were determined to implement the union without consulting the people, no matter what means they had to employ? Surely these historians should have expressed some opinion on the lengths to which political leaders may go in overriding an electorate which is unconvinced of the wisdom of their high policy.

Criticize Howe, if you will, for allowing his Nova Scotian patriotism to exaggerate the evils which might befall his native province under union. Criticize him for failing to recognize the feasibility of a united British North America in the 1860's. Criticize him for being so obtuse that he could not appreciate the complete unacceptability of his proposals for the organization of the Empire. But do not give undue weight to the hoary mythology which has perpetuated the charges of inconsistency, precipitate intervention, and bad motives foisted upon him by the partisanship of the Confederation era.

FURTHER READINGS FOR TOPIC 16

J.-C. Bonenfant. *The French Canadians and the Birth of Confederation*. Ottawa: CHA Booklet 21, 1966.

D. G. Creighton. *The Road to Confederation: The Emergence of Canada, 1863–1867*. Toronto: Macmillan, 1964.

Peter J. Smith. "The Ideological Origins of Canadian Confederation." *Canadian Journal of Political Science* 20, no. 1 (March 1987): 2–29.

Gordon Stewart. *The Origins of Canadian Politics: A Comparative Approach*. Vancouver: University of British Columbia Press, 1986.

P. B. Waite. *The Life and Times of Confederation, 1864–1867: Politics, Newspapers, and the Union of British North America*. Toronto: University of Toronto Press, 1962.

STUDENT REPLY CARD

In order to improve future editions, we are seeking your comments on *Change and Continuity : A Reader on Pre-Confederation Canada* by Carol Wilton.

    After you have read this text, please answer the following questions and return this form via Business Reply Mail. *Thanks in advance for your feedback!*

1. Name of your college or university: _____

2. Major program of study: _____

3. Your instructor for this course: _____

4. Are there any sections of this text that were not assigned as course reading? _____
    If so, please specify those chapters or portions:

5. How would you rate the overall accessibility of the content? Please feel free to comment on reading level, writing style, terminology, layout and design features, and such learning aids as chapter objectives, summaries, and appendices.

6. What did you like *best* about this book?

7. What did you like *least*?

    If you would like to say more, we'd love to hear from you. Please write to us at the address shown on the reverse of this card.